MAN
OF THE
FUTURES

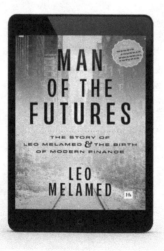

MAN OF THE FUTURES

*The Story of Leo Melamed
and the Birth of Modern Finance*

LEO MELAMED

HARRIMAN HOUSE LTD

3 Viceroy Court

Bedford Road

Petersfield

Hampshire

GU32 3LJ

GREAT BRITAIN

Tel: +44 (0)1730 233870

Email: enquiries@harriman-house.com

Website: harriman.house

First published in 2021.

Copyright © Leo Melamed

The right of Leo Melamed to be identified as the Author has been asserted in accordance with the Copyright, Design and Patents Act 1988.

Hardcover ISBN: 978-0-85719-748-1

eBook ISBN: 978-0-85719-749-8

British Library Cataloguing in Publication Data

A CIP catalogue record for this book can be obtained from the British Library.

Whilst every effort has been made to ensure that information in this book is accurate, no liability can be accepted for any loss incurred in any way whatsoever by any person relying solely on the information contained herein.

No responsibility for loss occasioned to any person or corporate body acting or refraining to act as a result of reading material in this book can be accepted by the Publisher, by the Author, or by the employers of the Author.

The Publisher does not have any control over or any responsibility for any authors or third-party websites referred to in or on this book.

Leo Melamed is a successful speculator and a recognized scholar, a far-out visionary and a down-to-earth realist, a skilled performer in Yiddish, dedicated to preserving that dying language, and an author of science fiction, a mover and a shaker, who has had a major influence on both private institutions and public policy.

He had the independence of mind and foresight to envisage the need for a public market in foreign currency futures, the imagination to invent a mechanism to make such a market feasible, and the courage and leadership ability to persuade his colleagues at the Chicago Mercantile Exchange to establish the International Monetary Market.

—MILTON FRIEDMAN

CONTENTS

Contents

FOREWORD

Keynote address by Christopher Giancarlo

Chairman of the Commodity Futures Trading Commission (CFTC), the US federal regulator of futures and derivatives, before the Futures Industry Association (FIA), Annual Conference, in Boca Raton, Florida, March 14, 2018.

GOOD morning. It is great to be here at FIA's 43rd International Futures Industry Conference. It is certainly the one annual event that brings together all participants in the global derivatives markets.

So, I am delighted to have this opportunity to speak to all of you about our work at the CFTC. Thank you for your attendance.

There is a comment attributed to Isaac Newton. He said that, if he saw farther than others, it was because he stood on the shoulders of giants.

Today, I can't help but think of one of the giants of the derivatives industry: Leo Melamed. We all see farther because of Leo. Many of you know Leo. Some of his colleagues and friends are here today. We have all, directly or indirectly, been influenced by him.

Leo is the Chairman Emeritus of the CME Group and one of the central figures in American commerce and trade. He has just announced his retirement. In the world of derivatives, he has been a leader who shaped and guided our thinking. In electronic commerce, he actually took us into a new world. He is often called the 'father of financial futures.'

Leo Melamed's vision, brilliance, and accomplishment have spread out from

xi

Chicago to include the entire world, a world that began for him with harsh clarity through escaping with his family from Nazi-invaded Poland. Then, the stuff of legend: crossing wartime Siberia by railroad and then by boat to Japan, crossing the Pacific by ship only months before Pearl Harbor. He and his family eventually found safety in America. From there, he stumbled into the world of finance by mistake, yet by pluck and hard work, he thrived and conceived great innovations in trade and commerce. He founded and chaired the NFA from 1982 through 1989, and provided direction and guidance of the Chicago Merc as it grew into one of the great institutions of American finance.

Leo has been a grand figure striding the world's financial landscape. A consummate professional, a creative visionary. And, what I admire most: a fearless believer in the promise of tomorrow.

Leo dared to define his own future, not have it defined for him. When he started out in Chicago seventy years ago, he found markets that were small, commodity based, and domestic. He leaves markets that are enormous, diversified and international. And, we are here today—standing on Leo's shoulders—participating in global derivatives markets that are legacy of a man who was not afraid to envision a brighter and more prosperous future. I dedicate my remarks today to Leo Melamed.

CHRISTOPHER GIANCARLO
March 14, 2019
Boca Raton, Florida

AUTHOR'S BRAG

THE phenomenal success of financial futures exemplified the power of an idea whose time had come. The financial revolution I describe blazed the trail for much of what has since followed in world capital markets. It established that there was a need for a new genre of risk management instruments responsive to investment applications and modern telecommunications. It led to the acceptance and integration of futures and options within the infrastructure of the financial establishment. It became the catalyst for the development of financial futures and derivatives worldwide. And, according to Nobel laureate Merton Miller, it introduced the modern era of finance.

In time, I became a singular voice with the foresight to recognize the gargantuan force of coming technology, as well as its ability to trample everything standing in its way. As I courageously told members in 1987:

> Anyone who has not seen the handwriting on the wall is blind to the reality of our times. One can no more deny the fact that technology has and will continue to engulf every aspect of financial markets than one can restrict the use of futures in the management of risk. The markets of the future will be automated. The traders of the future will trade by way of the screen. Those who dare to ignore this reality face extinction.[1]

I took it upon myself to revolutionize the 1,000-year-old open outcry transaction process and replace it with the magic of Globex—the CME's electronic transaction system.

What I did not set out to do was to make gobs of money. Don't get me wrong. As a trader I always wanted to make winning trades, but that was never the priority in my life. In first place was the drive to leave a mark, to make a difference, to

---

1 Leo Melamed, spoken at the unveiling to the members in 1987 and published in the 1988 Annual Report to CME membership.

deserve a word or two in history. The Chicago Mercantile Exchange (CME), once the Butter and Egg Board and later the house that pork bellies built, is today known as the house that innovation built—or, as most would say, the house that Leo built. As in most great endeavors, it must be underscored that without the countless devoted and talented people at my side, to whom I am eternally grateful and who I name wherever possible, this result could not have been achieved.

Needless to say, financial derivatives and futures also come with attendant risks and dangers. They are highly sophisticated tools. If used for illicit purposes, or applied in a negligent manner, they can become a causal factor for disastrous results, as the financial breakdown of 2008 demonstrated. Nevertheless, their successful application and efficiency continue to give them an indispensable role in today's trading and risk-management ecosystem.

I confess that some of the recollections in this book have been described in my other books: *Leo Melamed on the Markets*, *Escape to the Futures*, and *For Crying Out Loud*.[2] Why, then, write another book? The answer is simple. My previous memoirs were published in 1996. It was far too early to provide an in-depth assessment of what I had accomplished. So much has happened to markets since then that my achievements take on a much deeper understanding from the perspective of history.

Additionally, *Man of the Futures* contains a host of events and episodes that I have never shared before. It also is companion to a unique set of photographs taken over the span of five decades. *Man of the Futures* affords me the chance to delve deeper into past events and assess everything with the benefit of hindsight. In this manner, it represents a rare opportunity to evaluate my original rationale, examine my prognostications and offer a peak into the future.

Finally, I must admit that long ago I adopted Sam Zell's motto, "If it ain't fun, we don't do it."[3] Sam and I are friends. The fact we both ended up in Chicago is a rare coincidence. Although Sam was born in the US and I in Poland, Chicago was the resting stop for our respective parents, who separately escaped from Poland at the outset of the second world war, they from Sosnowiec, us from Bialystok. Both sets of parents followed the same escape route from Vilnius, Lithuania with a transit visa from one of the world's righteous—Japanese counsel general to Lithuania, Chiune Sugihara. Sam once wrote that as a result of that miraculous escape, he "grew up believing that anything is possible."

So did I.

LEO MELAMED
Chairman Emeritus, CME Group

---

2   *Leo Melamed on the Markets*, Wiley & Sons Inc., 1993; *Escape to the Futures*, Wiley & Sons, Inc, 1996; *For Crying Out Loud*, Wiley & Sons, Inc., 2009.
3   Sam Zell is an eminent real-estate tycoon.

CHAPTER 1

My Parents, Moishe and Faygl Melamdovich

W E were on the Trans-Siberian Express on our way to Vladivostok, Russia's most eastern seaport, when my father sat me down to explain the difference between Fahrenheit and centigrade. I was eight years old. We were not on a holiday excursion. We were on a critical leg of our escape from the horrors unfolding in Europe at the outset of the second world war.[4]

Before the bombing began, my father moved us to his family's brick building, near the outskirts of Bialystok, Poland, the city where I was born and where he said it would be safer. To protect us against bombing, he used black paint to cover the windows.

I was sitting in a barber's stool when we heard someone outdoors shout in Yiddish: "*Lost arop di zaluzjan, der gast is do.*" Close the grating the guests are here!

When we got home, I secretly took a key to scratch out a little peephole for myself through which I saw the first German tanks roll in to capture Bialystok and all its inhabitants. To a seven-year-old, they were huge monsters from an alien world—an image I will always remember.

Before the tanks came, my mother woke me in the middle of one night to

---

4   As everyone knows, on September 1, 1939, Germany declared war and the world became engulfed in the deadliest military conflict in human history. The war would last over six years, involve the vast majority of the world's nations and affect more than 100 million people from more than 30 different countries. It would mark the mass murder of six million Jews, along with the massacre of 1.5 million children, and millions of other nationalities. Poland fell within 27 days, and the citizens of Bialystok, the city where I was born and lived, were among the earliest victims to be captured by the Nazi onslaught.

say farewell to my father. It was known that the Nazis used prominent people as hostages and my father was one of 20 (or so) Bialystok council members who were in particular danger. At a council meeting it was explained that the mayor had made arrangements for a truck to take them away.

This meeting was held in the great synagogue, because the City Hall had been bombed out. The mayor had asked the chief rabbi of Bialystok, Gedalja Rozenman, for permission to hold the meeting, and was granted the request with the stipulation that everyone wear a yarmulke (skull cap) or a hat, as was the religious custom. Everyone agreed except my father. He was the only Jew elected to the council, but he was also an ardent member of the Bund, the secular Jewish socialist party. As such, he was an agnostic. Wearing a yarmulke would violate his principles.[5] The rabbi looked the other way.

I remember how tightly my mother held my hand as we ran through the darkness—interrupted only by flashes of light from the falling bombs and the constant *ack-ack* sound coming from what I later learned were machine guns. A tearful farewell scene followed in an empty lot with but one lonely truck.

When the Gestapo came a week later, my father was not there and we truthfully had no idea where he was. The ordeal became my first horrifying memory, one that has haunted me throughout my life. There were three of them. I remember their boots. They ransacked our house and slapped my mother around. One thought is indelibly seared in my memory—my mother never cried nor let go of my hand.

THE RUSSIAN DANCE

Several weeks later, Bialystok was turned over to the Russians, as part of the non-aggression treaty between Nazi Germany and the Soviet Union.

All of the city officials who had run in the face of German occupation now returned. To many, the Russians were a safer occupier than the Nazis, especially for Jews. It was a sad, life-or-death mistake—one *not* made by my father. As he later explained to my mother, he did not return because the Bolsheviks were not to be trusted. "Besides," he said, "the machinations between Hitler and Stalin were to be regarded as those of madmen."

Sure enough, within days we were confronted by the NKVD (precursors of the KGB) and at the time, the only difference I could discern between them and the Gestapo was that they were in plain clothes and not wearing boots.

5   See page 37.

All those who returned to Bialystok were arrested and never heard from again. Oddly, while not very prominent in the Bund hierarchy, my father was known enough to be included as an 'enemy of the state' by the Communist party. He had sympathized with a small group of Bundist loyalists in Bialystok who wrested the Jewish trade unions from communist control, restoring them to the influence of Jewish Socialism under the Bund banner.

What possessed my father to take flight and not return? What possessed him several weeks later to call a neighbor and direct my mother to get the last train that very night out of Bialystok to Vilnius (*Vilna* in Yiddish)? How did he know that Vilna would be turned over to the Lithuanians the next day and would therefore be safer? How did he know? Why Lithuania? What possessed my parents to leave their house, jobs as schoolteachers, relatives, friends and all possessions? And to go—where? There was no destination. And this was before anyone in the world knew of the Holocaust.

Later in life, when I asked my father the question, "What made you do it?" he shrugged and just said it was an instinctive reaction. "Something you feel certain is the right thing to do."

THE ESCAPE

That night was the beginning of our escape from Bialystok and the scourge that would befall the unfortunate souls who remained. My mother grabbed me and some bare necessities and made our goodbyes as if we would be back in a couple of days.

The train station was in chaos, with people shouting and running back and forth. Everyone was rushing but seemingly without a destination. We barely made it. The next 12 hours were a nightmare. My mother and I spent the night pressed against each other like sardines in a can. Somehow, she managed to steal a cardboard box from a grizzled old man for me to sit on. He alternated between smiling at me and giving me dirty looks in case I stole something.

The train stopped countless times, causing everyone to rush out in fear that it would be bombed. After the whistle blew again—an all-clear signal—everyone rushed back on the train to find their spot. No one argued about it. People seemed amazingly polite, but there were babies who never stopped crying. The journey, which normally took a couple of hours, lasted all night. It was my first sleepless night.

JEWS IN BIALYSTOK

Jewish history in Bialystok can be traced back to the 1500s. Their presence swelled over the years and in the 1700s, Count Jan Branicki gave Jews full-citizenship status. It was a historic event. Nevertheless, the Bialystok Jewish population was consistently subjected to waves of anti-Semitism and pogroms. The most well-known occurred on June 1, 1906, with more than 200 Jews killed and hundreds injured, along with the destruction of homes and businesses. For three whole days, June 1 to 3, 1906, Czarist murders ravaged the people and property of the Jewish community. Ironically, the police chief was a liberal and afterwards he declared "there will be no [more] pogrom in Bialystok." (Nice try, Count Branicki.)

Bialystok could boast of some very distinguished personalities, such as Icchok Shamir, who served as prime minister of Israel, and Dr. Ludwik L. Zamenhof, the inventor of the international language Esperanto. It was fitting that the founder of Esperanto was a Jew from Bialystok, a place where Jews encountered many ethnic groups and languages—Polish, Russian, German, Lithuanian, White Russian, as well as Yiddish and Hebrew. Dr. Albert B. Sabin, a microbiologist who improved the Salk polio vaccine by developing an oral equivalent, was also a Bialystoker. And, of course, Max Ratner of Cleveland Ohio, a most distinguished Bialystoker, who was a prosperous industrialist and leading philanthropist on the American-Jewish scene. Samuel Pisar, a renowned Parisian lawyer who spent his adolescence in Auschwitz, was also a Bialystoker.

Bialystok also thrived as a center of the Jewish labor movement, a revolutionary arena that produced many prominent personalities and writers. As early as 1882, 70 Jewish Bundist weavers went out on strike against the factory owner. This stoppage set a precedent for other job actions over wage disputes. However, more than the weavers, politicians and distinguished citizens, it was the bakers of Bialystok who achieved worldwide fame with their *bialy*, a breakfast roll.

THE GRIM TRUTH

In 1939, just before the Germans invaded Poland, there were 110,000 Jews living in Bialystok, representing over 60% of the city's population. It meant that Bialystok had the highest percentage of Jews among the world's cities and the greatest number of synagogues per capita.

Long after the war, when I returned with my family in 2000, Mayor Richard

Tur told us that there were no Jews in Bialystok. And little wonder! Nearby is Treblinka, to the southwest is Gross-Rosen, to the southeast is Majdanek and further south, behind Warsaw, is Auschwitz. In writer Elie Wiesel's words, "All the outcries of mankind, lead to this accursed place. Here is the kingdom of night, where God's face is hidden and a flaming sky becomes a graveyard for a vanished people."[6]

Hitler had turned Poland into a factory of death. All of my would-be classmates were gone; instead of learning geography, they were taken on cattle trains to killing camps, and instead of writing, they were taken to gas chambers, or starved and forced into labor. Many were individually executed or used for medical experiments.

Let the world never forget the atrocities carried out by the Nazis under orders from Adolf Hitler, Heinrich Himmler and Josef Mengele, to name just three villains of the Third Reich, who perpetrated the world's most heinous act of genocide, the Holocaust.

Nothing that happened thereafter can change or diminish this truth. As General Dwight D. Eisenhower asked, "How is it possible to do justice to demonic acts that beggar[ed] description?"[7] Alas, the world closed its eyes and shut its ears while a monstrous deed—one that left a permanent blot on human history—was inflicted on the Jewish people.

6   *Pilgrimage to the Kingdom of Night*, Elie Wiesel. *The New York Times*, November 4, 1979.
7   On April 12, 1945, General Dwight D. Eisenhower, then commanding the Allied military forces in Europe, visited the Ohrdruf concentration camp. After viewing the evidence of atrocities, he wrote in a letter to General George C. Marshall, dated April 15, 1945: "The things I saw beggar[ed] description... The visual evidence and the verbal testimony of starvation, cruelty and bestiality were ... overpowering ... I made the visit deliberately in order to be in a position to give first-hand evidence of these things if ever, in the future, there develops a tendency to charge these allegations merely to 'propaganda'." Source: The US Holocaust Memorial Museum (hereinafter: USHMM).

5

CHAPTER 2

High Finance

A WAKING NIGHTMARE

OUR miraculous escape, made possible by my parents and a Japanese diplomat, spanned two years, three continents and six languages. We took the Trans-Siberian railroad across the vastness of Siberia to Vladivostok, then travelled on to Tsuruga, Japan, and finally to the US. In this circuitous fashion, I was among the fortunate few who escaped the unspeakable horrors in Europe.

My parents had to make countless life or death decisions during this time, but their main concern, as teachers by profession, was that my education was being disrupted. So, they did two things. First, they enrolled me into school whenever we stayed somewhere for a few days. This was not fun for me, as I had to make new friends each time and learn a variety of languages, mostly now forgotten. Secondly, my parents became my private tutors. For instance, on the Trans-Siberian railroad, my father explained that to change Fahrenheit to centigrade, you have to subtract 32 degrees, then multiply by five and divide by nine.

I may fail to sufficiently recount that, for my parents, these years were a nightmare. Not knowing where they were heading, or what the future held, they carried a ceaseless anxiety that the next moment would be the end. They feared that a stranger might innocently divulge our plight, feared the police or secret service, feared because we were Jewish, feared not having enough money to carry on, feared our dependence on strangers, feared becoming separated, and feared for me. I was conscious of my parent's anxiety but, being a child, I could escape for hours into a child's imaginary world. My parents had no such refuge.

VILNA, POLAND
(TODAY THE CAPITAL OF LITHUANIA)

In Vilna, our first stop after leaving Bialystok, life was a drudgery for both of my parents. However, my mother had it a bit better, as she had graduated from the famous Vilnar Teachers' Seminary and had a number of friends there. Her close teacher-friends, the Manns, found her a job as a substitute teacher. The Mann's seven-year-old daughter, Esther, also saw to it that my refugee existence was bearable. She became my first girlfriend.

While my mother's days were at least occupied, my father's existence was very difficult. Upon arrival, my father would sometimes busy himself with activities for various Vilna Jewish organizations. However, once the Russians took over Lithuania, his life became a misery. Whenever there was a rumor of a Soviet hunt for foreigners or dissidents, he would hide for days in a nearby forest with other partisans.

We managed to gain a second floor, one-room loft in the middle of the Jewish ghetto. It contained a bed for my parents, a cot for me, a small gas stove and a tiny bathroom in the hall down the way. It also featured a very small portico barely big enough to fit one person. I would sometimes step out onto the portico to witness the strange world below. We were on Straszuna Street, in the butchers' quarter. Scurrying shoppers with shopping bags were everywhere, all trying to avoid the horse-pulled wagons and rickety trucks loaded with freshly cut carcasses of beef for the butcher shops. In their windows hung slabs of meat, geese and chicken which were attended to by butchers wielding cleavers and wearing blood-splattered aprons. A stream of blood ran down the gutters in a constant flow.

Some eight months later, Hitler broke the non-aggression treaty with Russia. This caused Stalin to invade and capture Lithuania, as well as the other Baltics, Ukraine, Estonia, Latvia and Romania. Falling under Russian rule was not good for my father. Being a member of the Bund and an outspoken anti-communist, his name was likely on an NKVD list for deportation to Siberia or worse. As a result, my father again went into hiding, only returning when my mother would place a dish towel on the portico railing as a safe signal.

Vilna, along with Bialystok, would ultimately fall into Nazi hands. The entire Jewish population would be herded into ghettos from which hardly anyone escaped.

A FUTURE THAT COULD HAVE BEEN

As my father predicted, the agreement between Hitler and Stalin did not last long. Operation Barbarossa was launched by Hitler on June 22, 1941, when he ordered the invasion of the Soviet Union. The same mistake Napoleon Bonaparte made in 1812. When the Nazis recaptured Bialystok, those that had returned were trapped and suffered an inhumane fate.

My parents never seriously considered returning to Bialystok, even when the Nazis temporarily left. My father's distrust of the Bolsheviks saved our lives once again. On Friday, June 27, 1941, five days after their return, the Nazis celebrated their recapture of Bialystok by marching at gun-point some 2,000 Jewish inhabitants, including my entire remaining family, into the famous Bialystok *Grosse Shul* (Great Synagogue).[8] This was just before candles were due to be lit in Jewish homes, to usher in the Sabbath. All the doors and windows to the synagogue were locked, it was hosed down with gasoline, and set on fire.

Everyone within was burned to death. My parents and I had to live with that memory. All that remains today is a memorial with the steel skeleton of its famous Byzantine dome.

MARKETPLACE LESSONS

My first private lesson with my father was on high finance. Early in our Vilna stay, my father sat me down to explain that every country had its own currency. He handed me a unit of paper money and asked if I knew what it was. Recognizing the Polish currency, I responded, "a *zloty*." He nodded and handed me another unit of paper currency. It was different looking and beyond my ken. My father explained that it was a *litas*, the Lithuanian unit of currency.

"What are they worth?" he then asked. "The same?" I ventured. "That is what the government says," my father replied, "but let's find out." We went to a nearby bakery and my father asked how much a loaf of bread was. "One *litas*," the baker responded. "We will take it," my father said. After the baker wrapped the loaf

---

8   Designed in 1908 by a renowned architect, Shlome Jakow Rabinowicz, the Great Synagogue's dome exhibited a Byzantine-Muslim influence and was famous throughout Europe. In this synagogue, open only on Saturdays and holidays, women prayed together with men, although in separate halls. Between the first and second world wars, national holidays were celebrated there, and the services were attended by such authorities as the mayor and the governor of the region.

of bread, my father handed him one *zloty*. The baker balked. "No, no," he said shaking his head, "one *litas*, two *zlotys*."[9]

As my father explained, the true value of the two units of currency could only be determined by what they can buy in the marketplace. While the official rate of exchange between the *zloty* and the *litas* may be one-to-one, in fact it would take two *zlotys* to buy a loaf of bread, but only one *litas*. Their purchasing powers were very different.

My father repeated this lesson later in Moscow with *roubles* and in Tokyo with *yen*. Only the marketplace, he lectured, can be trusted to ascertain value. Although I did not know it at the time, my first private lesson in finance proved to be an introduction to one of the fundamental truths of market dynamics.

Such lessons stayed with me and 30 years later, although not a registered student at the University of Chicago, I could not resist sneaking into the lectures of Milton Friedman, to listen to him explain that what I had learned from my father as a child was true: that true value is best determined in the free marketplace. Friedman went on to receive the Nobel prize in Economic Sciences in 1976. And by then, his 1962 seminal work, *Capitalism and Freedom*, had become my economic road map.

---

9   I do not remember the actual official rate between a *zloty* and *litas* in 1939. But I never forgot the lesson involved.

CHAPTER 3

Sugihara

THE origin of my affection for Asia is easy to understand. It began with Chiune Sugihara, the Japanese general consul in Kaunas, Lithuania in 1940. Over 10,000 Jews had somehow managed to escape their fate and now found themselves in Vilna. Many were elite Jewish intellectuals—actors, writers, leaders of the Bund and Zionist parties, and thousands of Talmudic students. Although Vilna offered a lifeline, we all felt the presence of the hangman, whether German or Russian, around the corner. The world was on fire and the flames would certainly reach the tenuous safety of Vilna soon. So, life in Vilna was both temporary and, since history had proven that Jews were expendable, conditional.

UNEXPECTED ALLIES

One escape plan emerged from two Dutch students, Nathan Gutwirth and Chaim Nussbaum, both attending the *Telshe Yeshiva* in Vilna.[10] Being Dutch citizens in Kaunas (then the capital of Lithuania), they had become friends with Jan Zwartendijk, a fellow Dutchman, who was left in charge of the Dutch consulate after the previous ambassador was expelled from Lithuania.

The objective of the students' plan was to reach the island of Curaçao, part of the Dutch West Indies, which had not yet been overtaken by the German onslaught. They speculated that if they could persuade Zwartendijk to stamp 'permission to Curaçao' on their passports, then it could act as an official visa.

10   A Yeshiva is an Orthodox Jewish college or seminary.

Zwartendijk was willing, but first asked for the opinion of the Dutch ambassador to Latvia, L. P. De Decke, who approved. Consequently, Zwartendijk ignored the other requirements of such visas and ended up issuing hundreds of visas to Surinam, Curacao and other such colonies—destinations which were still under Dutch official purview.

This was but the first leg of the plan; now came the hard part. Since there was no way to get directly to Curaçao from Lithuania, Gutwirth and Nussbaum went about seeking transit visas from countries they could pass through to get to their ultimate destination. This far-fetched scheme was turned down by nearly all embassies, including the US and the Swiss. However, when they came to Chiune Sugihara, the Japanese consul general who was aware of the Zwartendijk scheme, they found that he might consider issuing a ten-day visa to Japan.

AN HONORABLE ACT

Although it was a cursory procedure, Sugihara asked his Foreign Office in Tokyo for permission to do so. To his utter surprise and chagrin, the request was denied. Not accepting no for an answer, Sugihara repeated his request. "These are not criminals," he explained, "their only crime is being Jewish." After the second refusal, he tried a third time, and again was sternly ordered not to do so. "This is none of our business, follow orders," he was told.

Sugihara's instincts told him differently. He struggled with the decision but, in the end, humanity prevailed. Sugihara had by then converted to Christianity and solemnly stated to his wife, "If I obey the orders of my government, I would be violating the edicts of my God." His decision was to issue unconditional visas.

Overjoyed, Gutwirth went to his friend, Elieaer Portnoy, the rabbi of the famous Mir Yeshiva, and urged him to get a visa.[11] However, Rabbi Portnoy advised Sugihara that he could not accept a personal transit visa without first obtaining them for his entire congregation of 300 students. Sugihara acquiesced. It did not take long for this plan to become known to the Jewish community at large. Thousands of Jewish refugees, including my parents, Isaac and Faygl Melamdovich, and myself, Laybl, lined up at the Japanese consulate to appeal for similar transit visas.

It is reported that Sugihara and his wife, Uukiko, issued a total of 2,139 visas during the month of August 1940. This deed saved over 6,000 people, since each

---

11   Also known as the Mirrer Yeshiva, a Lithuanian Yeshiva located in the town of Mir, founded in 1815 by a wealthy householder, Shenel Tiktinski.

visa was to the head of household and therefore valid for an entire family. Chiune Sugihara is today among the most lauded humanitarians in world history and an outstanding example that every individual has the power to make a difference! We received our transit visa to Japan on August 31, 1940.

There was still a third leg to the scheme. While receiving a transit visa to Japan was like a gift from the angels, the odds of escaping remained in the hands of the devil. No one leaves Russia without approval from the Russian Foreign Office. Requesting permission to leave the *golden motherland* was, in itself, extremely dangerous, because once you applied you were considered a risk to the state. "Only undesirables would want to leave paradise." It became a rather cynical joke among refugees that those who voluntarily applied for permission to travel through Siberia, in order to get to Japan, might end up there permanently. It was like walking a tightrope without a net. Still, it was either take the risk, or forever remain a refugee and be recaptured by the Nazis.

For my father, the risk was larger than for most. He was a known Bundist. Nevertheless, after a great deal of soul-searching—they even asked for my advice—my parents decided to take the gamble. Our story would be the truth; we were after all refugees running from the Nazis with a transit visa to Japan.[12] If, in the confusion of world events, the Bolshevik officials did not catch on to the fact that my father was Isaac Melamdovich, the Bundist, anti-communist rabble-rouser, then we might get away with it. If the truth was discovered, my parents explained to me, the three of us would be arrested as political prisoners and either sent to a Siberian Gulag or murdered by the Germans.

Aside from these dangers, money was an issue. Corruption in Russia is legendary. The cost of a ticket included both an official amount and an under-the-table one. Most of the money was, of course, pocketed by the Russian officials, a deal between the Foreign Office officials and the government's Intourist agency, from whom tickets were purchased.

For Jews, the one-way fare for the ten-day trip from Moscow to Vladivostok, by way of the Trans-Siberian railroad, was $120 per person—five times the stated official rate for non-Jews. And that was excluding additional fees for food and the like. Where would we get the money, a sum that in those days was considered a small fortune? Again, the money was supplied by Jewish committees or friends of two Yiddish schoolteachers from Bialystok.

---

12 Bialystok, at that moment, was under Russian rule (based on the deal between Moscow and Berlin), so theoretically we could return there. But everyone knew the situation was fluid and my father was certain that back in Bialystok he would quickly be arrested since he was on the NKVD (KGB) list of wanted people. In any event, it wasn't long before the Germans recaptured Bialystok.

AN AGONIZING WAIT

An additional problem was that the money had to be paid in American dollars—which no one had since it was against the law to have foreign money. As always, there existed an underhand special scheme. We were secretly advised that if we went to the Monica Café, a black-market deal could be made to convert roubles to dollars at an outrageous conversion rate. Of course, this whole operation could have been a scam to "Get the Jewish money," a common saying in Russia. And if nothing happened, who could you complain to?

My father again went into hiding just in case. With me at her side, my mother and I would go every Friday to the Bolshevik Foreign Office, where the names would be posted for those whom permission was granted. Fear for the worst mounted with each passing week. This torture lasted for more than four months. Finally, our names showed up in approval.

When we originally left Bialystok, it was without warning and in the dead of night, the last moment before the borders closed. We thought it was but a temporary departure. This time, we knew our departure was likely to be permanent. All avenues of communication between us and Bialystok had ceased to exist. Instead, we left letters for our family members in Bialystok extending our well-wishes and love. We had no way of knowing that all of them were doomed.

We also made our goodbyes to our Vilna friends, particularly the Manns. I remember telling Esther that we would be together again as grown-ups. The Nazis made certain that she would not reach adulthood. Another young friend, Masha Bernstein (Leon) and her family also received a Sugihara visa and were prepared to leave with us. In the last moment, her father, Matvey, was discovered by the NKVD as a rebel Bundist. He was arrested and never heard from again. The Bernsteins had to decide whether to remain in Vilna in case Matvey was released or escape without him. They made the only decision they could. In New York, Masha became known for writing the gossip column for the Yiddish newspaper, the *Daily Forward*. We remained friends, often participating jointly in remembrances of Sugihara. Masha recently passed away but her daughter, Karen Leon, carries forward her mother's memory.

Sugihara and his family were punished by the Japanese Foreign Office for issuing transit visas by being transferred to dangerous posts in East Prussia, Czechoslovakia and Romania. When the Soviet troops entered Romania, Sugihara and his family were kept in a prisoner of war camp for 18 months.

Sugihara's humanitarian deed went unheralded for many years. However, once it became known to the world community, he received the deserved recognition together with a multitude of awards. In 1985, Israel named him in the *Righteous Among Nations*. He is similarly honored in the United States Holocaust Memorial Museum (USHMM). I took it upon myself to do what I could to publicize his humanitarian deed. Over time, my office in Chicago became a mecca for Sugihara's family members and officials of the Japanese government. Sugihara passed away on July 31, 1986.

CHAPTER 4

Moscow

OUR journey to Moscow was a strange experience. United by circumstance, almost every person on the train was forced to hide behind the façade of a carefree tourist. We became like a troupe of actors performing a play with no script, all hoping to regain their autonomy. But that was all it amounted to, a flicker of a chance that could quickly be snuffed out.

Despite my parents always being near, I found being on the run a lonely experience. And with this loneliness came a sense of displacement and a loss of innocence. The pulse of these bleak times coursed through me and I struggled to understand the world, which seemed doomed to go to hell.

The war had not yet reached Moscow, so when I got off the train and stepped outside the station, I thought I had entered another world. The streets teemed with Muscovites and traffic moved in every direction. There were towers, spires, golden domes, gardens, plazas, and blotches of red on tunics and flags. There were soldiers everywhere, too—the same kinds of soldiers I had seen goose-stepping along the streets of Bialystok.

HISTORY LESSONS

I knew nothing of Nicholas II, the Red Guards or the Bolsheviks. Nor did I know of Tolstoy, Tchaikovsky or John Reed, the leftist writer and only American to ever be buried in the Kremlin. Of course, my parents did their best to explain it all, but there was just so much to take in.

I didn't even know of Vladimir Ilyich Lenin until we silently marched past his embalmed body, lying uniformed in a mausoleum built in his honor. The soldier-guards, stiff and stern-faced, reminded me of the lead ones I had once played with. My father took pains to explain the October Revolution of 1917 to me, as well as who Lenin was and what he did. For good measure, he added that these events had all gone badly, and led to communism and Joseph Stalin.

My father also tried to give me a historical sketch of the city and explain that, throughout its history, Moscow had survived riots, plagues, revolts, sieges and foreign occupations. He told me of the Mongolian Tartars, as well as the armies of Napoleon in 1812. I, however, was too busy looking in every direction.

SIGHTSEEING

Moscow was massive. It was safe to say that the city had captured both my eyes and my heart. Its buildings, complete with great wooden doors, chunks of stone, tall pillars and lofty ceilings, were awe-inspiring. I also remember there being a giant bell and a cannon whose bore I could have squeezed my whole body into. And those frightening red walls of the Kremlin. They left an indelible impression on this eight-year-old refugee. I often dreamt about those red walls in the nights that followed.

Who would have ever imagined that almost to the day, 50 years later, I would return to Moscow—this time as a conquering hero of free markets—to be hosted by Mikhail Gorbachev within those dreaded Kremlin walls.

We stayed in Moscow for three days in December 1940, during which time we, more or less, had the run of the city. My family had just enough money to stay at the Novaya Moskovskaya, a third-rate (fifth-rate by today's standards) hotel which, with its mirrors, chandeliers and carpeted lobby with overstuffed chairs, I then considered a palace. But my eight-year-old self was most impressed by the show in the hotel's pretentious ballroom, which my father treated us to one evening. It featured scantily dressed female gypsies, who sang as they cavorted about the stage offering their rendition of belly dancing.

But, of course, we weren't tourists out to buy knick-knacks as a reminder of our trip. We were escapees, waiting to board the eastbound Siberian train for Vladivostok—and perhaps freedom.

My mother's anxiety was unceasing—she was convinced my father would be apprehended and disappeare. My father, too, was fearful and certain we were followed everywhere we went. For me, Moscow was a diversion, for my parents it was a potential sinkhole. Fear was their constant companion. I was traveling light, toting a child's curiosity, while my father lugged a fugitive's suspicion.

Better to act as tourists though, then hide as criminals. Thus, as we pretended to stroll leisurely along the streets like other tourists, we never lost sight of the fact that the hangman was no more than a few feet behind us.

Finally, it was time to leave. We packed and cautiously made our way to the railway station. The closer we got, the more soldiers appeared. While Russia was not yet at war with Germany, it had already fought—and captured—its small northern neighbor Finland. Stalin had taken a page out of Hitler's book by bombing the Finnish capital, Helsinki, in a blitzkrieg-style campaign waged in temperatures 60 degrees below zero. In Moscow, there were yet no traces of war like I had witnessed in Bialystok. It was the proverbial calm before the storm.

FORTY BELOW ZERO[13]

We departed Moscow on a bitterly cold December morning. I remember the conductor shouting what I assumed was 'all aboard' and the brake-man waving a lantern. The train hissed and, picking up speed, began to roar. Snow covered the countryside and within minutes the windows were glazed with moisture. It was a powerful locomotive, pulling a rickety chain of wooden cars that rumbled over narrow tracks.

We had a small, extremely crude compartment to ourselves that could be converted into sleeping bunks. There was a dining car as well, and two sittings for each meal, but we could only afford tickets for dinner. At various stops, my father would get off the train and buy bread, milk and other foodstuffs for breakfast and lunch. My mother would panic at each juncture that we might never see him again.

The trip was filled with the unknown and fraught with danger. As we moved along Siberia's spine, the train was a pinprick against the vast wilderness, which was otherwise utterly untouched. Begun in 1891, the 5,800-mile Trans-Siberian railroad was built to connect Moscow to Vladivostok and other Asian ports. You could travel for thousands of miles without seeing traces of man or beast.

The train kept at a steady speed, perhaps to conserve fuel, or because of weather conditions, or the fact that we were crossing treacherous terrain, its rhythm lulling us into a false sense of security. There were no shortcuts. Indeed, because there was only one track, we would often spend hours waiting at designated switching points (like Oms, Novosibirsk or Irkutsk) for our westbound sibling to pass us so that we could continue our trek to Siberia's most eastern point, the port of Vladivostok.

---

13   Much of my description that follows, I first wrote for *Escape to the Futures*, Wiley & Sons, 1996.

There was beauty in this frigid frontier, but a harsh and muscular beauty, where bears, tigers, sable, reindeer and wolves roamed freely among some of the greatest treasures on earth. To me, it was a bewildering kaleidoscope of marshy plains, dense forests, desolate plateaus and craggy mountains. A landscape where time and place were lost.

Described by many as a cash cow, Siberia accounted for one-fifth of the world's gold and silver, a third of its iron and timber, and contained an immeasurable wealth of gas, oil and coal. The eventual oligarchs figured this out. And at four million square miles—the size of the entire US—it was the largest region of the world's biggest nation.

Due to the harsh climate, hardly anyone would choose to live there. Yet, when war broke out, millions of workers and their factories were transported to Siberia from vulnerable areas, retreating like a turtle beneath its shell. It was also where Stalin banished criminals, Jewish intellectuals and political prisoners to mine and build in forced labor camps. In this way, it was a place where untold millions died long before and after the war. And our train, on its single track, was the ubiquitous carryall, the workhorse of this Siberian transport system.

BIROBIDZHAN

My father's lesson about Fahrenheit and centigrade was not in vain: he was preparing me for our visit to Birobidzhan. Practically in the middle of Siberia, about 300 miles north of Manchuria, Birobidzhan's temperature was rumored to be 40 below zero—so cold that a person's breath could instantly become an icicle and a stiff wind could freeze your eyelids shut. There was also the constant danger of frostbite.

I guess my father wanted me to experience what a frozen void felt like. My parents dressed me, being sure to cover everything except my eyes and a small hole for my mouth, and when I stepped onto the frozen steppe, my first breath froze and fell like hail to the ground. My father's lesson was proven, Fahrenheit and centigrade *did* meet in a frozen hell.

This ice city had been a gift from the Russian government to its Jewish denizens. Here, they were told, they could create their own sub-zero paradise. Indeed, there was a thriving community of Jewish poets, authors, journalists and professors who had been exiled to Birobidzhan. Many among this disaffected group, however, believed it was a far better option than ending up in the frozen grips of a gulag, or labor camp, for which Siberia had become synonymous.

Stalin had sent 17–25 million people to these camps from 1928 until his death in 1953. But this system's horrors didn't reach the West until the 1970s with Aleksandr Solzhenitsyn's *Gulag Archipelago*.

CHAPTER 5

Siberia

THE trip from Moscow to Vladivostok, scheduled to take ten days, actually took almost three weeks. And with every passing mile, it began to sink in that we might never again see the world we were leaving. My mother often told me that she never forgave herself for not taking my *Babba*, her mother, along with us. But, at the time, who could have known where we were headed or what our fate would be. Still, we never could have imagined the absolute nightmare that was to unfold behind us.

There were rumors, of course, and stories of Nazi atrocities circulated as fast as the Siberian chill. I myself had already witnessed the evil they sponsored, having silently watched through my peephole, with tears in my eyes, two German soldiers raping a screaming young girl. The scene will never be erased from my memory.

But Europe had not yet turned into the Jewish slaughterhouse it would become. Around 195,000 Lithuanian Jews, only a fraction of the eventual six million, were murdered during the 1941–44 German occupation. It later transpired that, in late 1943, Heinrich Himmler, chief of the Nazi SS, sent a letter to Heinrich Mueller, chief of the Gestapo, emphasizing the importance of burning and destroying all human remains so that there would be no evidence of the genocide.[14]

We were the fortunate ones, fleeing on a transit visa, brimming with hope even as we were hounded by the fear of discovery. At first, our train stopped at every

---

14   The word genocide was coined by Raphael Lemkin during his tenure as an attorney for the United Nations. By coincidence, Lemkin escaped from the Holocaust in much the same way as my family did, and met my parents and me aboard the *Heian Maru*, the ship that carried us to Seattle, Washington.

village depot, but as we got deeper into Siberia—known natively as the sleeping land—stops became fewer and fewer. Siberians knew what Muscovites apparently didn't care to know—that, provided you didn't mind battling the permafrost, elements and emptiness, there was joy to be found in such staggering space.

JOURNEY TO VLADIVOSTOK

Siberia could freeze a traveler both physically and mentally. Its vast stretches and solitude, coupled with short winter days, made one lose track of time. Like man's ancestors, we began to live in a kind of timeless present, with a diminished sense of the past or future. Despite the fact that we were speeding through eight time zones from the Urals to the Pacific, our surroundings forced us to live in the moment.

I spent most of our train journey staring at the changing landscape. Most notably, I watched the birch trees, which glowed orange in the autumn, slowly lose their leaves and the sky turn lavender as we moved through the lofty Urals, heading toward Sverdlovsk, Omsk, Krasnoyarsk and Khabarovsk—cities I could not then pronounce. While passing a frozen wasteland just after Omsk, the refugees on our Siberian express welcomed in the New Year, silently toasting with water to a better tomorrow.

When I wasn't surveying the landscape, I focused on the chess games my father played against fellow passengers. By the time we reached Japan, to my father's astonishment, I had learnt the game. At other times, he would tutor me, mostly in mathematics.[15]

During the night, I frequently woke to the screeching halt of the train. I would gaze upon the depot from my bunk and look at the people, all wrapped like mummies to ward off the cold. Siberians, or *Sibiryaki*, were a hardy bunch. They grew their own vegetables, picked berries in the forests, and ice-fished. Many patriotic Russian writers have lauded the Siberian way of life for its close ties to nature.

Founded in the nineteenth century by Russian sailors, the city of Vladivostok was built on a series of hills overlooking a bay. Life in the city centered around the port, which was the largest in eastern Russia. I find it ironic that today, Vladivostok boasts of an international stock exchange containing the most modern trading floor in all of Russia, located in a cavernous hall intended to house the regional archives of the Soviet Communist Party.

15   Ibid.

We arrived in Vladivostok on a bitterly cold, blustery morning. Carrying all of our belongings in three suitcases, and a number of little cases and packages, the three of us walked the length of the train to the *Vladivostok vagsal*, the station house, where we would be processed along with all the other refugees. The place was bedlam.

From here, we were scheduled to sail to Japan. Thereafter, our destination was uncertain. It depended on many variables and could be anywhere we were accepted.

EAST-COAST SHAKEDOWNS

Because of its strategic position near the Japanese mainland, fear and propaganda had overtaken Vladivostok. Such feelings were heightened by Japan bullying its way into China and Manchuria. Moreover, Soviet-Japanese relations had been simmering since 1905, when the Japanese soundly defeated the Russians in war. It wasn't surprising that Soviet secret police were everywhere and that port control was rigid.

Up to this point we were on a roll, but the wheels could come off at any moment—my parents were convinced that disaster was about to strike. A few feet ahead of us, one of my father's political friends from Bialystok, also on a fugitive list, was caught and literally dragged away by the police. We were only able to watch in petrified silence. It would be a nightmare to have come this far only to be captured by the Russian Cossacks.

Immigration officers searched each bag thoroughly, looking for valuables to confiscate in the name of security. Yosef and Lola Brumberg, family friends and fellow Bundists, asked whether my parents would agree to let me wear their son's gold watch. While they were certain that Amik, who had just turned 13, would be searched, they were hopeful that younger children would not be. My father acquiesced, and I proudly wore the watch for several hours while the family's meagre belongings were scrutinized. For my parents, as long as we remained on Soviet soil, losing a watch to a corrupt official was the least of their worries. The Brombergs remained friends of the Melamdoviches and Amik became an official of the US State Department—an expert, appropriately enough, in Russian affairs.

The queue seemed endless but, once at the front, we got through the questioning and probing. For whatever reason, my father's name did not appear on any list.

It was past two o'clock in the morning when we were permitted to walk up the gangplank to board the boat that would take us to Japan. While my mother clutched my hand in one of hers, the other wrapped around a suitcase and a package, my father silently trailed behind, lugging the remaining suitcases and clutching the papers to get us aboard. The sky and sea were both black and the waves smashed against the side of the boat, rocking it violently. As a Japanese junk vessel, the boat was small, dark and had a peculiar smell. We laid down on straw mats in the hold, our communal bedroom, together with several dozen other passengers—I never even knew when we departed.

SETTING SAIL

It was a wooden tub, my father said. A wooden tub that was never meant to haul human cargo. For the next three days, the boat groaned and creaked and the horizon never stood still. We were at the mercy of the sea, just as we had been at the mercy of the cold and the Bolsheviks. I awoke to scores of passengers with their heads buried in a bucket. The stench was nauseating. My mother took me up on the narrow deck for air, where relentless waves leaped high above the bow, drenching every inch of the deck. I don't know why, but I never got seasick.

At the end of the third day, an outline of something appeared on the horizon. Land. The entire boatload pressed against the ship's railings. Refugees learn not to make noise, but joy and relief spread across everybody's body. People shook hands and hugged each other. Soon, the unmistakable outline of mountains appeared. It was Tsuruga, a small Japanese seaport—a setting that seemed nothing short of idyllic. Upon arrival, we were greeted by citizens in traditional Japanese garb, my first encounter with kimonos, sporting straw hats and warm smiles, and offering us flowers and fruit. Perhaps, I wondered, this was really paradise?

Everyone was quickly escorted off the boat and led to the train station, where we were to travel to the city of Kobe. Everything had already been arranged and paid for by the Jewish residents in Japan, the Jewish Committee or JewCom.

My mother, holding my hand, whispered that it was the first time in two years that she could breathe freely, without the fear of something terrible waiting to happen. Her fear became an ingrained feature of my life. I call it the Bialystok Syndrome.

CHAPTER 6

Three Cultures

OUR stay in Japan was in total juxtaposition to everything before, with but one exception. To my chagrin, my parents again enrolled me in school and I had to suffer the pangs of attempting to learn yet another language.

Of much grander significance was my exposure to the totally dissimilar culture. Remember, our stay in Japan was before the war and its Western influence, per General Douglas MacArthur. My mother explained that they were a very proud homogenous nation and that their traditions dated back thousands of years. The most striking difference, of course, was their dress, particularly women's kimonos. I learned that a kimono represents longevity and good fortune, but my fascination was with their striking colors. In fact, I recognized that color seemed to play a significant role in everything the Japanese did.

Our stay included their cherry blossom season and it was obvious that colorful flowers and gardens were of singular importance. It was also a hugely curious discovery to learn how polite they were, especially to us as foreigners. I guessed that politeness carried over to their custom of bowing to each other upon meeting. In fact, it was clear that they went out of their way to help us in providing directions or in shopping for food as my mother did.

My father once insisted that we visit a Japanese restaurant, which turned out to be a mistake since the food was so totally different from our European norm that we found it quite inedible. But it was a revelation to learn that we had to remove our shoes, replacing them with some form of slippers, before entering. The proprietor handed me a pair of chopsticks as a gift. My father also took me to a public bathhouse, where I had the shocking discovery that the Japanese disrobed with hardly any separation between men and women. All in all,

I learned a great deal and could not help but appreciate their kindness, customs and culture.

Our transit visa was theoretically good for ten days but, in reality, it was good until the government ordered us to leave. After arrival we were required to submit a formal application to another country. The unanimous choice was of course America, but, as refugees know, you had to apply to many places—just in case. Canada, Australia and a number of countries in South America were also on the list.

As it turned out, many did get to go to Canada, but about half of the refugees from Vladivostok ended up in Shanghai—where they remained during the war that followed between the US and Japan. The Melamdoviches were among the precious few that got extremely lucky. Out of the many thousands who arrived in Japan, only 250 were accepted by the American government.

My father believed that it was his honest answer on the application that did the trick. My father said that the question, 'how do you plan to live in the US if you are approved?', was a trick. If you answered you would get a job, you would be displacing an American worker. If you answered that you would do nothing, it would mean that you would be relying on the government—not a good answer. My father said he answered truthfully that he would be a Yiddish school teacher—how many jobs would he be displacing then?

It wasn't until 50 years later, when the US State Department released its past documents that we learned why the Melamdoviches were lucky enough to be admitted to the US. Our name was on the list of Jews who were being chased by both the Nazi Gestapo and the Russian NKVD, in other words, *endangered species*. The list was submitted to the Department of State for special attention by the AFL and the CIO, the two politically powerful American Labor organizations who were aware of my father's standing as a member of the Bund—a sister organization in the world labor movement.

A QUESTION OF FUNDING

I have often been asked where our family got the money for our escape, since my parents, and the majority of other refugees, were unable to access their personal funds, or had very little. The answer was that the money came from long-standing committees such as HIAS (Hebrew Immigrant Aid Society) and JOINT (Jewish Joint Distribution Committee), and the generosity of friends. Later, in Japan, the Jewish Refugee Committee devised a plan using the black market. For me, another lesson in currency.

It was against the law for anyone in Japan to hold foreign currency. However, once someone got permission to leave Japan, that person was required to exchange a certain amount of yen for the currency of the country to which they were destined. In fact, one could not leave Japan without the required foreign currency in hand. In the case of the US, the amount required was $50. Today, that is the equivalent of about $1,000.

Of course, hardly any of the refugees had that kind of money. So, once permission to leave was granted, JewCom would open a bank account in the refugee's name and deposit (in yen) the necessary amount. On the day of departure, the refugee would go to the bank with a *friend* (a representative of the committee) and withdraw the money, changing it to dollars based on the current yen/dollar exchange rate. The refugee, accompanied by the friend (for goodbye purposes), would then go to the ship to register with the ship's purser and record that they had the necessary dollar amount to enter the US. This done, the friend would leave—surreptitiously taking the US money—to exchange it on the black market. In 1941, the official dollar-yen exchange rate was, let's say, one dollar to 300 yen. However, on the black market, you could sell that one dollar for *double*, or more, yen. The profit was used by the JewCom to fund assistance to refugees.

THE ONWARD JOURNEY

The ship that carried us across the Pacific was called Heian Maru. It was launched in 1930 as a Japanese ocean and cargo liner, operating out of Yokohama. During the war, the ship was converted to a submarine tender and was hit by American aircraft lying at the bottom of Truk Lagoon. Our trip to Seattle, Washington, took ten days, landing on April 16, 1941. I befriended a boy from India about my age and although I could not speak English, we found a way to communicate.

It was an uneventful passage but for two occurrences. By unusual coincidence, Raphael Lemkin, a lawyer similarly fleeing from the Nazis, was aboard. Lemkin became a United Nation's official and coined the word *genocide*, which was adopted in 1944 as the official word to describe the act of mass atrocities. Today the Lemkin Summit is the name of an annual gathering of world activists to end genocide. The other occurrence that piqued my interest, as my father explained, was when we crossed the international date line and had April 10, 1941, twice.

From Seattle, we took a four-day train ride to New York City, where my mother's older sister Sarah (who had come to the US as a teenager) and her children, Norman and Janet, were expecting us. It was a gathering of once-in-a-lifetime emotions. Words fail me in describing the impact of New York on a nine-year-old child who had never even seen a building over five or ten stories high.

The effect was both mind-boggling and permanent. The power and magnitude of the structures in every direction, the number of people on the streets, the rush and noise of everything, all caused a permanent shock to my being; one that to this day, I have not forgotten or overcome. The sheer size of everything was impossible to digest or comprehend. It was clearly an alien experience, one that takes years to accept or grasp, and leaves a truly permanent shock on one's existence. I loved it from the very first second, and do to this day.

Our stay in New York was short-lived, yet long enough for my parents to send me off to a four-week summer camp. A dastardly act. An intentional baptism of fire, executed by my parents as a means of forcing my survival in a do-or-die existence. I would either learn the language and culture, or perish in the attempt. I cried myself to sleep every night during the first week, promising never to forgive them. Talk about tough love. It worked though, like they were certain it would. Four weeks later, I could speak English nearly without an accent.

CHICAGO, IL

We settled in Chicago because my parents became employed as after-school Yiddish teachers by the Sholem Aleichem Folks Institute, a national Jewish educational organization. Chicago was hardly the best academic setting to learn the ways of world markets. Nor had it any connection to the centers of finance— New York, London, Zurich, Tokyo, or Brussels—which were affected by my introduction of financial futures. Yet my inner-city education managed to prepare me for the path I was to take.

As a nine-year-old, I very quickly became immersed in the so-called melting pot of American life, which included an assortment of Italian, Polish and Jewish people. I entered fourth grade in Lowell Grammar School before I had even mastered the English language—and was swiftly educated that to be called a 'Dirty Kike' was not a phrase limited to foreign environs. It toughened me forever, learning how to defend my presence with words and fists.

Alas, I was one of those *don't-give-an-inch* teenagers, so such encounters became commonplace. It was much harder for a foreigner like me to assimilate and learn the cultural demands of, say, baseball, when I had never before held a bat. I was always last to be picked when choosing teams for a baseball game. Of course, eventually I learnt the game and went on to become a life-long fan of both baseball and the Chicago Cubs.

It is also important to record that because my parents went to work after the normal public-school-day hours, I was left alone until they returned at dinner time. During those four or so hours, I was left to my own devices, resulting in a further opportunity to use my imagination and listen to radio programs. This had one rather unusual consequence—my love for Italian food. Nearby our third-floor walk-up lived the Capone family with five children.[16] In a sense, I became a sixth child of theirs and learned to love Ms Capone's Italian cooking.

I also have great memories of the Humboldt Park neighborhood, where I met a gaggle of people whose friendship lasted a lifetime. In a booth in Zob's drugstore, on the corner of Division and Kedzie, we would sit for hours, sip a chocolate phosphate and chat about girls. Or at the Spot, across the park at Division and California, where my father would search me out at 2am because I wasn't home in bed. And finally, the ubiquitous Itskovitch's Deli, whose corned-beef-on-rye with a slice of dill pickle was surely the best in the world.

BECOMING A TRUE AMERICAN

Roosevelt High School, on the north side of Chicago, was a blessing for me. Entering high school meant that everyone had to adapt to a new school environment, so I became just like any other student. What's more, basketball was the in-sport, rather than baseball, and hardly anyone my size knew about that game. Nobody knew of my immigrant history, nor did I divulge it. I wore jeans, smoked cigarettes and owned a leather jacket—a teenage requirement of the day. By then my accent had vanished, so for all intents and purposes I was no different than a born American.

At last, I could spread my wings. And while my grades got me onto the honor roll, I used my other talents to become popular. In my third year, I became president of the class and remained its leader through to graduation. To get elected, my mother helped me create election placards which I pasted on the school halls, depicting a lion's head with the caption: "Vote for Leo, the Lion." I also became an avid book reader. Upon entering Roosevelt I asked the librarian to give a list of 100 of the most important books I should read. I believe this was a new experience for her, but she provided the list and, to the best of my memory, I read many of them before graduation. I also became a sci-fi devotee. I held the role of locker chief, and obviously used the position to assign the prettiest girls'

16   No relation to the infamous Al Capone.

lockers near to mine. Likewise, I was a member of a social-athletic club, the Phi Kappa Tau, and even became its president.

I made many friends, but please allow me to name those who have lasted: Meyer Seltzer; Jerry Specthrie; Libbie and Jerry Rosenholtez; Alan Surgal and Rose Green; Phil Siegel; Zave Gussin; Bob Schey; Jack and Nina Bell; Sy and Marilyn Golden; Emil and Debbie Shafran; Karen and Ira Marcus; Helen and Willie Boris; and Sheldon and Joanne Mantelmann. During this time, I also had my first taste in entrepreneurship. Because Illinois had a law prohibiting the sale of firecrackers, I learned that there was a market for them as the Fourth of July approached. Since anyone could drive over the border to Indiana, where there were no such laws, to buy firecrackers, I quickly determined that such laws were unenforceable and that there was a profit to be made in selling these goods to kids in Chicago. So I went into business and did quite well—until I got caught by two of Chicago's finest, who brought me to the harsh jury of my parents. Suffice to say, my parents did not appreciate my adventurous spirit.

However, that experience did not deter me from going into partnership again with my buddy Meyer Seltzer to become our high school's main purveyor of condoms. This business wasn't exactly illegal, but neither was it something welcomed by the authorities. We bought them in bulk, again in Indiana, and sold them to our classmates at an enormous markup. In those days possessing a rubber was a sure macho sign—even though most of them ended up rotting in a guy's wallet.

And I cannot forget my summers as a counsellor at a Jewish children's camp, appropriately called "Kinderland." Those nights around the fire singing Yiddish songs with fellow counsellors—Sheldon Mantelman and his wife-to-be Joanne, Janet Faber, Sy Golden, Jack Bell, and of course Cece Sigalowsky—were some of the finest moments before I left my teens. It was a well-known secret that my love affair with Cece was at the summit of my summer.

I dated many girls throughout high school, but none made their mark as much as Betty Sattler, a cute, blonde sophomore who I met in my senior year. Betty was not only attractive, but very smart, affable and, as I learned later, had an iron-fist memory. By sheer curious coincidence, she was an immigrant from Germany who arrived in Chicago as a three-year-old before the war. A romance blossomed and, in spite of a number of break-ups, our love affair led to marriage right after her graduation—and has lasted to this day. What also lasted to this day is my enthusiasm for the game of duplicate bridge, playing often with Betty as my partner in weekly tournaments.

HARVARD ON THE ROCKS

I must forever be grateful to Chicago's internationally known Mayor, Richard J. Daley, who, as a state senator, introduced legislation calling for the creation of a university in Chicago. Daley relied upon a passage from the GI Bill, which sought to reward veterans for their military service with things such as educational funding. As a result, in 1946, the University of Illinois opened what was to be a temporary branch campus, the Chicago Undergraduate Division at Navy Pier (a former Naval station), which became known as Harvard on the Rocks. It grew to become the forerunner of the University of Illinois' Circle Campus, which, with over 30,000 students, is the largest city university in the US today.

Along with veterans from the second world war, first-generation college students like me could enroll for $50 per semester. That fit my pocket book, although both Jerry Specthrie and I were accepted to Harvard. The small entry fee to Chicago was, of course, the main attraction. It also meant that those of us supporting ourselves with part-time jobs were able to begin climbing the educational ladder.

Some of my Navy Pier co-students included eventual luminaries, like Illinois Governor Jim Thompson; national commentator and former CNN lead news anchor, Bernie Shaw; and White House chief of staff to President Bill Clinton, John Podesta. And as far as part-time jobs go, I did nearly everything: paper delivery, magazine salesman, phone-book delivery man, Stop & Shop counter clerk, Marshall Field stock-boy, Fuller Brush salesman, hot-dog-stand clerk, greeting-card-machine operator, children's counsellor, and taxi driver—to name a few!

In high school, I learned to drive in a real jeep (stick shift) brought home by Arnie Warshawsky's dad after the war. Arnie would charge 50 cents per lesson plus gas. Indeed, all my buddies—male and female—who chose Navy Pier also learned that they would have to contribute 25 cents for gasoline if they were to get a ride to school in my spiffy 1941 Pontiac, purchased nine years after it was built for $125.

Ownership of a car was the goal of every male student in high school. In my case, ownership required partnership with my friend, Meyer Seltzer. Our first purchase was a 1920 Ford Model T, at a cost of $20, and then a 1928 LaSalle, which took two of us to navigate (one for steering, the other for pulling the wire, since it had no gas pedal). I later became the proud sole owner of a 1936 Chrysler, which really only functioned in the summer months, and a terrific 1941 Pontiac.

While at college we also learned to drink beer and coffee, and play Hearts for money (a precursor to my love of tournament bridge). Oh, and we also went to class. To our surprise, we discovered that Navy Pier was no piece of cake—still, not a real problem either.

Upon receiving the equivalent of a bachelor's degree, I nixed summer plans with my pal Alan Surgal to work as deckhand on a Norwegian ocean liner to Europe. I then entered John Marshall Law School in the summer of 1952. John Marshall was a tough, highly regarded law school where, for the first time in my formal educational life, I actually had to study. Upon graduation in 1955, I earned a Juris Doctor degree.[17]

17 My Juris Doctor degree was awarded by Illinois Governor Otto Kerner.

CHAPTER 7

Enter Fate

IT was an accident of course. Serendipity at its finest. I thought I was applying for a clerking job at a law firm and, instead, I wandered into a world I had never known to exist—a world of fantasy that changed the direction of my life, and the lives of countless others, forever.

There is no mystery to what happened. Like many inner-city college kids, I had to work to support myself and fund my education. So, once I was admitted to law school, I immediately began to look for employment as a law clerk, the best stepladder to success as an attorney. And as fate would have it, one Sunday morning I got a call from my buddy, Meyer Seltzer, who directed my attention to an employment ad in the *Chicago Tribune* placed by Merrill Lynch, Pierce, Fenner & Smith (years later, in a merger, Mr Smith was replaced by Mr Beane). Surely, to a couple of unworldly 20-year-olds, an enterprise with such an impressively long name *must* be a law firm.

They were looking for a runner to work from 9am to 1pm. A runner, I surmised, referred to running dockets to a lawyer in court—and since my first class that fall term would be at 2.15pm, the job was ideal. As you may have already guessed, I ended up working as a runner not for a law firm, but for the nation's pre-eminent investment broker, Merrill Lynch, on the floor of the CME for the sum of $25 per week.

Yes, from the moment I entered the futures scene and opened the door to the arcane world of shouting and gesticulations, I was bewitched. This may not be the surest road to a successful law career I realized, but providence was not to be denied. Besides, I fell in love.

The tumult, the colored garb, the frenzy of activity, the people rushing about, shouting at the top of their voices, acting out their mysterious incantations, served to instantly inflame my young and unworldly soul, awaken some unknown and uncontrollable passions deep within, and cause me to irrevocably conclude that this, *whatever* it was, was for me.

As history records, I didn't just become a part of the CME, I seized and *transformed* it. It's a very long story, and I cannot possibly record the full history of my efforts and achievements in these pages, but I shall single out some of the salient episodes I encountered and the many critical decisions I made in my 40 years spent leading the CME board.

ASSUMING LEADERSHIP

There's an old adage about it being easier to follow than lead. Well, for me, it was the opposite. I have little doubt that I could have continued as chairman for a number of decades. Yet I judged that my holding onto the title of CME chairman for a long, continuous time would be detrimental.

First, I reasoned that denying others the opportunity to hold the title would result in animosities, which would diminish my ability to lead. Second, because I felt it would be fairer for the chairman title to rotate between other senior CME board members.[18] Third, and most importantly, I never was a strong believer in titles. Rather, I believed, and do to this day, that leadership is an inherent ability that no title can provide: you either are a leader or you are not. I am reminded of a story about Winston Churchill who, upon arrival to a private dinner, tried to sit down at the side of the table. A hostess noticed and quickly moved to take his hand, stating: "Mr Churchill, your place is at the head of the table." Churchill promptly replied, "Madam, wherever I sit is the head of the table." Pompous, certainly, but no less true. In a similar fashion, I was the Merc's Grand Poohbah, its CEO, regardless of my title.

To this day, I firmly believe that my rationale was correct. While I made certain that the chairman title rotated every two years or so—always, I must add, to a board member of my choosing—this was to serve the best interests of the institution, avoiding wrangles and jealousies. We remained unified. At no time did anyone on the board, or in the world-at-large, ever doubt that I was always the de facto chairman. This may well have been one of the factors allowing our exchange to continue to grow. In comparison, there were bitter fights within the Chicago Board of Trade board nearly every year or so. As Tom Donovan,

---

18 In every instance I selected and assured support for the chairman to be elected.

the long-time president and extremely able CEO of the CBOT, once said, "the constancy of Leo Melamed at the CME helm was the biggest difference between our two exchanges, and the reason for the Merc's success."

TO RETREAT OR MOVE FORWARD

My CME stewardship began in 1967, as board secretary under then Chairman, Bob O'Brien. I was elected chairman in 1969 and remained as de facto chairman under a variety of titles pretty much until after the merger with the CBOT. My role, of course, lessened thereafter.

Upon becoming chairman in 1969, I tried to make it clear to members that I did not intend to tread water:

> I do not know to whom to attribute the following sage advice. I am certain, however, that all of you have heard these or similar words before: "we have only two choices, to retreat or move forward."
>
> The inherent implication of those words is that there is no middle ground. In business, to 'stand still' is the equivalent of 'retreating'. I am, of course, aware that any large business, corporation or institution, once it is fully geared, can coast for a number of years and continue to do well. But, the nature of the animal is such that while you mark time, you fall behind. When the coasting period is over, and the need for growth and progress is again felt, you find that you are unable to move. At best, you will find that much time and effort will be required to regain your momentum. Simply stated, I believe that a large business enterprise inherently follows the physical laws of motion and inertia. Rebirth is certainly more difficult than continuation.[19]

And so it came to pass. Although I finished law school, and even successfully practiced law for some six years, my heart, mind and soul never left the world of futures, nor the floor of the CME. So, whether it was my high-school teacher, Ms Wheelock, who made the subject of economics seem fascinating, or my easy understanding of economic principles dictating supply and demand, or even just the consequence of my new-found passion to consume everything written about markets, I was hooked.

I quickly understood futures' inherent contribution to the growth of capital

19   Message to members by Leo Melamed upon becoming chairman in 1969.

markets, its singular ability at risk management, its unique impact in liquefying cash markets, its intrinsic value in price discovery and its overall contribution to the national economy. In other words, I just *got* it.

Besides, I had an abundance of teachers—those hard-bitten professionals who prowled the exchange floor. And while many looked and acted more like characters found in a Dickens' novel of the 1850s than a financial institution a century later, many took a liking to this young law student. Some even took him under their wing.

CHAPTER 8

Yiddish

M AMME LOSHN,[20] the Yiddish language, was the lingua franca for Jews throughout the world. For me, however, Yiddish played a much more significant role than simply as a means to communicate. As noted, both my parents were devoted Bundists—a movement which embraced Yiddish as a foundation upon which to build a cohesive society. The movement urged Jews to embrace secular nationalism, encouraging them to become citizens within the nation they lived, rather than being a separate, religious sect.

As defined by Motle Zelmanowitz, one of its leaders, the Bund is "a vision of democratic and liberal socialism—not as a dogma, but as a way of life—as a garland of values which incorporate social justice, internationalism, and brotherhood of nations."[21]

The Bund had existed in Bialystok for a long time. It was deeply rooted and possessed a glorious history. When Poland still belonged to the Czarist empire of Nicholas II, Bialystok was the headquarters of the central committee of the then outlawed Bund.

My father was an intellectual and, forgive me, an agnostic. He had gone to a *chedar* (a traditional elementary school teaching the basics of Judaism and the Hebrew language) like all Jewish children, but was attracted to the Bund, a Yiddish Socialist movement that was growing throughout Poland and Lithuania before the second world war. They were the enlightened new guard of Jewish life,

---

20 In Yiddish, meaning mother tongue.
21 Motl Zelmanowitcz, *Memories of the Bund, In Love and in Struggle*, New York, 1998.

demanding freedom and equality for Jews—adamantly opposed to communism—and grounded in Yiddish language and culture.

Their mentor was Isaac Leibush Peretz, who has to be regarded as the most influential Yiddish writer of all time. He wrote from 1890, when he settled in Warsaw, the capital of Poland, until his death at the beginning of the first world war. Peretz shaped Yiddish literature into an instrument of national cohesion. As described by historian Ruth R. Wisse, he led Jews "away from religion toward a secular Jewish existence without falling into the swamp of assimilation."[22] He defined Jewish identity in its culture, common historical memory, high ethical standards, holidays, music, literature, theatre and song—all wrapped up within the Yiddish language. He preached that Jews must leave the ways of the *shtetl*, an exclusively Jewish community, to immerse themselves in the greater society.

GROWING CULTURE

My parents' generation embraced Peretz's ideals as gospel. Under Peretz's influence, Warsaw became the epicenter of a rapidly growing modern culture that was based in the Yiddish language. Peretz appealed to intellectuals like my parents and gained millions of followers. As a result, Warsaw evolved into a vibrant and dynamic center of secular Jewish life

The Yiddish school in Bialystok, where my parents worked, was named the *Grosser shul*, after Bronislaw Grosser, a Bundist writer and theorist. The Grosser school had the distinction of being the first to be accredited by the Polish government, meaning that its graduates could attend the Polish gymnasium (high school). This was a defining moment in Poland's history, a sign that the population was largely accepting the integration of Jewish and Polish cultures. As a mathematician, my father's published work was accredited and used in some Yiddish schools in Poland. Although anti-Semitism remained endemic, with vicious pogroms throughout Poland and Russia, Bialystok was far and away the leader in advancing cultural equality. My father was also an authoritarian—rules were made to be followed. Oddly, he had a knack for repairing nearly anything that became broken around the house. Our home boasted of indoor plumbing, which my father installed on his own.

His secularism, however, was so pervasive that years later, at my daughter's wedding, my father again refused the ritual custom of wearing a skullcap, as he once did in Bialystok. I had a devil of a time convincing him that he should

---

22   Ruth R. Wisse, *I. L. Peretz and the Making of Modern Jewish Culture*, University of Washington Press, 1991.

put principle aside, just this once, for his only granddaughter. My mother, on the other hand, was a sensitive and compassionate soul. As the saying goes, she would not harm a fly. However, as an equal breadwinner in our household, she was outspoken and one of the earliest proponents for equality and women's suffrage. She was also a brilliant teacher, with a remarkable intuitive sense for someone's feelings and problems. Many years after her passing, her former students would stop me on the street to tell me how much they loved their *lererkeh* (teacher).

MY CHILDHOOD AS A JEWISH YOUTH

Before the war, I could speak in both Yiddish and Polish. Due to my parents' convictions, we never spoke anything other than Yiddish in our household. On my 13th birthday, instead of a traditional Bar Mitzvah in a synagogue, my parents planned a celebration which required that I write my autobiography, in Yiddish of course, to read out loud to the invited guests. The event made the Jewish papers.

My aptitude for recitation in Yiddish, unblemished by English words that had crept into the language, caused my parents to encourage me to perform by reciting Jewish poetry. They arranged my appearances at many of the Jewish cultural events: banquets, celebrations and the like. Under my parents' tutelage, I spent countless hours preparing poems and learning to properly emote the poet's words and meaning.

These public undertakings brought me a measure of local fame. It also led me to participate as an actor on the legitimate Jewish stage in Chicago, as well as to partake in soap operas on Jewish radio programs. Subsequently, when the Chicago Yiddish Theatre Organization was organized under the direction of Dina Halperin, I became a proud member of its permanent cast. It led to my becoming an amateur Yiddish actor and receiving roles in Chicago theatre productions alongside famous Jewish actors like Maurice Schwartz, Molly Picon and Dina Halperin.[23]

For a number of years, I played an ongoing role in a Friday-night Jewish radio soap opera. In Jewish circles, I was considered a prodigy from the age of ten— *Leible der actior*, Leo the thespian. I even semi-seriously considered Hollywood. One of my memorable moments was partaking in a major New York concert, sponsored by the YIVO (the Institute for Jewish Research), starring Theo Bikel

---

23   Dina Halperin made her debut in the 1920s in the famous film, *The Dybbuk*.

who sang a couple of Yiddish songs. After my recitation of a ballad in Yiddish by the famous Jewish poet, Kadya Molodowsky, Bikel came out onto the stage to embrace me in front of the applauding audience, stating loudly, "You were unbelievable, where have you been my whole life."

I knew that I had become very good at public speaking. The larger the audience, the better I emoted. I have been told by many that I was as good as any professional speaker they have encountered. I was the designated poetry reader at many Holocaust commemorations—of which there were countless throughout the nation.

A VISIT TO ISRAEL

My parents' love for Yiddish, which I inherited whole cloth, is best illustrated by my first trip to Israel in early 1974, just after the Yom Kippur War. The idea came about through my fundraising for the JUF, the Jewish United Fund, and I soon found myself leading a delegation.

The highlight of the trip was to be a visit to the military bunkers and perhaps lunch in the *Knesset* (Parliament) hosted by no less than the Prime Minister, Golda Meir. Because Yiddish was being depressed by the Israel government in favor of Hebrew, my parents insisted that I ask the PM how she could allow that to happen when she herself spoke perfect Yiddish. It was a tall order, but I promised that I would ask if I could. The lunch itself was cancelled, but I got to be with Golda for about 20 minutes—enough time to carry out the request. Her indignant response was, "Tell your parents it was Ben Gurion, not me."

Over time, our house became a mecca for Jewish intellectual gatherings, which were often attended by prominent literary figures visiting Chicago. One of the most memorable events occurred in honor of Avrom Sutzkever, the great Jewish poet who was a Holocaust survivor from the Vilna Ghetto. My parents insisted that at the gathering I recite one of his most powerful Holocaust poems, 'The Boy of Steel,' and spent a good deal of time with me in preparation.

After I finished the recitation, the author, sitting directly in front of me, rose to embrace me and whispered that the poem's story was based on a true incident. It happened some months after the war ended. The author was walking along a desolate war-torn path just outside of Vilna. Suddenly, he saw in the distance a young boy, perhaps 13 or 14, hurrying towards him:[24]

---

24   For audiences that did not know Yiddish, I translated some of my favorite poems into English and would pass out the translation before I spoke.

A scorched Star of David on his forehead
Hair of tangled thorns
His eyes—ice in spring
With yellow ribs beneath torn rags
Strides a boy, assisted by a twisted staff,
Hurrying along Konigsberger Way.

Large willows double in the water
Cornflowers beckon through the stalks
But the boy, leaning on his stick, hurries forward
The foliage was not for him…

Except, from time to time
He tosses his head behind him
Like a bird searching—how far is yet the storm…
He imagines still—he's being chased.

We meet.
"Tell me child, what is your hurry?
Awaits for you a home, a father-mother?"

He freezes for a moment
As if the world endured a sudden eclipse:
"I have no one," he responds.
"They say in Vilna there's a school for children.
I'm headed there.
Is it far from here?"

We place ourselves together on a hill
And I show him where to go.

He lifts all the world in his sack
And hurries off through sticks and stones.

I shout to him from a distance:
"Young man! Young man!
And you, yourself—
From where are you? From where?"

Like glowing embers,
His wrinkles unexpectedly illuminate,
A smile forms in the corner of his lips,

His eyes begin to shine—bluish gold,
And from his voice a boldness suddenly emerges:

"From where am I you ask? From where?
Sir, I am from steel."

CHAPTER 9

Committee On Conscience

MY father passed on October 15, 1990; my mother on February 22, 1993. At my father's Shiva,[25] many people came from all over the US to pay their respects. There was an outpouring of many who I did not remember. One gentleman shook my hand and introduced himself as Benjamin Meed. I had no recollection of knowing him until he explained that he was a Warsaw ghetto resistance fighter, original name of Benyomin Miedzyrzecki, and the husband of Vladka.

Vladka Meed, whose given name was Feigele Peltel, was a teenage member of the Jewish underground in the Warsaw ghetto from its first days. In our household, her name possessed a near holy status. Her book, *On Both Sides of the Wall: Memoirs from the Warsaw Ghetto*,[26] has been translated into 12 languages. In it, she describes how she served in the resistance to Nazi rule by passing as a Christian. Because of her typically Aryan appearance, fluency in Polish and resourcefulness, she was a heroic underground warrior.

Not only did Vladka smuggle weapons across the wall to the Jewish Fighting Organization, the *ZOB*, but she helped Jewish children to escape from the ghetto to be sheltered in Christian homes. Additionally, she assisted Jews hiding in the city and established contact with those in labor camps. She even communicated with partisans in the forest. Vladka's exploits and bravery have become legendary in Jewish history. Vladka Meed died in Phoenix, AZ, on November 21, 2012.

---

25   Shiva is the mourning period in Judaism for first-degree relatives.
26   *On Both Sides of the Wall: Memoirs from the Warsaw Ghetto*, Vladka Meed, Schocken Books Inc. (first published 1948). Published November 1, 1999.

A FITTING MEMORIAL

When Benjamin Meed asked what I was doing to honor my father, I told him that I had helped to publish a set of books by Isaac Leibush Peretz, my father's Bundist mentor, and also donated money to Bar Lian University, Israel, to begin a Yiddish language course in my parents' names. However, Mr Meed said this was not enough. When I asked what he had in mind, he suggested I should join the ongoing effort to build the United States Holocaust Memorial Museum (USHMM) in Washington DC.

The USHMM is one result of a commission, established by President Jimmy Carter on November 1, 1978, to determine an appropriate memorial to those who perished in the Holocaust. Eliezer Wiesel, a Romanian-born, American writer, political activist, Nobel laureate and Holocaust survivor, was appointed chairman (and later became founding chairman of the museum). A report issued by the commission on September 27, 1979, suggested three components of remembrance: a memorial museum, an educational foundation, and a *Committee on Conscience*. It also called for official days of remembrance.

I received the necessary nomination from President George Bush, and a later reappointment from President Bill Clinton, and was quickly appointed to the museum's executive committee, where I served for the following 15 years.

President Clinton officially opened the museum, located among our national monuments on the National Mall, on April 22, 1993. The USHMM (as stated on its website) "provides a powerful lesson in the fragility of freedom, the myth of progress, and the need for vigilance in preserving democratic values. With unique power and authenticity, the Museum teaches millions of people each year about the dangers of unchecked hatred and the need to prevent genocide."

Since its opening, the museum has had nearly 40m visitors, including more than 10m school children, 99 heads of state, and more than 3,500 foreign officials from over 211 countries. The museum's visitors come from all over the world and fewer than 10% are Jewish.

The USHMM in our nation's capital inspired similar museums to be established throughout our nation and the world. I have visited many of them. I am especially proud of the museum created in a Chicago suburb, Skokie, named the Illinois Holocaust Museum and Education Center. Much of the original money to create the museum came from the present governor of Illinois, J. B. Pritzker. Like others, it offers pictures and memorabilia which depict the horror that befell the Jews in Europe, but, as its title indicates, it is created to act as a facility of education on hatred, bigotry, and anti-Semitism.

ESTABLISHING THE COMMITTEE

Most of Wiesel's recommendations were instituted, with the exception of the Committee on Conscience, whose mandate it was to alert the national conscience, influence policymakers and work to halt acts of genocide or related crimes against humanity. The critical reason blocking its inception was the belief that such a committee might run afoul of secret agreements between the US State Department and countries being accused of genocide by the museum. Such an occurrence, it was thought, would bode ill for both the museum and Jewish people in general. I refused to accept this rationale and told Elie Wiesel as much— he encouraged me to pursue the idea.

At the same time, I privately explained to Wiesel that I had trouble considering myself a survivor, because I didn't have a tattooed number on my forearm. Mr Wiesel just smiled and said: "You were captured by the Nazis and escaped, that makes you a survivor."

Shortly after the museum's opening, I established an ad hoc committee to vet the issues preventing the creation of a permanent standing Committee on Conscience. I could not accept a full-time position, so became vice chair of the committee, while Professor Ruth B. Mandel, director of the Eagleton Institute of Politics (a division of Rutgers University), became the committee's chair.

My uncompromising belief was that no entity in the world was more qualified to act as a sentinel against genocide than the USHMM. Another strong proponent of this belief was Deborah Esther Lipstadt, professor of Modern Jewish History and Holocaust Studies at Emory University. Professor Lipstadt is best known as author of the books *Denying the Holocaust* and *The Eichmann Trial*. A Hollywood movie, *Denial*, was released in 2016 based on Lipstadt's book, *History on Trial*, which dramatized her victory in a libel suit in Great Britain over Holocaust denier, David Irving.

Although my effort took several years, I succeeded. In a final drive to overcome objections, I invited a US State Department official to a committee meeting. I don't remember the official's name, but her Irish brogue was unmistakable. Mincing no words, she lashed out against those who were worried about stepping on the State Department's toes. "We want our toes stepped on," she loudly stated. "We *need* them stepped on. We must know if genocide reappears, and there is no one more qualified in the world to do so than the USHMM!"

The Committee on Conscience was established in 1996 as a standing committee of the USHMM. It has become one of the principal pillars of the museum.

THE MARTYRS OF BIALYSTOK

While I quickly embraced American culture and a new way of life, it was a more difficult transformation for my parents. In many ways, my parents never really came to America. Instead, they were befriended and surrounded by people who lived the American version of Jewish culture, with Yiddish as their common denominator. After the war, when I offered to arrange a family excursion back to our roots, to Bialystok, my father declined. "There is nothing there left for us," he explained sadly. And he was right.

It took a while for the barbaric truth to be understood by the European Jewish population. It is not easy to comprehend, let alone accept, that nominally civilized human beings, as Germans were generally perceived, would set about murdering an entire ethnic nation. The concept is insane.

The Warsaw Uprising occurred on April 19, 1943 and lasted to May 16, 1943. For Jewish people it has been given exalted status and became equal to other famous Jewish battles throughout biblical history. The ghetto fighters were prepared to die fighting. Against impossible odds, without military training, they inflicted considerable casualties on the Germans and were victorious in forcing the invaders to leave the ghetto and regroup. Although the outcome was a foregone conclusion, it took 28 days of intense fighting and the full might of the German *Wehrmacht*—tanks, artillery and fighter planes—to firebomb the ghetto and quell its defenders.

Six months before the Warsaw Uprising, in November 1942, Mordechai Tenenbaum, a 26-year-old activist, was sent by the Warsaw Jewish Fighting Organization to arrange a resistance movement in the Bialystok ghetto, as was being planned in Warsaw. Upon his arrival, Tenenbaum convinced Bialystok leaders of the unbelievable truth, that the Germans meant to murder them all, and advanced this powerful and prophetic message:

Let us fall as heroes, and though we die, yet we shall live.

However, there were two thorny problems: disunity in the ranks and a lack of arms. The ghetto stood alone in its struggle, as no help could be expected from Polish underground forces. As in Warsaw, arms had to either be stolen from German armories or purchased at high prices outside the ghetto; only the hand grenades were of home manufacture. Tenenbaum's efforts succeeded in unifying the various underground factions, which included Bundistins, Zionist religious factions and others, who then formed the Bialystok Organization of Jewish Self-Defense. The new organization issued the following manifesto:

> Don't be lambs for slaughter! Fight for your life to the last breath.... Remember the example and tradition of numerous generations of Jewish fighters, martyrs, thinkers, builders, pioneers and creators. Come out to the streets and fight!

On Sunday night, August 15, 1943, the call was answered. Two days later, Bialystok was a city under siege. It was the second largest ghetto uprising organized in Nazi-occupied Poland.

THE BIALYSTOK UPRISING

Led by Mordechai Tenenbaum and Daniel Moszkowicz, 300–500 insurgents, armed with 25 rifles, 100 pistols, home-made grenades and bottles filled with acid, attacked German forces. The main objective was to halt mass deportations to death camps and enable as many Jews as possible to escape into the neighboring Knyszyn Forest. The fighting lasted six days; the Germans used tanks, artillery and airplanes to quell the uprising. Unofficial data and eyewitness accounts put Nazi losses at 100 soldiers killed or wounded.

The name of one of the heroes of the uprising was strangely similar to my father's, Icchok Malmed. After throwing acid in the faces of some particularly savage Nazi soldiers, Malmed gave himself up when the Germans threatened to retaliate by shooting 1,000 Jews. He was executed by hanging. A plaque in his memory was placed on Malmeda Street, named for him.

The news about the Bialystok Uprising came to my parents and their Bundist friends quickly. It proved to be a mixture of pride and mourning. For weeks on end nothing else was discussed. While the Warsaw Uprising gave birth to a feeling of great pride, the one in Bialystok was wrapped in great sorrow. My parents knew the parents of some of the fallen fighters.

Mordechai Anielewicz, leader of the Warsaw Jewish Fighting Organization, couldn't have foreseen the full significance of the Warsaw and Bialystok Uprisings, yet he sensed that the ramifications would go far beyond military reports and casualty statistics. In a defiant act, reminiscent of the heroic deed taken centuries earlier by his brethren at Masada, Anielewicz and several other brave compatriots took their own lives in their Mila Street bunker in Warsaw, rather than allow themselves to be captured alive. In his last letter, written two weeks before his death on May 8, 1943, Anielewicz wrote: "I feel that great things are happening and that this action which we have dared to take is of enormous value."[27]

News about the uprising inspired Jewish underground resistance elsewhere. There were revolts in more than 60 ghettos and in about 100 regions, such as those documented in Kovno, Vilna, Minsk, Bialystok, Lachva, Novogruok, Lublin and Krakow.[28] And ignoring the certainty of severe retribution, and irrespective of fences, guard towers, machine guns, searchlights and vicious dogs, uprisings occurred in death and concentration camps, including those in Treblinka, Sobibor and Auschwitz/Birkenau.[29] Of a different dimension, and of incalculable magnitude, is the fact that the Warsaw and Bialystok Uprisings will forever remain an exalted flashpoint of pride for Jewish people everywhere.

Memorials commemorating the fighters, on April 19, the date of the Warsaw Uprising, have become a major tradition throughout the world. In the US, there is an annual memorial held at the Rotunda, where the US Navy Choir sings in Yiddish the partisan's theme, *'Zog Nisht Keynmol Az Du Geyst Dem Letzten Vog'* (Never say that you are on your last march). I have often spoken at such events. On the 75th anniversary of the Bialystok Ghetto Uprising, I was invited by the Polish/Bialystok officials to speak at a commemoration.

27   Resistance During the Holocaust, USHMM.

28   The armed revolt in Vilna took place in September 1943 under the command of Itzak Witenberg and, upon his death, under the command of 23-year-old Abba Kovner, after the issuance of a manifesto by its Jewish Fighting Organization, the FPO, imploring the remaining 14,000 Jews to resist deportation. The most successful organized resistance was carried out by members of the underground in Minsk, who helped between 6,000 and 10,000 people flee to the nearby forests. The Jews in Lachva, lacking guns, set fire to the ghetto and attacked Germans with axes, knives, iron bars, pitchforks and clubs. Source: USHMM.

29   *The Holocaust Chronicle*, Publication International, Ltd., Louis Weber, CEO, 2000.

CHAPTER 10

Capitalism

LAW school was tough, but I loved it. In my opinion, the study of law was preparation enough for almost any profession undertaken. It taught me to think. Not only that, it taught me how to quickly find the crux of an issue, as well as understand the *other* side. That aptitude is precious when dealing with a large contingent of people—like pit traders—who hold different views and hard-nosed opinions which have to be harmonized. In other words, without demeaning other lines of education, I believe that law school is the best route to prepare for a leadership role. I doubt very much that I could have reached the success I did without my education at John Marshall Law School.

I had an epiphany during one of my Constitutional Law classes. The subject, my favorite at the time, put into focus the rights of the individual as measured against the rights of the state. These ideas gave me a key to understanding capitalism, and essentially opened up an entirely new thought process to me. Whereas my father's socialism focused on the betterment of society as a whole, capitalism focused on the betterment of the individual to the ultimate benefit of society as a whole. A monumental difference.

And there was no denying which system worked better. One need only compare the US standard of living in the 1950s with most of the rest of the world to see the truth. It brought this young American patriot to the realization that his parents' socialistic beliefs were antithetical to the very essence of the American success story.

QUINTESSENCE OF THE FREE MARKET

As Milton Friedman lectured, the American free-market ideal was born in the Declaration of Independence, when Thomas Jefferson and his fellow revolutionaries declared that every person was born with the right to life, liberty and the pursuit of happiness. By curious coincidence, Adam Smith authored his economic magnum opus, *The Wealth of Nations,* across the ocean that same year, 1776.

During the two or more centuries that followed, the fused application of both ideals by the offspring of the US revolutionaries, in unison with a flood of immigrants that came to the shore seeking freedom, produced an unprecedented result: a crucible of innovation. Their unique features aligned to become a lightning rod for ideas—it created the free-market ideal.

To understand how and why this outcome came about, one must recognize that the American free-market ideal is not simply an economic principle giving an individual the right to produce goods and services without coercion or government intervention. Instead, as British economist Fredrich Hayek explained, "it is a social philosophy encompassing ethics, moral values, jurisprudence, ideas and a way of life." Capitalism is embodied in the American free market ideal— they are one and the same. And at its core is liberty, the right to act pursuant to one's judgment; the right to confront old truisms and examine new ideas; the right to experiment and explore; and fail without the stigma of failure.

The right to be wrong, to get another chance, is one of the most significant elements of capitalism and is an American tradition. In nations soft on capitalism, failure often defines your future. But we believe that failure can become the driving force of eventual success. It means that when our nation is hit by war, recession or even depression, Americans roll up their sleeves, push the innovation button and zealously overcome the calamity. Here is how 'economist' Rocky Balboa puts it in *Rocky*:

> The world ain't all sunshine and rainbows. It's a very mean and nasty place and I don't care how tough you are it will beat you to your knees and keep you there permanently if you let it. You, me, or nobody is gonna hit as hard as life. But it ain't about how hard ya hit. It's about how hard you can get hit and keep moving forward. How much you can take and keep moving forward. That's how winning is done!

Ask Bill Gates and he will agree. He was a Harvard dropout. He owned Traf-O-Data with Paul Allen, a business which was going nowhere. However, he had two things going for him: he was in the capital of capitalism and passionate about computer programming. The end result is Microsoft.

Or take Abraham Lincoln, who had a nervous breakdown in 1836 and was defeated in his run for presidency in 1856. America gave him another chance in 1861... and he won.

The liberty to think, invent and experiment, coupled with the right to fail, is a collective consequence of the free-market ideal. It attracts investment and has made the US number one in the world for innovation. The past century is a great example. Some of the most significant and astounding inventions—from within the fields of space exploration, information technology and medical advancement—have an American stamp.

But the free-market ideal did not materialize without thought-leaders in academia, in government, in business—and, of course, in economics. Throughout history there were giants, like Alexander Hamilton, our first secretary of the Treasury, whose expertise in economics designed our financial system; David Hume, Scottish philosopher, historian, and economist; Adam Smith, the other Scottish economist and philosopher known as the 'Father of Capitalism'; and John Maynard Keynes, the British economist, whose ideas fundamentally changed the theory and practice of macroeconomics.

FREE TO CHOOSE

Milton Friedman, the 1976 Nobel prize winner in economics is one of those giants. He dominated academic thought during the latter half of the twentieth century and became one of the greatest economists of all time. From his pulpit at the University of Chicago he preached free-market capitalism. He became best known for promoting Monetarism, a method which advocates for the control of money supply to stabilize the economy. In this regard he differed from John Maynard Keynes, who advocated for increased government expenditures and lower taxes to stimulate demand and pull the economy out of calamity.

In addition to his economic concepts, Milton Friedman had strong views on public policy, always with primary emphasis on the defense of individual freedom. His advocacy in the 1970s to transform the US military into an all-volunteer force was heroic. He and his wife, Rose—an economist in her own right—established the Milton and Rose D. Friedman Foundation for the purpose of promoting parental choice over where their children attend school. They espoused that School Choice programs improve educational outcomes by expanding opportunity and access for historically disadvantaged students. School Choice options include open-enrolment policies, magnet and charter schools.

Throughout the years, Friedman gained a universe of admirers. None were as significant as Bob Chitester, a brilliant TV producer who had an idea and the resources, energy and determination to make it happen. He got together with Milton and Rose to conceive *Free To Choose*, an internationally acclaimed, award-winning, ten-part PBS TV series which premiered in the US on January 11, 1980. It changed the world's direction. It featured Professor Friedman explaining the basic principles of how markets work and their relationship to one's personal, political and economic freedom.

Free To Choose provided answers to sophisticated economics questions in Friedman's unique and simple language. For example, Friedman worked through an explanation which enumerates all the components, countries, and people (in the thousands) involved in producing a pencil. This pencil exemplified the beauty of free-market globalization, which provides a profit incentive and cooperation to make things happen. As Friedman explained:

> No one sitting in a central office gave orders to thousands of people to make the pencil. No military police enforced the orders that were not given. These people live in many lands, speak different languages, practice different religions, may even hate one another—yet none of these differences prevented them from cooperating to produce a pencil. How did it happen? Adam Smith gave us the answer 200 years ago.

Free to Choose literally overwhelmed ingrained and erroneous market beliefs, capturing the minds of millions of viewers and teaching them why the free-market ideal is the most commanding economic system for civilization. The program was an epic success.

AN IDEAL IN ACTION

Forty years later, on October 13, 2010, there occurred a most riveting real-life example of Friedman's miracle pencil—33 men trapped in a Chilean mine for 69 days made the 2,041-foot journey safely back to the surface. No one in recorded history has ever survived so long trapped beneath the earth. *The Wall Street Journal* reported that the "Chilean miners owe their lives to the free market ideal." "The rescue effort," said the *WSJ*, "stands as an amazing feat of human faith, ingenuity, and engineering." It included groups ranging from the miners and their families to NASA, involved experts from the Center Rock Drill company in the US, and innovations from Germany, Japan, South Korea, and, of course, Chile to achieve the miracle.

Make no mistake, not only was this a triumph of the free market but, equally, of Wall Street. Without the ability to encourage investment, achieve capital formation, assume risk and offer vast financial resources, the free market might never have flourished. The internet, Google, Microsoft, Apple, Facebook, Amazon, YouTube, the airplane, atomic power, antibiotics and even our own International Monetary Market (IMM), as well as an endless list of other enterprises, were primarily American ideas inspired by the free-market ideal—and to the largest extent underwritten by American business and Wall Street.

Oh, and one more thing, it *changed the course of civilization*. The advance of liberty and democracy, the freedom to think and explore, the advance of rights for women, the advance of higher-education institutions, the right for human dignity, the incredible advances in technology, improved life expectancy, exploration in space, the embrace of US jurisprudence as a showcase for others to follow, and so much more, can be directly traced back to the American free-market ideal.

THE MARCH OF THE FREE-MARKET IDEAL

In the course of time, the world recognized the value of this ideal. It became an elixir for the oppressed, a weapon for the enslaved and a model for those who dreamed of freedom and craved liberty. And, as Hayek also noted, economic freedom can be the pathway to achieving political freedom. The basic tenets of the American free-market ideal could be seen wherever freedom flourished. In France, the ideal became *liberté, égalité, fraternité*; in Japan, see the 1947 constitution, which promotes life, liberty and property. In the constitutions of Canada, Australia and New Zealand similar references can be found.

Thirty years after my escape from the Nazis, I combined the formative economic truths embodied in the US Constitution, Milton Friedman's free-market philosophy, Hayek's definition of capitalism, as well as my parents' practical wisdom, and turned them into reality on the floor of the Merc.

As I applied my talents to build the CME, I never lost sight of the fact that it was here in the US, the land of the free and home of the brave, that I was given the opportunity to enter the world of futures markets. It was here that a child who escaped from the Nazis, a refugee from Bialystok—without

American roots, without wealth, without proper credentials, without clout or influence—was given the opportunity to climb to the top of its complex structure. It is highly doubtful that this would have been possible in any other country in the world.

CHAPTER 11

The Merc

WHEN I started working as a runner in 1952, the old guard that founded the Merc had already seen its best days. They, the so-called equivalents of the infamous Wall Street Robber Barons, had enjoyed their day in the sun. In their place was a second generation of traders. They were the *new* old guard: sons, in-laws, relatives or close associates of the founders.[30]

Although it was known as the Jewish exchange, Jews never comprised more than about 30% of the membership. Nevertheless, when the inevitable comparison was made with the Chicago Board of Trade (CBOT), the only other futures market in Chicago which happened to be the largest futures exchange in the world, the characterization seemed valid. The CBOT also had a Jewish contingent but boasted a very large assemblage of Irish members and consequently was labelled the Irish Exchange. Although the rivalry between the two exchanges was legend, any comparison was unreal; the CBOT was a hundred times larger by size, transactional volume and world recognition.

A WILLING STUDENT

My earliest market lessons originated from the desks of Merrill Lynch and its chief broker, Joseph Seeger, whom I quickly learned to both love and fear. Seeger was

---

30   Among them Saul Stone, Sam and Phil Becker, Harry Redfearn, Elmer Falker, Harold Fox, Sam and Sol Schneider, Chuck Borden, Joe Seeger, Izzy Mulmat, Miles Friedman, Gilbert Miller, Hy Henner, Bill and Izzy Katz.

a tough, no-nonsense Dutchman who was the power of the exchange, not only because Merrill Lynch was the biggest US broker and a primary source of CME business, but also because Seeger was the current chairman of the institution. I also became a close friend to Seeger's associate broker, Kenneth Birks, who was much younger he became one of my senior lieutenants in the takeover I led some dozen years later.

From Joe Seeger and Ken Birks I learned rudimentary lessons about an exchange: order flow, liquidity, rules, trading etiquettes, trade-execution, floor procedure and clearing. I also learned that while runners are on the lowest rung of the ladder, they are of indispensable value to the broker. A runner is merely a clerk who runs (delivers) orders received from customers at the firm's floor-desk to the broker in the pit for execution and then returns executed orders from the broker back to the desk. In its most sophisticated application, however, a runner is the first control point to prevent broker errors and achieve good execution for the customer. A good runner acts as another pair of eyes, ears and hands for the broker. This is accomplished by being alert, watching the market and remembering what orders are in the broker's deck.

I was an ardent and willing student, and quickly became a useful assistant to Seeger and Birks. In fact, Seeger soon began to reward my efforts with a weekly cash bonus of ten or 20 dollars, a sum greatly appreciated. Of course, Seeger could be as brutal as he was generous. On one occasion, as a result of a particularly bad error, Seeger threw one of the steel chairs that surrounded our desk at his entire floor staff—his phone clerk and two runners. Had his aim been as accurate as his anger was fierce, it might have been the end of my career.

By the time I started, the old quarters on South Water Market had long been replaced with the large (75ft by 125ft) modern trading floor at 110 North Franklin. In those early days most of the trading was on blackboards that surrounded the back walls, although there were pits for trading when things got active. On the blackboards, board-markers standing on a platform scribbled in chalk bids and offers that were shouted at them by members.

CME trading activity during the 1950s and early 1960s had fits and starts, with many a quiet period of hardly any trading at all. Some of those times it got so bad that those who didn't partake in gin rummy or pinochle, which were quite popular, created a back room for playing ping-pong. One factor contributing to a downturn in work was the increasingly obvious fact that storage eggs themselves were a disappearing commodity. The normal egg production cycle was very quickly waning and with it, the need for a futures storage-egg contract. Still, the egg contract remained a mainstay for the exchange, with its onion contract a close second. There was also talk of developing a pork belly contract.

LIFE-LONG FRIENDS

In 1955, I duly received my law degree and formed a law firm with one of my classmates, Larry Mayster. The firm was later restructured with Maury Kravitz, one of my closest chums, to become Melamed & Kravitz. One of Maury's distinguishing features was his size. While not tall, he kept gaining weight. I personally believed he was modelling himself after someone—Nobel prize author Ernest Hemmingway comes to mind. Not that Kravitz was a great writer, what appealed to him was Hemmingway's adventurist spirit: big-game hunting in Africa, bullfighting in Spain and deep-sea fishing in Florida. Kravitz did none of that, but he possessed an incredible imagination, along the lines of Walter Mitty. At my suggestion, he romanced and married my secretary, Mona Wallace, a highly intelligent women who was another of my dearest life-long friends.

Among his many travails, Kravitz formed a 'sword of the month' club and made a deal with a Spanish sword company to that end. At one point, he went through the rituals to become a Free Mason. At another, he advertised for Seminole Indians to become our clients in a class action against the State of Florida for the land stolen from them. The idea failed miserably, as did many of his adventurous ideas, but that never stopped him.

Kravitz eventually followed me to the Merc, leaving behind my firm in order to register with the CFTC. Once there, his considerable charm made him very popular. He gravitated towards the gold pit, where his presence as a gold broker became legendary—alas, with some negative overlays. He also published a member's gossip letter, *View from the Pit*. Kravitz's ability to tell tales and attract people who fell prey to his charms was one of a kind. He could walk into a room of 50 people he did not know and come out knowing most of them on a 'best friend' basis.

Yet Kravitz was most notorious for becoming an expert on Genghis Khan, specifically his claim that he knew where Genghis and his fortune were buried in 1227. Toward that end, now styling himself as an Illinois Indiana Jones, Kravitz travelled to Ulan Bator and convinced Mongolian officials to give him exclusive rights for an expedition to find Genghis' tomb and treasure.

In 1994, he convinced the archeology department of the University of Chicago to help him organize such a near-science-fiction undertaking. Together they created an expedition to Kuala Lumpur led by Kravitz and Dr. D. Bazargur, a member of the Academy of Sciences of the Republic of Mongolia. Parenthetically, Maury offered me 30% if I took over running the project. I respectfully declined. The expedition found nothing.

A BALANCING ACT

While our law firm was successful, my heart and soul were not in it. My unmistakable first love was trading. From the first whiff of the trading floor, I was smitten, and my dream was to buy a membership even before I graduated. It speaks highly of my father that he lent me $3,000, nearly all of his savings, to buy a seat in 1953 to enter into this strange world, when in truth he was proud that his son was going to be an attorney, a profession for which he held the highest regard. Of course, he made me promise that the CME membership would not derail my school attendance or prevent me from graduating as a lawyer. A promise I kept.

In the six years following my graduation, our law firm reached a level of success sufficient to provide a decent income. It enabled me to buy a home in Skokie, a nearby Chicago suburb, father a couple of offspring and own an expensive Corvette to satisfy my life-long proclivity for driving fast. In the course of those years, I tried doing both crafts—running from the trading floor to the courtroom, or to a deposition, and back again—but in my heart I knew that such a regime would only serve to detract from success in both vocations.

On the other hand, my futures-trading capabilities were questionable at best. I would go through streaks where my trading was quite successful, only to then lose most of what I had made. Nevertheless, my fascination with the market never waned. I became convinced that trading required a full-time approach. My instincts also told me that in trading I could reach unlimited heights, whereas lawyering seemed to have severe limitations. The mystery of figuring out the next day's market was thrilling and an unrivalled attraction, while practicing law was humdrum for me.

Aside from that, I was full of ideas on how to make the Merc bigger and better. Thus, the goal of becoming a full-time trader would not let me be, becoming an inexorable obsession, a belief that my ability at trading would only blossom if I actually depended on it for a living. I constantly wrestled with the dilemma. I knew my parents would vehemently disapprove. For them, the fact that their immigrant son, without clout or money, was able to reach that lofty status of *advocat* (Yiddish for attorney) was an attainment of high achievement and great pride. On top of that, I had made a promise. But the devil on my shoulder kept whispering that I had kept that promise; now I should follow my dream.

YOU SHOULD NOT TRY TO DANCE AT TWO WEDDINGS AT THE SAME TIME—OLD YIDDISH ADAGE

I could record many situations and incidents that led me to my fateful decision. The following is an example of what I was facing. The occurrence that topped the cake was a situation worthy of an Abbott and Costello routine. I was in the Circuit Court of Cicero, a suburb of Chicago, representing someone whose previous attorney allowed a default judgment to occur. I was there to reopen the default, a simple procedure as long as it is within 90 days after the default. But you better be there when the case is called.

At the time, I also held a long position in September eggs. Suddenly, I got nervous and decided to get out of the position. There was a telephone box across the hall and thankfully I had a dime, the cost of a call. Believe it or not, it took only one dime to make a telephone call, but you needed the exact coinage. I had three dimes.[31]

When I called the desk of Miller & Company, where I did my business, old man Mr Miller picked up the phone. Did I mention that Mr Miller was old? Well, he was also slow, hard of hearing and often got confused. Our conversation went like this:

"Hi Mr Miller, it's Leo…"

"Leo, I will look…"

With that Mr Miller laid the phone down and went to look for me. Frustrated, I took the opportunity to see if my case had been called. Finding that it had not, I ran back to the phone in time to hear Mr Miller say, "Leo not here." With that, he hung up before I could say anything.

Again, I ran to see what was happening with my case and then ran back to the phone to use my second dime. Mr Miller again answered and I said loudly, "Mr Miller, it's me, Leo."

It was of no use. Mr Miller said, "Just a moment, I will go look." Again, when he returned, he said, "Leo not here," and hung up.

I thought I was living in a comedy—except I wasn't laughing. Again, my case was not yet called, so I used my last dime. This time I shouted, "Mr Miller don't hang up, this is Leo." And sure enough, Mr Miller simply hung up.

The long and short of it, I won the court motion but lost a rather sizable amount on my position in eggs.

In the summer of 1965, waiting until my parents were away on a driving

---

31   A telephone box required that the money be deposited in one or more of the slots.

vacation, I made the fateful decision. I sold my law ownership to my partner, Maury Kravitz, without asking for any immediate payment. He would pay my share, I suggested, when he was certain what it was worth. The deed was done. I was a happy man.

At the age of 33, I embraced a full-time career as a pit trader. My father was so upset that he hardly talked to me for over a year. That changed materially when one day the *Chicago Sun-Times* reported (picture and all) that I had been elected chairman of the exchange. My father finally warmed up to the idea and suggested that my law degree would no doubt help my new position. He was ever so right.

CHAPTER 12

Rules Are for Sissies

IN-HOUSE CORRUPTION

BEFORE I came on the scene, the CME was often described as a den of thieves. And while that definition was well-deserved, the manipulations involved, except for the onion debacle, were of a local nature compared to some of the global rip-offs that had come before.

Still, they were of a nature that often made the exchange a laughing stock. One small example occurred in 1939 and was allegedly perpetrated by the CME's chairman, Miles Friedman. In that era, blackboard trading was the traditional transaction methodology for trading. Each morning, board-markers would record on blackboards located on the exchange walls the bids and offers brokers and traders shouted to them in every contract month. In other words, the entire inventory of bids and offers (updated continuously throughout the day) was listed on the blackboards and available for purchase or sale. Talk about transparency.

Mr Friedman was a likable, mild-mannered guy, whose trademark was a daily, fresh boutonniere pinned in his right lapel. One fateful morning, he calmly walked over to the blackboards listing all the bids and offers of eggs futures in the September, October, November and December contracts and shouted to the board-markers that he was buying the entire listed inventory of offers. In that one action, he cornered the egg futures market.

What prompted this unusual action? No one knew. It came out later. As chairman of the CME, he had just received a confidential notice from the US

Department of Agriculture stating that it was going to announce a nationwide school lunch program. This meant that the government would be in the market to buy large quantities of eggs during the coming months—talk about inside information! Friedman knew that with his advanced notice he could make a fortune.

An emergency board meeting was called to determine what should be done. If you thought that Mr Friedman would be expelled, or even asked to resign, you have *no idea* how the CME worked in those days. Rules and ethics were for sissies—after all, these board members were Chicago's version of New York's Robber Barons. Instead, the CME board ruled that the punishment for Friedman's bullish act would be for him to sell a portion of his gain so that other board members could also enjoy the windfall. The penalty certainly offered a new definition for a slap on the wrist.

Another common manipulative activity was coat-tailing. Tagging along in a manipulation was an unholy tradition at the Merc. Essentially, coat-tailers followed the lead of the manipulator, thus aiding and abetting the manipulation by acquiring and holding positions, collusively in line with the direction (usually up) of the manipulation. In this fashion, manipulators exceed the exchange rules that limit the position owned or controlled by any one given trader. However, one was hard-pressed to prove collusion, so the *squeeze* usually worked—creating a stranglehold on the market and causing prices to go well above their inherent or street value.

There was a code of silence among those involved, as well as an unholy agreement that nobody leaves the deal until the end, lest it cause an unravelling which would foil the entire operation. (Sometimes the trick for a coat-tailer was to exit the deal before something went wrong.) Such corners and squeezes went on year after year. In truth, to successfully execute this type of manipulation, it often required a sinister agreement with the powers that be, i.e., the board or one or two board members. The Merc's old guard remained mum—it is believed that they benefitted.

THE ONION CAPER

The onion fiasco in 1958, the consequence of a grand manipulative scheme,[32] nearly sealed the death of the Merc. Onions were not alone in being a commodity subject to manipulation. From the 50s to the early 60s, the storage-egg contract

32 Fully described in a subsequent chapter.

became a constant attraction for would-be manipulators and attempted corners. It was one of the things that I wanted to fix. By the time I arrived, the Merc's public image as a place of risk-management was overtaken by its image as a corrupt enterprise for highly-trained professional sharpies in the money world. I privately thought that I would work to change all that.

In the Fall of 1955, Sam Siegel, a Merc member, and Vincent Kosuga, a prominent onion grower, hatched a plan to corner the onion market. They achieved this by buying enough onions in the cash market to control 95% of the crop in the US. Then, they went long in onion futures. Millions of pounds of onions were shipped to Chicago warehouses so that the conspirators owned enough of the supply to make it nearly impossible for sellers to deliver. By controlling the supply and being long futures, the pair drove futures onion prices sky high—effectively cornering the market.

To capitalize on their hugely profitable long positions, the conspirators had a plan not only to get out of their longs, but to get short. They convinced US onion growers (farmers) to buy onion futures, promising to keep their massive supply from the market to drive onion prices higher. Word got out in the onion growing community and the farmers all went long in onion futures. It was a sure thing.

Surreptitiously, the two manipulators began to establish a short onion position by selling futures to the very farmers and growers who were eager buyers. When they were finally the primary shorts in the market, they double-crossed the growers and began to flood the markets with onions. The price of onions began cascading downward in a panicked state. In the spring of 1956, the price of a 50-pound bag of onions fell from $2.75 to 10 cents—less than the value of the bags in which they were held.

COLLUSION—A NATIONAL DISGRACE

There can be little doubt that the board was aware of the shenanigans going on, since one could hardly miss the fact that millions of pounds of onions were being shipped to Chicago and stored in local warehouses. There was a strong belief that many CME governors were either in cahoots with the manipulators or were coat-tailers, holding profitable short positions in the market. Siegel and Kosuga made millions of dollars while many onion farmers went into bankruptcy.

As a consequence of public uproar from onion farmers, the Commodity Exchange Authority (CEA), precursor of the Commodity Futures Trading Commission (CFTC), held hearings. Congressman Gerald Ford of Michigan, who went on to become the 38th US president, sponsored a bill known as the *Onion Futures Act*, which proposed banning onions from futures trade. E. B. Harris, then president of the CME, lobbied against the bill by lamely saying it was like, "Burning down the barn to find a suspected rat." I guess the barn he was talking about was the CME boardroom—there was certainly an abundance of rats. The Onion Futures Act passed on August 28, 1958, nearly sealing the death of the Merc with it.

Although the CME filed a lawsuit in federal court alleging that the ban unfairly restricted trade, a judge ruled against them and the board declined to appeal. To this day, onions remain the only product banned from futures trade. In my humble opinion, by enacting this legislation, Congress violated the range of powers granted to them by the US Commerce Clause and set a dangerous precedent that could be used to restrict free trade within the US. Worse still, no actions were taken against the manipulators, the CME board or the CME itself. It was the darkest chapter in the Merc's history, humiliating the membership and leaving public confidence at an all-time low.

In the aftermath of the onion debacle, trading slowed to a crawl, causing the exchange to lose money year after year. Annual CME deficits mounted to $500,000, a frightening amount in those days. Membership prices sunk and, in 1960, in an unprecedented move to hold up the membership price level, the board voted to institute a support program, authorizing the exchange to purchase seats at $3,000. It was a desperate move. Annual trading volume in 1964 was about 249,000 contracts, the lowest post-war volume.

IT'S NOT ALL BAD!

Allow me to turn the page. In fact, allow me to turn many chapters and offer a glimpse years into the future at the other side of the coin.

First, the beauty of the Merc's open outcry. There is no fool-proof way a clearing firm can control what a trader does on the floor during the trading day. It is based on *trust*. In the course of a trading day in open outcry, trades are made with a shout, a wave of a hand or a nod. No matter if the trade ends up giving the buyer or seller a million dollar win or loss, a shout, wave or nod is like a written guarantee drafted by a bevy of lawyers. The fallout of legitimate so-called 'out-trades,' where an honest mistake is made, was less than 3%. Often in such instances, the value of the profit or loss involved is evenly split between the two traders. A very small percentage of out-trades end up before the arbitration committee for final adjudication. A trader's word was a bond, it was the only way that open outcry could function.

My son, Jordan, an accomplished movie maker, made a superb, highly successful documentary, *Futures Past*, depicting the Merc's transformation from open outcry to Globex. It also detailed the life of his father and relationship with his son as a trader turned movie maker. Having been a trader himself, Jordan was perfectly placed to capture this bitter-sweet moment. It was the end of the open outcry era, which had defined futures markets for centuries. In my obviously biased opinion, Jordan caught the moment on tape for posterity in a way no other ever could.

Second, equality at the exchange. During the course of my stewardship, I ran a small trading firm called the Dellsher Investment Company. (*Dellsher* was devised in honor of the daughters that Maury Kravitz and I were fortunate enough to have; my first born was Idelle, Kravitz's was Sheryl, ergo: *Dellsher*. Initially Dellsher was the name of Kravitz and I's jointly-bought 33-foot cabin cruiser. When I left the law firm, I got the rights to the Dellsher name.)[33]

I ran the Dellsher Investment Company alongside my appointed COO, Valerie Turner, my former law secretary. She had been studying futures and ran the firm with an iron fist. It is important to note the fact that Valerie Turner was black, and that her becoming chief operating officer of a recognized CME clearing firm, owned by the CME chairman, did not go unnoticed. With this appointment, it was my intention to signal to all floor and clearing members in 1967 that the chairman of the exchange meant it when he preached equality.

I was once visited by Jesse Jackson on behalf of his Rainbow Coalition.[34] He explained that he was meeting with me to promote the hiring of African Americans. I asked Mr Jackson to come to the Merc's gallery. After we were seated, I asked him to take a look at the floor below. As Jesse Jackson could plainly see, at least a full third of the many hundreds of employees in blue or gold jackets were minorities. Smiling, Mr Jackson stood up, shook my hand and left, saying "I have no mission here."

It had been one of my personal efforts, making certain that the CME hired a fair number of minorities and women, and that our member firms equally did so. I owe this feeling to my mother's efforts. Even as a child she made sure that I understood the meaning of Johann von Schiller's theme for universal brotherhood of mankind—set to Beethoven's 'Symphony No. 9,' known as his 'Choral Symphony.'

---

33   Years later, the name was changed to Sakura Dellsher when the Japanese Sakura Bank bought a majority stake in my company.

34   The Rainbow Coalition was an effort organized by Jesse Jackson, a prominent Civil Rights leader.

DEMONSTRATIVE EQUALITY

There is yet one more aspect of the exchange floor that was special: its *demonstrative equality*. Even as it grew to an immense size—housing over 5,000 individuals—and required a second floor to accommodate all the markets—with its population of traders, brokers, and their personnel—the entity maintained a special characteristic, one which I proudly had a hand in advancing. It represented a defining example of American exceptionalism. In the open outcry trading environment, with very few exceptions, the primary goal was to achieve a price based on fairness, competition and within a framework of full disclosure. Nothing else mattered very much.

I am not discussing the lives, relationships, virtues or problems of traders off the floor. But on the floor, the trophy went to the company or person who operated *within* the rules and understood the economic principles of supply and demand. One's personal pedigree, family origin, physical infirmities and gender were to the greatest degree meaningless when measured against one's ability to figure out the direction of the market. Little else mattered.

One's success in the market did not depend on whether you were a Catholic or a Jew, white or black, man or woman. The market rewarded you when you were correct, or when your quality was high and your service good, and punished you when you were wrong or your quality was inferior and your service poor—no matter *who* your parents were, no matter *what* they did for a living, and no matter *where* they came from. No, it was not a utopia—the system had its flaws and exceptions—but I knew of no other private-sector enterprise, institution or system of that day and age, that was freer of human prejudices and less concerned with ethnicity, race, religion or gender, than the trading floors of American open outcry futures markets.

CHAPTER 13

The Broker's Club

IN 1960, five years before I became a full-time trader, I was invited to join a half-clandestine group of Merc traders, known as the Broker's Club, who were hell-bent on change. I do not recall the exact date when this club was formed, but the motivation of each of its 20 or so members was quite clear: to clean up the place and elect board members who would move to end corrupt practices.

Clearly, my lawyer status combined with my gift for public speaking gained me recognition and admittance to this underground sanctum—or the Young Turks, as it was later called by the old guard. The composition of the Broker's Club was in dramatic contrast to that of the then CME board of governors. The Club's members were young, without a stake in the establishment, financially insecure and, for the most part, had little to lose. They were clearly dissatisfied with the status quo and looked to grow the exchange and change its low image.

Any comparison between us and the other Chicago exchange, then Board of Trade, was a joke. The CBOT was internationally known and enjoyed a measure of respect. We, on the other hand, were considered more or less a den of thieves. The onion debacle served to prove this point.

The CME board was primarily comprised of sons, in-laws, relatives and close associates of the founders of the exchange. They held total power over the decisions of the exchange, were financially secure, and merely gave lip-service to the notion of change or ideas that originated on the floor. In truth, they were happy with the status quo. Even though the exchange was on a major downturn after the onion debacle, the board's composition did not change—mainly because they *owned* the votes from the major brokerage firms as well as the outside members. Their annual re-election to the board was always a more or less foregone conclusion.

The Broker's Club did include a couple of well-knowns, which gave it a little bit of standing. One of them, Robert J. O'Brien, was the son-in-law to a leading figure in JV McCarthy & Company, a founding firm of the exchange.[35] A close relationship between us quickly developed as I helped him become the unofficial chairman of the Broker's Club. Working mostly in secret, because no one wanted to take on the board openly, we met in a hotel room for which everyone chipped in $20.

Our clandestine efforts in the late 1950s had some positive results, such as the election of several new and younger governors to the board—albeit not members of the Club. Our most effective achievements were in bringing to surface board decisions which were self-serving and, in our opinion, contrary to the best interests of the exchange. This served to create a more open, antagonistic environment between the board and the Broker's Club, which lasted through the early 60s, but without meaningful results. The board continued to rule, not paying much attention to floor's ideas or the growing dissent mostly generated by the Club. *Status quo* is what the board wanted—and that's pretty much what they got.

ADDRESSING THE QUORUM ISSUE

With O'Brien at my side, I explained to the members of the Club that to really achieve change, we had to change the bylaws of the institution. The structure and math of the exchange guaranteed that nothing could be done unless the board said so, and that was not going to happen. The exchange had 500 registered members. Only about half were active and came to the floor on a regular basis. The other 50% were owned by out-of-towners, commercial entities, relatives of members who had inherited the seat and others who had little reason to become active.

The rules of the CME, written some 40 years back, were devised to give total control to the founders. In order to hold an official members' meeting, the rules required a quorum of 300 members: a 60% requirement. This effectively prevented an official meeting of the membership from ever occurring. Indeed, to the memory of most, there had not been an official meeting of members since the rule was written in 1927. Annual member meetings did take place, but none with a quorum present and therefore of no official consequence. Without a reasonable number for a quorum, there was nothing the membership could accomplish.

---

35   Destined to become the hugely successful modern RJO enterprise.

Although young and a relatively inexperienced lawyer, I made a strong case that the membership could not effectuate any change unless the quorum requirement was reduced to a reasonable number. My rationale was clear and won over many floor members. When the board heard of the idea, they thought it was a joke. "The board need do nothing they don't want to," was their response. The idea of lowering the quorum rule would never happen, and if it did, "it would not be something the board would abide by."

It must be difficult for anyone in today's information age to believe that an American entity could reject such an obvious legal principle. But this was the 1950s, an entirely different world. Of course, I knew differently and would be ready for that fight.

I persuaded the Broker's Club that, no matter what the board thinks, "the Merc is subject to the Constitution of the United States." In other words, as an Illinois corporation, the CME board would be compelled to follow any resolution adopted by its membership at a duly-constituted members' meeting. Ultimately, I convinced Club members to go for a quorum requirement that was a practical number, say 100 CME members, otherwise they would never have an effective voice in exchange proceedings. Of course, to reduce the quorum requirement, you needed a one-time official meeting with the full quorum of 300 members—a sort-of catch 22.

It proved to be what was the corporate version of an old Western shoot-em-up—*Gunfight at the O.K. Corral* comes to mind. In today's parlance, a corporate takeover by the membership. Carl Icahn would have been proud.

We made the quorum requirement our *raison d'être*. Under my direction, we officially called for a special meeting for the express purpose of reducing the quorum requirement to 100. I was meticulous about following the necessary legal requirements so there would be no procedural flaw in the process. Then we set about gaining support from floor members. Hardly anyone objected to this effort, but the hard part was making sure they attended the meeting. The harder part fell on Ken Birks—my boss and a fellow member of the Broker's Club. He offered to use his Merrill Lynch stationary to gain credibility and receive a signed proxy from the member-firms as well as non-floor members. Otherwise we would not get to the necessary number of 300 in attendance to make the proposition legal-proof.

I give Birks full credit for getting enough signed proxies to reach more than the required amount. Birks followed up his letter with telephone calls to as many people as he could. My assignment was to energize the floor members; all they had to do was come to the meeting so that we would reach 300. Our efforts proved successful. History has recorded that on June 14, 1961, a duly constituted members' meeting, with more than 300 members in attendance (in person or by proxy), took place. On a motion made by me and duly seconded by Mr Birks, the proposition for a reduction in the quorum requirement from 300 to 100 was presented to the membership. The proposition was adopted in near *unanimous* fashion. It was historic.

TALE OF THE UNDERDOG

At first, no one was certain what would happen. This was the first legal confrontation between the board and its members. The CME chairman, William Katz, publicly stated that nothing the members did at the meeting had any validity. A successful egg merchant, whose family was among the founding fathers of the exchange, Bill Katz had been chairman of the CME for the past ten years. He was a powerful figure at the institution and wielded dictatorial rule. As anticipated, his view was endorsed by the other 11 board members as well as Lee Freeman, the CME's attorney.

Mr Freeman, an established Chicago lawyer, was tough, feisty, and known for his two-fisted defense of clientele. Yet for all the bravado he was a savvy lawyer, and he knew that I had led the Broker's Club onto solid legal ground. Moreover, he was probably worried about the potential for the case to proceed to court, knowing, as both Katz and Freeman did, that if we went to court and won, it would wrest control from the board.

Instead, Freeman persuaded the board to do the prudent thing: publicly deny that the member's quorum resolution had any validity, but officially adopt the rule on its own volition. It was clever. An amendment to Rule 109—the CME quorum requirement rule—was established, which lowered the quorum requirement to 100 members. The façade, however, failed. This represented the first major victory for the Broker's Club and the board knew it. It also made me a bit of a folk hero and set the stage for what followed.

Although the exchange was still in its doldrums, the Merc introduced a pork belly contract (uncured bacon.) This futures contract was destined to become a huge winner and bring life back to the moribund floor. The CME soon became known as the pork-belly exchange.

CHAPTER 14

The Right to Referendum

F IVE years had passed since the members had taken issue with the quorum requirements—years during which the makeup of the board had not materially changed. There was also little evidence of any progressive programs regarding members' rights and opinions, or new ideas and products. We were resting on the success of pork belly contracts without any thought to growth or change in the future. That was not enough for my ambitions. I wanted our voice to make a difference and stop the shenanigans, the squeezes and corners, from continuing year after year.

After the onion scandal, you would think the board would have cleaned up its act. But no, they were well taken care of, so why would they? In December 1966, I decided to do something about the situation. It was a radical idea. I proposed to the Broker's Club the adoption of a rule in the bylaws giving the members the *right of referendum*.

This would spell fundamental change, giving the members a voice in the CME's governance. Again, it was the kind of thing Carl Icahn might have advanced in current times. I judged that it was the only way to force the board to listen to its members. Although the right of referendum is one of the most basic principles in the American concept of law and justice, it was not without its dangers. For one thing, it would place actions of the board in jeopardy, as decisions would always be subject to countermand by the membership. To prevent frivolous applications, I proposed difficult conditions before this rule could ensue. Since nothing else seemed to work, this rule would prove to be a critical threat to force the board to be more responsive to the opinions and demands of its members.

Proxies were again needed, this time to have sufficient votes to pass this amendment to our bylaws. And again, we were advised by the board that such a proposal would not be binding. Nevertheless, we proceeded and mustered the required number of proxies and called for a meeting to vote on the proposition.

I vividly recall the floor of the exchange where the meeting was held after the markets closed. There were easily over 200 of us, so there was no doubt about a quorum. I had made certain that the notice for the meeting was ironclad. You could cut the tension with a knife. Bill Katz, the chairman, and Lee Freeman, the exchange attorney, opened the meeting by denouncing the proposition as an attempt to wrest control from the duly elected board of governors. That was true. However, I had the legal argument and the ability to speak passionately.

My rebuttal explained that the board had been totally unresponsive to member complaints about the Merc's reputation. It ignored our pleas to clean the place up. No one listened to any of our ideas and proposals for new markets. Those of us who planned a career in futures did not want to tolerate the alleged 'deals, squeezes and corners' that were going on. It was business as usual, like the onion debacle never happened. The CME, I stated, was rotting from within and we were going nowhere as a futures market. The members loved it and gave me loud applause. I also outlined that, if passed, this resolution would be legally binding.

Lee Freeman, an experienced trial lawyer, wasn't even close to matching my passion or logic. The motion was made, seconded, and overwhelmingly approved—the membership had resolved to adopt, under carefully structured conditions, the right to a referendum. And as it turned out, no court battle was necessary. In fact, the controversy ended right then and there. An annual election was only weeks away. The members had won, and the board knew it.

BEGINNING TO MAKE WAVES

In January 1967, I was duly elected to the board of the CME with the highest number of votes ever recorded—around 98%. Officers of the board were to be chosen by the board the following week. Robert J. O'Brien, son-in-law to one of the founders of the exchange, urged me to run for chairman, but I reasoned that his becoming chairman would actually better serve our cause. As I explained, I wanted a peaceful revolution; I wanted to lead with meaningful innovations, rather than spend my time justifying my presence. As son-in-law of one of the founders, he was more likely to be accepted by the old guard as a *legitimate* heir to the throne. I was considered a bit of a rabble-rouser, and my appointment would not go down well.

Bob reluctantly agreed on the condition that I assume the leadership role right from the beginning of his tenure and then officially become chairman two years later. I agreed. We also decided that I should run for secretary, so that I could use that post to institute my idea of publishing regular reports for the membership. A first of its kind.

My first act as a board governor was to enact rule 206, giving the CME membership the right to a referendum over any decision of the board. After the Broker's Club victory, this was no longer much of a battle. However, with O'Brien's support, I also sponsored the removal of the male-gender membership requirement, a rule that had been in place since the CME's creation. This was hugely controversial, given that it would probably be the first US exchange to allow women on the floor not simply as employees, but as traders.

The main objection was that women on the floor could become a huge distraction to the all-male floor makeup. One board member actually stated: "It will cause brokers to walk around with a hard-on." This was followed by a discussion about a female dress code. How high above the knee would a dress require? O'Brien and I could hardly keep straight faces throughout the five-hour debate. We settled with the need for dresses to be at least three inches below the knee. Between us, Bob and I had the votes to pass the rule with a 7–5 victory. I like to say that real credit goes to my mother, an active agent for female equality back in Poland—she taught me well.

THE EVOLUTION OF THE CME

Flash forward. In 1972, my bridge-playing partner, Carol 'Mickey' Norton became the first female trader to go into the pits. We had made a deal; I would teach her trading and she would teach me bridge. The result, she became a successful trader and I became a *Life Master* in bridge in record time. Carol adopted the masculine nickname Mickey, which probably tells you a lot about her character and how she was able to stand her ground in a male-dominated place where brawn was as important as brains. But Mickey had both and used them to become a legendary speculator at the IMM.[36]

Another unexpected decision I made was to insist that Lee Freeman remain in his position as the CME attorney. Previously one of my main adversaries, I now wanted him to use his skills as forcefully as he had for the old guard. It proved to be a very wise decision. As did my decision to keep old E. B. Harris on as

---

36   Margie Teller, a former trader in the eurodollar contract holds the current title.

president. It was mostly a ceremonial office anyway, but Harris knew everyone in the industry and that would be very important to my plans.

Looking back, these were my first steps towards transforming the CME. My leadership had been broadly accepted and my popularity made it certain that I would be elected chairman at the next election.[37] My avowed goals were ambitious: reformation and enforcement of the rules, elimination of 'corners and squeezes', establish departments and a public relations team, seek new products, create a viable membership committee structure, consider a new trading floor and promote the diversification of futures products.[38] A progressive agenda, to be sure, but I meant every bit of it.

The Merc's image as a den of gamblers, cut-throats, and financial wolves was well deserved. Upon becoming chairman in 1969, I was hell-bent on reform. It is, after all, the reason I fought to lower the quorum requirements, to create a referendum rule and to become chairman. On the day following my election, I was given a set of bylaws by Ken Mackay, the Merc's executive vice-president. I could hardly keep myself from laughing. Not only had they not been seriously altered since their original adoption in 1919, but they were in disarray, kept together with scotch tape, paste and paper clips, with hand-written revisions and explanations.

THE AGENDA

Clearly, my first project was to rewrite and modernize the bylaws, adopt current corporate practices and most emphatically expand and enhance the rules and penalties for violators. So I set into motion what I called a *constitutional convention*, the first major assignment for the newly appointed General Counsel, Jerrold Salzman (Jerry). He became an indispensable ally and advisor and, some 45 years later, still acts as primary legal advisor to the exchange.[39]

It was Lee Freeman, the tough and savvy old-line lawyer with whom I had locked horns in my early days but no less admired and respected, who gave the Merc Salzman, a gift I readily accepted. Jerry began his post with the Merc right out of Harvard, when he joined the small but respected law firm of Freeman & Freeman. As soon as Salzman joined his firm, Freeman said to me that he was going to give him the Merc account because the "stuff" I was planning required

---

37　The original exchange, the Butter and Egg Board, formed in 1898, became the Chicago Mercantile Exchange in 1919.

38　The exchange had no rule endorsement department.

39　Recently retired.

"someone of my generation to understand." To underscore this point, upon the launch of the IMM, Lee Freeman presented me with a sculpture depicting me as Don Quixote fighting windmills.

I was extremely happy with Salzman's appointment. I learned very quickly that he was a solid lawyer on whom I could depend. He was present throughout the difficult twists and turns that we endured. I often sought him out for help and advice in critical moments—of which there were an infinite number. I am happy to say that Salzman was key in bringing the Merc to a safe shore. Although there were a few times we disagreed, at no point did I ever doubt that his opinion was based on what he thought would be the best legal advice for the exchange. He then applied his legal knowledge and professional talent to carry out the result I was looking for.

Over time, Jerrold Salzman became one of the most, if not the most, respected futures-markets attorneys in the world. I could fill a whole other book just recording his efforts on behalf of the Merc as we held hands to realize some of my impossible dreams. Jerry was indispensable, as I have recounted throughout this memoir, and was in a class by himself. He would always give me his unbiased view, which I always welcomed and, with few exceptions, followed.

Once, some 40 years later, when I spoke before a Chicago Bar Association assembly to recount our growth and success, Jerry introduced me by saying, "Nothing of any consequence would have happened at the CME without Leo Melamed." On more than one occasion I have returned this compliment by stating that Jerry played an outstanding role in our journey.

As promised, my second goal was to bring law and order to the CME. The two of us spent the better part of a year and a half meeting with every committee chairman and rewriting the committee charters and practices. The new rules gave me the power to meaningfully enforce regulations and therefore alter our lawless image.

My third goal was to diversify our product line. In 1969, the old storage egg contract was on its last legs and our strongest product was pork bellies, with cattle and hog contracts still in formative stages. We were basically banking on meats—a risky business if something happened to diminish the need of futures on this product line, like occurred with butter and eggs.

One other action that required my immediate attention was the 50th anniversary of the exchange. I wanted to use this event to underscore to Chicago, and the nation, that something really special had occurred at the CME. We settled on gifting the city of Chicago a Farm-in-the-Zoo, a farm in Lincoln Park where children could see how chickens lay eggs. We handed the city a $50,000 check to build the farm so that children could learn first-hand about our heritage in agriculture. It made headlines.

Point is, things at the Merc were happening and membership values were rising—a sure sign of optimism.

CHAPTER 15

Old Traditions Die Hard

THE full meaning of my election became clear to the old-line would-be violators some months after I took office. This was a time when the exchange handed down some of its stiffest new penalties to members for rule violations. It was an unprecedented move, one that served to make it clear that this young Turk was determined to change the CME and its reputation. But it was no bed of roses. While I got plaudits from the rank and file, I became highly unpopular in some quarters. Members who had been doing things a certain way for years, suddenly found their practices were illegal. I am talking about trading rules, like not running through bids and offers, exceeding position limits, roughhousing in the pit, breaking up potential squeezes, and so forth. This did not make them happy. But it is one thing to say, 'we have taken a hard line,' and quite another to prove it.

My new policies were frequently put to the test—there are always those who scoff at rules or believe they can circumvent them. I had to prove to the membership that every member was subject to the rules, that no one was exempt. Often it gave rise to heated conflicts, sometimes even lawsuits. This occasionally hurt business, but I knew the principle was sound and the measures were necessary. I once whimsically asked our president whether our CME market could work without corners. To my surprise, Harris replied: "I really don't know." Well, I had to hope that it would. Futures, I knew, performed valuable economic functions. Why not without shenanigans?

I do not for a moment wish to imply that we became totally clean of rule violations at this exchange. That would be a utopia. Instead, I sought to heavily punish, and thus deter, misconduct. This was primarily achieved through my creation of a department of Audits and Investigations, to which I appointed William Phelan, an attorney with a reputation of being straight and tough. He eventually went on to become an Illinois Circuit Court judge. Looking back, I know these steps were a critical factor in the eventual success of the CME.

From the beginning of my tenure, I also wanted our administration to be open with the membership. It is near impossible for anyone today, who was not around when an exchange was structured with a floor-based community of hundreds of brokers and traders, to understand how imperative it was to have the members support the actions of their board. Most notably, I instituted writing to them to explain my actions and to issue annual and special reports. For instance, my 1970 report explained what we had done:

> We have now witnessed the conclusion of a year-long intensive effort to reconstruct and revise our rules, an effort which required the cooperation and service of every exchange committee and which resulted in a total revamping of most of the important exchange rules and concepts.
>
> The new rule book, which was published the previous March, expunged archaic requirements and standards, and attempted to replace them with modern concepts within the framework of present-day standards and the current volume of business. I would be the last to state that our present rule book is perfect, but I certainly believe that our rules, for the most part, have now caught up with, and are suitable for, present and future administrative needs.

UP AGAINST RESISTANCE

I knew from the start that both myself and the new rule book would be put to the test. As I said, I had to prove that what was written was now law. Almost immediately, a pork-belly manipulation was carried out. It was achieved in full violation of our rules and included several members in collusion. The evidence was solid. I knew the floor was waiting to see what I would do. Here was my first opportunity to prove to the floor that the perpetrators would not get away with it.

I decided to do something public. I spoke to our new general counsel, Jerry Salzman, about an actual trial. I explained to him that we needed a showcase to prove to members that it was a new era—a line had to be drawn. Although Salzman probably never considered this kind of work when he became our lawyer, he understood and agreed. After all, we had re-written the rules for this very reason.

For the first time in CME history, there was an actual trial for a rule violation—I was the challenger; Salzman, the prosecutor; and the board were the jury. Salzman proved his worth. It took several days, but the exchange had the proof and the jury were unanimous in their guilty verdict. The floor members were duly impressed and applauded the result. I was relieved, but I knew that there would be more to come.

THE HAROLD FOX RULE

It was not too long before another manipulation arose. The difference was that the violation had not yet been executed—the pieces were in place though. The would-be culprit was Harold Fox, a major player at the exchange. He and his cohorts were in position to corner the 1970 September egg contract.

Harold Fox was a bit of a floor trademark. A heavy-set man who was a dyed-in-the-wool chain smoker, with a cigarette dangling from his lips as if it was a permanent fixture. He never seemed to take it out for a puff, instead he allowed the cigarette to burn itself down to a stub with the ashes falling onto his vest. Harold Fox was a senior member at Fox Deluxe Inc., a national food operation that also processed poultry, eggs, dairy products and its own national line of beer. He and his family were time-honored members of the Merc's old guard. They were among the founders of the Butter and Egg Board, and two of his family members, Harold's brother and uncle, were past Merc chairmen.

Reputedly, Harold Fox and his cohorts had done this before. They had the money, reputation and power to carry out their intentions. No one dared stop him. Big money was at stake. What made matters much worse was that many of the Fox family were floor members. Worse yet, not only were they stalwart members of the Merc but they were generally on my team, openly applauding what I stood for and had achieved. Bill Muno, a family member by marriage, was a strong friend of mine and an influential member of the board. So, this situation was not only a test for the exchange, but also for my integrity. Since the corner had not yet been carried out, I wanted to prevent it from happening. Our new rules provided for this very situation.

The rule, written with Salzman, could have been named the Harold Fox rule. It provided that owning a controlling interest in the deliverable supply of the actual product traded, complemented by a large long futures position, was against the law. In other words, I knew that to have a successful corner on a futures product, you not only needed a commanding long position in the futures market, but also control of enough of the actual cash product as well. The rule went on to state that anyone found in violation could be forced to liquidate their futures position and face additional disciplinary action.

When the 1970 September futures egg contract began to rise steadily, an indication that another Fox squeeze may have been put in place, Marlow King, one of my advisors, said, "Lee, you can stop this." I had Phelan do a careful review of the situation. Satisfied that the facts bore me out, I decided to bite the bullet and apply the rule for the first time. I met privately with Harold in his office. I politely explained why I was there. He chuckled when I showed him the undeniable evidence Phelan had gathered. It proved that he was in violation of the rules and in a position to squeeze the shorts in the September egg contract. Harold kept silent. I then sternly stated that I was ordering him to reduce his futures position by 50% by the end of the following week. I explained that no one would know of the order, so that the liquidation could be at his own pace. Harold laughed out loud when I finished and said, "Or what?"

Undaunted, I responded quietly, "Or I will send brokers into the pit to sell out your positions as the rule allows me to do." He offered a full belly laugh. As I left his office he shouted: "You and what army?"

AN IMMOVABLE OBJECT

I left his office a little scared but satisfied that I had done well.

The first two days of the following week passed without any change in Harold's futures position. I again went to his office to repeat my warning, even going so far as to read him the rule so that he fully understood that I had the authority to do as I threatened. He continued chuckling, but I had a feeling that he finally believed me. No one except Phelan and Salzman knew of my action.

The following morning, to the surprise of everyone on the floor, there was wave after wave of selling in the September eggs. When I checked the books after the market, sure enough, Fox's egg position was considerably reduced. The selling continued the next day, bringing the market below the daily permissible limit. By Friday morning, Harold Fox had no positions in September eggs. He and his coat-tailers had lost a ton of money and the potential for an illegal big profit.

Late that Friday evening, as I descended the marble steps of the Merc building as I normally did, I suddenly heard behind me the echo of heavy footfalls. It was like someone had been waiting for me to appear. A shudder went through my body as I realized it might be Harold Fox, who was easily twice my size. Had he purposefully waited for me to leave as I normally did each day?

"Hey Lee," Harold shouted as I stepped outside the building, calling me by my trading acronym. His deep voice was unmistakable. "Hold up a minute." I turned and waited, hiding any fear. "Lee," he said after he got closer, "I'm going to Paris for the weekend with a couple of friends, want to join us? It's on me! We'll have a ball." It was hard to hide my shock, "Gee, Harold, that is a very nice offer. I wish I could, but I have plans with the wife." He smiled and said, "Sorry, maybe next time."

It was vintage Chicago: we had a fair fight and you won—let's move on.

The Fox standoff was pivotal. The floor understood what had happened. From that day forward, the old way was no longer acceptable, and everyone knew it. And not just around the Chicago environs either, it was an *inside* story nationwide. I had faced down the powerful Fox Deluxe, broke up a corner in eggs, and gained huge respect from the membership: I accomplished what many believed could not be done. That episode says quite a lot about the new Merc, the traders, and me.

I was overwhelmingly re-elected for a third straight term as chairman.

CHAPTER 16

Conception

DIVERSIFICATION was always on the top of my agenda and continued as a motivating force during the following nearly 50 years of leadership. I had witnessed first-hand what can happen if an exchange has but one or two products for trade and something goes wrong.

Jump ahead a few decades or so and you can readily see that the CME Group is the most diversified institution of its kind. Some of that was achieved through merger, but most was the consequence of a conscious and determined effort to diversify. In my search for new products, foreign currency as a futures product sometimes crossed my mind as a fleeting thought, only to be quickly dismissed. Agricultural products were so entrenched and ingrained in the very existence of futures that the idea of a brand-new asset class was beyond consideration. Anyway, had I presented currency as an asset class for futures directly after my election, it would have been laughable at best. So, during my first year in office I remained fully committed to the norm and stayed within the acceptable parameters of the futures ecosystem. I tried potatoes, turkeys, lumber, shrimp and apples. Except for lumber, none of them succeeded.

Successful or not, none of those products satisfied my deep desire for something else—something brand new. By 1970, the diversification issue morphed into a fundamental consideration: if futures are truly an insurance and price discovery tool as I earnestly believed, then can't they be applied across the board? I mean, for almost anything? Clearly there exists an economic and commercial need for forward-pricing, risk management and speculation potential in products well beyond a limited menu of commodities. It was a reoccurring, even nagging, thought. It wasn't long before this radical thinking led me to the global rumblings of the day, especially as they related to foreign exchange.

THE END OF BRETTON WOODS

In the late 60s and increasingly into the 70s, news about changes in foreign exchange began to appear regularly in the financial press. What was causing this attention was the news about sudden foreign exchange devaluations and revaluations. In some instances, they even made the front page of *The Wall Street Journal* or *The Times* in the UK. It seemed as if, suddenly, one finance minister after another found it necessary to announce a revaluation of its country's currency in order to stay in line with global dictates.

By 1971, you could hardly open a daily newspaper or listen to a radio news program without learning about the financial implications of an announced change in FX values. It seemed like a game of dominoes, where one nation's change in FX value would cause a knock-on effect on several others. The Bretton Woods fixed-exchange-rate system seemed to be the cause of the problem. The need for a new and better system became a topic of serious discussion.

The Bretton Woods fixed-exchange system was devised in a small resort town in the mountains of New Hampshire in 1944. It was there, at the Mount Washington Hotel in Bretton Woods, that an assembly of 730 delegates from 44 allied nations gathered to establish financial order after the second world war. The conference lasted three weeks, from July 1 to July 22. Its two principal architects were the celebrated British economist, John Maynard Keynes, and well-known Harry Dexter White of the US Treasury.

You have to understand that after the second world war, the US was the only country left standing. The dollar was supreme and the only viable currency. Under the agreement reached, all currencies would have fixed price parities for both gold and dollars. The dollar, in turn, would not have a fixed parity but would be freely convertible into gold at the fixed price of $35 an ounce. The finance ministers planned to meet on an annual basis to review or change the evaluations as conditions dictated. This Bretton Woods fixed-exchange system was ratified on December 27, 1944, and was hailed as a seminal achievement.

There was but one noted dissenter, Milton Friedman, who argued that the agreement was doomed to failure. From his view, it tried to achieve incompatible objectives: freedom for countries to pursue an independent, internal monetary policy; fixed exchange rates; and relatively free international movement of goods and capital.

I had been a devoted follower of Milton Friedman since my college days. As I mentioned, I have great memories of sneaking into his lectures at the University of Chicago, even though I wasn't a student, to listen to the great man expound on the free market. He quickly became someone whose ideas were my bread and butter. I had no doubt that soon Milton Friedman would be proven right about Bretton Woods. Although it took much longer than he anticipated, here is how Friedman saw it:

> From the time Bretton Woods became effective, it was inevitable it would break down ... It tried to achieve incompatible objectives: freedom of countries to pursue an independent internal monetary policy; fixed exchange rates; and relatively free international movement of goods and capital ... As one of the architects of Bretton Woods, Keynes tried to resolve the incompatibility by providing for flexibility of exchange rates through what he intended to be frequent and fairly easily achieved changes in official parities. In practice, this hope was doomed because maintaining the announced parity became a matter of prestige and political controversy. Countries therefore held on to a parity as long as they could, in the process letting minor problems grow into major crises and then making large changes.

THE RISE OF A NEW ERA

For the first decade and into the second, the system worked well. Milton looked as if he made a mistake. However, in the late 60s, Bretton Woods began to fail. Its rigidity was the problem. By 1970, it became obvious to many that the Bretton Woods fixed-exchange system was dying; it was no longer viable. For one, the economies of developed nations had mostly recovered from the war and were well on their way towards becoming competitive with the US. In other words, the dollar now had competition. And every nation was now competing against every other nation. As Friedman predicted, each country had an independent monetary policy.

Aside from this, revolutionary advancement in information technology made the Bretton Woods agreement an anachronism. When it was first enacted, information travelled slowly around the globe. In the information age the world had entered, news affecting currency and other financial values was instantly recognized by the marketplace. Values changed in immediate fashion. This reality often forced financial ministers to play catch up and rush to announce sudden currency revaluations in rapid and repeated order so as to keep pace with what was happening. The realities of the marketplace could not wait for a meeting at Bretton Woods to officially accept changes. It was full confirmation that Friedman's opinion was correct. The fixed-exchange-rate system was a relic of the past.

By then I had a fairly good understanding of how currency values affect the internal economic policy decisions of governments—FX rates are one of the most important means by which a country's level of economic health is calculated, while changes in inflation and interest rates affect currency value. I also knew that a country's political state, economic performance, and prospects affect valuations in currency. I began to contemplate that what the modern world needed was a system that would allow currency values to adjust in an ongoing fashion.

In other words, a system wherein FX prices reflected continuous changes in response to the constant flow of new information. Such an open system would allow risks to be managed and opportunities to be captured in real time, eliminating the need for after-the-fact official catch-up announcements. The system I visualized was precisely what a futures market can provide. Wouldn't a futures market in currency be the exact prescription for what ails the world? The thought was like an atom bomb explosion in my head—it scared me half to death as I fully recognized the enormity of the idea I was considering.

PEER REVIEW

At first, I kept it inside of me. But I was bombarded with internal questions. Would such a market work in futures? Why hasn't anyone else thought of this? How dare I consider a financial instrument for futures? Was there a reason futures mostly served the agricultural arena? Would everyone just ridicule me? Who of the traders knew how to trade currencies? I could laughingly imagine some of the old geezers in eggs bidding in Swiss francs. Was this just the crazy notion of someone who was not an economist? If I was right, why hadn't the banks said so? Was I ready to be known as the village idiot? Besides, until Bretton Woods was officially abandoned, how could a futures market even operate?

While I had few answers to these questions, the idea would not leave me. *Why not money futures*, kept repeating like a beating pulse.

When I quietly broached the subject with a couple of traders, I would often get blank stares and funny smiles, sometimes even laughter. Some looked like they were questioning my sanity—like I had suggested putting my hand in a tiger's mouth. There were exceptions though. Most notably, a fellow trader, Dick Boerke, who assured me that it was a grand idea. He ultimately became my strongest ally and advisor.

The concept soon became an obsession, a gnawing thought and a constant companion. It got to the point where I could think about little else. Day in, day out, the idea plagued me. But neither did the doubts and fears ever leave me. In fact, there was a physical effect. I developed a tightness in my stomach which caused constant pain. My smoking in those days went up to an ungodly four packs a day. It was a tug-of-war. My rational side continued to dismiss the idea as too grandiose, too off the charts, while my innovative side kept insisting it was brilliant.

A RENEWED SENSE OF PURPOSE

One day something caught my eye that pushed me over to the innovative side. It was a news story about Milton Friedman's desire to short the British pound since he thought, quite correctly, that it was out of line with world conditions. During the 1960s, the UK economy was facing lower productivity compared to its competitors, making its goods less competitive, which led to an increased deficit. Being right was not Friedman's problem, it was that no bank would take the professor's money to institute a short position because "He did not possess a commercial reason to sell short the pound."

That story really got to me. "A commercial reason?" Does one have to be a bank to try to increase the value of one's estate or income? Is there a law against it? Doesn't the US Constitution give everyone the right to pursue any legal course of endeavor? Is enhancement of one's personal estate not guaranteed as an inalienable right? That issue put a wind in my back.

As the Bretton Woods system began to suffer its terminal pains, I began testing my idea on market aficionados outside of the trader community. I soon learned that most people believed the idea of a futures market in FX was a non-starter, especially for a Chicago backwater exchange like the Merc—*what, at the pork belly exchange?* The onion debacle exchange? Apart from a tiny cadre of trader-friends, no one would give it much of a second thought.

Fortunately, the Merc's president, good old E. B. Harris, became a supporter—although I never really knew whether he really liked the idea or was humoring me. On the other hand, Mark Powers, whom I appointed as chief economist for the CME on the basis of his pork-belly-futures dissertation, became my greatest supporter inside the Merc. I had no doubt that he fully believed in the idea, urging me on, for that I am eternally grateful. In fact, later on, when I asked him to prepare a draft for the actual specifications of an eventual FX contract, Powers had them ready within 24 hours. Powers eventually became the chief economist for the CFTC.

THE PREVAILING SENTIMENT

In early 1971, when I finally summoned up the courage to introduce my idea to the CME board of directors, I saw that some of them had to stifle their laughter. How could Leo Melamed, lawyer turned trader, realistically consider foreign currency futures? How could such an idea ever succeed within the strictures of a futures marketplace, one designed for butter and eggs, pork bellies and soybeans? Weren't futures exchanges created to exclusively serve farmers? Wasn't there some fundamental economic reason why no one had, in the long history of futures markets, ever attempted to apply futures to finance? Why hadn't the CBOT or New York Stock Exchange (NYSE) thought of it? Surely, this was just Melamed's attempt to get a headline.

Simply stated, there wasn't nearly enough support for me to proceed. I needed a majority of seven votes for approval. Similar negative sentiments prevailed not just in the Merc boardroom, but around the world. Futures markets, I was told, were suited for the traditional agricultural products and could never be applied to the sophisticated world of banks and bankers. Besides, detractors pointed out, "If your idea had any validity, it would be initiated in New York, the US capital of finance." Such arguments were prevalent, powerful, and convincing.

Indeed, on the eve of the launch of the IMM in May of 1972, a prominent New York banker stated in *The Wall Street Journal*: "It's ludicrous to think that foreign exchange can be entrusted to a bunch of pork belly crapshooters." And that sentiment was universal. *BusinessWeek* echoed thus: "The New Currency Market: Strictly for Crapshooters." But I did not buy it. As I have often stated, derogatory comments, defamatory innuendos, inflammatory jokes, false accusations, misleading opinions, half-truths and out-and-out lies have all been the burden and fate of futures markets. And why not? From time immemorial, predicting the future has been a hazardous occupation—*behead the messenger of bad tidings!*

Even after our successful launch, *BusinessWeek* made this cynical statement: "The new currency market: strictly for crapshooters, if you fancy yourself an international money speculator but lack the resources... your day has come!" But never mind the opinion of the media, without board approval, I did not have the ability to move forward anyway.

On top of all that, rather than being dissuaded, I soon became paranoid that someone would steal my idea. While unlikely, as most everyone was sneering at the concept, I was concerned—and I was right to be. After all, my idea was now an open secret. I had mentioned it to many people, anyone could give it a try. And sure enough, I soon heard that the New York Produce Exchange, an almost non-entity, had changed its name to the International Commerce Exchange (ICE).[40] My heart sank. Were they going to list currencies? CME President Harris and I immediately flew to New York to pay a visit.

It was more of a joke than anything else. There was hardly anyone in the room: no traders, no brokers. It turned out that the ICE was on the order of a large currency exchange—similar to a Western Union shop. It seemed to be mostly for wealthy tourists who were looking to exchange, say, $5,000 or $10,000. It was a huge relief. What they were doing was nothing close to what I had envisioned. They were exchanging short-term money, I wanted to change the world's foreign exchange system. The ICE closed soon after the IMM was formed.

PRESIDENTIAL INTERVENTION

Throughout all the machinations, I was also aware that the viability of currency futures would depend on the abandonment of the Bretton Woods fixed-exchange system—something outside of my control. Although I believed its end was coming, the timing was unpredictable. I authorized Mark Powers to write to Friedman, economist to economist, to inquire how much longer he thought the Bretton Woods system would last. His answer was non-committal.

Nonetheless, my mind was made up to proceed. With inflation rising and the dollar falling, I could see that the US economy was in trouble and in need of a new order. But the toughest obstacle remained my own board—the majority remained convinced that my global system of floating exchange rates was without merit. This coming from a group of people without credentials in that arena! There was but one person I could turn to: Milton Friedman, my mentor and idol. Friedman's words and ideas were, for me, holy scripture. More than anyone in the world, he could validate my idea. At the same time, I was scared to reach out to him—what if he gave a negative response? That would certainly make me despondent.

40   Not related to the current ICE, owner of the NYSE.

This feeling didn't last long though, as reality soon exploded with nuclear force. On August 15, 1971, President Richard Nixon closed the gold window, an action Milton Friedman had advised from the outset of his administration, dropping the US dollar convertibility to gold. President Nixon's action was primarily the consequence of the cumulative effect of fixed exchange rates. The dollar was falling continuously, inflation was rising, and the world was making a run on the dollar by converting their currency to gold. It so disadvantaged the United States that, by the time they were discarded, our nation's financial structure was crumbling and drastic measures were in order.

I was certain that this presidential action represented the end for Bretton Woods. For the world, it was a financial tsunami whose reverberations would still be felt a decade later. For me, it was the moment of truth—I had to act immediately. I directed E. B. Harris to get an appointment with the great man.

CHAPTER 17

Genesis

MILTON FRIEDMAN, E. B. Harris and I met for lunch on Saturday, November 13, 1971, at the Waldorf Astoria in New York. The moment has forever been engraved in my memory. I began by asking him to promise not to laugh. Then, wasting no time, I put forth my idea: "I am thinking of launching a futures market in world currencies." To my total surprise and my indescribable gratification, Friedman did not hesitate. "It's a wonderful idea," he said, adding emphatically, "you should do it!"

Stunned, I could hardly believe my ears. E. B. Harris remained silent. After my heart began beating again, I pressed forward, "Isn't it possible that foreign currency might not work in futures markets?" He chuckled, "None that I can think of." For a moment, his words hung in the air. When my voice again returned, I said, "No one will believe you've said that." He chuckled again, "Sure they will. You can tell them I said so." I shook my head, "No, I need it in writing."

Friedman hesitated for a brief moment, "Are you suggesting that I write a feasibility paper?" I wasn't sure, but I emphatically said, "yes." "You know I am a capitalist?" he said. I laughed. We shook hands and settled on a $5,000 fee for a feasibility study on the need for a futures market in currencies. This was one of the best trades made in the history of finance, as the street value of the CME Group today is in the billions. A friendship was formed that day between us, one that lasted a lifetime.

GAINING MOMENTUM

The Bretton Woods system was officially abandoned on December 13, 1971, when ten of the leading industrial nations gathered at the Smithsonian Institute in Washington, DC, to scrap the fixed-rate era and permit the world's major currencies to fluctuate against the dollar. At first, this was only by 4.5%, but this percentage was gradually increased until it was entirely removed.[41]

Luckily, by then I held in my hand the holy grail for the CME: Friedman's 1971 paper. Within those 11 pages, Friedman provided the intellectual credibility upon which I could build the CME's financial futures superstructure. The following is an excerpt:

> Changes in the international financial structure will create a great expansion in the demand for foreign cover. It is highly desirable that this demand be met by as broad, as deep, as resilient a futures market in foreign currencies as possible in order to facilitate foreign trade and investment. Such a wider market is almost certain to develop in response to the demand. The major open question is where. The US is a natural place and it is very much in the interests of the US that it should develop here.[42]

Friedman's words were magical. I used his paper as a sword and a shield; a sword to attack naysayers of the idea and a shield to defend against those criticizing my lack of financial credentials. In December 1971, the IMM was officially incorporated as a futures exchange which exclusively listed financial instruments for futures trade. My 1971 report for members was modest and simple:

> On December 20, 1971, we called a news conference to announce a concept we believe and hope will be of paramount significance in the years to come—the decision to develop a futures market in foreign currencies so

---

41   If you had to pinpoint the birth of globalization, you can't do much better than August 15, 1971, when President Nixon dropped the US dollar convertibility to gold. It led to an irreversible breakdown of the system of fixed exchange rates, initiated the modern era of globalization, and provided the rationale for the launch of financial futures by the Chicago Mercantile Exchange (CME). Indeed, few things are more emblematic of the era of flexible exchange rates than the International Monetary Market (IMM) launched by the CME directly after President Nixon's action. The birth of this financial futures exchange is inextricably intertwined with the death of Bretton Woods.

42   Friedman, Milton, 'The Need for Futures Markets in Currencies', 1971.

that those engaged in international trade will have an additional mechanism with which to hedge the risks associated with fluctuations in international currencies. This entailed the formation and chartering of an entirely new exchange, the International Monetary Market of the Chicago Mercantile Exchange, the opening of which to occur on May 16, 1972.

IF IT'S LEGAL, GET IT DONE

After I was officially elected chairman in 1969, E. B. Harris thought I would fire him as CME president since he had sided with the old guard against me and the Broker's Club. I thought differently. I specifically kept him around for his wealth of connections and friends.[43]

Sometimes this was difficult. Harris was not only an odd soul, he was also old guard in his thinking. I had several interactions with him that made me rethink my decision to keep him on. For example, early in my administration, E. B. asked to speak with me privately. During the meeting, he nervously asked me not to get mad because he said, "You have a temper." I promised not to get angry and he proceeded to ask why I was exclusively hiring Catholics? Did I know that the people I hired to head up the new CME departments, Mark Powers, Ron Frost and William Phelan, were Catholics? Since I was a Jew, he said, "I would understand if you hired Jews, but why Catholics? You know they are very cliquish?" Of course, I had no idea what religion they were, nor did I care. So, trying to control my temper, I told Mr Harris that if he ever broached the subject again, I really would fire him as he believed.

In my haste to open the IMM, I had a real serious issue. I knew that before the market could do business, there had to be a delivery system. Without delivery capabilities, the IMM could not function. Sometimes customers who were in the market would want to receive delivery of the currency they were long in. In other words, we needed to secure the cooperation of one or two foreign banks in each of the seven countries whose currency we were trading.

E.B. Harris now justified my reason for keeping him around. He introduced me to Tilden Cummings, president of the Continental Illinois National Bank, Chicago's largest bank. The Continental had branches in every country whose foreign currency we listed for trade—if we could come to an agreement, we would not even need the agreement of an outside bank. Cummings heard me

---

43   Prior to becoming CME president, E. B. Harris held the office of secretary at the CBOT.

out, but he had very little idea of what we were talking about—to the uninitiated, futures trading in currency sounded like science fiction.

He did, however, come around, given that Harris was an old friend and my passionate appeal convinced him of the legitimacy of my request. I also liberally dropped the name Milton Friedman. Cummings decided to bring in "someone more my age," who might understand what I was talking about. In came John McPartland. I carefully went through the explanation again. "Do you get this?" Cummings asked. McPartland confidently responded in the affirmative. "Good," said the president of the Continental Bank, "if it's legal, get it done."

With this directive, Cummings appointed John McPartland to our case. McPartland was a dream come true; he instantly understood the nature of our request and set about creating the necessary delivery facilities in the Continental's branches in those seven countries. I am forever grateful to him for using his innovative capabilities to breathe life into the IMM. The essence of McPartland's system operates to this very day, with trillions of dollars delivered over the years at the maturity of our currency contracts. John McPartland went on to become senior policy advisor for financial markets at the Chicago Federal Reserve.

AS SOLID AS THE NEW YORK STOCK EXCHANGE

Of course, the IMM was a brand-new entity without any history of legitimacy. Ensuring its financial credibility was critical. This was partially achieved by promoting our link to the CME—the very reason I created the IMM as an offshoot, a division, of the CME in the first place. It worked. Still, I knew that eventually the IMM's wherewithal would require that it stand on its own feet. Association with the CME could only go so far. The strength of an exchange lies in its clearing house, upon whose shoulders the safety of all customer money depended. I made sure to adopt all the CME's rules, so the same people operated both sets of books, but I had much more in mind.

At the time, CME clearing members operated under a common bond: if any of them failed, the others would pick up the default and proportionally restore the failed capital. In other words, the CME's financial strength was based on an unwritten, 'good to the last drop' principle (any loss would be covered until nobody had any money left).

However, aside from being unrealistic, this understanding had never been applied or tested. And there were many who questioned (me among them) whether it was enforceable. In reality, whenever there was a potential failure, the Merc would quietly get another clearing member to assume the failing customer positions and make good any default. The exchange, in turn, would find a way to make up the cost to the intervening member. I thought that the IMM offered an opportunity to fix this gap.

My advisor in financial matters was Barry Lind, who I appointed chairman of the IMM clearing house upon its creation. Together we discussed our goal for the IMM to be regarded as being as solid as the NYSE—the archetype of financial strength at the time. We also agreed that the clearing members of the CME, many of which were Wall Street brokerage houses, would automatically become clearing members of the IMM. The clearing entity Lind devised became the foundation for the edifice upon which the Merc's financial integrity stands. It withstood all the financial demands and stresses of the decades ahead.

Barry Lind was without a doubt my closest chum, as well as someone upon whose advice I depended throughout a myriad of issues we faced. Barry had an outstanding talent for math, was an excellent trader, and a specialist in finance. In 1965, he created Lind-Waldock, the first discount-commission brokerage firm in futures. It served to influence Charles Schwab in 1971 to similarly pioneer a discount-brokerage firm in securities. Barry Lind also had an unusually competitive streak— in everything. We both drove fast and owned Porches. Barry always compared our driving skills. He said as many times as he tried, he failed to beat my time from his house to the Merc. On January 24, 2013, to my deep grief, Barry Lind died after he was struck by a car in Southern California. He was 74.

Lind and I held hearings, carefully advising Wall Streeters that we were setting very high financial standards. In fact, I had adamantly insisted that the IMM bylaws, which had been written by Barry Lind, Jerry Salzman, and myself, included this 'good to the last drop' principle in writing. While we carefully avoided using this phrasing, we did emphasize that each clearing member would be obliged to be part of a common bond that would secure the IMM's clearing structure. Incredibly, the rule was accepted without objection. Over time, the common bond became a carefully defined formula based on annual transactions, open interest and other factors.

A QUESTION OF INTEGRITY

I knew that the reputation of the people serving on the board of directors (I insisted that they be called directors, instead of governors) was central to building a strong image. I needed to set the standard with as high-caliber appointments as possible. It was a measure of my own reputation that I was able to appoint extremely credible and well-known people to sit on the IMM's first board of directors. Of course, the appointees were all free-market advocates who strongly believed in the IMM itself. It began with Beryl Sprinkel, chief economist at Chicago's Harris Bank (today the BMO), a Milton Friedman disciple who went on to become chairman of President Reagan's council of economic advisors.

This first prestigious appointment enabled me to reach out to other prominent people: Robert Abboud, EVP of the First National Bank of Chicago; William J. McDonough of First Chicago, who later became president of the NY Federal Reserve Bank; Robert Aliber, noted professor of economics at the University of Chicago; and Dr. Henry Jarecki, chief arbitrageur at the Mocatta Metals Corporation, to name but a few. Truly a star-studded platform. In doing this, I broke the tradition that board members were exclusively elected members. For obvious political reasons, I also appointed all the board members of the CME.

Appointed members of the board were changed from time to time. We did not offer payment, so it was purely for the prestige that directors accepted a seat. Aside from the value of their presence, directors provided advice based on years of experience. But gaining credibility cannot be attained solely through the board. The growth of the IMM would also greatly depend on my leadership, as well as the senior executives that myself and the board would appoint over time.

While consolidating the IMM's credibility and integrity, I also made sure to keep up with evolving technological tools. I sought with a fierce determination to apply any new advancement in order to provide the safest form of clearing both for ourselves and our clearing members. It was no accident that the CME website underscores this caveat:

> The CME Group is vitally aware of its role in global markets and is confident that our operational standards paired with our financial safeguards provide an effective set of risk management tools and capabilities that result in industry leading risk management capabilities. Risk management and financial surveillance are principal functions of CME Clearing's financial safeguards system.
>
> The Financial and Regulatory Surveillance Department monitors the capital requirements of clearing members based on the risk associated with each clearing member's positions as well as our assessment of each clearing member's internal controls, risk-management policies, and back-office operations.

MY *ANNUS MIRABILIS* (REMARKABLE YEAR)

Looking back, we opened a centralized marketplace on the American shore for a commodity that had been traded on a decentralized basis for over 1,000 years. We entered into an arena that was considered taboo for anyone outside the banking community. We redesigned a business tool that was unused—and not even fully understood—by a large portion of the world. And we opened the door to a new philosophy which could revolutionize the system of exchange-rate determination.

My 1972 annual report to the members followed the Texas saying, "If it's real, it ain't bragging":

> So much has happened since opening day that one is tempted to think of the IMM as an established marketplace when, in fact, it has yet to reach its first birthday. Yet, when our accomplishments of ten months are measured against the magnitude of this undertaking, one begins to realize that in some respects our progress has been monumental.
>
> Today the IMM is known from coast to coast with benefits to the Chicago Mercantile Exchange that should not be underestimated. We have received recognition in offshore financial centers and have won acceptance both here and abroad from many who were initially skeptical. The IMM's business, by any standard, has exceeded all reasonable expectations for a market less than one year old.
>
> When the concept of the IMM was first announced, we were but singular pioneers who favored flexible exchange rates. Today, current events have proven our philosophy to be sound, vital, and the inevitable trend of the monetary world. We are heartened, therefore, to be in tune with the economics of the years ahead, and we are certainly encouraged to expand our efforts.
>
> Finally, we believe the IMM is larger in scope than currency futures alone, and accordingly, we hope to bring to our threshold many other contracts and commodities that relate directly to monetary matters and that would complement the economics of money futures.

Like most great ideas, however, its merit was not immediately or universally recognized. The history of the IMM and the start of financial futures trading is as much a story of persistence, determination and conviction as it is one of brilliance, insight and inevitability. To borrow from Thomas Edison, the birth of the IMM was the result of both perspiration and inspiration.

To fully comprehend the revolutionary impact of the IMM on the history of futures markets, one must first understand that, from its inception, the IMM represented both a specific and general departure from traditional futures. Although the IMM began life with foreign-currency contracts, itself a revolutionary departure from the established agricultural base for futures, it represented a much broader concept. It introduced the idea of instruments in finance that would forever change and advance the concept of investment.

Two decades later, Nobel laureate Merton Miller would call the introduction of financial futures, "The most significant innovation of the past 20 years."

CHAPTER 18

Gestation

WITH everything I could think of in place, I became a modern-day evangelist—or a Don Quixote, as our attorney Lee Freeman stated—crisscrossing the country many, many times, meeting a variety of groups and travelling to every foreign center of finance whose currency we were about to trade.

To achieve my grand design, I needed to gain the support, or at least recognition, of respected economic authorities and high-level government officials. I had already gained the approval of, arguably, the highest academic authority with Milton Friedman, but it would still be a meaningful boost if, in addition, the chairman of the Fed, say, understood and liked what we were doing—perhaps even made a favorable public comment about it. At a minimum, I wanted them to not be surprised about our plans when asked for a comment by the media. For that exact reason, even before the IMM's birth, I insisted that we meet with US officials to advise them of the IMM.

Our attorney, Jerry Salzman, opposed this idea. "It's like putting your hand into the tiger's cage," he cautioned. Perhaps I was naïve, but I ignored his advice—looking back, I was right to do so.

MEETING AT THE US TREASURY

I met with most of the top officials of our nation: chairman of the Fed, Arthur Burns; past and present chairmen of the Council of Economic Advisors, Alan Greenspan, Herbert Stein, Martin Feldstein and Beryl Sprinkle; US secretary of the Treasury, George P. Schultz; undersecretary of the Treasury, Paul Volcker; past and present secretaries of agriculture, Clifford Hardin and Earl Butz; secretary of commerce, Peter Peterson; reputed to become next secretary of Treasury, William E. Simon; and a host of other officials.

I correctly judged that current officials more or less belonged philosophically to the free-market ideal and would favorably view our new market in that light. In every case I received a favorable nod to proceed, or at least no words of discouragement. Of course, Friedman's feasibility paper was of incomparable value; "You don't have to believe me," I would state, "but believe Milton Friedman."

This was particularly applicable in the case of Treasury Secretary George Schultz, to whom I sent the paper prior to our meeting. I was aware that Schultz had been a professor at the University of Chicago. While my knees shook as I stood for the first time in the immense office of the secretary in the US Treasury building, Shultz simply said: "Listen Mr Melamed, if it's good enough for Milton, it's good enough for me." I used that historic quote wherever I went.

ADAPTING TO YOUR AUDIENCE

When I visited with businessmen and members of the financial community, I was aware that many, if not most, would be skeptical. So, I would adjust my words accordingly. Often it was a case of the bigger the crowd, the better my explanation. To any audience, however, I found it important to explain that my plan for the IMM went beyond currency futures. The following is from my address to the Society of Security Analysts, a large group of expected skeptics:

> I am honored to have this opportunity to address the Society of Security Analysts on the eve of the birth of the International Monetary Market. I am pleased that you were sufficiently interested in our invention to invite me to appear before you.
>
> As I see it, my mission here is threefold. First, to address the question of why there should be a futures market in currency. Second, in what manner will such a market be different from the existing interbank forward system which the commercial world uses? And third, why we think the IMM will succeed and be applied with other instruments of finance. A formidable task, but I shall try.

Flashing forward to November 27, 1973, a year after the launch of the IMM, I could afford to be more confident at a trade conference before a friendly audience at the Continental Plaza:

> Last year when I addressed our First International Monetary Conference, I spoke of the successful launching of the International Monetary Market of the Chicago Mercantile Exchange. I pointed out, with a great deal of pride, that we had ventured into an uncharted sea, that our journey was motivated by the obvious necessity of the times; that our goal was grandiose, unique and revolutionary. Those sentiments are no less true today.
>
> But, last year, the International Monetary Market was but a mere five months old. We were no more than an embryo whose life could be snuffed out by any one of a hundred eventualities. We had little proof of success, no credentials or credibility, little evidence of existence. We were but an idea which we ourselves forced upon the scene. Some of the same birth pangs are still with us today.
>
> But, today, the International Monetary Market is a year and a half old. Our embryo survived and is now an infant. We have passed from the crawling to the walking stage.

I often tried innovative approaches, especially when addressing faculty or students at a university. For example, to gain the approval of students at Northwestern University, Evanston, Illinois, on November 7, 1973, I may have been the first to compare the biblical Joseph when explaining futures:

> And after Pharaoh summoned Joseph to interpret the dream, Joseph said to Pharaoh: there will come seven years of great plenty throughout all the land of Egypt, but after them, there will arise seven years of famine. And Joseph proposed: Let them gather all the food of these good years are coming, and lay up grain under the authority of Pharaoh for food in the cities, and let them keep it. That food shall be a reserve for the land against the seven years of famine which are to befall the land of Egypt, so that the land may not perish through famine. Thus, the concept of a futures market was born.

WHY CONSTRUCT A WHOLE NEW EXCHANGE?

From the outset of the idea, I insisted that financial instruments listed for trade must reside in a separate exchange, rather than as a CME product. I did this for several reasons. First, I knew that I wanted to list additional financial instruments in the future and an exchange specifically designed for this purpose seemed right. Second, the IMM's catchy moniker would offer a better sales pitch to the world. Third, many officials and traders at banks and securities firms were concerned that they would be sending business to the pork-belly exchange, an act that might have injured their financial standing. Creating the IMM as a separate entity would skirt this issue. I chose to not explain that its financial products would be trading on the CME floor, often adjacent to the pit where pork bellies traded.

Fourth, and perhaps most important, I needed committed traders to start the engine. In other words, there had to be a group of traders focused entirely on creating liquidity in the currency market. Their separate membership restricted trade to the IMM, including any new financial instruments we launched. This proved to be critical to the success of the IMM—not only did its traders create liquidity, but they also did extremely well for themselves too.

Finally, we established the IMM in order to attract young people looking for a new career. By then, CME membership had risen in price to over $100,000—a record high.[44] However, very few people in their 20s or 30s had a spare $100,000 to launch a new career, especially in a field that was reputedly difficult and fraught with danger. I reasoned that the people we were looking for would be hungry and willing to take a chance on learning a new profession—I thought they could perhaps scrape together one-tenth of the CME membership price.

So, we opened the IMM seat sales at the fixed price of $10,000, with a caveat that the buyer had to hold it for at least a year—this offering remained open for one year. Afterwards, IMM membership would be priced subject to the free market.[45]

We were initially able to sell 150 seats, raising $1.5m, which we used to develop the new exchange. This group of buyers became known as the Melamed IMM Army. With an average age in the early 30s, these new members came from a mixture of previous occupations, such as law, real estate, accounting, salesman and shopkeepers. Some were even without particular skills, simply looking for a profession.

---

44   A decade or so earlier I purchased my CME seat for $3,000.
45   The IMM seat price never fell below $8,000.

On a side note, I bought one of those initial seats for my father, a sort of repayment for the $3,000 he lent me to buy my original CME seat. Years later, when the IMM seat was worth $250,000, I asked him if he wanted to sell it out and take the profit. He answered in Yiddish, *"kain mol"*—never.

CRITICAL DECISIONS

One of the first decisions we faced was determining the size of the new currency units. I encountered a similar issue when I first became chairman in 1969. At the time, everyone was pinning their hopes on cattle, the first live product in the industry. This came with its own set of complications, as delivery at maturity meant providing transportation facilities for on-the-hoof animals. Although this problem was successfully handled before I got involved, the real issue seemed to be that the cattle contract was going nowhere. After investigating, the answer stared me in the face: our delivery unit was too big. Reducing the unit size to 40,000 pounds, equal to what one truckload could handle, worked like magic.

While there is a huge difference between cattle and FX, the issue of size was very similar. Bankers advised us that the interbank market trades in units of $1m, so if the IMM was going to compete, it would be logical for us to use the size to which FX traders were accustomed. The problem was that $1m per contract was, in 1972, far too big for our locals to handle. Again, since liquidity is the holy grail of any new product, and without local participation the contract would not become sufficiently liquid, I *needed* local participation. It came down to a tug of war between the commercial world and the futures market. That tug of war applied to nearly every new product that we launched.

We settled on half a million dollars per unit. After several weeks, I realized that this size was too large for our locals. I quickly pushed for a two-for-one contract split, a tactic used in securities to increase the number of outstanding shares by issuing more shares to current shareholders. At the IMM, this meant issuing two contracts for every one owned—we waived the commission requirement for the second unit. Almost immediately, we saw a constructive result. Not long after that, I moved to another two-for-one split. The new contract value came down to the range of $100,000–$150,000, which worked perfectly.

DEVELOPING THE QUARTERLY CYCLE

One of the most critical decisions in the life or death of a new instrument of futures trade is the listing of trading months. As everyone knows, financial markets throughout the world are almost universally listed in what is known as the quarterly cycle, i.e., March, June, September, December. I am given full credit, some even said genius, for this listing, since the IMM currency contracts, the first financial instruments, used the quarterly listing cycle. Nearly everyone followed suit. It worked well for accounting purposes as well as other financial issues. Well, I guess genius takes many forms. Here is how this happened.

The decision on which months to list the IMM's new currency contracts was the decision left to the currency committee. In agricultural products, months chosen for listing were governed by the production cycle, growing and harvesting months, seasons of the year, or similar criteria. Eggs, for instance, were listed in September, October, November and December. Cattle, on the other hand, were listed in February, April, June, August, October and December. However, currency has no production cycle, or rather, has a *constant* production cycle. Accordingly, there was a strong view that we should have a continuous 12-month listing.

Remember, in 1972, blackboards, especially for new products, were the mainstay of trading because trading was sporadic and traders were loath to stand in the pits waiting for something to happen. By listing bids and offers on blackboards (in price/time priority) a trader was assured that his potential offering would not be missed. For currencies, we planned that each blackboard would represent a given month of the trading year. Eventually, as they became active, each currency would go into a pit.

Blackboard trading was a partner to open outcry. When a market was not very active, it was futile to ask brokers and traders to stand around in a pit waiting for someone to have an order for execution. Instead, blackboards were the solution. At the morning opening of every market a bell would ring and the members with orders (or speculative intent) would shout to the board-marker for listing of their offerings (bids or offers), which the board-marker would record in chalk on a blackboard in price/time priority. You could, of course, change or remove your offering at any time.

Normally, each blackboard would represent a month of a given product, but extra blackboards sometimes became an issue. Once a trade was made, it was recorded on one of the blackboards, becoming the final proof of the trade. In addition, of course, the brokers and traders would record their transactions on one of their trading cards and submit it to the exchange for clearing purposes. The amount of errors or mistakes was surprisingly very small. If a given market would suddenly become active, the bell would ring and the market would move into the pit and into the primary form of open outcry.

I was opposed to the idea of a continuous 12-month listing. I thought that, to be successful, we should inject a bit of uncertainty. So I argued for and convinced the committee to list every other month. After we adjourned the meeting, Thomas Peak, CME floor manager, privately told me that we did not have sufficient wall space to fit six more blackboards for each of the seven currencies. "That would require space for 42 new boards." It stopped me dead in my tracks. "How much wall space do we have?" I cautiously inquired. "Well," he replied, "we have just enough to squeeze in 32 new blackboards."

It took me about ten seconds to call the committee back into session. The decision was unanimous. We would go with a quarterly listing: March, June, September and December.[46] That would only require 28 new boards. As I said, genius takes many forms.

---

46   A December contract was considered necessary for certain tax purposes. It became known as the March cycle.

CHAPTER 19

Birth

A S scheduled, the IMM opened its currency contracts for trade on May 16, 1972. Seven currencies were launched: the British pound, Canadian dollar, French franc, German Deutschmark, Japanese yen, Mexican peso and Swiss franc. For the first time, a tool that offered risk management, price discovery and economic opportunity became available within the dominion of finance. It was a historic moment.

Although I was ecstatic, my emotions had to wait. For the opening day, I had chosen to be in the pit along with the IMM traders. I was overcome by the size of the crowd, the thunderous sound of voices shouting numbers as loud as their vocal tract would allow, the pushing and shoving, the waving of arms, the scribbling of numbers in the four currencies that were board traded, as board-markers frantically tried to keep up with the bids and offers hurled at them.

The atmosphere on the trading floor was electric. These were all members I had convinced to share my dream; they believed in it and would go to the end of the earth to make it happen. It mattered not who won or lost—that day was to make a market, to prove to the world that, against all odds, this idea was becoming a reality. Our first day success was a huge victory. When the day ended, and both physical and emotional exhaustion took over, one thought kept repeating in my mind: *if it works in currencies, the sky's the limit.*

The IMM quickly became known for successfully creating liquidity. Exchanges who tried to mimic our product line or compete with a new product soon learned that Leo Melamed and his IMM officials were extremely adept at motivating locals to liquefy new products or protect a product under attack. One reason for this success was that I was, first and foremost, a trader myself.

I set about becoming the motivator in chief. Not only did I bombard members with an array of motivating speeches and lectures, currency news stories, relevant information and charts, but I chose to lead by example, spending time in the pit with other traders and putting my money, as it were, where my mouth was. Trading initial listings when the market is still immature and illiquid can be quite costly, but I was driven by something far stronger than the consideration of making money.[47]

THE NEW ERA OF FINANCE

Nobel laureate Merton Miller recorded the day: "That first truly successful innovation in financial futures can be pinpointed quite precisely, as can the name of its inventor or at least its prime mover. He was Leo Melamed of the CME (the Chicago Mercantile Exchange.)"[48] A couple of years later, he added a critical sentence: "With the launch of financial futures, Leo Melamed introduced the modern era of finance."[49]

Many years later, I asked Professor Miller to explain what he meant. "Because, Leo," he said, "the launch of currency futures was the very first public step to provide the financial world with a new and relatively direct way to manage their risks in financial dealings and investments."

He went on to explain that before the launch of currency futures, it was near impossible to limit or alter the considerable risk in business transactions containing a currency component. With the IMM, suddenly there was a practical and simple way to do it. It also provided opportunities to make money.

"Clearly," he said, "by creating a brand-new financial tool, your idea ushered in a new era in finance, one in which currency risk could be managed and adjusted." The IMM proved that there was a need for a new genre of risk-management tools available for financial dealings. And as Victor Hugo told us: "No force on earth can stop an idea whose time has come."

---

47   Years later, after open outcry was replaced by electronic trade, the methodology used to liquefy a new product was to rely on professional market-makers assigned to a product by paying them to provide the necessary flow of bids and offers.

48   'Financial Innovation: The Last Twenty Years and the Next', Merton H. Miller, University of Chicago, Selected Paper Number 63, June 1986.

49   Endorsement on the opening of Globex, June 25, 1992.

A LITTLE BIT OF LUCK

Of course, success did not come easily. The IMM's currency contracts endured a difficult process of acceptance from the US brokerage community and the world's banking establishment. It took several years. In fact, at the outset the US FX Association sent out a memorandum to all US bank dealers stating that it did not approve of interaction with an unauthorized entity like the IMM.

But in time, just as the professor suggested, the IMM captured the imagination of every segment of the business world. They came around for several very good reasons. First, it was a terrific idea embraced by many in the economic realm—not least two Nobel prize winners in economic sciences. Second, I will take some credit, I was indefatigable in my efforts to gain credibility; I rushed about the US and the world extolling the virtues of currency futures. Third, US officials with whom I visited were generally very constructive whenever the IMM came under review.

But most importantly, in markets luck almost always had to do with timing. And in this case, we were exceptionally lucky. If global upheaval creates market volatility, causing market prices to gyrate, and price gyrations demand insurance and offer speculative opportunity, then our timing could not have been better. Indeed, if the good Lord allowed me to design the global circumstances that would best validate a need for currency futures, I could not have imagined anything better than the actual conditions.

Allow me to start with the Middle East, from where most of the world's energy was derived and its prices determined. In 1970, a conflict known as Black September ensued between King Hussein and Yasser Arafat of the Palestine Liberation Organization and by 1972, the Yemenite War began—such events coincided with the IMM's opening. Then followed the Turkish invasion of Cyprus and the Lebanese Civil War. All of this was background for the eight-year conflict between Iraq and Iran.

The foregoing, of course, does not include the Six-Day War in 1967, between Israel and its neighboring states of Egypt, Jordan and Syria; nor the three-year war between the Israeli military and the combined forces of the Egyptian Republic, the USSR, Jordan and Syria; and finally, lest we forget, after the surprise attack on Israel by a coalition of Arab states led by Egypt and Syria, the Yom Kippur War of October of 1973. This then led to an oil embargo on the US during 1973–4 by Arab members of the OPEC (Organization of the Petroleum Exporting Countries)—ostensibly in retaliation for US support of

Israel during the Yom Kippur War, but mostly to gain leverage in the post-war negotiations.

As if the above was not enough to create volatility, there were also domestic factors that were exponentially more controlling. Front and center was President Nixon's August 15, 1971 act to break up the Bretton Woods system and cancel the long-standing policy of converting dollars to gold at the fixed price of $35 per ounce. This was the pivotal action that triggered my decision to no longer wait to create the IMM. The "closing of the gold window" exacerbated the repudiation of the dollar by most to the rest of the world. Predictably, the US inflation rate went from below 5% at the beginning of the decade to over 11% by 1974; as a direct result, interest rates rose to historic levels of 20%. It took the appointment of Paul Volcker as chair of the Federal Reserve in 1979 to put the US financial system back together again.

To add to the economic tumult, prices were rising, especially in food products like hogs and cattle. Gerald Ford's response, believe or not, had been to issue WIN[50] buttons to try to spur on voluntary action to stop inflationary forces. That worked like applying cupping to a corpse.[51] President Nixon went with one better—our so-called 'right-wing' Richard Nixon embraced price controls. He issued Executive Order 11615, imposing a 90-day freeze on wages and prices to counter inflation. This was the first time the US government had enacted wage and price controls since World War II.

As Milton Friedman correctly predicted, Nixon's gambit ended "in utter failure and the emergence into the open of the suppressed inflation."

I used the opportunity to show off my poetic skills.

Ode to price controls

I wish to record—just for fun,
How price controls happened in '71.
The story can serve as a future lesson
Should we again with economy go a-messin'

So now that they're going some six-feet under
How did we make such a classical blunder?
To future generations, this ode I christen,
Ladies and gentlemen, just listen.

---

50   A WIN button (Whip Inflation Now) was Ford's attempt to inspire a grassroots movement combating inflation. He combined this with public measures.
51   Old Jewish saying.

Said the Democrats:
The next issue with which to contend
Are the rising prices and what they portend.
We need a remedy which will look good,
One that is appealing and understood.

"Price controls," of course, they fit the need!
A solution to the problem with instant speed!
Of course, they might turn out to be bad,
Cause shortages, disruptions, and that would be sad.

But that should not be our main concern,
We'll create the issue, and then it's their turn.
The G.O.P. will never approve this solution,
It's against the free-market institution.
Then we can blame the rising prices
On Republican inaction in times of crises.

Thought the Republicans:
The Dems have created a clever trap,
An issue on which we could take the rap.
This could cost us many a vote,
Inflation is at the public's throat.

But we, too, can play this game of tag
In political know-how, we don't lag.
We'll turn the tables on their little scheme,
We, too, will join the price-control team.

Of course, they might turn out to be bad,
Cause less production, and that would be sad.
But the president will never play this tune
And allow the country to go to ruin.
He'll ignore controls without any shame
And then nobody will be to blame.

Said the media and press:
To report the news is our obligation,
To seek the issues or their mutation.
Inflation has become a terrible woe,
We need a quick solution to keep it in tow.

Congress had enacted what sounds so good,
Why doesn't the president do as he should?

Of course, they might turn out to be bad,
Prove counterproductive and that would be sad.
But at least they would serve us for a time,
The raising of prices would become a crime.

Thought the Labor leaders:
Our workers have had it with rising prices;
Something must be done to end this crisis.
A free economy is good and well,
But not when our dollars are going to hell.
Controls on prices are what we need,
(But not on wages—heaven forbid!)

Of course, they might turn out to be bad,
Cause less employment and that would be sad.
But then we can blame the legislators
For being bad-law perpetrators.

Espoused the Consumer Advocates:
Big business runs our USA
They make the little guy pay and pay.
To help the citizen is our job,
We're his saviors—the ignorant slob.
What we propose is a magic wand
That'll bring down prices with a wave of the hand.

Controls are the thing, they work like magic,
They'll stop the profits, and that's not tragic.
Of course, they might turn out to be bad,
Cause hoardings and panic, and that would be sad,
But should they work like some ancient voodoos,
Then we'll get the credit and take the kudos.

Said business management:
The crisis really must come to an end,
Our public image we must mend.
Controls will placate the public's mood
If we're for them, it will look good.

Of course, they might turn out to be bad,

Cause a business slowdown, and that would be sad.
But if we object too strongly,
It certainly will be interpreted wrongly.
So let's hope they're what we need,
To the free-market economists—pay no heed.

Counseled the president's advisors:
That controls are bad, there's no denial,
But if we applied them for only awhile,
A sort of in-between election trial,
It really wouldn't cramp our conservative style,
And maybe they wouldn't much harm compile.
Meanwhile we would derive a political mile
By quieting the housewife's growing rile.

Said the president:
I'm against controls in any form,
They're not the answer to this storm.
They'll disrupt the economy of our nation,
Create shortages and cause us to ration.
They create bureaucracy like the O.P.A.
They cause inequities and disarray.
But wait—let's look at the facts
Controls were created by Congressional Acts.
The Dems and G.O.P. have had them adopted
To pass me the buck, they have opted.
The press is for it, the media too
The dissenters are quiet and very few.
Labor is pressing for action at once,
If I don't do it, I'll look like a dunce.
Consumers think it's a magic spell,
Prices will come down at the ring of a bell.
Business is for it and they must know
What's good for the country to make it grow.

My advisors agree, if applied for a while,
They might not much harm compile.
How silly of me not to see the light,
If everyone's for it, they must be right.
They'll help diminish the public's ire,
They could break the rising spiral fire.

Maybe they are magic—you can't be sure,
Any action could be the right cure.

Of course, they might turn out to be sad,
But Congress passed the law—too bad, too bad!
This tale is funny, if it weren't so sad,
Ladies and gentlemen, we've been had.

Who could have asked for more when initiating a market that thrives on volatility? For us, it was the perfect scenario, proving that necessity is the mother of invention. Three years after the birth of the IMM, my 1975 annual report recorded this fact:

> Timing, which is a combination of planning and luck, was exactly the element present when, in 1972, the International Monetary Market was established. A market designed for the trading, initially, of foreign currency futures could not have begun at a better point in history. Bretton Woods was dead, currency floats replaced fixed parity rates, and those engaged in international trade needed an alternative means of hedging their risk from fluctuations in the value of currencies vis-a-vis the US dollar.

Following the IMM's continued growth and success, markets around the US and in foreign domiciles benefitted by similarly creating new financial products. Traders came from all over to discover the opportunities opened up in futures as well as in spot markets. Many went on to become very successful and wealthy, some even becoming the luminaries of today. To name a few: Lloyd Craig Blankfein, Peter Borish, Gary David Cohn, Richard J. Dennis, William Eckhardt, John William Henry, Henry Jarecki, Paul Tudor Jones, Bruce Kovner, Ralph Peters, James Harris Simons, George Soros, Vinnie Viola, and others.

FENDING OFF THE COPY-CATS

In truth, I knew it was very foolish to attempt the launch of seven different futures contracts at one time. I knew how difficult it was to introduce just *one* new futures product, let alone *seven* in a brand-new asset class. But I was motivated by the fear that what we were doing would be copied by the CBOT, the NYSE or some other exchange. By listing for trade all major currencies, I made it that much harder for someone to steal my idea.

Which brings me to an issue that has been plaguing futures since their invention. In most business sectors, government authority can protect an inventor for a period of time by prohibiting others from copying (pirating) the original invention—not so with futures and options trade. There is no protective patent available. Yet, no differently than in most other business endeavors, before a new futures product is created there is the cost for research and development, marketing and advertising, and for PR, literature and lectures. Not to speak of the cost of choosing the actual product, which often requires testing and rejection of the unsuitable. But still, intellectual property protection is not available.

In effect, any exchange can copy a futures contract with the exact specifications as the inventor-exchange designed. In fact, time and time again, exchanges have tried to do so with CME/IMM products. Although they seldom succeeded, we had to spend both time and money fending off the would-be pirates.

Some exchanges have even tried a back-door approach, by creating methodologies to poach the open interest from a successful product at another exchange.[52] We have consistently fought off such piracy by arguing that open interest is the futures equivalent of a patent, since it represents the successful result of a listed product. In this way, open interest is a good way to determine the success or failure of a new product. Jack Sandner often liked to point to our large open interest as proof of IMM viability—he was correct.

APPOINTING REALITY MONITORS

In retrospect, my fear of another exchange copying us was very misplaced. There was no rush to imitate; it seemed precious few thought currency futures were a good idea. Except for Chicago banks, which fully supported our revolutionary undertaking, the event went largely unheralded by the mainstream global financial players. To tell the truth, for the first couple of years we continued to be regarded as a nuisance, if not a joke.

Soon after the IMM launch, I ran into one of the consequences of simultaneously listing so many new markets. Our seven listed currencies did not always actively trade at the same time, or in the same direction; each currency traded sporadically and sometimes not at all. This meant that some of the currency prices would occasionally become out of line with the price movement of their counterpart in the cash (spot) market. They were, therefore, out of sync with the

---

52 Open interest is the total number of outstanding derivative contracts, such as options or futures, that have not been settled. It is commonly associated with the futures and options.

global market. This was a major problem, as it related to the closing (settlement) price at the end of the day.

To solve the problem, I appointed a couple of traders to act as *reality monitors*— Maurice Levy comes to mind. Before the end of each day, they would bid or offer the price of a given currency as necessary to bring their settlement into line with the closing price in the interbank market.[53] Fortunately, all of this was before the CFTC and its rules preventing fake trading.

This solution did not, however, solve the underlying problem. Even the most active of the IMM currencies—the Swiss franc, German Deutschmark, British pound and Japanese yen—quite often failed to sync with price movements at the interbank market during periods of volatility. What was needed was a much more comprehensive solution than reality monitors at the close of day; I realized that we needed an arbitrage operation between cash and futures to keep them in line.

B-CLASS ARBITRAGE

An age-old operation, arbitrage functions to mediate between different markets whose prices are related but not always in sync. An important by-product of arbitrage is that it helps keep the price movement of related markets in line with each other. Banks naturally perform this task as a matter of course, but our problem was, during the formative stages of the IMM, the banks did not participate in our market. Without the ability to keep IMM's currency in line with the movement of interbank cash markets, our market would lose all credibility. I went to the banks for assistance, but only those in Chicago would listen; and they pointed out that they could not do the business of arbitrage because the IMM traders were not sufficiently capitalized. It was true.

The solution I devised was called a B-class arbitrage clearing operation. An IMM member would open a spot account at a bank for the purpose of trading spot-currency positions. The member would then simultaneously trade an equivalent, and opposite, futures position in his B-class account at his IMM clearing firm. This B-class account would be for the single purpose of arbitrage with a given bank; the account was required to always be equally counter-balanced with the spot positions at the bank. To satisfy the need for sufficient capital, the IMM member's B-class futures account would be legally owned by

---

53   That effort was not exactly kosher, it required an intentional pre-arranged trade, not what the CFTC would have approved.

the bank. Effectively, the bank was financially secure because it controlled both sides of the arbitrage transaction.

This was an iron-clad system, one that would not need additional capital from IMM members for financial security purposes. Thus, our relatively cash-poor members were able to go into the arbitrage business. Matter of fact, this B-class operation literally saved the IMM. The constant flow of arbitrage transactions provided liquidity to the IMM markets while continuously bringing our prices in line with movements in spot. I used my own clearing firm, Dellsher Investment Company, as a model for others to follow and retained Bert Norton, husband of Mickey Norton, the first female trader at the IMM and my bridge partner, to run the arbitrage business.

At its peak, there were nearly 30 B-class IMM operations each with mostly different banks. Some banks mimicked the idea by purchasing an IMM seat and sending one of their own traders to the IMM floor. After a number of years, as the IMM matured and the competitive spread between spot and futures tightened, B-class operations dwindled and eventually went out of business. By then, the IMM's success was assured.

As promised to the membership, I advanced the IMM in its first decade by initiating new markets in the financial realm, specifically in interest rates and equity indices. These markets proved hugely successful and were aided by the introduction of the Black-Scholes model at the Chicago Board of Options Exchange (CBOE) a year after the IMM launched. This model furthered the capabilities of financial risk management. It also served me personally to develop a life-long kinship with both Myron Scholes and Robert Merton, inventors of the Black-Scholes options model and Nobel laureate recipients. We've found many reasons over the years to remain close associates and friends.

CHAPTER 20

Don Quixote

L EE FREEMAN, legal counsel for the CME in 1972, gave me the moniker, the *modern Don Quixote*. Freeman recognized that I would be fighting unknown windmills, among which would be the status quo. And I did indeed spend my time challenging the existing state of affairs in central banking, the US government and inside the Merc.

Shortly after the launch, I planned to visit every central bank whose currency was listed at the IMM. While I knew I didn't need their approval, I realized that a courtesy call could prove advantageous. So, with the help of Curtis Hoxter, an international advisor we hired, I arranged a visitation program for myself and several CME officers. We prepared handouts in French, German, Italian and Spanish. To my disappointment, this largely turned out to be a bit of a failure— very few foreign officials cared, or even attended. I gathered that no central banker gave the idea a second look.

It was as Lord John Maynard Keynes once said: "The greatest difficulty in changing any enterprise lies not in developing new ideas, but in escaping from old ones."

One visit, however, was different and encouraging. When meeting with officials at the Bank of England on June 24, 1972—who wished us luck and offered their support for the free market ideal—one official asked, as a courtesy, whether there was anything they could do to help. Knowing that the pound was a fixed currency, I jokingly responded that "it would be immensely helpful if the UK could float the British pound." Instead of the chuckle I expected, there was just an embarrassing silence; no one even smiled.

We left, feeling bad that my obvious joke laid an egg—and here I always believed the Brits had a great sense of humor. Our next stop was Milan, Italy. Whilst there, we were stunned to read the *International Herold Tribune* headline: "Bank of England floats the British Pound." Coincidences do occur throughout history, but this one takes the cake. No doubt the British central bankers thought they had a leak and that I was tweaking their nose.

The *Chicago Tribune* commented that:

> "The move is a de-facto devaluation that will allow free-market forces to set a new and lower international price for sterling. It ends the purchases the Bank of England has been making in the foreign exchange markets in a vain effort to halt the pound's slide from its official parity price of $2.6057.

It is the exact reason Milton Friedman was trying to go short the pound.

OVERSIGHT

From 1972–1973, futures markets played an insignificant role in the national economy. At the time we were under the regulatory authority of the Commodity Exchange Authority (CEA), a tiny operation with little authority and less than a dozen employees. It was headed by Alex Caldwell, a well-intended official without a meaningful budget or a strong authority.[54] But, as we grew, I knew that the US government would soon be knocking at our door to gain oversight.

The agency I thought most likely to be given authority would be the Securities and Exchange Commission (SEC). Dealing with securities and the like, this organization was a powerful, long-established bureaucracy. I quickly realized the SEC was the last place I would choose for regulation over futures, as the people were anything but innovators. As Jerry Salzman once said in jest, "the SEC regards the NYSE as its first-born son and the CME as the bastard daughter of a Nubian slave taken in battle." Indeed, the SEC epitomized Milton Friedman's book, *The Tyranny of the Status Quo*. Happily, the SEC wanted no part of us. The idea of regulating the "people that deal in pork bellies" was repulsive and beneath their dignity. This changed over the years, especially after my friend Mary Shapiro became SEC chairperson.

Meanwhile, US national politics were in high gear with the Watergate Scandal.

---

54 Once, during a suspected corner in eggs, I invited Mr Caldwell to the floor to view trading in an attempt to scare the would-be manipulators. This indicated to the squeezers that I had the backing of the CEA in my efforts to break up the potential corner.

On August 9, 1974, facing likely impeachment for his role in covering up the scandal, Nixon became the only US president to resign. Gerald Ford, who had replaced Spiro Agnew upon his resignation amid charges of corruption, was a congenial guy trusted by both sides of the aisle. Ford became the first non-elected president in US history.

More important House agriculture committee staffer, John Rainboldt, and the assistant secretary of agriculture, John Damgard, sponsored legislation to create the CFTC. Their advisors were Philip Johnson, a prominent Chicago attorney at Kirkland & Ellis, and Leo Melamed of the CME.[55]

JOURNEY TO THE CFTC

Philip McBride Johnson had spent 15 years representing clients in the commodities industry. He was a new appointee at the Kirkland firm in 1974, who were then legal counsel for the CBOT. Yet, the CBOT hierarchy did not particularly care for him, as Johnson did not bow to the belief that the CBOT was the king of the hill, nor that it alone could dictate the rules applying to a new federal agency. Even before he became CFTC chairman, Johnson took time off from the Kirkland law firm to write a Commodities Regulation treatise. Published by Little, Brown and Company, it became the futures bible on futures regulation.

Johnson and I hit it off famously well. I think he appreciated my innovative approach, my can-do attitude and my unbridled passion for the free markets. To me, he was someone outside the exchange who understood what futures were about, how they functioned, and how they could greatly serve our nation's best interest. Johnson also recognized the revolutionary value of our launch in currency futures, perceiving that our industry would grow large as a consequence of the new financial arena—and would continue to do so, far beyond the sphere of agricultural products. He reasoned that this would result in our stepping on the jurisdiction of other federal oversight committees (say coal, gas, lumber or housing), who would then demand a role in the process.

In light of this, Johnson drafted a provision in the CFTC Act making them the sole regulator of the US futures industry, a provision explicitly applicable to all manner of products—tangible and intangible. He also ensured that exclusive oversight was awarded to the agriculture committee, which has remained the case until the House financial services committee was given joint jurisdiction. This was a great achievement, which proved fundamental to our industry's success.

55   John Rainbolt became the first vice chairman of the CFTC.

However, Gerald Ford soon made it clear that he was a small government kind of guy, who didn't see the need for yet another federal agency. This opinion was shared by the secretary of agriculture, Earl Butz, who threatened to advise the president to veto our legislation. In order to gain a better understanding of the situation, the president called his close friend, Texas Congressman William 'Bob' Poage, chairman of the House agriculture committee, for advice.

A TWO-MINUTE PITCH

Critically, it was around this time that the CME chairman, Larry Rosenberg, and I decided to move ahead with plans to open an office in Washington, DC. Our first representative to head up the office was Dayle Hennington. This was a fortuitous appointment. Coming from the same town in Texas, Hennington and Bob Poage were lifelong buddies. In fact, after Poage was elected to Congress, Hennington became his administrative assistant. And later, when Poage became chairman of the agricultural committee, Hennington counselled him in favor of our developing legislation. It was Hennington who secured a meeting for me and the congressman.[56]

Poage listened politely but concluded that someone from the futures industry needed to explain the complexities directly to the president. While he was reluctant to be seen doing such a big favor to our industry, Poage agreed to arrange a confidential meeting between the president and myself.

I briefly met the president as he was leaving the house where he had been minority leader before he became vice president. I was given two minutes, but in Washington that can mean at least half an hour. He remembered me from the many American Enterprise Institute (AEI) meetings we attended together in Beaver Creek, Colorado, when he hosted us at his home nearby. He also remembered a meeting I chaired between Alan Greenspan and five other central bankers from around the world where we discussed interest rates. He said that he was very impressed.

I began by reminding the president that he had sponsored the Bill to ban onion trading, which made him laugh. I then explained that my idea for finance in futures was a million miles away from onions and would instead grow the

---

56 Commodity Futures Trading Commission (CFTC) Act of 1974 (P.L. 93-463) created the CFTC to replace the US Department of Agriculture's Commodity Exchange Authority, as the independent federal agency responsible for regulating the futures trading industry. The Act made extensive changes in the basic authority of Commodity Exchange Act of 1936, which itself had made extensive changes in the original Grain Futures Act of 1922 (7 USC 1 et seq.).

economy by providing the ability to *hedge risk*. I explained that if I was right, the idea would become of national interest. I brazenly stated that Congress would then want an oversight agency anyway. The president chuckled and said, "So you want to be the guys to create this agency, is that it?"

I agreed, but gave full credit to John Damgard, whose memo to the president I believe had already convinced him not to veto the legislation. While this meeting may have sealed the deal with the president, the Act still had to pass both Houses of Congress. Again, I assign the lion's share of the credit for the CFTC Act passing to the same three people who crafted the legislation: John Damgard, John Rainboldt and Philip Johnson.

Today, some 80% of futures markets are conducted in financial (or non-agricultural) products. In 1972, however, the idea of financial futures was considered as wild a concept as the airplane was to a culture that had just finished building the railroads. In this way, the battle against the wider financial world was expected; the principle windmill which would take years to conquer. It represented a long and painful battle with the status quo. What I did not anticipate was the windmills developing on the CME trading floor.

UPROAR AT THE EXCHANGE

Truth be told, the IMM's success was turning into a double-edged sword. A schism was being created between the old-line of the Merc and the new IMM members. The biggest complaint from the CME's old guard was that IMM members were taking up space on the exchange, using the floor and its facilities, without contributing much to its well-being. In private, I had to admit that this was true; I was advancing the growth of the financial markets on the shoulders of the CME. The bottom line, however, was that CME members had no use for the new markets, especially when pork bellies were doing well, setting volume records and offering profitable opportunities. They just couldn't visualize the huge potential of financial contracts, nor would they consider the IMM as the future for the Merc.

When I broached the problem privately, even the average CME trader admitted that they resented the IMM members. The old guard was more explicit. One old-timer, Izzy Mulmat, verbalized the viewpoint by stating: "Lee, they are using our floor space. They are crowding us out. They are using our blackboards, and our employees, even our chalk and our coffee. And what do we get? Bupkis! We don't use their markets. They don't bring any business to pork bellies, cattle, or hogs. We are better off without them!"

On the other hand, IMM members did not take the complaints well. Just as I had hoped, they had become enthusiastic, committed traders who saw the future and brought business to the growing financial markets. IMM Members said to me: "Lee, more than anyone, you know we are the future! In a couple of years, the markets in finance will be vastly larger than in agriculture. Our potential is a thousand times bigger than theirs. Pork bellies and hogs, or even grains, will never be as big as currencies or interest-rates or whatever else you will think of."

It was the truth and a potent argument. My concerns multiplied with every passing day as the estrangement between the two factions continued to grow. While I totally agreed with the IMM's view, I also saw that it had a serious flaw: the IMM *needed* the Merc's floor. In fact, the IMM had none of the infrastructure or employees of an exchange, nor the resources to create or support one. It had little in terms of assets and with its comparatively meagre transaction volume, would be unable to carry the underlying costs. And where do we go to trade?

The anti–IMM movement began to represent a fifth column within the exchange.[57] I visualized that if I did nothing it would end up ripping the exchange apart from within. The IMM was still in its infancy, if something derailed it at this juncture in its life, my dream for the future of financial markets would be endangered.

I held serious discussions with my inner circle. Not all of them saw it as a critical problem. I insisted that a crisis point was not very distant. I minced no words when I explained that the IMM were the interlopers, the offspring of the CME parents. They could not last six months without the Merc's support. Although the CME view was short-sighted and lacking in substance, I realized that in order for the IMM to reach its immense potential, it needed to be fully embraced by the CME. I proposed a radical solution: merge the CME and IMM.

A UNIFIED EXCHANGE

My proposal was well thought out. I proposed that every CME member would receive a free IMM membership to either keep or sell. Our exchange attorney then said I had to establish a price value for tax purposes, so I settled on $100—since IMM seats were going for some $15,000, this amounted to a substantial gift. Additionally, my proposal resulted in the IMM becoming a division of the CME and all CME

---

57   A fifth column is any group of people who undermine a larger group from within, usually in favor of an enemy group or nation. The activities of a fifth column can be overt or clandestine.

members, present or future, received the privilege of trading in the IMM or any other division the Merc might create. For sure, I got the plan approved by Salzman.

I tested this idea on the floor. CME members, generally speaking, were accepting, but I came up against the expected IMM opposition. Randy McKay, a strong IMM member, good trader and all-around smart guy, voiced the solid reasoning: "Lee, you know we are the future. Why should we give our markets to the old fogies? We don't need their help or want their contracts." My answer was equally solid, "I am giving the IMM a guarantee to life in order to achieve the enormous future that you correctly envision."

This divisional concept, transforming the IMM into the financial division of the CME, was the perfect plan to achieve peace before the schism grew unmanageable. The CME received a huge bonus and the potential of becoming a financial futures behemoth. The IMM received an exchange infrastructure to build its future and forgiveness for all cost in its birth and formative life of the past four years.

There were many additional benefits too, as we would become larger, stronger and more diversified as a merged institution. For instance, the IMM's original membership of 150 would become 650, while the CME markets could serve both agricultural and financial constituents. In fact, I proposed this same idea for yet another division, the AMM, to attract additional new members at a cheaper seat price for underdeveloped markets. This division eventually became the Index and Options Division (IOM) with the launch of the S&P futures contract.

It was a formula for success. However, the plan was still difficult to sell to both parties. My lobbying for the proposition was extensive. I put my reputation and leadership on the line because I was certain that a unified exchange had much more potential than two separate structures. Even though I believed the future was in finance, I also knew that the agricultural markets were central to a successful futures exchange. Randy McKay, an influential IMM member, told me that he was opposed to the merger but would vote for it "because you, Lee, could sell ice to Eskimos."

The referendum passed overwhelmingly. At the CME, the vote was 343 in favor against 23 opposed. At the IMM, it was 396 to 57. A unified exchange was born, another division (AMM) was created and a future crisis was avoided.

AN EYE TO THE FUTURE

I truly believed that my look ahead proved to be the critical move that saved the IMM as well as the CME. The structure that resulted became the foundation upon which the phenomenal future could be built. I cannot prove what might have happened had the merger failed. At a minimum, the merger at the CME avoided the kind of years-long legal and acrimonious battle between the CBOT and its offspring the CBOE, one that sapped the strength from both structures.

In my 1986 annual review to the members, I applauded our achievement:

> Without a doubt, the highlight of the year was the implementation of our Plan of Merger and Reorganization. By becoming a division of the Merc, the IMM gained a sound financial base, representation on the Board, and full rights to adequate space and facilities. But, more importantly, merger with the CME meant the IMM's future was safe so that its immense potential could be fully explored and realized.
>
> Merger with the IMM was equally important to the CME and its members. Not only did CME members thereby permanently gain new and diverse markets, but the IMM also gave the Merc an international and monetary division. The field of monetary instruments will someday prove as significant a factor in futures markets as have agricultural contracts in the past; thus, the Merc now has the broadest and most potent base for growth and expansion of any futures exchange in the world. There is no doubt in my mind that the merger was a most important milestone in the history of both institutions and will prove to be the primary ingredient for continued prosperity of the CME.

In 1977, the first year of the merged exchange, I once again accepted the title of chairman. I was, and still am, interested in historical junctures. For that reason, I wanted history to record that I was the first chairman of the new (merged) CME. I only wanted one year at the helm, but the membership would not have it. They overwhelmingly demanded the board find a way to keep me at the helm without the need for an election.

In 1978, the board created a new and permanent role for me: *special counsel.* Although this title kept changing as conditions warranted, I liked the fact that I would not need to be elected by the membership. It may sound a bit haughty, but I felt like I deserved a permanent position in the structure of the CME. And after putting my heart and soul into resuscitating the dying Butter and Egg Board, and then inventing an entire new asset class for futures trade, the vast majority of members agreed.

CHAPTER 21

Mexican Hat Trick

TODAY, Mexico's fiscal house is more or less in sync with world standards. The Mexican peso floats and is now an accepted global currency unit—the eighth most traded in the world. Since its relisting in 1994, it has become one of the IMM's established currencies, providing wholesome transaction volume and international business. But this was not always the case.

As I mentioned before, it's important to understand that listing seven currencies at once would usually be a big *no*. Every new product for trading requires a good deal of marketing to both internal and external communities. You need a cadre of traders to help generate the initial liquidity needed for a product to survive, traders who would have to leave other markets and risk trading something brand new with no guarantee of income. Obviously, it was nearly impossible to keep seven currencies alive and aligned with the real world.

BRAZIL CALLING

Several weeks after the IMM opened its doors, or should I say pits, in May 1972, I received a phone call from Brazil. The gentleman, speaking English with a South American accent, introduced himself as a major Brazilian coffee grower. He explained that he had just read a newspaper account of a new market in Chicago called the International Monetary Market (IMM), which would allow trading in foreign currencies. Since he was a major exporter of coffee and often received payment in foreign denominations, he was calling to see if this was truly so.

I was thrilled to hear that news of the IMM had reached Brazil and assured the caller that our market was open for business and trading the British pound, Canadian dollar, French franc, German Deutschmark, Japanese yen, Mexican peso and Swiss franc. The IMM, I explained, would give businessmen, bankers, financial managers and of course speculators, the same risk transfer opportunities that their agribusiness counterparts had been successfully using for more than 100 years.

Hearing my response, the caller was silent for a couple of seconds. He then asked, "Excuse me, sir, did you say the Mexican peso?" I responded that, yes, we were trading the Mexican peso. I was about to explain why we did not list the Brazilian real when the caller interrupted, "Perhaps it is a bad connection, you are trading in the Mexican peso?" I assured him that this was correct. Without a pause, the caller continued, "Are you saying that I will be able to sell the Mexican peso to hedge the money I expect to receive in payment for a coffee sale and you will pay me the value of the peso at the time of my sale, no matter if the Mexican peso price goes down in value after the sale?"

"Yes!" I responded emphatically, "That is precisely how the market will work." The caller had no further questions. Instead, I distinctly heard a giggling sound at the other end before the caller hung up.

DIPLOMATIC IMPLICATIONS

That giggle haunted me for years—I fully understood why the Brazilian coffee grower might laugh though. Remember, this was 1972, a time when the Mexican currency's value was arbitrarily controlled and heavily supported by its central bank. Hardly anyone knowledgeable, in and outside of Mexico, trusted the official rate of exchange, since they knew the peso was worth a lot less. Indeed, from time to time the Mexican government would announce an official devaluation, bringing the peso down to a more realistic level. My caller, the Brazilian coffee grower, knew this and found it comical that anyone would let him sell the Mexican peso short—it was like a dead certain annuity.

When I began contemplating which currencies to list for trade on the IMM, the Mexican peso was not on the list. I had chosen currencies that were all more or less floating, that is, their value was determined by respective economic factors of supply and demand, not by government edict. This was the fundamental premise on which the IMM was built; its futures contracts would represent the anticipated value of currencies by virtue of economic supply and demand dictates.

But then a very strange thing happened: my office received a call from the US State Department requesting an appointment. I could not for the life of me figure out why the State Department of the United States was interested in the IMM. At the allotted time, two State Department officials showed up and explained that the IMM currency market had the potential to create a major diplomatic flap. "Mr Melamed," one official somberly stated, "listing for trade the currency of our neighbors to the north while ignoring our neighbors to the south can be viewed as an American insult to the Mexican government."

I was flabbergasted. I clarified that I had not meant to insult anyone, and that our reason for not listing the Mexican peso was because the "exchange rate is controlled by government fiat—how can we trade a currency in which the government can decide at any time what the value shall be?" Although they understood my reasoning, the argument made no impression on the officials.

PLAYING THE GAME

This was the last thing I needed. There I was in the midst of trying to convince a skeptical world to embrace the idea of futures on foreign exchange, with no guarantee that it would work, and suddenly I'm faced with causing a potential *diplomatic flap* as the State Department called it. In the end, I decided that prudence was the better part of valor and bowed to government pressure. The IMM committee determined that the currency of our southern neighbor would be traded alongside the floating currency of our northern neighbor.

It didn't take long before the flaw in trading the Mexican peso made itself known. Right from the start the market knew the truth, as it generally does. While the price of the nearby futures in Mexican peso maintained a price relatively close to the official rate of exchange, the forward price of the Mexican peso was heavily discounted. The further out the price, the deeper the futures discount—which could sometimes be as high as 10–15%. The market knew that at the time of maturity, the spot and futures price must converge.

This backwardation created a valuable tax gimmick, a so-called *tax straddle*. One could go long the heavily discounted forward futures contract and go short the nearby. If there was no devaluation, the long position had to rise as it neared maturity. If the long position was held for six or more months, the resulting profit would be a capital gain with a favorable tax rate, while the nearby short position was an ordinary loss. This tax straddle became a highly lucrative and popular market play, attracting many wealthy investors. Some brave souls would even play this tax gimmick wide open, simply going long the discounted forwards and betting against devaluation.

PREPARING FOR THE INEVITABLE

One of the most distinguishing differences between futures and other markets is that futures operate on what is known as a mark–to–market regime.[58] Futures clearing houses charge participants two types of collateral: an *initial* and a *variation* margin. Margin is actually a security bond, usually a relatively small amount to cover the initial credit risk, calculated on a standard deviation formula. A variation margin is the money due daily to offset losses, if any, which occur as a result of unfavorable market movements. In both cases, the exchange clearing house looks for payment from the member clearing firm carrying the position.

So, here's the rub. If an unfavorable daily movement is far beyond normal expectations, the initial margin will be inadequate to cover the loss, and the variation margin will be far larger than most clearing firms could handle immediately. For instance, if each Mexican peso contract was worth $100k, the initial margin might be $3,000 for every contract bought or sold. But, if there was a highly unusual change, by virtue of, say, a 30% devaluation, the clearing firm carrying the investor's long position would owe the exchange $30,000 for each peso contract before the next day's opening. Many of the IMM's clearing firms did not have that kind of reserve. In other words, if that were to happen, the integrity of the IMM would be at stake.

In early 1976, the rumblings I heard made me feel that Mexico was in trouble and that at some point soon the government might devalue the peso. I conveyed my opinion to Barry Lind, the chairman of the IMM clearing house committee. He asked whether I had any idea about the amount of such a devaluation. I responded that it might be as much as 30%. We agreed that neither the CME clearing members nor the CME clearing house could afford to pay the losses involved if that were to happen. The exchange would be in default, an unacceptable situation.

Fortunately, our new IMM rule book provided a solution. It was an emergency provision that I privately called the *Mexican rule*. Were an emergency situation to occur or be expected to occur, the CME chairman and president, with consent of the chairman of the clearing house committee, could demand additional margin from either the longs, the shorts or *both*.

---

58   The Dodd Frank legislation requires certain over the counter positions to apply a mark–to–market regime.

PREVENTATIVE MEASURES

In August 1976, the clearing house issued an executive order requiring a 30% margin for long positions in the Mexican peso within a week—this meant about $30,000 per contract. It was an unheard-of margin requirement. There were many screams from clearing members, but the loudest voice was from a company called Maduff and Co., an IMM clearing member whose books contained the largest long position in the Mexican peso. The owner of the firm, Sidney Maduff (no relation to the infamous Bernard Madoff), quickly began shouting that his company did not have sufficient capital to meet the new margin requirement and that they would be ruined. He demanded a withdrawal of the order.

I explained why we had to do this and that it was within our authority to do so, but Maduff rejected my rationale. "Do you realize who my customer is?" he asked. "It's Lamar Hunt, one of the sons of the Texas oil tycoon, H. L. Hunt. The Hunts," Maduff shouted, "are wealthier than the CME and IMM put together!" "I don't care who your customer is," I responded. "My concern is only the integrity of the IMM." I then suggested to Maduff that maybe he get the required money from the Hunts themselves.

Maduff insisted that I would have to tell the Hunts this myself. And, sure enough, a couple of days later, Lamar Hunt and his attorney showed up. After the yelling ended, I showed Hunt's lawyer the emergency margin rule and he explained to his client that we had acted within the rule. The solution I offered was to move Hunt's peso position to a clearing member who could afford the required margin. The lawyer agreed so long as the exchange would not make additional charges. Lamar chose E.F. Hutton. Mr Maduff was livid.

Less than a month later, the Mexican Government devalued the Mexican Peso by 50%. The devaluation, of course, caused financial chaos. Among the many calls I received the next day, one was from William Butcher, the chairman of the Chase Manhattan Bank, one of the largest banks in the world at the time. Having spoken to the chairman before, I knew that Butcher and his board of directors were very much in the IMM corner and highly approved of what it represented. He explained that in light of the peso devaluation, his board authorized a line of credit to the IMM of up to $100m to cover the variation margin our clearing house would need. This was about the amount of loss the longs in the peso futures market owed the clearing house. It was a fantastic offer.

The fact that I could say, "No, thank you, the IMM clearing house is fully covered," was a stunning revelation to the Chase Manhattan chairman. After congratulating me on our foresight, he said that he would personally ensure that his colleagues in the financial community heard about this. He did. I began receiving congratulatory calls from a large number of banks and financial institutions. It turned out to be one of the defining moments in IMM history.

Ten years after this peso devaluation, I published a review to the world and our members, 'Making A Market, Making History.' This is what I wrote:

> The devaluation of the Mexican peso in 1976 put the IMM to the test. The overnight devaluation sent shock waves throughout the foreign exchange market. Though banks would no longer trade the Mexican peso, the IMM continued to make markets in that currency. The futures market in Mexican pesos at the IMM helped to facilitate the transfer of hundreds of millions of dollars affected by the devaluation. It was an impressive performance and gave the IMM credibility throughout the world. That year was the turning point in the life of the IMM.

CHAPTER 22

His Honor, Da Mayor

HISTORIAN Michael Beschloss described Chicago's legendary Mayor, Richard J. Daley, as "the pre-eminent mayor of the twentieth century." Folksinger Steve Goodman, on the other hand, said that "No man could inspire more love or more hate."

On the 50th anniversary of Chicago Mayor Richard J. Daley's first election, several dozen Daley biographers and associates came to the Chicago Historical Society to celebrate the event. The Irish Choir offered this poem about the working-class, dominantly Irish American citizens in Bridgeport, a neighborhood on Chicago's South Side, where the Mayor lived his entire life:[59]

> We're the South Side Irish, as our fathers were before,
> We come from the Windy City and we're Irish to the core,
> From Bridgeport to Beverly, from Midway to South Shore
> We're the South Side Irish—Let's sing it out once more!
> We live on the South Side,
> Mayor Daley lived here too
> The greatest Irish Leader that Chicago ever knew
> He was always proud of his South Side Irish roots!
> So here's to his honor, to his memory we'll be true.

Mayor Daley, who never lost his Irish, blue-collar accent, was also known for butchering the English language. One of his most notable verbal gaffs occurred in

59   Written by Tom Black and Terry McEldowney.

1968 during the Democratic Convention, when he defended the ruthless action of the Chicago Police. "Gentlemen," the Mayor said, "get the thing straight once and for all, the policeman isn't there to create disorder, the policeman is there to *preserve* disorder." In 1971, the iconic Chicago reporter, Michael Royko, published *Boss*, a (mostly unflattering) best-selling biography of Mayor Daley and the City of Chicago under his rule.

MEETING THE MAYOR

The mayor knew me for various reasons. We first met on September 30, 1969, at the 50th anniversary of the CME, where I presented the city of Chicago with the gift of $50,000 to build a Farm-in-the-Zoo within Lincoln Park Zoo. Next, he saw my name in the headlines as the chairman of the CME, when I appeared in newspapers and interviews on radio, during the launch of the IMM.

A few years later, on a sunny July afternoon in 1975, I walked the ten or so blocks from the CME to Chicago's City Hall. I was armed only with some rolled up blueprints prepared by Skidmore, Owings and Merrill (SOM), our architectural firm, ready for my appointment with the mayor. Upon arrival, I was ushered into his inner office—yes, there were two. The outer office was for group visitors, with plenty of sitting room, while the inner, just as big in size, held only two chairs in front of the mayor's desk.

I was certain he remembered me. I had no trouble making the appointment and wasn't even asked to explain my purpose. This may have been because alongside the Chicago Board of Trade (CBOT), the largest exchange in the world, our smaller, innovative exchange dominated the futures markets. It was a point of pride for the mayor. After I sat down, we exchanged the normal pleasantries before he asked, "What can I do for you?" It is difficult to describe my feelings as I began my explanation. Here I was sitting in front of this legendary figure, whose dictates were the equivalent to commands by, say, Moses, daring to be here after once rejecting a political offer that people die for, to make what I was advised was an outrageous request.

Brazen was not the word for it. Neither was fear. Instead, it was a sort of *what the hell* attitude. I went right into it, since I didn't know how much time I had and how much I would need to explain. It really wasn't complicated. The building presently owned by the Merc to house its trading floor, which now also included the IMM markets, had become too small for our burgeoning financial instruments.

At the time, all futures markets were conducted in open outcry fashion on a trading floor which housed both the trading pits and the desks from which emanated the orders that runners would literally run into the pit for execution. This execution architecture was more or less the same whether the market was in futures or securities. Electronic competency, as we know it today, was still over a decade away. Although it was a fairly new facility, built at my direction on Jackson Blvd and the Chicago River several years before, the pace of the IMM's success was without precedent. Our new financial markets were growing at a transactional rate of 45% a year. Our trading floor had quickly run out of space again and we still had many new instruments on our drawing board to launch.

To put it succinctly, we had reached the physical limitation of space on the floor. If we did not expand our trading floor, I didn't know what we would do. We retained SOM, who several years earlier built the present facility 50% larger than the original CME trading floor at 110 North Franklin, where the exchange was born. But SOM had bad news for us. They explained that since we could not extend our building over the river's edge, the only way to expand was to cantilever our building over the sidewalk of Canal Street, the street behind the exchange building.

If we did this, we would gain at least 40% of additional floor space. But there was an insurmountable problem. To do what SOM suggested required that we use the air rights owned by the City of Chicago. The City Building Department summarily turned down SOM's request without a second thought; the air rights, they explained, belonged to the City of Chicago and nobody, but *nobody*, can get such permission. This reality dealt a near fatal blow to my IMM dreams and the future of financial futures. Only the mayor could save us.

GETTING THE GO-AHEAD

When I finished my brief explanation, I started to unroll the blueprints that SOM had provided. The mayor raised his hand with a wave and shook his head. "I don't need to see the plans," he said as my heart pounded. "Instead," the Mayor continued in his Chicago Irish-style brogue, "tell me what your IMM will do for the city of Chicago?" Wow!

"Mr Mayor," I said without hesitation, "if you allow our building to expand, these markets will continue to grow and the IMM will move the center of financial gravity out of New York and toward Chicago." The mayor clapped his hands and laughed. "I like that!" he shouted. "I like that! Build your building."

Richard J. Daley had become mayor in 1955, just as I graduated from Law School, and was to remain in that office until his death in 1976. I went to his funeral. He was, of course, the father of Richard M. Daley, who took over his father's role for a subsequent 22 years. Bill Daley, the youngest of Mayor Daley's sons, once told me that his father knew that I kept my promise. Bill Daley was appointed by President Clinton as secretary of commerce and by President Barak Obama as chief of staff.

I got to know all the Daleys over the span of many decades. Taken together, the Daley family dominated Chicago politics during much of the twentieth century. I liked them and I believe they liked me. They were all Chicago and so was I.

A NEW FACE

After Everette B. Harris retired, we needed a new president. We found the perfect choice. Clayton Yeutter had degrees in both agriculture and finance, and held a sub-cabinet appointment in the department of agriculture. But Jack Sandner and I had a difficult time bringing him in. Yeutter was reluctant because the Merc's reputation might sully his résumé. We finally convinced him that our past reputation was history and that we were now on a path to greatness. He believed us.

Yeutter became the Merc's president in 1978. He did so with the understanding that I would remain, in his words, "Mr Inside" and, given his education, credentials and international standing, he would be the Merc's "Mr Outside." It was a perfect match and for the next eight or so years our partnership blossomed.

While Yeutter was never actually in the inner circle, he played a critical role in advancing the Merc's reputation. He was the only president the CME retained who was without futures market credentials. He remained president for several years, during which time he gave the CME an international presence.

But our close friendship held the unwritten understanding that Yeutter was destined for a national office. The CME was just a stepping stone in that direction. And as much as I wanted Yeutter to remain as CME president, I equally hoped to lift his national presence. As it happened, in 1985 the position of US Trade Representative opened up. I called Yeutter and urged him to go after the post. He said, "I am off to speak in Germany, but Leo, if you can make that happen, I would be thrilled." I think he was afraid that it wasn't in the cards.

I spent the next several weeks turning the political world inside-out. My son, David Melamed, spent a week with me in our Arizona house and watched first-hand as his father called on a dozen or so influential American officials to lobby for Yeutter. Of critical influence was my friendship with Senator Bob

Dole, the US Senate's strong man, who agreed to the idea. At his suggestion, I talked with Don Regan, chief of staff for President Reagan, who I knew from his days as chair of Merrill Lynch. He made it happen. Clayton Yeutter went on from US rep to US secretary of agriculture, and later to the chairmanship of the Republican Party. When I visited him during his time as secretary of agriculture, he made me sit in his chair, saying, "It really belongs to you, Leo."

As a Chicagoan, my efforts on behalf of the nation were duly recognized. In the book, *Chicago and the American Century*, author F. Richard Ciccone, former editor of the *Chicago Tribune*, enumerates the Chicagoans who in his opinion made the greatest impact on America during the twentieth century. He divided the book into ten of the most obvious categories. politics, sports, crime, business, media, law, performing arts, literature, architecture and business.

The following are Ciccone's choices in the field of business: [60]

1. The franchiser: Ray Kroc
2. The manager and the general: Julius Rosenwald and Robert Wood
3. The king of power: Samuel Insull
4. The spin doctor: Albert Lasker
5. Moon to earth: Paul Galvin
6. Butter to billions: Leo Melamed
7. Double your pleasure: William Wrigley
8. Color it yellow: John Hertz
9. Paddy and me: Joseph Kraft
10. Foot fetish: William Scholl

60   *Chicago and the American Century*, F. Ciccone, 1999.

CHAPTER 23

The Unreal 1980s

JUST as the 1970s—with the creation of the IMM and introduction of financial futures—was the most innovative and revolutionary decade in the Merc's history, so the 1980s served to lay the foundation for the CME to become the most successful, diversified, and international institution of its kind.

Whenever I am introduced to an audience, it is standard procedure to explain that I am the founder of financial futures and initiator of Globex. Those plaudits are true and represent two of my most pronounced accomplishments. Without them, I dare say, there may not have been a CME exchange today—certainly not of its present scope. However, I candidly and unabashedly state that those two achievements do not sufficiently recount my continuous role in making the Merc the most successful futures exchange in the world.[61] For that to be achieved took years of my constant attention, a plethora of ideas and innovations, some historic defensive strategies, and, as I have said before, many devoted and talented people.

Here is how Nigel Foster, the former managing director of Blackrock, the world's largest hedge fund, explained it:[62]

> It needed something more than the intellectual thinking and influence of Hayek or Friedman to bring markets in financial derivatives into being. So many great ideas flounder in delivery and practical implementation. This did not happen with financial futures and the credit for this achievement goes principally to the energy and persistence of a determined Chicago trader

---

61 Nor does it recount my efforts in helping create the futures industry that exists today.
62 *The Derivatives Game*, Nigel Foster, 2018, p93.

called Leo Melamed. Without him Hayek and Friedman's vision might not have come into being.[63]

The actions were of such magnitude it may be hard to accept that one person could possibly have led all efforts involved. Looking back, even I have trouble believing it, and yet, it was so.[64] To effectively touch on the record of these undertakings, I will introduce them in a year-by-year basis with a brief explanation of each. I will begin with the description of 1980, which represented the creation of cash settlement.

1980: LIFT OFF

I have often been asked to assess the value of our regulatory agency, the CFTC. Let me put it as succinctly as I can: passage of the 1974 Act, which created the CFTC, opened the curtain on a vast array of financial instruments, enabling futures markets to reach unimagined heights which serve the best interests of our nation. It made me one of its strongest proponents.

But passage of its legislation was a touch-and-go affair, and I had a hidden motive. To explain, I must single out Elmer Falker, my personal Old Turkey, who took me under his wing when I first appeared on the floor of the old Merc. Elmer, who was a fount of information when it came to the type of contracts that were traded around the world, said to me one day, "Of course, the ultimate contract would be Dow Jones Futures."

I immediately got it. "Wow," I nearly shouted, "Why hasn't it been tried?" He propelled an oyster with precision into a nearby spittoon and responded, "Can't make delivery."

I needed no further explanation. The reason Elmer's Dow Jones stock futures could not be carried out was the requisite for *physical delivery* at maturity of futures contracts. In simple terms, at expiration, i.e., on the final day or days of trading, every futures contract had to include a system which enabled the product traded to be delivered to those longs remaining in the market. An index, such as the Dow, could not (at least not easily) be delivered.

---

63   Friedrich August von Hayek was an Anglo-Austrian Nobel prize economist and philosopher best known for his defense of classical liberalism. Milton Friedman is widely regarded as one of the most influential economists of the twentieth century and possibly of all time.

64   Fortunately, there are the members who witnessed first-hand what I had done and what I was doing. There are countless local, national, and international newspaper articles and other publications which over the years recorded the range of these activities. Finally, there is a vast assemblage of financial executives and participants, national and global, who observed, assisted, recorded, and sometimes copied, my actions.

The legal reason for the delivery requisite was established by Justice Oliver Wendell Holmes Jr in 1905 in the *US Supreme Court Case Board of Trade v Christie.* Justice Holmes delivering the majority opinion established the principle that the difference between gambling and futures was that futures contemplate delivery. His decision made futures trading not only legal, but desirable.

The practical reason for the delivery requirement was to ensure that, at maturity, the futures price would converge with the actual spot price of the product. This provision served to prevent manipulative activities, acting as a sort of policeman to keep futures honest and, at maturity, in line with the spot market for that product. But in truth, only a very small fraction of futures contracts were ever physically delivered. Futures markets were never intended to be a substitute for the actual market delivery procedures in place for all products grown or manufactured.

CHANGE IN PERSPECTIVE

This conversation with Elmer had a lasting effect on me. First, it gave me the idea for stock futures. Second, it gave birth to an ancillary thought in the back of my head—the concept of cash settlement in place of delivery. In simple terms, cash settlement would create a method of settling forward or futures contracts by way of cash (money), rather than by physical delivery of the underlying product. Presto! An index on stocks or anything would become tradeable. I believed that indexation was precisely the direction the financial world was headed, and cash settlement would allow futures markets to capture that trend.

When I broached Salzman about cash settlement, he doubted it was possible and told me I would need a federal law to make cash settlement a legitimate methodology. Now, how would I go about doing this? Well, a *federal agency* could do that. Suddenly, a federal regulator was not such a bad thing. But, being a less-government advocate, that seemed like a heretic thought. I wrestled with that for a bit and concluded that I was never dogmatic about the principle. I believed in being *practical* above all else. Milton Friedman once explained that you need government to enforce the rules. Well, how about government to help make the rules? I become an advocate on behalf of a federal regulator—but not simply for cash settlement. There was a lot more to my rationale.

After passage of the legislation, my role in the process took an unusual turn. The legislative focus now turned to the actual staffing of the new agency. To do that, President Ford appointed his own White House personnel chief, Beverly Splane, who ultimately became the new futures agency's executive director.

It also wasn't very hard for me to immediately become a close friend of Ms Splane, a free-market thinker with an MBA degree from the University of Chicago. At her request, we held meetings in the old Washington Executive Building, as I became her private futures advisor in the appointment of CFTS personnel. Often, she would send me a résumé of a prospective high-level candidate and seek my advice or selection between two or more competing candidates. I like to believe that as a result the first panel of CFTC staffers was outstanding, laying the foundation for its difficult rise as a first-line market regulator.

It included a host of devoted and talented people like Howard Schneider, its first general counsel, and Ken Raisler, who followed in that office; Andrea Corcoran, who headed up the division of trading and markets; Dennis Klejna, the CFTC's director of enforcement; Tom Russo, who began his career as deputy general counsel of the CFTC and rose to become general counsel for AIG, helping to bring that enterprise back from near extinction; Jack Gaine; Paula Tosini; and many others.

I learned to hold Beverly Splane in such high regard that once she finished her stint as executive director of the CFTC, I offered her the position of executive vice president of the CME. She accepted, and in doing so became perhaps the first high-ranking female official at a major American exchange in 1975. Her many years of service at the Merc helped me fill some of the important CME staff positions, including that of Fred Arditti, our brilliant chief economist, who became one of my closest friends. In 1984, Splane's knowledge of Chinese enabled us to appoint her as coordinator for the newly-formed Singapore Exchange, the SIMEX, and to help establish another of my revolutionary innovations called *Mutual Offset*—a clearing system for two separate exchanges, the CME and SIMEX.

RACE TO LAUNCH

It was about this time that I turned my attention to the potential of interest rates as futures instruments, and was counselled by our then chief economist, Mark Powers, to think about 90-day Treasury bills. His advice was well-reasoned, since T-bills were highly liquid and could physically be delivered, as futures markets still demanded in 1975.

About the same time, the CBOT began to realize that what Melamed was doing at the CME might be of value. They retained Richard Sandor, a very engaging, very bright economic professor from Berkeley, to devise for them a financial-futures instrument. Sandor too thought about interest rates, but his focus was on the mortgage-backed notes, known as Ginnie Maes (GNMA).

In addition, the CBOT had retained as consultant, economist Roger Gray, the highly regarded Holbrook Working Professor emeritus of Commodity Price Studies at Stanford University. Professor Gray flew in to visit me in Chicago to counsel us to stay away from Ginnie Maes, since they would be a problem in the delivery process. It was the same conclusion he provided the CBOT, but it seemed they were about to ignore his advice. Gray's opinion served as additional proof for me to stick with the T-bill market. Although the GNMA contract was first to get CFTC approval, it unfortunately failed miserably and was quickly delisted by the CBOT.

In January 1976, the Merc's T-bill contract was launched, becoming the first *successful* interest-rate futures product in the world—with Milton Friedman as the guest of honor and bell ringer. To Richard Sandor's ever-lasting credit, he quickly admitted his mistake and turned his attention to the 30-year US bond market as a substitute to GNMA. US Bonds proved to be a huge success and finally brought the CBOT into financial futures in a big way.

Sandor and I developed a friendship over the years. Indeed, I greatly admire his deep understanding of futures and the fact that he played such a major role in saving the CBOT. The foregoing history sometimes prompted Richard Sandor to claim that his GNMA futures were the first interest-rate instrument to be approved by the CFTC. However, they were far from being the first financial futures instrument to be *launched*. Currency futures were launched in 1972, two years before the CFTC even came into existence. [65]

THE SEARCH FOR A LIKE-MINDED LEADER

Within about a year after the 1976 launch of the CME 90-day T-bills, I again picked up the issue of cash settlement as a substitute for physical delivery. Of course, in the back of my mind was Elmer Falker's stock-index futures. In 1979 I asked our legal counsel, Jerry Salzman, and CME chief economist Mark Powers, to educate CFTC staffers about this concept.

The first CFTC chairman, Bill Bagley, a President Ford appointee, was a very nice guy and somewhat of a card, but he had not a clue about our markets and admitted this. I judged that he was not the guy to take on major changes to a just-formed federal agency. The second CFTC chairman, Jim Stone, appointed

---

65   The failed GNMA interest-rate contract was the first interest product to be approved by the CFTC but was quickly delisted by the CBOT. The CME's US T-bill contract launched in 1976 was the first *successful* short-term interest-rate futures contract.

by President Jimmy Carter, was a very savvy guy who knew a lot about insurance. He was appointed chairman because of his experience as insurance director of the Commonwealth of Massachusetts. But while futures have the ability to insure, they were eons removed from Stone's expertise.

For one reason or another, Stone was not popular with the hierarchy of the futures world. As far as I could tell, I was the only one within our industry that Stone befriended. I used this fact to explain and convince him of the cash settlement concept. In truth I was somewhat successful, because at least he seemed ambivalent to the idea. However, cash settlement was for him such a radical idea (which it was) that I soon realized he would never shake that tree. Thus, I began to look ahead to the next CFTC chairman.[66]

Once Jim Stone's term was up, the person I had in mind was Phillip McBride Johnson, who helped write the CFTC Act and whom I privately asked whether he would accept such an appointment. Johnson was skeptical that this could happen because he had been the attorney for the CBOT and it would be like appointing a fox to the chicken coop. Oddly, the CBOT also sort of opposed the idea but, for me, there was no sound second choice.

What everyone missed was my strong friendship with Senator Robert Dole of Kansas, who was elected to the Senate the same year I became CME chairman. Although I was politically independent, it was an instantaneous bond of politics and patriotism. He told me that he lost the use of his left arm in the war so that I could live in freedom. In 1985, Dole became Senate majority leader and in 1996 was the Republican candidate for president. It was my honor to be in his Illinois leadership circle during the election which he lost to Bill Clinton.

Once on an airplane, Dole asked me what I wanted. I responded, "Nothing!" To which he said "Awe comm'on Leo, everybody wants something." I insisted that I didn't, but he would not give up. Finally, I said, "OK, I won't get it, but I would accept CIA director." He roared, "You are right, you won't get it."

In June 1981, President Reagan appointed Phillip McBride Johnson as the third CFTC chairman. With Johnson as chairman, we finally had someone who was an expert in our markets. Johnson later wrote the three-volume book, *Derivatives Regulation*, which became the holy bible of the industry.

---

66   Upon returning home, James Stone founded the highly successful Plymouth Rock family of insurance companies.

JURISDICTION ISSUES

Again, it was important for Salzman to soften the ground with the CFTC staff, while I pressed cash settlement on the new chairman. Johnson easily understood the value of cash settlement, in fact, he included the words "tangible and intangible" in the CFTC Act defining futures, which certainly included the definition of an index.

As Johnson and I discussed, cash settlement would open futures to nearly anything one can imagine. All that was needed was to adopt or create an index for a given product and *presto*, the product's index could be listed for trade. But it was as revolutionary a concept as one can imagine. Physical delivery was ingrained in futures' DNA. There was never anything else. When I once tried to explain it to Barry Lind, my futures' soul mate, his reaction was: "Leo, you have gone off the rails." In a very real sense, it was nearly as revolutionary as the idea of financial futures.

Still, Salzman assured me the CFTC had the power to make it legal and I was certain Phil Johnson had the brains and brawn. However, when the SEC learned of talk about stock-index futures, it went into shock mode. With futures on securities, such as Dow Jones or the like, our markets would be encroaching on the sacred jurisdictional territory of the SEC.

It led to a major jurisdictional bruhaha between John S. R. Shad, chairman of the SEC, and his counterpart at the CFTC. Again, I must credit and praise the fact that Phillip Johnson stayed the course. Without Johnson's tenacity, it would never have happened. In the end he needed a compromise. We huddled about this and agreed to accept a compromise offered by the SEC that would divide the jurisdictional territory.

The agreement became known as the Shad-Johnson Jurisdictional Accord of 1981. Without this agreement, there might never have been futures on stock-index products or little else. The Accord granted broad-based indices (as defined in the Act) to remain under the CFTC's jurisdiction, while narrow-based stock indices (such as single stocks) remain defined as security futures and therefore under the joint jurisdiction of the CFTC and the SEC.[67] It was a near miracle.

---

67   To be acceptable as a futures product, the instrument must satisfy the definition of a broad-based index. To be broad based, it must be composed of ten or more securities, no single component constitutes more than 30% of the weighting, the largest components by weight collectively constitute no more than 60% of the weighting, and each component is a 'large' stock (defined as one of the top 500 stocks common to rankings of both the largest market capitalization and largest average daily trading volume). An index

Kudos to Phil Johnson. If the CFTC never did anything else during its existence, the Shad-Johnson Accord fully justified its presence.

But there is more. As it is said, 'the Lord moves in mysterious ways.' What happened is that the SEC's Mr Shad suddenly became concerned that the settlement procedure of stock-index futures within a physical-delivery procedure might disrupt the securities market. Heaven forbid! Shad suggested that the only way to overcome this concern was to make certain that such futures instruments be cash settled. I kid you not! My dream for cash settlement was conceived as a *concession* to the SEC. Will wonders ever cease?

---

that does not qualify as broad-based under the conditions stated, would be defined as a security future subject to the joint jurisdiction of the CFTC and SEC. Enacted into law in 1983.

CHAPTER 24

1981: Dollars Everywhere

T HE instant success of the T-bill contract in 1976 was an easy pathway to thinking about more interest-rate products. Aside from adding or subtracting one or another currency, there wasn't too much else one could list as it relates to FX.[68] In contrast, interest rates were like a candy store with nearly unlimited delights.

However, there was now competition. The genie was out of the bottle. As the scuttlebutt went, 'Melamed's idea of finance in futures was, after all, not so crazy.' The CBOT and even the newly formed New York Futures Exchange (NYFE) by the NYSE made a mad dash in the direction of interest rates. Certificates of deposit (CD) were the immediate target. A certificate of deposit is a product offered by banks and credit unions that provides an interest-rate premium in exchange for the customer agreeing to leave a lump-sum deposit untouched for a predetermined period of time.

I expected and didn't fear competition. The odds favored us because we were the first financial exchange and, as I often said, "the firstest with the bestest, wineth." Second, I had the IMM liquidity army behind me. Finally, a key element in creating liquidity was by way of spreading—similar to arbitrage. Once we had T-bills liquid in the 90-day interest sector, all other instruments with parallel specifications could be used for spread trading. This made it most likely that we would win the liquidity contest.

We did, but it turned out to be a pyrrhic victory. Problem was, the CD interest rates offered by banks depended on the strength of the bank itself. Not all of

---

68   In time, we found plenty of additional FX related products.

them were equal. Successive commercial deficits in the US, for instance, brought about problems at the Continental Illinois bank, causing them to withdraw from issuing CDs. Similarly, Chase Manhattan's encounter with Drysdale Government Securities, who failed to pay interest due, meant they too withdrew from issuing CDs. On top of this, the Federal Reserve placed a ceiling on domestic deposits during the high inflation of the 1970s. As a result, CD futures became unattractive and could not provide a valid benchmark. Still, this did not disprove my theory about spread trading to create liquidity.

RISE OF THE EURODOLLAR

Our focus turned to eurodollars, perhaps the largest pool of potential trade in the world. To understand this subject requires a little history review. We have to go back to the end of the second world war, when the only nation left standing was the USA. Simply stated, the US dollar was the Babe Ruth of currencies. Everything of importance was marked and paid for in US dollars. The Marshall plan was a large contributor, as were geopolitical forces and global trade imbalances. Some countries, such as the Soviet Union, always held large deposits in US dollars abroad, as did other Communist governments. It is also believed that Communist China in 1949 moved all of its US dollars into a Parisian bank.

All of this combined to create enormous amounts of US dollars in foreign banks. After a decade or two, the world outside the US had more of the dollar currency in its possession than in the country that issued it. And because this stash was outside the US, it escaped regulatory oversight by the Federal Reserve, or anyone else, and resulted in higher interest rates, willingly paid, for these so-called eurodollars.

The term eurodollar referred to US dollar-denominated deposits at foreign banks or at the overseas branches of American banks. They were stateless and allowed companies and countries to borrow and repay while dodging domestic regulation and taxes. Over time, these 90-day interest-rate deposits were used in transactions around the globe, and its name never changed. Problem was, every bank had its own interest rate. In effect, one had to go shopping from bank to bank to negotiate the best rate. It was wild.

In addition, in the early 1980s, banks and hedge funds began trading something called derivative options based on loans, which promised high returns. However, both parties to the transaction had to agree on the interest rate of the underlying loan into the future. In other words, they needed a method to agree on an interest rate that a bank would charge for a future loan. There were two imponderables.

One, there was no such methodology; and two, you cannot deliver an interest rate. Well, I knew the answer to the second problem—cash settlement—CFTC Chairman Phil Johnson was on the way of solving it. And as to the first, enter Fred Arditti.

One day, our executive vice president, Beverly Splane, came to me with the name Fred Arditti, head of the department of economics at Florida State University, with a PhD in economics from MIT. I don't know how she found him, but I needed only a few minutes in an interview to conclude that he was the perfect pick. His lightning-fast thought process and depth of economic knowledge were second to none. His extensive understanding of derivatives, that at the time hardly anyone understood, coupled with his knowledge of the IMM were more than I could expect. I quickly agreed to bring him aboard as our chief economist.

Fred and I spent a long time getting to know each other and discussing the potential of interest rates for futures. We came to the conclusion that the world needed a uniform price in short-term interest rates. A futures market that could accomplish this feat would capture a ton of business. How to achieve this idea was the problem. We were aware that the London Interbank Offered Rate (Libor), which evolved in the 1970s to meet rising demand for a reference rate, was a good start. But Libor was not a futures market. What the reference rate needed, we agreed, was a 90-day futures contract with a pricing methodology at final settlement that would be accepted by the big European banks as the global common-denominator. If we found that formula it could become the most traded futures instrument in the world. It was a most enticing mission. We talked about it incessantly.

Finally, we agreed that Fred should spend some time with the London banks and elsewhere in Europe to gain an idea of what they would agree to. He went and a couple of weeks later came back with what turned out to be an ingenious solution: an acceptable methodology, embraced by the world's banks, for determining the final settlement price at maturity of a proposed futures eurodollar contract. This achievement, coupled with cash settlement, could solve the world's need for uniformity in 90-day interest rates.

WORKING OUT THE DETAILS

Arditti found the solution by remembering his days at the Rand Corporation and their publication, *A Million Random Digits with 100,000 Normal Deviates*. It led him to a design which enabled replication of a random-order selection process based on a defined but selected-at-random starting point. Today, computer modelling makes such a random-ordering process easy and common, but that technology was not available in those days. Fred's brilliant solution was a manual process by which to determine the 'correct' interest rate of the final settlement at maturity of the eurodollar contract.

Arditti's plan called for two bank surveys, one reading at 9.30am, and the other at a randomly selected time within the prior 90 minutes—so between 8.00am and 9.30am Chicago time (2.00pm to 3.30pm London time). For each of the two bank surveys, the clearing house would select at random 12 reference banks from a list of no less than 20 participating banks that are major banks in the London eurodollar market. Each reference bank shall quote to the clearing house its perception of the rate at which the three-month eurodollar time-deposit funds are currently offered by the market to prime banks.

These rates must be confirmed in writing by telex before they are accepted as official; only after confirmation will they be used to determine the final settlement price. The two highest and two lowest quotes shall be eliminated. The arithmetic-mean of the remaining eight quotes shall be the Libor at that time. If for any reason there is difficulty in obtaining a quote within a reasonable time interval from one of the banks in the sample, that bank shall be dropped from the sample, and another shall be randomly selected to replace it.

When I asked Fred if he played it on the New York banks, he said, "yes, and they don't like it." "In that case," I laughed, "for sure we will do it." We called it the IMM Index. On December 9, 1981, the IMM's eurodollar contract was launched, becoming the first cash-settled product in the history of futures.[69] The price of eurodollar futures reflected the interest rate offered on US dollar-denominated deposits held in banks outside the US. More specifically, the price reflected the market gauge of the three-month US dollar interest rate anticipated on the settlement date of our contract.

A HARD SELL

It was left to me to convince the financial world. It took nearly four years and required my crisscrossing the planet to explain what the contract was about, and how the settlement at maturity was to be determined. It also required my continuous coaxing and begging of a small fraction of IMM traders to remain in the pit day after day, month after month, year after year (even when nothing

69   Cash settlement had been approved.

much was going on), and convince them not to abandon their continued time and resolve to provide liquidity. Even Barry Lind was hesitant. "Leo," he said to me, "a futures contract without delivery? Haven't you let your imagination run too far?" Ultimately, of course, eurodollars provided the world with a universal benchmark for short-term rates. It became the most successful futures instrument of all time. The IMM eurodollar contract, at times, represented over 50% of the CME's entire open interest.

Fred Arditti served as the Merc's chief economist from 1980 until 1982. After a stint at Drexel Burnham at my personal urging, he returned to the CME in 1997 to assume a leadership role in the development of the exchange's weather-derivatives market, among other things.[70] Arditti's work embodied a passion both for innovative thinking and practical benefit to commerce and markets. The department of finance at DePaul University in Chicago established the Arditti Center for Risk Management, to honor his lifetime achievements and continue this important work in the areas of education, research and practice. Arditti's book, *Derivatives: A Comprehensive Resource for Options, Futures, Interest Rate Swaps, and Mortgage Securities,* is one of the most assigned books on the subject of markets in many universities.

Phupinder Gill was discovered by Fred Arditti, who was in charge of our staff. Gill was Indian by birth, Singaporean by citizenship, and brilliant as an American. He came to the Merc by way of the CBOE. Arditti, Gill and I soon became a devoted trio of friends. Gill and I maintain our close relationship to this day. He became like the brother I never had. Gill's talents made it easy for him to move through the CME ranks and reach CEO status. Our collaboration and common efforts, especially relating to China and other Asian principalities, where my reputation was extremely well received, made the Merc the number one exchange in that arena and a trustworthy partner in foreign affairs around the world. What impressed me most about Gill was our similar ability to see beyond the immediate.

During his service as CEO, Gill used his skills to attract and bring to the fold hugely talented officials who to this day continue to provide us with strong management and innovation. Among them was Kim Taylor, recruited by Gill in 1989, who rose to become president of the clearing house. Kim's talents proved to be without equal. I would ascribe to her the fact the CME clearing house became the model for the futures industry, its integrity and financial strength second to none. Her talents are the reason the CME clearing entity went unscathed during the 2008 financial crash and other calamities. When Paul

---

70   I too had just returned to CME leadership, which gave Arditti a strong reason to return.

Volcker called me after the crash to see if we would open the following day, I called Kim to get the answer.

In addition to Taylor, Gill attracted Derek Sammann, who headed up our commodity and options products; Sean Tully, global head of financial and OTC products; and Jason Weller, who stood at the highest level of the Merc's vision. Weller in particular was an outstanding logician with whom I often discussed plans and strategies.

Fred Arditti passed away from pancreatic cancer on October 31, 2005. His loss left a permanent void in my life and at the Merc. At his passing I suggested an innovation prize in his name but our chairman, Terry Duffy, insisted that it be named the Melamed–Arditti Innovation Award.

CHAPTER 25

1981: NFA

WHILE the launch of eurodollars was an all-consuming undertaking, I was once again knee-deep in fending off federal legislation that would institute a transaction tax on futures. Congress wanted our industry to fund the CFTC. Not an outlandish idea, but we knew that this approach would place our industry in jeopardy to additional taxation and ultimately the potential to make us non-competitive.

The legislation was triggered by some unsavory and illegal acts that caused great losses to investors in futures. The CFTC blamed lack of funding for their failure to adequately protect every arena in the vast universe of futures. It was true. The futures world had many parts, with regulations over both exchanges and their members being the easy part, since the exchanges themselves did most of the policing. But the CFTC was not equipped to cover the *rest* of the industry, which included non-member activities by future commission merchants, commodity trading advisors, introducing brokers and a vast array of other operators in futures. I knew well that those individuals and firms not regulated could cause investors and the industry great harm and stunt its growth—but I also knew that funding this job by government was a bad idea.

The creation of the National Futures Association (NFA) was historic. Few other industries ever became authorized by Congress to regulate themselves as futures do. To this day, the futures industry maintains and funds the regulatory framework on which its markets continue to grow and succeed without the need for federal funds in the form of a transaction tax. My testimony in Congress on this issue explains in detail how this came about.[71]

---

71 I continue to act as the permanent advisor to the NFA.

THE POWER OF PERSUASION

Believe it or not, it was harder to convince the members of our industry than the members of Congress. I had a devil of a time explaining to our members why we needed an NFA. Why they should support the creation of a *second* CFTC, one limited to non-member activities. More than that, members of the markets would not pay or otherwise be subject to this new authority. It would be funded by non-member money. A concept that on its face sounded impossible.

At the Merc, the members had learned to trust me. But not at the CBOT—its membership was fiercely opposed to any new regulatory body and Leo Melamed was a competitor which made him untrustworthy. At one point I asked their chairman, Leslie Rosenthal, to allow me to face his board of directors in person. It was something that had never before occurred. But Rosenthal was a close friend and on the NFA organizing committee. He believed in the power of my personal conviction. It worked. To almost everyone's surprise, I convinced the CBOT, fanatical anti-government folks, that they should agree to the creation of a federal agency that would help regulate our markets.

The NFA exists to this day, and does a superb job at regulating the vast non-member world of futures. Without the NFA, the CFTC would have long ago failed—which likely would have meant the end of the futures industry. Or that a federal transaction tax or whatever name it was given would have been imposed on our industry and limited its value to the nation. The NFA has grown to become one of the hallmark industry-wide self-regulatory organizations for the US derivatives industry. I continue to be its *permanent special adviser*. The NFA website records this history:

> In 1976, Leo Melamed, chairman of the Chicago Mercantile Exchange (currently permanent special advisor to the NFA executive committee and board of directors), persuaded other industry leaders that a title III organization would unquestionably benefit the futures industry and the public it serves. Mr Melamed created an NFA organizing committee comprised of industry leaders which he chaired and which included himself as chairman, David T. Johnston, vice-chairman; John J. Conheeney; George D. F. Lamborn; Warren W. Lebeck; Leslie Rosenthal and Howard A. Stotler.

A CULTURE OF EXCELLENCE

Although I accept the praise for creating the NFA and chairing it for the first ten years of its life, it was Robert Wilmouth, former CEO of the CBOTs, who, as the first president and CEO of NFA, created the staffing, culture and structure of this unique self-regulatory agency. I brought Wilmouth in as CEO of the newly formed agency right from the start, when we were but an empty shell. He took charge as if he had done it before, which he had not.

The NFA under his leadership took shape and became a highly regarded regulatory body. He created a culture of excellence and job devotion. He also knew how to deal with the difficult and sensitive issues of dividing the regulatory authority and responsibilities between the CFTC and the NFA without taking away the CFTC limelight. Very quickly he established himself as an industry spokesman without getting into the hair of the hierarchy of the futures exchanges. The NFA is the respected regulatory body it is today *because* of his leadership. He also served as a model for Dan Roth, who followed in his footsteps to preside over the vast expansion of futures markets that followed, and kept the NFA on a stardom course for the following 15 years. His successor, Tom Sexton, is from the same cloth and I am certain will continue to lead with equal integrity and vigor.

The following is my written testimony presented in 1981 before the US senate committee on agriculture which served to deny a transaction tax on our industry and thereby gain US Congressional approval to create the NFA:

> Mr Chairman, members of the committee. My name is Leo Melamed. I am chairman of Dellsher Investment Company, special counsel to and a former chairman of the Chicago Mercantile Exchange. Since 1976, I have been an organizing director and president of the National Futures Association. I am delighted to appear before you today on behalf of the NFA. Accompanying me today are Patricia Carlile, NFA's acting executive director and John Stassen, a partner of Kirkland & Ellis, NFA's general counsel.
>
> I appear before you today to acquaint you with what may be the very short biological history of the life of an entity conceived by Congress, the very same body which all of you proudly represent—a life which is today in your hands and whose future depends on your decision; a life which represents the hope and promise for our industry; a life which you sponsored, we devised and the CFTC ordained. I speak of the very short life of the National Futures Association, the NFA.

Conception of the NFA occurred in 1974 when the United States Congress adopted the Commodity Futures Trading Commission Act and provided, under title III thereof, for the birth of a new self-regulatory organization for the commodity futures industry.

Two years of incubation followed the act of conception. The first signs of fertility occurred in 1976 when a not-for-profit corporation, sponsored by leaders of our industry and called the National Futures Association, was registered under the corporate laws of the State of Delaware.

What followed was one of the most difficult periods of gestation ever recorded in private sector embryology. It was a five-year pregnancy, painful and dangerous, during which the prognosis for a healthy birth was often in doubt. There were many from within and without our industry who were against its conception from the beginning.

The antagonists from within argued that NFA would represent but one more body of regulatory authority in a world already possessed of too many regulators; that this new organization could not and would not fairly represent all the diverse sectors of the industry; that it would be too costly to ourselves; that it would duplicate functions of the CFTC; and, yes, some cynically asked why we should regulate properly and forcibly in areas where the CFTC had failed.

The antagonists from without argued simply that the NFA represented a ruse to divert authority from the CFTC and that no self-regulatory private-sector organization could be trusted to do a proper job.

I led the fight for the protagonists who were both from within and without our industry. We claimed to be much more responsible and farsighted. We insisted that NFA could be the potential savior of the futures industry and of its federal regulatory agency. NFA could, we fervently espoused, save the industry from unnecessary duplicative regulations, carry out regulatory functions in a more proficient manner, relieve the CFTC of some obligatory burdens so that it could better carry out its oversight mandate in areas where it had failed to so do expeditiously, and that it would prevent the onerous onslaught of those who proposed a user fee system to defray the cost of regulation. It was the only time I disagreed with CFTC chairman, Philip Johnson. Aside from these specifics, we argued with what amounted to religious fervor that NFA was consistent with the banner of self-regulation which the futures industry has so proudly hailed for over 100 years of its existence.

I am delighted to report that in the end the protagonists prevailed. In March of 1981, the NFA went into heavy labor by filing its application before the CFTC for designation as a futures association pursuant to Section 17 of the Commodity Exchange Act. As delineated in the comprehensive application package filed with the CFTC, NFA was devised to do the following:

- To effectively police the futures industry itself as well as those segments operating outside the system of exchange standards and surveillance.

- To achieve better cost control over regulatory expense by eliminating duplication and conflict between governmental and self-regulatory programs.

- To facilitate a reduction in the costs of federal regulation for the benefit of taxpayers in general and market users in particular.

The labor pains were extreme. A lengthy and exhaustive, as well as constructive, review process followed. All went well, however, and with no small measure of pride the CFTC, acting as midwife, announced the NFA birth on September 22, 1981. The National Futures Association was designated as an official 'registered futures association.' The baby was born.

At first our industry went into shock. It had been so long and arduous a process that we were not fully prepared for the event. But soon the realization of parenthood took place and with it, preparations for the offspring's wellbeing began. I am pleased to report that our progress has been swift and impressive. Since December 15, when Pat Carlile was chosen as acting executive director, substantial sums of money have been committed to the project. The core of a full-time professional staff was brought on board to develop programs and systems for membership qualification, member registration, FCM financial audits and NFA's professional standards and compliance programs. The national headquarters of the NFA were opened at 120 South Riverside Plaza in Chicago.

An advisory was mailed to all exchanges and 3,500 futures industry professionals apprising them of the next immediate stages of NFA formation and the expected timetable for membership. A plan was formulated to appoint the first 40-person board of directors of NFA which would represent every segment of our industry. Additionally, the agenda was prepared for a full briefing of our industry at the Annual Futures Industry Convention later this week. In short, we were well on the way to fulfilling our objectives and on target for meeting the goal of being a significant self-regulatory factor in our industry by October 1 of this year. The NFA proposes to enhance regulation by assuming the following obligations:

- comprehensive FCM audits;

- introducing broker oversight and ethical standards;

- pool operator and trading advisor oversight and ethical standards;

- sales practice reviews;

- options program oversight of FCMs and introducing brokers;

- registrations and fitness standards for industry professionals including sales personnel;

- speedy, inexpensive, equitable customer claim procedures;

- enforcement of ethical rules on all industry professionals.

We propose an emphasis on self-regulation by the nation's eleven commodity exchanges. If implemented, NFA estimates that it will permit the CFTC to reduce its staff levels by at least one-third and result in a substantial reduction of its 1983 budget request.

But a large cloud now hangs over the NFA. Suddenly its very existence is being threatened, even before it can justify its existence; before it can produce any of the benefits it was so painfully programmed to carry out; before it is even one year old.

The NFA program, in fact the NFA's very existence, is threatened by the CFTC's recent decision (supported by the office of management and budget) to propose a special regulatory tax on all futures market participants including hedgers and market makers.

Mr Chairman, members of the committee, I am here to plead for the life of the NFA and to impress upon you why the enactment of the CFTC tax is unnecessary, unwise and incompatible with the premises upon which the NFA was created. The CFTC's proposed tax would deprive NFA of its funding base, destroying the underlying reason for its creation (i.e., to absorb some of the regulatory burdens in a cost-efficient manner) and remove the single most effective incentive of a self-regulatory organization—to prevent duplicative oppressive regulation. Our industry cannot rationally be expected to pay twice for the same regulatory process. It makes little sense for our industry to fund a self-regulatory organization if the CFTC plan is enacted.

CFTC Chairman Johnson is and has been for many years a foremost protagonist of NFA. I know because I worked with him on its behalf during the many years of gestation. But, he is in error when he now says, as he recently did, "that proponents arguing abandonment of NFA if a fee system is adopted are largely the same people who earlier opposed NFA for other reasons."

Mr Chairman, I represent the chairman of the seven organizers of NFA who toiled against bitter odds to give birth to this entity and I am here respectfully to advise you that we cannot in good conscience tell our industry members that NFA represents the same purpose, the same promise, the same productive result, if the CFTC tax system is imposed.

Justice John Marshall said: "The power to tax involves the power to destroy." That is clearly the central view of the present Administration. President Reagan has repeatedly spoken out against burdensome taxation and its destructive force on the private sector. Succinctly, he set the tone for the administration by declaring in his State of the Union address that his plan for recovery is "removing unnecessary regulation to spark productivity." Moreover, both Republicans and Democrats alike have gone on record against excessive regulation and to urge a system of self-regulation in its place wherever possible.

A futures transaction tax is not merely perverse in economic terms and a dangerous incentive for growth of federal economic regulation, it represents the antithesis of the agreed-to theme of both the Administration and Congress.

Ours is not an instance where an industry is shirking its responsibilities. Quite to the contrary. The futures industry is exemplifying the finest tradition of participation in the burden of government. We are prepared, willing and capable of sharing the regulatory burden and costs, estimated at $6–8m annually, if given a chance. We are not prepared to duplicate these costs, however. We agree with CFTC Commissioner David Gartner:

- This organization (NFA) will be totally funded by the industry to the tune of millions of dollars annually. And NFA will take over many of the functions performed by the Commission.

- Having mandated the NFA, I do not believe ... that the Commission should place an additional burden on market user(s) by way of the transaction tax.

In a separate document of legislative recommendations, NFA has set forth many compelling reasons why a transaction tax is indefensible from the standpoint of economic policy, principles of regulatory reform and legal/historical doctrines. This document also contains recommendations which relate directly to NFA's ability to act as a self-regulatory unit which will improve the level and efficiency of regulation at significant cost savings to the US taxpayer.

I respectfully request that this document and the accompanying complete text of a 'Futures Trading Regulatory Improvements Act of 1982' be made a part of the record of these hearings and be given your most serious consideration.

We submit that if NFA is allowed to function and if our recommendations are implemented, then there is no reasonable or proper fiscal rationale for the imposition of a special regulatory tax on futures transactions. Not only will a significant cost savings to the Federal Government be accomplished through NFA, not only will the government have advanced its cause in favor of deregulation and on behalf of self-regulation, it will have avoided the danger seen by Federal Reserve Chairman Volcker when he cautioned: "One danger from ... the imposition of heavy costs [on organized futures markets] is that activity will shift to unregulated channels here and abroad ..."

To put it precisely, NFA is the self-regulatory, deregulatory answer to increased CFTC budget demands in an era of diminishing federal resources. NFA is an answer which cuts taxpayer costs significantly but actually enhances the level and quality of customer protection. It is an answer which requires no new taxes.

Finally, our economic system, our social system, our political system already are staggering under the excesses of those who trust government regulation and distrust freedom. Of late, however, there is a general recognition that this country and the Congress must move in the direction of lessening the burdens of regulation.

The CFTC's bill, including its tax plan, is a giant step in the opposite direction. I do not believe that the members of this Committee will want to add to the burdens already imposed upon our free and functioning futures markets by supporting such legislation. It is a measure that is ill-conceived and ill-considered. If enacted, it could only have the worst of ill effects.

NFA respectfully urges Congress to reject the CFTC's legislative and taxing plan and to choose the NFA alternative instead—an alternative which is the only sensible and certain means to lower the costs and burdens of federal regulation while at the same time assuring that the public interest is well protected.

Thank you. I will be happy to respond to any questions you may have.

It has been 39 years since this testimony was presented to Congress. As promised, the NFA is today the industry-wide self-regulatory organization for the US derivatives industry, including on-exchange traded futures, retail off-exchange foreign currency, and OTC derivatives (swaps). It is designated by the CFTC as a registered futures association. The NFA's role is to safeguard the integrity of the derivatives markets, protect investors and ensure members meet their regulatory responsibilities.

NFA membership includes swap dealers (SD), futures commission merchants (FCM), commodity pool operators (CPO), commodity trading advisors (CTA), retail foreign-exchange dealers (RFED), introducing brokers (IB) and the associated persons (AP) of FCMs, CPOs, CTAs and IBs.

In 2017, the NFA board of directors agreed to increase the fee to 0.02 per contract for futures and options starting January 1, 2018, in order to "fund its operations without compromising the quality of its regulatory programs, and maintain adequate reserves."

CHAPTER 26

1982: SIMEX

ARLY in 1982, to my naïve surprise, I learned that London was the 'right' place. It was a rude awakening. As people in real estate like to say, there are three priorities: location, location, and location.

Perhaps I should begin by explaining that I am a believer in competition. I mean, I *really* believe in it. As I explained to IMM members when they asked why I was helping John Barkshire, a London money broker, to create a competitive market in London, my answer was that the competition would be good for us. Not only would it keep us on our toes and force us to push forward with new ideas, but it would expand the universe of futures users and thus create new customers for us. Besides, gaining acceptance in Europe would accelerate our markets' validation throughout the world. I did not expound on the fact that there was no patent for our idea anyway, meaning we couldn't stop others from copying us.

BEYOND OUR AMERICAN BORDERS

In 1980, John Barkshire realized that we were on to something really big in Chicago. He sought my help—which I happily gave—in establishing a London futures exchange based on the IMM architecture. Michael Jenkins, their first CEO, and Jack Wigglesworth built the London International Financial Futures Exchange (LIFFE) into the most successful European futures exchange. And my view about competition paid off. Not only did European business come to

LIFFE, it also came to the Merc—so much so that we soon opened a London office. Of course, competition can sometimes produce difficult ramifications too.

The eurodollar market that Arditti and I launched in 1981 was destined to become the biggest futures market in the world. But there was a maturation process of several years. During this hiatus, the Brits launched an exact copy of our contract. We took notice, but there was nothing we could do. As I said, there was no patent for ideas.

One other fact was becoming clear. The Far East was awaking and would soon need financial futures to continue its growth. Asia's potential was immense and the eurodollars contract had special appeal. Suddenly, there was a worry. Why? Because London was the right location.

London has, for centuries, been the preferred site of world business—its location captures the final business hours in Asia, the entire business day in Europe, and the opening business hours in North America. That may not matter in many endeavors, but with respect to eurodollars, it was of huge significance. News affecting interest rates happened round the clock.

When a hedger or speculator took a position in eurodollars at the IMM from, say, Tokyo, they would be covered for the American time zone. But if they did so at LIFFE, they would get interest-rate coverage for nearly the entire 24-hour business day and at the cost of only one commission. The same coverage at the IMM would require at least two commissions. Clearly, London is in the perfect time zone—not Chicago.

QUANTUM MECHANICS

The problem was very real and very serious. LIFFE's open interest began to beat the IMM's almost immediately. And while I had done some very smart things to make the IMM in Chicago a most successful entity, I could not move the world's time zones around.

Or could I?

The solution didn't come to me overnight, but it didn't take very long either. For the IMM to provide cover in the Asian and European, as well as American, time zones, the IMM had to be situated in both the US and Asia. So how could the IMM accomplish this miracle? How could we be in two places at the same time?

The answer, I realized, was a full-scale cloning of the IMM. In other words, we needed an Asian exchange as a partner, one who had sufficient financial strength and experience and could be trusted to share our clearing responsibilities. That way, a eurodollar trade made in Tokyo—at an Asian cloned copy of the IMM—would provide coverage through to the close of business at the IMM in Chicago. It would then, of course, be cleared at the original IMM. It would be as if the Tokyo trade was made in Chicago at the IMM and vice versa. I might add, it was the futures market equivalent of quantum mechanics.

Were we crazy? No one in the world had ever done anything like it—a simultaneous eurodollar transaction on two different continents and in two different time zones! It would make two separate contracts into one.

In retrospect, the idea would be unnecessary within a couple of years. Globex, the Merc's electronic-trading system, would provide coverage on a 24-hour global basis. But that was still ten years away. In the meantime, if nothing was done the IMM would lose its eurodollar contracts to LIFFE. You will note that our eurodollar was of such great value that it became the single most sought after futures contract.

SEEKING APPROVAL

To execute this outlandish solution in the twenty-first century would have been a tall order. To do so in 1983 required a near miracle. First, I had to gain acceptance from then CME chairman, Brian Monieson; followed by Barry Lind, clearing house chairman; Jerry Salzman, our general counsel; and finally Clayton Yeutter, CME president.

Brian Monieson, founder of GNP, a sizeable clearing firm, was elected CME chairman in 1983. He was a colleague of mine who, like me, always sought to find the hidden pitfalls that surely lurked in our groundbreaking undertakings. Brian quickly became a personal friend, and one of my strongest allies during many of the hurdles we faced. In 1986, our tournament-bridge team (myself, Brian and two other players) won a National Bridge championship.

Brian had three passions in life: his family, computers and horses. In 1990, his two-year-old, Art's Place, won the Breeders Crown and set a two-year-old pacing record of 151.1—breaking the previous record, held for 18 years, by two seconds. His partner in this was George Segal, an outstanding trader and someone whose views I often sought. George was a bedrock common-sense guy and never one to say anything that wasn't 100% factual.

Sadly, in the 1980s, Brian was accused of having failed to supervise two salesmen in his firm, GNP, who allegedly cheated customers out of $300,000. The CFTC offered to settle with a fine of $100,000. Brian rejected the offer because he felt he was not guilty. In 1992, a CFTC panel fined him $500,000, which was reduced on appeal to $200,000. Brian battled cancer for a number of years and passed away in 1999 at the age of 62.

Having received agreement from the highest CME officials that the solution had merit but would be near impossible to achieve, I still had to convince officials at the CME clearing house, as well as those on the clearing house committee. Next was getting the CFTC on board—they agreed mainly because it was my idea, or so they told me.[72] This was followed by my persuading all the member clearing firms, a daunting task since the money at risk was ultimately theirs. Finally, I had to satisfy the principal component—a trustworthy Asian partner who could pass the stiff requirements we had set, one that perhaps did not exist! And finally gain CFTC approval again.

And that was just the beginning. The Asian entity itself, once chosen, would subsequently have to deal with a ton of delicate issues. To name just a few, the exchange would have to gain their government's approval, comply with their country's trading regulations, establish their independence as an exchange, create financial safeguards, implement the technology to transfer open positions and set up sophisticated clearing capabilities. I was now ready for the journey to Asia.

SCOUTING PARTY

I asked Brian Monieson to travel with me. He had a good head for finance. Should we get anywhere with this venture, as CME chairman, he would be helpful in getting board approval. For similar reasons, I also asked Jack Sandner to accompany us. Although Jack did not become an active CME member until long after the launch of financial instruments, he was a quick study. Jack was personable and smart, as well as a lawyer, so it was easy for us to become friends. In 1978, I helped get him elected to the board and, two years later, I sponsored him for chairmanship. Jack was also chairman of RB&H, a major CME clearing firm known for its expertise in the cattle market.

For many years Jack and I worked as a team, with Jack always publicly endorsing and supporting my leadership. I admired Jack's skill as a public speaker, a talent that we shared, which was necessary for leadership. During sessions when I needed to convince group members of something, it was comforting to know that Jack could follow my lead without a hitch. During his extended service as

---

72   Years later, I was told that no one else could have convinced the CFTC to approve this revolutionary idea.

chairman of the CME, Jack was a strong voice and an able ally. As a result, Jack often escorted me to difficult foreign environs.

There were three natural venues: Tokyo, Hong Kong and Singapore. We began our exploration in Tokyo. Remember, I had special affinity for Japan, given my personal history, and was rather well known there. Yet, as was the case everywhere we went, we had to convince the government before anything could happen. And Japan was nowhere near ready for the complicated mission I was describing—I am certain our pitch must have sounded like financial sci-fi to some of the government officials whom we met with. At this early stage in their global market rise, it was far too early to consider what I was selling.

But Japan did advance. Many years later I was able to convince their finance minister, Toyoo Gyohten, to give license to the CME for the listing of their Nikkei index. Years after that, I was able to convince another finance minister, Makoto Utsumi, to approve the use of Globex in Japan. No small accomplishments, I mention this background to record my strong recognition in Japan—I am today still an advisor (without pay). But at that early stage in Japan's global marketplace, it was a non-starter.

From Japan, we tried Hong Kong—the location on which I had high hopes. Larry Rosenberg, the new CME chairman joined Jack and I for this segment. Market wise, Hong Kong was advanced, with a going futures market. They readily took to the idea. However, they simply would not consider giving up the control that our idea required. Also, their financial community was divided into three factions: the mainland Chinese, the Hong Kong Chinese and the Brits. Each of them wanted to be the partner, but none of them necessarily wanted the other two communities involved.

THE RIGHT FIT

Finally, we went to Singapore, widely regarded well for its incorruptible, meritocratic government as well as its fair judicial system and strong rule of law. Singapore desperately wanted to be chosen, since that would mean a huge step towards becoming a Far-Eastern financial center and maybe even overtaking Hong Kong. The country already had a futures gold market. Its chair was Elizabeth Sam, a very bright and assertive person. Elizabeth was willing to restructure the gold exchange to suit our demands. This was a good starting point, but far from sufficient.

The power behind their markets lay with the Monetary Authority of Singapore (MAS)—nothing of significance happened in Singapore without its approval. After preliminary discussion, Lim Ho Kee, MAS chairman, was so insistent that Singapore was the right country for my idea that he followed me back to Chicago—a move that went a long way towards convincing me that he might be correct.

The discussion went into high gear after Mr Kee was succeeded as MAS chairman by Ng Kok Song, who turned out to be a hugely resourceful and brilliant official. The chemistry between us was instantaneous. I have to believe that without Song, SIMEX would never have been born. Mr Ng was a graduate from Stanford; he was far-sighted, sophisticated and fully aware of what such an agreement would mean for Singapore. During our many visits I gained the utmost respect for him, the nation of Singapore, and its founder and prime minister, Lee Kuan Yew. Commonly known by the initials LKY, Yew not only created the city-state of Singapore, but was, in my opinion, one of the smartest world leaders in history. LKY presided over Singapore from 1959 to 1990, during which time Singapore became the most prosperous country in Southeast Asia.

PROBLEM SOLVING

There were many internal concerns of course. The monetary consequences were frightening. The chance for fraud or failure was enormous. How would the margining work? These intricate questions were satisfied by the Merc's economic department, which included two former Federal Reserve officials, Michael Asay and Roger Rutz, who were brilliant economists. Together they came up with the foolproof system eventually named the Mutual Offset System (MOS). This was key to the guarantee needed. It was an outstanding bit of work. Negotiations took over a year.

To progress, we needed to be sure that the government of Singapore would have our back and that the MAS were willing to pass rules compatible with CME and CFTC regulation. For that, Song took me to meet with the prime minister. Straight up, LKY asked me the critical question: what was stopping our partnership?

I explained that this was an untested idea and that, with Singapore, I was dealing with a country that hardly had a history and questionable market rules. I had seen how loosely the gold market operated. "Who makes the rules?" Mr Lee asked. I replied that ultimately it was the CFTC. "Do they have a book?" he pursued. When I responded in the affirmative, he said sternly, "Send me their book." The long and short of it was that Singapore adopted all the critical CFTC rules.

The new exchange, christened the Singapore International Monetary Exchange or SIMEX, opened its doors on September 7, 1984. Jack Sandner and I did the honors by joining the traditional Asian Lion dance. From the moment SIMEX opened, LIFFE's open-interest began to fall. The IMM eurodollar open-interest rose and never looked back. On December 1, 1999, SIMEX merged with the Stock Exchange of Singapore (SGX).

At the 15th anniversary celebration, I was seated next to LKY. During his address, he called me up and introduced me—at the black-tie event of perhaps 3,000 people—as the person most responsible for making Singapore a financial center. I give equal credit to Ng Kok Song. He and I were inducted to the Singapore Hall of Fame. When I describe my accomplishments, the quantum mechanics of time zones is always near the top.

CHAPTER 27

1982: The Libor Debacle

ALTHOUGH it took several years for the banks to discover the importance and beauty of the IMM's eurodollar contract, once they did, it began to achieve the full measure of its potential. By the time I returned to the board in 1997, 15 years after its birth, the IMM's eurodollar contract had become the global benchmark for hedging and speculating short-term interest rates.

However, unbeknownst to me, it had recently undergone a major and dubious transformation. Beginning in 1995, a plan evolved at the CME to hand over the calculation for pricing to Libor. By then, Libor had grown to become the final authority on the average interest costs to most international London banks when borrowing from each other for durations ranging from overnight to one year.[73] It was believed that this change would bring additional futures business for the CME, since Libor would be perceived as a more impartial party than the CME clearing house.[74] Libor was happy to agree. It turned out to be a very serious mistake. Our own hands are the safest.

I am quite certain had Fred Arditti or I been around we would not have supported the idea. First, we both were in the 'If it ain't broke, don't fix it' camp. More to the point, in conversations with Fred just after he first unveiled his plan, I questioned him on whether the banks could be trusted not to manipulate their rate submission to favor their market position—moving it by the tiniest fraction would affect borrowing costs on everything around the globe.

---

73   It was estimated that the Libor rate influenced $350trn of securities and loans around the world.
74   Reuters, Special Report by Marcy Engel, 'How gaming Libor became business as usual' 1996.

Arditti responded, "Not likely," making two points: first, that our clearing house managers were expert in determining what their bank counterparts and bank traders were doing and would be watchful for collusion; second, his plan was based on a random-order selection process. This was key, he said, "to preventing any serious gaming attempts." The explicit requirement was that the 12 reference banks were chosen at random from a list of 20 or more participating banks. It meant that it would be far too costly for any one bank to fiddle with the rate submitted and then not be chosen again. Even if chosen, he explained, no one bank or even several in cahoots could affect a meaningful rate change unless a majority of the banks, including all the biggest, joined in such a fraud. This was unthinkable.

In his opinion, as long as the CME clearing house was in charge, any fiddling by banks would have been detected. And it wasn't likely that such an attempt would be considered, since an outside third party (the CME clearing house) would be the recipient of the fiddled quotation. We never considered that the fox might be guarding the chicken coop.

IGNORED ADVICE

During the CFTC comment period for approval of the move, the agency did receive a letter from Marcy Engel, an attorney at Solomon Brothers, warning that a change in how and who priced the eurodollars "would put at risk the integrity of a key interest-rate in the global financial system." Specifically, the attorney said, tying the futures contract to Libor "might provide an opportunity for manipulation of the interest rate."[75]

Unfortunately, Ms Engel was very right. It is true that a single objection is usually not enough to prevent legislation, instigate an investigation or, as in this case, insert some safeguard procedure. However, this letter came from an officer of Solomon Brothers, a highly qualified expert, and should have carried weight. It is analogous to when the SEC ignored the lone warning from the accountant, Harry Markopolos, about the Bernard Madoff Ponzi scheme. The CFTC approved the transfer. On January 13, 1997, the CME officially turned over to Libor the pricing of eurodollar interest rates.

Libor followed Arditti's formula. It was published daily to the financial world announcing the average interbank interest rate at which a selection of banks on the London money market lend to one another. The average rate was compiled

---

75   Letter to CFTC by Marcy Engel, a lawyer at Solomon Brothers in 1996.

by submissions to Libor by the selected banks of their own average rate. On the basis of the published Libor rate, the rest of the world established its own rate upon which it did its business. Libor included a self-policing committee composed of the world's largest and most respected banks to make certain its published rate was on the up and up. It failed miserably. The Libor rate-fixing scam remained undetected for nearly a decade.

MARKET MANIPULATION

It could not, however, remain under wraps during the financial crisis of 2008. Frauds of many sorts lose their covers during times of crisis. On April 16, 2008, the headline on the front page of *The Wall Street Journal* read: 'Bankers Cast Doubt on Key Rate Amid Crisis.' The story written at the *WSJ*'s office in London began, as follows: "One of the most important barometers of the world's financial health could be sending false signals. In a development that has implications for borrowers everywhere, from Russian oil producers to homeowners in Detroit, bankers and traders are expressing concerns that the London interbank offered rate, known as Libor, is becoming unreliable."

It was the first of several *WSJ* articles that questioned whether banks were submitting honest borrowing costs to calculate Libor. Suddenly, allegations of price fixing and manipulation were everywhere. Among the financial institutions that became caught up in the scandal were Deutsche Bank, Barclays, UBS, Rabobank, HSBC, Bank of America, Citigroup, JPMorgan Chase, the Bank of Tokyo Mitsubishi, Credit Suisse, Lloyds, WestLB, and the Royal Bank of Scotland.

If banks were lying about Libor, it wouldn't just affect interest rates and derivatives payments—it would skew reality. The scope of this Libor rigging scandal was far larger than any previous financial scandal in history, even larger than the old Ponzi scheme and the most recent Madoff fraud. Essentially, any person or company lending or borrowing money was affected. Like the prime rate in the United States, it is also often used to help determine how much interest banks and other financial institutions should charge consumers.

It was comical that the bank manipulation scam began to unravel with an offhand email in 2006 that went viral. A swaps trader sent a jubilant message to a counterpart at Barclays Bank who had rescued his interest-rate trading position by helping *fix* the daily Libor rate. "Dude. I owe you big time! Come over one day after work and I'm opening a bottle of Bollinger." Here is another example, Barclays Bank trader in New York to submitter on September 13, 2006: "Hi

Guys, we got a big position in three-month Libor for the next three days. Can we please keep the Libor fixing at 5.39 for the next few days? It would really help. We do not want it to fix any higher than that. Thanks a lot."

Talk about deadly incriminating evidence. It turned out that there were mountainous stacks of emails such as these from traders at nearly all the banks, all of whom were in cahoots. It was like the saying goes, 'if you ain't cheating, you ain't trying enough.' Traders begged, pleaded, offered champagne and who knows what else to their counterparts at other banks and to employees at their own banks who were in charge of submitting daily estimates of interbank borrowing rates to the official Libor calculation process.

Investigators collected the following sampling of email gems, from Deutsche Bank, just before the bank agreed to a record fine of $2.5bn for rigging Libor settlement price:

February 2005: from one trader to another, "Can we have a high 6mth libor today pls gezzer?"

March 2005: "Could we please have a low 6mth fix today old bean?"

February 2005: "Can we have a high 6mth libor today pls?"

November 2006: A manager replies when a submission is lowered, "I love you."

September 2007: A Deutsche trader asks one at Barclays, "I'm begging u, don't forget me... pleasssssssssssssssseeeeeeeeeee ... I'm on my knees."

January 2008: a Tokyo manager says after a rate is left high, "You owe me a drink!"

August 2008: A trader on learning the rate is unchanged: "Oh bullshit ... strap on a pair and jack up the 3M [month]. Hahahahaha."

May 2009: An external trader asked a Deutsche Bank trader: "cld you do me a favor would you mind moving you 6m libor up a bit today, I have a gigantic fix." The next day, the Deutsche Bank trader confirmed the yen Libor submission had been raised: "u happy with me yesterday?" The trader replied "thx."

FAR-REACHING REPERCUSSIONS

It was the worst, most disgusting scandal in banking history, demonstrating an immeasurable arrogance and total disregard for the truth and law. For years, traders colluded to rig Libor, potentially affecting the price of some $350trn financial products, from mortgages and corporate loans to derivatives.[76] Some traders were seeking to adjust the benchmark to complement their open positions; others to enhance or advance the value of a bank deal, or a prospective arrangement; while some sought to make themselves look stronger during the financial crisis when low borrowing rates were viewed as a sign of strength.

In June of 2012, Barclays became the first bank to reach a settlement with government cops by admitting to rigging the rate and agreeing to pay a then-record £290m in fines. Once Barclays settled, it created a political storm. London's Serious Fraud Office, which had previously resisted such a probe, reversed its position to issue a statement saying that it would be undertaking a criminal investigation.

Marcus Agius, chairman of Barclays, resigned from his position. One day later, Bob Diamond, Barclays chief executive officer, also resigned. On December 19, 2012, UBS agreed to pay regulators $1.5bn ($1.2bn to the US Department of Justice and the CFTC, £160m to the UK Financial Services Authority and 59 million CHF to the Swiss Financial Market Supervisory Authority) for its role in the scandal. It was just the beginning.

Among the financial institutions that became caught up in the scandal were some of the world's premier banks: Deutsche Bank, Barclays, UBS, Rabobank, HSBC, Bank of America, Citigroup, JPMorgan Chase, the Bank of Tokyo Mitsubishi, Credit Suisse, Lloyds, West LB and the Royal Bank of Scotland. The total fines levied were over $10bn, a number of people served time in jail and many others lost their careers. By everyone's assessment, it was the worst banking manipulation in human history and the ramifications will continue well into the future.

As one would expect, this horrific tale meant the demise of Libor as the benchmark of short-term interest rates. In 2017, the UK's Financial Conduct Authority officially closed Libor down. Since then regulators and banks have been wrestling with the difficult challenge of finding a replacement. The US Federal Reserve assembled the Alternative Secured Refence Rate Committee,

---

76   Today that amount is in the neighborhood of $240trn.

consisting of several large banks, to find and agree on an alternative reference rate benchmark.

Easier said than done. The committee chose SOFR, a rate based on transactions in the Treasury repurchase market, which represented a broad measure of the cost of borrowing cash overnight collateralized by Treasury securities. In 2019, the Federal Reserve Bank of New York began publishing the rate as part of its effort to replace Libor. So, for now, Libor and SOFR exist side by side. By 2021, it is expected that SOFR will become the benchmark for dollar-denominated derivatives and credit products. Let's hope so.

Fortunately, the CME eurodollars, the futures contract designed by Fred Arditti, continues unabated to serve the best interests of the marketplace as the benchmark for the world's short-term interest rates.

CHAPTER 28

Academics, Academics

U PON Fred Arditti's passing from pancreatic cancer in 2005 at the age of 66, the CME board created the Melamed–Arditti Innovation award, with chairman Terry Duffy making the motion on its behalf. It has become one of the most coveted awards in the US financial sector.

Choosing the annual Melamed–Arditti Innovation award winner became one of the responsibilities of the Competitive Market Advisory Council (CMAC), a CME Group think-tank, founded by Nobel laureate Myron Scholes and myself. From its inception in 2005, CMAC included four Nobel prize winners, Gary Becker, Myron Scholes, Robert Merton, and Bob Shiller; later, Lars Peter Hansen replaced Gary Becker upon his passing.

CMAC also includes some highly regarded financial luminaries such as Andrew Lo, professor of finance at MIT, Michael H. Moskow, former president of the Chicago Federal Reserve, Randall S. Kroszner, former Governor of the US Federal Reserve, and my personal friend of many years, Jacob Frenkel. Not only was Frenkel the former Central Banker of Israel, and currently the chairman of the Group of Thirty, he and I could converse in *mame-loshn*. I have the distinct honor of continuing to co-chair this elite group together with Jack Gould, former Business School Dean at the University of Chicago. The idea served to bring together some of the most regarded financial thought-leaders in the US to provide the CME with advice, opinions, and ideas that are on the cutting edge of finance.

SUPPLEMENTARY ACTIVITIES

I was privileged to befriend Myron Scholes when he served as a professor of finance at the University of Chicago in the early 1970s. It was the natural thing to do given that he was a co-originator of the Black Scholes model upon which the CBOE was founded in 1973. My launch of financial futures a year earlier gave us immediate common ground, although he hung around with academic untouchables like Fischer Black, Gene Fama, Robert Merton, Merton Miller and the like—all eventual Nobel prize winners. However, our common embrace of Milton Friedman's free-market ideal brought us intellectually together as well as the fact that I brought Merton Miller onto the CME board.

In 1997, Myron Scholes and Robert C. Merton, in collaboration with Fischer Black (who passed away two years prior to the award), developed the formula for the valuation of stock options—later known as the Black-Scholes model. The pricing model is used to determine the fair price or theoretical value for a call or a put option based on six variables such as volatility, type of option, underlying stock price, time, strike price and risk-free rate. It was a watershed moment in finance. Their methodology has paved the way for economic valuations in many areas and generated a host of new types of financial instruments facilitating efficient risk management tools.

When Merton Miller passed away, it was obvious to me that Myron Scholes was the natural candidate for that board seat. He agreed. Few American corporate institutions had the honor of including his name on its board of directors. Scholes served until 2008, when the nominating committee opted not to re-nominate him. This was a disgrace. There was no reason given, perhaps simple jealousy. Unfortunately, I could not change the result. During the merger re-write of bylaws, the nominating committee was given finality in the nomination process without review by the board. I vented my displeasure with the full force of my feelings, but ultimately it represented my first major loss on the board. The rule has since been changed.

The CMAC think-tank, however, continues unabated. It is important to record the winners of the CME Melamed-Arditti Innovation award from its inception to present day:

2005: William Sharpe, STANCO 25 professor of finance emeritus, Stanford University, Nobel laureate in economic sciences (1990)

2006: Leo Melamed, founder of financial futures and initiator of Globex; chairman emeritus, CME Group

2007: Eugene Fama, Robert R. McCormick Distinguished Service Professor of Finance at the University of Chicago Graduate School of Business, Nobel laureate in economic sciences (2013)

2008: Michael R. Bloomberg, founder of Bloomberg LP and mayor, city of New York

2009: Harry Markowitz, Nobel laureate in economic sciences (1990)

2010: David A. Ferrucci, leader of IBM's semantic analysis and integration department at T.J. Watson Research Center

2011: Robert C. Merton, School of Management Distinguished Professor of Finance, MIT Sloan School of Management, Nobel laureate in economic sciences (1997), and Myron S. Scholes, Frank E. Buck Professor of Finance Emeritus, Stanford Graduate School of Business, Nobel laureate in economic sciences (1997)

2012: Jimmy Wales, founder, Wikipedia

2013: Sal Khan, founder, Khan Academy

2014: Ben Bernanke, chairman, board of governors of the Federal Reserve System (2006–2014)

2015: Elizabeth Holmes, founder and CEO, Theranos[77]

2016: Tim Berners-Lee, inventor of the World Wide Web

2017: John C. Bogle, founder & former chairman, Vanguard Group, and John A. 'Mac' McQuown, entrepreneur

2018: Steve Wozniak, co-founder, Apple

2019: Kenneth C. Griffin, founder of Citadel

In addition, Myron Scholes and I continued our quest to support education in Math and Science by establishing the Mathematical Sciences Research Institute prize in 2006. The prize is awarded to an individual to recognize originality and innovation in the use of mathematical, statistical or computational methods for

---

77   Ms Holmes was chosen for the 2015 award before the facts relating to the fraudulent actions and testing results became public. Her award has been officially withdrawn by the CMAC council.

the study of the behaviour of markets, and more broadly of economics. This coveted annual MSRI award has often become the precursor to winning the Nobel prize.[78]

EDUCATIONAL OUTREACH

Both the advisory council and Innovation Award were an extension of my recognition that education must play an unequalled role if I was to achieve a transformation of futures from a tertiary role in national economics to one of the primary tools in the development of capital markets.

Aside from setting the tradition for a constant flow of the Merc's written educational material for both the members and potential participants (materials I either wrote, directed or edited), I began a continuous program of convincing colleges and universities to initiate courses in futures markets.[79] This included sums of money for the introduction of futures classes as well offering myself as a visiting lecturer—to this day, I annually accept four or five such engagements. Much of my career had a direct connection to the two major universities in the Chicago area. For starters, without denigrating any of the other outstanding US schools of higher learning, from my earliest days in the USA, I was partial to the U/C, one of the great universities in the USA on the South Side of Chicago, as well as Northwestern University (in Evanston) on the North Side

As their websites proclaim, both are private, non denominational, culturally rich and ethnically diverse co-educational research universities, proudly situated in Chicago. The U/C was founded in 1890 by the American Baptist Education Society and John D. Rockefeller, while Northwestern University was founded in 1851 and named for John Evans, after whom the city of Evanston is named. Both universities hold top positions in various national and international rankings. Had I had the financial wherewithal, I surely would have chosen to become a student at one of them. It was an honor to bring Donald P. Jacobs, Dean

---

78   2018: Albert Kyle, University of Maryland. 2017: Paul Milgrom, Stanford University. 2016: Robert Wilson, Stanford University. 2015: Douglas Diamond, University of Chicago. 2014: Jose A. Scheinkman, Princeton University. 2013: Bengt Holmstrom, MIT. 2012: Robert J. Shiller, Yale University. 2011: Thomas J. Sargent, New York University. 2010: Jean Tirole, University of Toulouse. 2009: Sanford J. Grossman, Stanford University. 2008: Lars Peter Hansen, University of Chicago. 2007: David M. Kraps, Stanford University. 2006: Stephen A. Ross, MIT.

79   At the time, the principle reference on futures came from the material written by University of Illinois, Professor Hollbrook Working, such as 'Price Effects of Futures Trading', *Food Research Institute Studies* 1(1960), 3–31.

Emeritus of Kellogg School of Management at Northwestern University, onto the CME board of directors.

However, without question, my strongest connection to the U/C was Professor Milton Friedman, whose views on free markets changed the world's direction and whose embrace of currency futures gave the idea credibility, leading to a friendship that had no equal. As a very close second was U/C Nobel Professor Merton Miller whose recognition of my achievements led to a lifetime bond of mutual respect, as well as his service on the CME board of directors.

Of special significance was my embrace of Friedman's tenets on free markets. Those same principles were included in the U/C monetarist beliefs about the economy, contending that free markets best allocate resources in an economy and that minimal government intervention is best. The foregoing led to the establishment in 1975 of the Leo Melamed prize for outstanding research in finance, and eventually for the CME to honor me by establishing the U/C Leo Melamed chair. The above were reason enough to establish a futures course, Financial Instruments, under my name, which was brilliantly conducted by Professor George Constantinides. It is reason also for my personal involvement with the establishment of the Becker-Friedman Institute.

It should be clear by now, that Milton Friedman and I became close personal friends. Betty and I were honored to frequently visit with Rose and Milton at their home in San Francisco, as well as to receive them as house guests at our home in Arizona. Rose Friedman was an economist in her own right—it is said that she was the only one in the world to ever win an economic argument with Milton.

Being friends with the Friedmans exposed us to many of their friends, often the who's who of academic circles, and meant that we were invited to scores of events in which Milton was the guest of honor. I fondly recall being invited to Milton's 90th birthday, where former secretary of state George P. Schultz sang a ditty about him which was often repeated in his classrooms at the U/C. It underscored Milton's demand of his students that they not theorize without proof based on facts:

> A fact without a theory, is like a ship without a sail.
> Is like a boat without a rudder.
> Is like a kite without a tail.
> A fact without a theory is as sad as sad can be.

But if there's one thing worse in this universe, it's a theory... without a fact.
It was my great honor to be a part of Milton Friedman's commemoration after

his passing. Held at the University of Chicago's Rockefeller Chapel on December 7, 2006, I appeared as a presenter alongside Nobel laureate Gary Becker, Nobel laureate James Heckman and US Federal Reserve chairman, Ben Bernanke. It served as an opportunity for me to explain to the attending dignitaries from around the world how Milton's feasibility study on currency futures became my holy grail, and that "I personally have lost my mentor and closest ally in our common cause on behalf of the principles of free markets."

I similarly want to mention my strong connection to three other Chicago-based universities. First, the University of Illinois, Chicago Branch, where my higher education began; DePaul University, which I hold in very high regard and where I have often lectured; and, of course, the John Marshall Law School, which provided me with the legal education I so often use. Thus, while I am well regarded and lecture at many American universities, no other schools have the history nor level of connection to me personally than the ones I have called out.

CHAPTER 29

1982: The Mayflower

ONE hundred and twenty years earlier, in 1860, Henry Varnum Poor published a historical guide book, *The History of Railroads and Canals in the United States*. A competitor, Luther Lee Blake, then showed up in 1906 publishing *Standard Statistics Bureau*, a financial information publication on non-railroad companies. The two companies merged in 1941, becoming Standard & Poor's Corp, and in 1966, the company was acquired by the McGraw-Hill Companies.

The Dow Company, founded by Charles Dow, Edward Jones and their silent partner, Charles Bergstresser, began its publication in 1885, becoming the second-oldest US market index after the Dow Jones Transportation Average also created by Dow. Acquired in 1902 by Clarence Barron, the leading financial journalist of the day, the Dow company was passed on upon his death in 1928 to his step-daughters, Jane and Martha, children of his first wife, Jessie Waldron, and was run by Jane's husband Hugh Bancroft. When he committed suicide in 1933, the remaining family members maintained ownership through ensuing generations.

The above history meant little to me until 1980, when I became passionately focused on launching the S&P index as an instrument for futures trade. That product ultimately became the zeitgeist of the CME, making equity futures a permanent fixture of the global equities market and financial establishment. As I have explained, I began internally thinking and preparing for Elmer Falker's stock-index futures long before cash settlement was officially approved by the CFTC. But, being an incurable optimist—you cannot have big ideas or dreams by being anything else—I was certain it would happen and that the competition in futures for this asset class would be fierce. It could only turn into a battle royal.

I was quite certain four American futures markets would plan for an all-out effort to win this derby: the CBOT, the oldest and largest futures exchange; the NYSE, the big kahuna in New York that had taken a page out the IMM playbook to create the NYFE, a special financial-futures division; the KCBOT, the Kansas City Board of Trade, the smallest of the futures markets; and, of course, the CME/IMM, the youngest member of the futures-market industry.

There were five well-known indices to choose from: the Dow Jones index (DJI), the most known and popular index; the NYSE composite index, by far the broadest index containing at the time some 1500 listed companies; Standard & Poor's 500 index; the NASDAQ index; and the Value Line index. Point in fact, for a short time, all of these indices had their 15 minutes of fame in the mad race that followed.

FORMING AN ORDERLY QUEUE

As the rules required, the CFTC would consider applications for a new product on the basis of first in line. The KCBT, being the underdog, hurried to be first even before cash settlement was approved. Their application included a physical delivery component (a wild idea) for stocks in the Value Line index. Before they got approval, cash settlement was passed and the Merc became first in line.

I was called by CFTC Commissioner Susan Phillips, soon to be appointed the next chair of the agency, with a very odd request. She explained that the KCBOT had withdrawn its original Value Line index application and re-submitted a cash-settled version. But now it finds itself third in line for approval, behind the CME and the newly created NYFE. "Leo, these are very small exchanges with hardly a chance to be victorious. Would you agree to let the CFTC approve them before the Merc's application? It's only a difference in a couple of days." I granted the CFTC's request.

Ms Phillips was correct that several days would not make a big difference. However, as it turned out the NYSE creation of a financial division turned out to be a big deal. The NYSE was still the biggest name on the block and their index a serious contender. Although they were a late-comer to futures, and had already failed in their aborted attempt to compete with the IMM's currency and T-bill contracts, they became a most serious competitor in stock indexes. They had a well-known benchmark index, they had the backing of their traders and specialists, they placed their futures' stock index pit right next to where the actual securities were being traded and, most important, when it came to securities, none of the Chicago exchanges had anywhere near the credibility of the NYSE.

Nevertheless, I was an optimist. The success of the IMM was in no small way based on the fact that it was born as a separate exchange for the exclusive trade of financial products and whose members were exclusively qualified to trade those products. They represented an army of traders with a limited menu. No other exchange could make that claim. And, with all humility, because I gave birth to their existence as traders, most would follow me wherever I led them. That army represented liquidity with no equal—and as I have often stated, liquidity is the holy grail of markets.

IN THE PUBLIC DOMAIN

Meanwhile, the CBOT made it clear that they had chosen the Dow Jones index to be their futures product. I was not surprised and even pleased with their decision. First, I reasoned, if our two exchanges went head-to-head for the DJI, it would surely be a humongous battle, but one we would win. Second, I had serious reservations about choosing the Dow as the index for futures. In retrospect, this decision was a critical factor in the eventual growth and success of the CME. Of course, I understood the Dow was the most known gauge of the equity marketplace. I understood it to be the 'popular index' based on the movement of the most important 30 industrial stocks. But I was far from convinced that it was the best index for attracting commercial participants, ones who could use this new tool in executing hedging strategies. That was the critical question.

I spent considerable time debating this question both internally and externally. Internally, my committee members held mixed views. My most trusted advisor, Barry Lind, whose company Lind-Waldock could be an important element as a liquidity provider, favored the Dow. It would best fit his retail business. But that was far from the view held by fund managers. They were quite unanimous in choosing the S&P as the measuring stick for their portfolios. They won me over. I held fast, until I convinced Barry Lind. Soon the committee became unanimous—which is what I needed. I would rate this decision among the most critical of my career.

Across the street a colossal blunder was brewing. Based on their attorneys' opinion, the CBOT concluded that the Dow Jones index was an instrument in the public domain. In other words, a public utility—it was like predicting the weather, you needed no license to do so. This wasn't an illogical conclusion. After all, the Dow gave their index to the world free of charge. Everyone could print or quote the price of the Dow index with impunity. It was a public daily barometer for what the American equity market did each day. That's the case to this day. And the Dow organization seemed to approve and encourage this free notoriety and use of its product. Thus, the CBOT attorney's opinion seemed logical and the CBOT board relied on it.

That reasoning was equally the case with respect to the S&P index. The S&P organization, no differently than the Dow, were happy with the extensive free use of their index by the media and public. It should therefore be no surprise that the CME's general counsel, Jerrold Salzman, believed no differently. He too counselled me that the S&P 500 index was a public utility, and that the CME could list this index for trade without permission or license from the S&P owners or anyone.

A MATTER OF PRINCIPLE

I strongly disagreed. It felt wrong. I learned something about intellectual property both in law school and from Milton Friedman—it was holy.[80] For me, the S&P 500 index was the private property of the Standard and Poor's company and we would need their consent to use their product as a futures instrument. I was in good company. As P. J. O'Rourke, the humorist and political commentator once said, "If we want something, we should pay for it, with our labor or our cash. We shouldn't beg for it, steal it, sit around wishing for it, or euchre the government into taking it for us by force."

Salzman and I argued the issue at length, but I refused to budge. "Okay, Leo, if you want to throw away money," he said with finality. As I have noted earlier, lawyers sometimes miss the forest for the trees. I contended that even if there was the slightest chance that the lawyers were wrong, this asset class was of such critical value for the future of the CME that I did not want to take any chances.

As it turned out, it became one of the most significant decisions I ever made. On February 18, 1980, two years before they were launched, I had arranged for a meeting with Brent Harries, chairman of the S&P company. I came with Jerry Salzman and Jack Sandner, who was the CME chairman at the time and fully supported my rationale. From the S&P side were Brent Harries and his general counsel, George Baron. They had invited us to dinner at Mr Harries' penthouse. It started out as a weird conversation. I recognized that it was a historic moment: Harries US ancestry I presumed started with the Mayflower, mine started in Bialystok.

---

80   As an aside, the issues pertaining to intellectual property are front and center in the current trade war with China.

"You mean you want to pay me for something I give away for free?" Mr Harries whimsically asked, stifling what I thought might be a giggle. What wasn't lost on me was the fact that here I was, a Jewish immigrant kid from Bialystok, negotiating a revolutionary idea in a luxurious penthouse on New York's Fifth Avenue, with someone who probably can trace his lineage back to the Mayflower. It was a scary but delightful reality.

"Well, yes," I replied, "because I believe it is your intellectual property and I am looking for an exclusive license." George Baron, S&P's lawyer, kind of gestured to his client to keep quiet. ("Let's humor this guy to see where it goes.") It came down to how much we were willing to pay—a difficult question. To my knowledge, no one had ever wanted or needed a license for a futures product, say, for corn, or cattle, or Swiss francs. Salzman and I came prepared. We offered a novel approach. We suggested a long-range exclusive contract at ten cents per trade up to an annual cap set at the highest level of daily volume ever attained in any futures instrument, say, 10,000 per day.

The S&P trusted our opinion. An agreement was inked on February 28, 1980. Imagine that? Before cash settlement was allowed and two years before the S&P futures were actually launched, I held in my hand an exclusive contract for the rights to trade the S&P as a futures instrument. As it turned out, the S&P futures contract was of such exceptional attraction and value that it wasn't too long before the S&P futures daily transaction volume set records over all existing futures markets and of course also exceeded the limits of payment in our contract with S&P.

We were also given the right to license the index. Our first such license was to the CBOE. They were on the securities side of the market and therefore no threat to us. In fact, by virtue of arbitrage, it made our S&P futures contract much stronger—our success made the S&P name as big as it is today.

Two years later, in 1984, I was contacted by Ira Herenstein and Bob Andrialis, two senior officials of McGraw-Hill, the new owners of the S&P. They called to say that the S&P company made a bad bargain in what was an unknown concept. To some, they suggested, it might look like that a couple of Chicago sharpies in futures markets took advantage of a couple of neophytes. Would I consider renegotiating the deal?

I quickly convinced them that it was nothing of the kind. It was simply unchartered territory and the S&P executives were hardly neophytes. However, I told them, probably to their utter surprise, that I would have our board tear up the original, renegotiate a new contract, and make it into a long-term deal. I was Ecclesiastes casting bread on the water. I then authorized Salzman and Rick Kilcollin, our executive VP, to renegotiate a long term but fair agreement based on what we had learned. This unusual action in annals of corporate history was not forgotten. The CME continues to partner with McGraw-Hill to this day.

THE ALTERNATIVE PATH

Across the street at the CBOT things did not go well. Just before the CBOT's Dow Jones futures was to be launched, the Dow Jones company filed for an injunction. They contended, just as I believed, that the instrument in question, the Dow Jones Industrial Average (DJIA), was the intellectual property of the Dow Jones Company.

Although the CBOT won in Chicago's Circuit Court, on appeal to the Illinois Appellate Court the lower court's ruling was overturned and the injunction was granted. On appeal to the Illinois Supreme Court, the Appellate Court's ruling was affirmed.[81] In other words, without an express license by the Dow Company, the CBOT could not launch their equity index for futures trade. It was impossible for the CBOT to get the necessary license from the members of the Bancroft family. For the next 15 years, the CBOT was excluded from a major equity futures index. I guess my commitment to the sanctity of intellectual property won the day.

The battle royal now ensued between the CME-IMM and the NYSE-NYFE. The first thing I did was to take a page out of our own book to propose to the board that we create yet another Merc division, the Index and Option Division (IOM), which would be limited to index and option products. CME and IMM members would automatically have full rights in the IOM and could purchase additional IOM seats at the price of $30,000. The price of IOM seats for non-members would be $60,000.

Again, the idea worked extremely well—1,039 existing members bought an IOM seat as did 125 new members. An additional 123 were converted by the members of the AMM (a division created during the Merc and IMM merger). We raised a ton of money for the exchange and our membership rolls expanded to a total of 2,724. In my opinion, it created a nearly invincible liquidity force.

Our S&P futures contract was launched on April 21, 1982. It is important to record that three months after our opening, on August 12, 1982, the DJI closed at 776.92—the lowest recorded price since the 1930s. From there, a major secular

---

81   98 Ill 2nd 109; 456N.E. 2d 84, October 21, 1983; Justice Philip P. Simon, wrote a dissenting opinion.

bull market ensued. There are some analysts who correlate the US equities bull market, at least partially, to the fact that our futures contract provided an efficient safety net—allowing investors to take larger long positions in US equities.

BEHIND THE SCENES

Creation of the IOM division had a side story. Jack Sandner and I had been in pursuit of William Brodsky for the position of CME executive VP. I felt we needed someone with stock market expertise to help us in the equity asset class we were entering. It was a difficult decision for Brodsky, since he knew little about futures and even less about us. Besides, we were the second city and New York, well, you know the answer. He was well regarded there as an executive of the American Stock Exchange and clearly would have had a very successful reign there. But as Brodsky later told me, "The fact that you could raise several million dollars over a weekend by creating a new division convinced me to take your offer and come to Chicago."

Brodsky was the perfect choice for us. He was instrumental in solving some of the intricate issues which arose from trying to coordinate our futures instrument with the securities traded in New York. He negotiated and instituted the settlement procedure for the so-called 'triple witching day' (the convergence of cash, futures and option prices). This linkage feature removed the risk of ending the coupled transactions at different values at the close of the contract. Linkage also created index arbitrage, a market procedure that kept futures prices more or less in line with the underlying cash-index price. It was key in the success of the S&P contract.

It was an easy choice to promote Bill Brodsky to take Clayton Yeutter's post as CME president. Indeed, Brodsky's move to Chicago turned out to be a blessing both for Chicago and his career. He parlayed his formidable talents to later become the outstanding chairman of the CBOE, the options exchange created by the CBOT, a post from which he recently retired.

A CALL TO ARMS

Thus, our S&P futures instrument began trading with only one competitor, the NYSE index. Having only one adversary is quite different than needing to fend off two or more. However, the remaining adversary would not be easy pickings. As I noted earlier, the NYSE-NYFE had a good product, a ton of experienced traders right on their floor where the major components of the NYSE index were traded, and had the NY financial community in their corner. On top of all that, we were in Chicago, not exactly the capital of US finance.

Still, as always, liquidity would be the final determinant. I went into overdrive, pulling out all the stops. It was a herculean effort which included workshops, seminars and a continuous flow of reading material to the members. I held meetings with small and large groups reminding them who our opponents were and that this liquidity battle was for the life of the CME. I called on every major securities firm. For some of our most successful traders, I demanded do-or-die promises of support. I created a *WSJ* full-page ad showing a picture of something like 300 traders standing in their trading jackets, arms folded, ready to take on the battle royal.

I called everyone in the world I could think of, saying "Give us your business!" I usually got a positive response. In one instance, I called on my bridge playing buddy, Jimmy Cayne, who had become the CEO of Bear Sterns. He responded by taking out a further full-page *WSJ* ad stating that Bear Sterns supports the S&P contract at the Merc in Chicago. He also gave me an opening day order of 50 lots, not caring whether I buy or sell.

In another heroic instance, I called on my friend Ralph Peters. Ralph was without a doubt the most successful trader at the CBOT. I told him that, since he cannot support the CBOT effort in this matter, would he give the Merc all he can? He responded: "What do you want?" I told him that we needed to show open interest to prove that our equity product was being embraced by the investment community. Ralph nodded and agreed to help. In those days in order to be listed on the financial page of the *WSJ*, your open interest in a new product had to reach 5,000—no easy matter. About three weeks after the opening of trade, Ralph Peters came to my office to show me his profit and loss records. It showed that Ralph was long 1,000 S&P contracts. It was an unbelievably huge number—far, far more than I anticipated.

Each contract represented a value of $500,000. "Where is the other side?" I innocently asked, expecting that he had put on a spread. Putting on a spread, say, with one side long in a contract month and the other side short (in the same amount) in a different contract month was the safest way to create the impression of open interest without taking on the risk of an open position. "I have no other side, Lee." Ralph responded, "You see, I am bullish." It gave me pause. Remember, this was 1982, when the US equity market was at the bottom of what was to be a 15-year bull market. When I checked months later, I learned that Ralph was still long, having made an incredible killing on the trade.

These efforts worked. We came out of the gate swinging, getting an easy early lead. Our IMM army responded to our call. After a couple of weeks, it seemed like we were on the road to victory. I thought I could relax and accepted an invitation to speak at a London conference.

FIFTEEN MINUTES PLEASE

A couple of days after Jack Sandner and I arrived in London, I received some calls from people on the floor in Chicago that the NYSE had turned up the heat. The key indicator of open interest was starting to go their way. It was turning into a touch-and-go battle. Jack and I immediately decided to leave for Chicago directly after my remarks. On the flight home, I reasoned that the tide had turned because of overconfidence on my part. Our traders were returning to their own habitats, believing the battle was over. They probably felt that they had done enough. In addition, my personal presence on the floor was missing.

I realized that was to be a much longer confrontation than I thought. My IMM army would have to support an extended liquidity effort. But I knew that the traders eventually had to go back to their own market domain. How can we make them do battle perhaps over many months? Suddenly, I had a thought. We don't need the traders to abandon their business for a long period of time. If we could get them for some little time period each day, it would do. The idea gave birth to the 'fifteen minutes please' appeal. In other words, instead of asking traders to leave their own pits for days on end, we would ask every trader to spend no more than 15 minutes every day in the S&P pit. I knew that, being traders, during the 15 minutes they would do some trading. Many of them would remain longer. If enough of them responded, it could do the trick.

Upon arrival, we had 'fifteen minutes please' buttons created. Jack Sandner and I stood at the door to the floor and handed a button to every trader upon their entry. Our limited-time appeal was understood and made sense to the trader community; it was not too much to ask. They responded with gusto. Many traders even came over to me to show me their trading cards at the end of the day to prove that they were with the program.

As I expected, while they were in the pit they made some trades. It is difficult for traders to stand around and not trade. The market is enticing. Some of them never left the S&P pit. Within several weeks the S&P contract showed results. Our S&P open interest was rising again. We were on the way to an astounding victory. Of course, I spent most of my trading day in the pit with the other traders. My personal commitment defined the spirit of the time. It became my

MO for the opening of every new product on the floor. It cost me a bundle though, since trading illiquid products is not a profitable operation.

The S&P equity futures instrument put the CME on the financial map in a big way. A host of banks and financial entities that had ignored Chicago's brazen entry into their turf finally gave us a serious look. I rate this victory as one of the primary reasons the CME is the success it is today.

Our success was the consequence of three critical decisions: first, the choice of which index to use; second, the legal right to do so; and third, the marketing strategy to beat the competitors—primarily the NYSE. The first two decisions were mine to make after a good deal of internal machinations. The third depended heavily on a positive response by our floor community. With strong assistance from Jack Sandner and the floor at large, we achieved a triumphant victory over the NYSE. It took more than a year, but its conquest provided business flows from a brand-new major asset class and, like nothing else, gained the Merc tremendous credibility and notoriety in the financial world.

CHAPTER 30

1982: The last piece of the puzzle

DURING the same year came the resolve to proceed with construction of the CME's new premises; the twin towers on Wacker Drive where our two trading floors existed and where our permanent headquarters remains. I labelled this undertaking as the last piece in the puzzle—meaning, to finally achieve equal world-class status with the CBOT, whose premises at the head of LaSalle Street defined Chicago's business sector.[82] The complexities of moving an exchange—a trading floor with 2,000 traders and brokers, and an almost equal number of employees—without interruption to the market is, to say the least, most challenging. I must give due credit to John Geldermann, the board director I appointed to head up the real-estate project.

At the very outset, we had to resolve one of the most contentious issues: whether to build a second (spare) trading floor in the event we continue to grow at the present pace. "We can't keep building new buildings," said Bill Muno, an influential board member. But many were opposed. The cost of an additional $15m "for something we will never use" was a strong argument. At the end of the day, the Muno contingent won, making me a happy man. In time, nearly the entire second trading floor became a giant pit (historically, the biggest pit ever built during the open outcry trading) for the eurodollar contract, which provided 90-day interest-rate coverage extending out as far as ten years. It housed a thousand traders and a substantial number of support personnel.

---

82   Mayor Richard J. Daley once told me that our decision to build the CME Center on Wacker Drive was instrumental in the financial growth of downtown Chicago.

A bit of building history is in order: the Merc started its modern life in its 1927 location at 110 North Franklin and Washington Street. During the 1929 crash, CME governors panicked and sold the building to the legendary tycoon, Colonel Henry Crown. The plan was to rent back the trading floor. By 1970, as tenants, the Merc was paying Crown an annual rental fee equal to the price he had bought the premises from them.

From the time of my election to the board in 1967 and then as chairman in 1969, things had begun to boom. My first year in office witnessed our income grow by an astounding 100% and the idea of financial contracts was but an idea in my head. Along with others, I decided the old CME floor would be too small for the plans I had in mind.

This was not a new idea, just one never instituted. It was always a very controversial subject. The old guard lined up against it. "When you have a successful restaurant and you make it bigger, it becomes an unsuccessful restaurant," I was warned over and over again. The opposition became so intense that they called on the owner of the building, Colonel Crown, at the time one of the richest men in the country (he owned the NY Empire State building), to talk me out of it.

It was an unnerving moment for this young new chairman, a classic case of one-upmanship. At his invitation, we met in his penthouse for lunch. He had a butler serving. He told me in no uncertain terms that I would be making a big mistake; the country, he confided, will soon be facing another depression and it was the wrong time to take the risk. "It will put the Merc in jeopardy," he warned.

It was a heavy load to carry. Here was a legendary tycoon, cautioning me, an immigrant from Bialystok, of a depression. How could I ignore his dire prediction? Still, I knew that the CME was his biggest tenant. To lose us would deal him a blow. I also knew what my instincts were telling me. I knew that in my first year as chairman of the Merc, our growth was exceptional. I knew that CME memberships were going for a record $100,000—up from about $30,000 when I first took over.

I knew I had big ideas and innovative plans, and I knew I needed space to implement those plans. It gave me one sleepless night, but I did not change my mind. I arranged for a referendum and promised the membership that I would not exceed the $6m we had in the kitty. I promised I would not go into debt to pacify some of the old guard. In other words, the building would not put us in hock. I thought that the rank and file membership would follow my lead. It did, I won the referendum easily.

A TAXING DEVELOPMENT

But out of the blue, just as I began talking to architects, I was confronted by the US Revenue Service. It was unreal. Because the CME was a not-for-profit entity who in the previous decade made little or no money, the exchange had failed to file any income tax returns.[83] For some unknown reason they got away with it for a couple of years. However, in 1970, the IRS woke up and sent a bill to the exchange for $6m covering back-taxes plus interest. There went my $6m!

I cursed my bad luck and went to a buddy of mine, Ira Marcus, for help. Ira Marcus was a fine tax attorney, having been an IRS examiner. I asked him to review the tax bill and for advice. The bad news was that the IRS was more or less correct. We owed about $6m, precisely the amount the referendum authorized for new premises. My choice was to go to a bank for a loan, exactly what the referendum promised not to do, get a new referendum, or scuttle the building plans.

I wrestled with the problem for a few days and suddenly had an idea. It was to create a public trust fund and deposit our $6m to shelter the money from taxation. The fund would be used to provide financial protection to customers in the event a CME clearing member firm became insolvent. I presented the idea to Marcus and explained that I had always believed that such a trust fund was necessary to strengthen the image and integrity of our futures exchange. In my opinion, such a fund would be applauded by the government and the IRS.

Marcus was amused. "Leo," he said, "Nice try, but the IRS will never allow it. You cannot avoid paying the back taxes." We discussed it for a long time, but I would not change my mind. I told Marcus that I had great faith in his expertise and that he should not underestimate his talent. I said that I didn't mind failing, but I refused to not give it a try. In the end, he agreed to give it his best shot. That is all I asked for.

As you may have guessed, it worked. My faith in Marcus was justified. The idea went all the way up to the Federal Appellate Court. A public trust fund was found to have sufficient merit for approval. Marcus saved the day and was clever enough to include the right of the trust to use its money for certain investment purposes— like building the Merc's second home with a mortgage back to the trust.

I met with Colonel Crown to pay my respects and thanked him for the many years of service to the Merc. To his credit, and that of the Crown family, they

---

83   In my investigation of how this came about, I was told that some of the directors were under the impression that being not-for-profit meant they did not need to file a tax return.

did not turn against the Merc. In fact, Lester Crown, the son of Colonel Crown, became a valuable supporter of the CME in Washington politics. Lester Crown is today one of the most influential and respected voices in Washington—and one of this country's leading philanthropists.

THE CME GROUP CHARITABLE FOUNDATION

But that was not the end of the story. Each year our accountants, under board direction, would contribute to the trust to shelter additional income. The trust continued to grow, but the exchange grew much faster. Decades went by and the underlying purpose of the trust fund became inadequate for guarantee purposes. In addition to the trust fund, the CME clearing house established a much bigger and stronger guarantee fund based on a complex formula for protecting customer money.

By 2005, we no longer needed the trust fund to shelter income. Our attorneys proposed that we petition the IRS to allow us to use the trust fund for charitable purposes. We were granted approval and created the CME Group Charitable Foundation, which would use its annual income to advance education and charitable purposes primarily in the Chicago region. I chaired the foundation's first year.

Today, the foundation partners with universities, school districts, and non-profit organizations to ensure at risk young children be prepared for kindergarten; provide effective K-12 education that prepares disadvantaged students for success in college and career; prepare university students for careers in financial services and risk management, and conduct academic research in areas that advance derivatives knowledge and best practices.

The foundation has grown to over $100m and has done an outstanding job in advancing education, especially for disadvantaged communities. Not too bad a result from an unpaid $6m IRS tax bill.

A PERMANENT SOLUTION

The new premises were built overlooking the Chicago River at Jackson and Canal Streets without exceeding the cost of $6m. The new premises were not an architectural marvel, but a boxlike protrusion at the edge of the Chicago River; they included modern facilities and greatly advanced member morale. Lenny Feldman, a captain in the IMM army, famously said "It felt like we just took a great shower." However, the IMM growth rate continued to be on fire. It was an unwelcome problem in a hugely successful story—the new premises into which we moved just two years earlier were again inadequate.

Our architect, Skidmore, Owings and Merrill (SOM), had a plan to gain an additional 50% of space by cantilevering the building over the Canal Street sidewalk. It was the only plan possible without disrupting the current markets. However, it required mayoral approval, which was miraculously achieved. The expanded space sufficed for the next seven years. However, the space problem followed us like a trained animal. In 1981, as I prepared for the stock-index battle, I was aware that a successful victory would be limited by virtue of lack of space to expand the pit and support facilities. We needed a permanent solution.

I began examining space availability around the city for the construction of a new CME building. The cost was no longer an issue. The search led to an accidental conversation between real-estate developer Larry Levy and myself, which not only led to the Merc structure, but for Levy, a host of real estate developments and the creation of an international food service company. Of equal importance was my meeting Holly Duran, Levy's executive assistant, who became the Merc's and my personal real estate maven in the many subsequent moves we encountered during the decades ahead. Of equal note, our conversation carried me to funding discussions with Judd Mulkin, Neil Bluhm and Robert Judelson of the JMB Realty Group, whose history is like a fairy tale of young entrepreneurs on their way to becoming the largest and most respected managers of real estate in the US. I have to believe that the twin-towers building of the CME premises, built in 1983 on Chicago's Wacker Drive, had a strong hand in their great American success tale.

As an interesting side note, before the first of the two towers was built, I did negotiate a 10% equity ownership for the Merc in the first tower. The investment cost was $889,000. Some seven years later, in a refinancing of the premises, the CME was paid for its equity interest $27m. Surely, the second-best trade I ever made, next to the $5,000 cost for a feasibility study by Milton Friedman. JMB also asked me whether I wanted something personally. The answer was of course not, but I did get a designated parking space in the garage which I still have and pay for.

NO LAUGHING MATTER

The third challenge of this year was punctuated by a hilarious statement made by New York Senator Patrick Moynihan on the floor of the US Senate: "I always thought that a butterfly straddle must refer to a highly pleasurable erotic activity popular during the Ming Dynasty."

It was classic Moynihan, the charismatic Senator from the state of New York was well known for his controversial but clever public statements. Those were his opening remarks in promoting legislation dealing with tax straddles in futures. And although it was witty, it was no laughing matter. It could have spelled the demise of futures markets, and it fell on my shoulders at the CME and the capable shoulders of the CBOT chairman, Les Rosenthal, and its president, Tom Donovan, to defend our markets.

As I have previously mentioned, Tom Donovan and I, fierce competitors that we were, were actually strong friends when it came to the defense of futures markets. Donovan had come to the CBOT from the fifth floor of Chicago's City Hall, where for many years he was Mayor Richard M. Daley's go-to guy, and was as smart a politician as there ever was. When he joined the CBOT, where he rose to its presidency, he brought to their exchange a solid guy, who knew his way around the political landscape, could speak forcefully, and be my partner in matters of Washington, DC—and there were *no end* to those.

In the issue at hand, Donovan had me invite Senator Moynihan to a lunch at the Chicago Metropolitan Club, on the 67th floor of what was then the Sears Towers, in order to convince the Senator that he should reverse his stand on the legislation. We failed to do so, but, as Donovan would remind me time and again, the Senator, known for his drinking problem, consumed several bottles of very expensive wine.

It was a complex issue. The IRS contended that a futures-market tax straddle was illegal because it was a market position without risk and executed solely to avoid income tax or to transpose ordinary income into capital gain. It was a glaring tax loophole which brought futures market a ton of business. In fact, Merrill Lynch and other firms *advertised* this procedure to wealthy clients because it provided huge commission revenue.

Senator Bob Dole called me to his office to show me how people were taking advantage of the so-called 'tax spread,' and that he was out to close the loophole. I agreed that the loop hole should be closed, but not in the fashion he proposed. His legislation would force all futures traders to 'mark-to-market' their open positions on December 31 and pay the income tax at an 'ordinary' tax rate. This meant that users of futures would be forced to pay income tax on unrealized income, dramatically different than in the case of securities transactions, or real estate, or art, or a host of other asset classes which pay tax only after the income has been realized. I pointed out to Senator Dole that his legislation could mean the demise of futures since it would drive the legitimate business away along with tax straddles.

REACHING A COMPROMISE

Dan Rostenkowski, the powerful Illinois chairman of the House Committee on Ways and Means, offered to come to our rescue as he often did. He assigned Illinois Congressman Marty Russo to introduce legislation that would keep the futures income tax in line with securities and the like. To prepare Congressman Russo, Les Rosenthal and I locked ourselves up with him for a full day in a rented room in the O'Hare Hilton so that we could educate him on how futures markets worked, how the application of tax straddles could make the present income be thrown into a subsequent year, and the potential loss of business for futures markets if the proposed legislation was enacted.

Congressman Russo became a veritable expert on the issue and gave it his all. His sponsored legislation in the House closed the loophole without the onerous tax provision. Under his and Rostenkowski's leadership it passed in the House of Representatives. However, Senator Dole's legislation passed in the Senate. It meant that both bills would go to the Conference Committee. I recall it was well past midnight when Les Rosenthal and I were ushered into Rostenkowski's office to be told by Russo the sad news that his provision failed in the Conference. We were in shock. Tax on unrealized income could mean doom for our industry.

I refused to let it stand. I began another round of discussions with Senator Dole. I explained that I was all for closing the loophole, but not to have it close our markets. Senator Dole was sympathetic and asked me to come up with a fair solution. Research led me to Brad Ferguson, as innovative an attorney as one can find. He thought the IRS should be willing to accept a compromise which compensated our industry for being taxed on unrealized income. I then conducted a round of discussions with both Senator Robert Dole and the IRS.

In the end they accepted Ferguson's plan. While futures traders' positions would be marked-to-the-market at the end of each year, thereby closing the tax loophole, our industry would be compensated for the loss of business with a favorable *blended* tax rate, whereby the resulting income would be taxed at 60% capital gains and 40% ordinary income. It was a stellar and fair compromise that not only saved our industry from doom, but resulted in attracting additional futures business. The 60/40 rule remains in force to this very day.

(*Left*) Bialystok between the wars, by Henryk Poddębski (public domain)

⟨*Left*⟩ Leo at age 18

(*Right*) Leo's parents, Moishe and Faygl Melamdovich (1982)

(*Above*) CME Board of Governors, 1969. Leo is at the head of the table.

(*Right*) Leo announcing the creation of the IMM, 1971

(*Left*) Leo in the Pork Belly pit, 1970

(Above) International Monetary Market (IMM) Opening Day, May 16, 1972

(Left) Professor Milton
Friedman, Opening of
T-Bills, January 6, 1976

(*Left*) Leo and Milton Friedman, 10th Anniversary of IMM, 1982

(*Above*) Closing of the CME trading floor at 444 West Jackson Blvd, November 23, 1983

(Left) Bridge Nationals Tournament, Chicago, IL, 1975

First-place winners: Randy McKay, Brian Monieson, James Cordes, Leo Melamed, Burt Norton, and David Joyce.

(Right) Leo and Hillary Clinton, 1994

(Above) CME Traders, 1986. Liquidity advertisement on the eve of S&P Futures.

(Above) Leo heads delegation to the Kremlin, 1990. William J. Brodsky, Tom Donovan, Leo Melamed, William O'Connor, and John Geldermann (Vladimir Lenin's headshot on the wall)

(Above) Leo with Mikhail Gorbachev, President of the Soviet Union, May 8, 1992

(Left) Globex
Launch 1992—
CME Chairman
Jack Sandner, Leo
Melamed, CME
President William J.
Brodsky

(Right) Leo and Federal
Reserve Chairman Alan
Greenspan, 2005

(Left) Leo and Nobel Laureate Myron Scholes, May 25, 2007

(Right) Leo and Nobel Laureate Merton Miller, May 25, 2007

(Left) Leo and Federal Reserve Chairman Ben Bernanke, July 10, 2009

(Right) Leo with President Ronald Reagan, March 17, 1980

(Left) Leo with President Bill Clinton, 2000

(Right) Leo with President George W. Bush, March 6, 2001

(Left) Leo with Chinese President Li Xiannian, first Chinese President to visit the United States, July 26, 1985

(using hands for pit trading)

(Right) Leo meets Chinese Vice Premier Wang Qishan, November 17, 2009

(Left) Chiune Sugihara, Japanese diplomat who issued over 2,000 lifesaving Japanese transit visas for Jewish refugees fleeing the Nazis, 1940

(Below) Leo and Betty at a tribute to Chiune Sugihara in Tsuruga Japan, May 2014

(Left) Leo awarded The Order of the Rising Sun, Silver and Gold Star by the Emperor of Japan, November 3, 2017

(Left) Leo and Federal Reserve Chairman Jerome Powell, 2019

(Right) CME Building on Wacker Drive and Monroe, Chicago, IL (the last piece of the puzzle)

CHAPTER 31

1982: Carl Sandburg Melamed

WERE the foregoing reminiscences all that happened in 1982, it would have been the prime candidate for the title of *most important year* in the Merc's decade. But there was yet one more event that must be recorded: the IMM's tenth anniversary black-tie dinner, featuring guest of honor, Milton Friedman.

And lo and behold, the fact that Milton Friedman made rousing congratulating remarks and lavished praise upon me was *not* the highlight of the event, *nor* was it the fact that Friedman was the only one to dare come to the celebration, as was his wont, without wearing a mandatory monkey suit.

Rather, the highpoint of the 1982 tenth anniversary celebration was when the world's most noted economist, Nobel laureate Milton Friedman, stood up together with the *entire* audience for a five-minute applause for the ballad written and delivered by Chairman Leo Melamed—in which I dedicated the IMM's incredible success to the traders themselves:

Only Yesterday

It seems like only yesterday:
There is the new/old floor at 110 N. Franklin,
The bronze chicken in front of the door,
There are the new wooden desks,
The blackboards and board markers,
The glass recording booth,
The old ticker tape machine,
Ken McKay with a rule book and Walter Kowalski in statistics.

And there is the Western Grand Champion steer, on the floor of the exchange—defecating.

It seems like only yesterday:
There is the old guard,
Harold Fox with ashes on his tie,
Count DeLattre whispering in French,
Sam Schneider shouting "lackity, lackity,"
And Irving Manaster reminding us to "trade small and last all Fall."

And the new guard,
Lou Madda thinking of retiring from action and getting married,
Marlowe King accusing someone of cornering the egg market (or was it bellies),
And Dave Henner low-ticking the bellies (or was it eggs).

And there is Billy Muno screaming at a board marker,
And Lenny Feldman shouting to stop trading because he thinks he is broke,
And Jack Sandner making his debut to our family by slapping Eddie Cahill and punching out Wally Wizlewski.

I remember it like it was yesterday:
There are all the young Turks, secretly meeting as the "Broker's Club," to change the status quo.

And here is our first victory, the election of Bob O'Brien as chairman, and a new era for the Merc!

Then our 50th Anniversary, we build a Poultry and Egg Building in Lincoln Park Zoo,
and we try to launch Idaho potatoes—for the seventh time.

Wasn't it just yesterday when we were told
That you had to have an egg squeeze a month to bring business to the Merc,
That scrap steel and frozen shrimp were the contracts of the future,
That you could not trade a live commodity, such as cattle,
That pork bellies was the wrong name,
That women on the floor would destroy our ability to think,
That a new building would bankrupt the Exchange,
That the IMM was a loser.

It seems like only yesterday
When I sat around with Ron Frost, E.B. Harris and Mark Powers
debating what to call this crazy new division we were about to launch.

I was chairman, so my choice prevailed.

Only yesterday when the price of an IMM seat was ten thousand
and Arnie Ruben rushed to sell it out for eleven.

Only yesterday, when our newly-self-appointed international financiers,
the first IMM board of directors, took their very first European trip to
tell the world about our great idea—and no one came to listen!

And Barry Lind discovered that you can go broke just exchanging
currency from one country to the next.

Only yesterday
When Maurice Levy was in charge of closing 36 inactive currency
contracts in line with his version of Interbank prices.

Only yesterday
When the gold window was closed,
and George Fawcett and I could not cover our short Swiss francs for the
next ten limit ups.

Only yesterday
When a high NY bank official politely asked us to leave his office
in fear we might become violent.

And Fed chairman Arthur Burns, no doubt humoring us, wondered
how Milton Friedman got entangled with a bunch of hog traders from
Chicago.

Just yesterday when the Mexican peso was devalued,
and the world assumed that it meant devaluation of the IMM as well.

Just yesterday when Henry Jarecki scared the daylights out of us
by conclusively proving, with a mile-long computer run, that the
IMM would bankrupt the bank of England.

Only yesterday when Nobel winning economist Paul Samuelson came to
the IMM opening banquet to tell us that the IMM would fail.

Yes, only yesterday when E.B. Harris confided in me that our trouble was
that we did not know it could not be done! So we did it!

Who were we?

We were a bunch of guys who were hungry.

We were traders to whom it did not matter—
whether it was eggs or gold, bellies or
the British pound, turkeys or T-bills.

We were babes in the woods, innocents,
in a world we did not understand,
too dumb to be scared.

We were audacious, brazen, raucous pioneers!

Too unworldly to know we could not win.

that the odds against us were too high;
that the banks would never trust us;
that the government would never let us;
that Chicago was the wrong place!

CHAPTER 32

1983: Putral

I N *Escape to the Futures*, my first published memoir, I recorded my immediate emotions upon seeing the trading floor for the first time:[84]

> I was Alice stepping through the Looking Glass into a world of not just one
> Mad Hatter, but hundreds. The shouting among the traders, the movement
> of their bodies and hands, captivated me like nothing before. Dumfounded,
> I watched the clerks darting across the floor at road runner pace with buy
> and sell orders in their hands for brokers in the trading pits. If it wasn't the
> Looking Glass then it must have been the Twilight Zone, a dimension of
> sight, sound and mind. Maybe it was both. Whatever it was, there was a
> life-force on that floor that was magical and exciting, and though I didn't
> understand what was going on, I wanted to be a part of it.[85]

Yes, to the uninitiated, the open outcry trading floor of an exchange was a nearly indescribable spectacle. The vast expanse of human figures moving to and fro, the sea of their colorful trading jackets, the noise level emanating from the pits where the transactions occur and the electronic boards ceaselessly flashing numbers is a sight simply too difficult to process at one time. For me it was love at first sight. It was where my life as a trader in eggs and pork bellies began and where I cut my teeth as a student of the market. It was where I learned why these markets exist, how they work, and how they serve the nation's capital markets.

84 *Escape to the Futures* by Leo Melamed, John Wiley, 1996.
85 Ibid.

It was the reason I gave up my successful practice of law and ended up at the Chicago Mercantile Exchange rather than what my professional career dictated.

OPEN OUTCRY

For those who were born too late to actually see the old markets: open outcry represented a trading architecture by which a group of traders and brokers gathered in a pit (also known as a ring) and competed for transactions by using their voices and hands to shout out the quantity and price at which they were willing to buy or sell a specific product.

Until very recently, this methodology universally described and defined the markets of futures. It was a practice as old as the markets themselves, intertwined with their official birth which, it is said, occurred in Osaka, Japan in 1730. Feudal lords established warehouses to store rice paid to them as land-tax by their villagers. In order to protect their booty from wild price fluctuations between harvests, they formed the Dojima Rice Market in the house of a wealthy rice merchant named Yodoya—ostensibly the first organized futures exchange. The merchants gathered there and with shouts and gestures negotiated the price of their rice tickets.

Even before I became a full-time professional trader, I was embraced by the floor crowd as a welcome addition to their world. After all, I came up the ranks; beginning as a runner, advancing to become chief phone-clerk for Merrill Lynch, and then buying a membership. Moreover, upon graduation I owned a law degree, which in time became a Juris Doctor. That gave me special recognition with the floor community and, as I previously explained, led me to be included in the (semi-secret) Broker's Club. In summary, I was an accepted citizen of the floor establishment and a loyal constituent of open outcry.

Little wonder then that as a product of the floor, I believed as did virtually the entire world that open outcry was the quintessential element necessary to produce liquidity, the continuous flow of bids and offers—the holy grail of a marketplace. Besides all that, it is the intuitive expectation. A bunch of traders standing in a confined arena, a pit, shouting at each other prices and numbers, each trying to buy low and sell high in a competitive auction or to execute an order for a customer, is bound to result in a continuous flow of competitive bids and offers, precisely as intended. It had been so throughout the world for the past 250 years. To this very day, when a visual description of futures is needed for television or the movies, it is depicted in open outcry fashion.

To be clear, as futures markets became more and more successful, open outcry was really the only practical solution for executing transactions. But remember, historically, open outcry shared the execution architecture with blackboards.

PARTING WITH TRADITION

At one juncture in the growth of the CME/IMM, someone came up with a solution for the lack of space for blackboards. The idea was to take a Polaroid camera shot of a blackboard that had the record of the executed trades recorded so that the blackboard could be recycled for use. One of our floor officials was put in charge of this operation. The process worked famously well for a while. Suddenly, we were anonymously advised that the official in charge had assigned himself a back room for his photography equipment and such—and began using the room for Polaroid shots of prospective employees. Trouble was, one of his requirements for prospective female employees was that she expose her upper body for the picture. This incident quickened the demise of blackboard trading and the Chicago Police did the rest.

In 1971, the Nasdaq exchange, a subsidiary of NASD, actually became the world's first *electronic* stock market. To begin with it was merely a computer-generated bulletin board and did not have the ability to connect a buyer with a seller, but they were working on that.

In 1975, the SEC proposed the creation of an automated Central Limit Order Book for securities markets and the following year issued a formal call for automation. Professors Junius W. Peake and Morris Mendelson responded to the SEC, proposing an electronically assisted auction-market for securities. The idea drew heated negative repercussions. It was strongly opposed by the broker-dealer community, who stated that such an idea would "destroy capital markets." The NYSE joined in opposition.

The pressure caused the SEC to withdraw the concept entirely. Junius Peake persisted though and in 1981, launched the very first electronic futures market. The exchange—called INTEX—was based in Bermuda. The exchange world rose up in opposition, calling it an acceptable black box. Upon meeting with Professor Peake, I applauded his bravery but told him that in my opinion if automation ever came to pass, it would succeed only if an established futures exchange undertook the effort.

In 1977, I wrote an article at the request of the *Hofstra University Law Review,* in which I categorically declared that futures markets could *only* succeed within an open outcry transaction architecture. It is, I claimed, the only and best methodology to achieve liquidity. This opinion was, of course, founded on the known reality and wisdom of the day and the technological capability of that era. After all, in 1977, personal computers were in their infant cribs, Bill Gates had just recently left Harvard, windows were what you peered through, a screen kept the flies out of the kitchen, a mouse was a rodent, and the apple was a fruit.[86] It was natural to conclude that "Eyeball-to-eyeball interaction provided the only successful means of generating liquidity."[87]

SCIENCE FOLLOWS ART

But things change. Technology moved on. A decade later, I could not help but recognize the incredible advances in technology and the fact it was unleashing all kinds of revolutionary changes onto civilization.

What had the greatest impact on my thinking was the fact that, in 1983, I was in the midst of writing my first science fiction book, *The Tenth Planet*.[88] This was published in 1987. In the story, I let my imagination loose and created many new technological advances. Believe it or not, some of which over time have actually been invented or whose creation is nearing.

Among the characters I created was a master-computer named Putral, who could carry out a limitless number of actions and responsibilities, at the same time for an advanced alien civilization inhabited by 50bn intelligent beings. Putral was central to their civilization, representing a combination of Google, Wikipedia, Twitter, Facebook, We Chat, PayPal, the UN, the Pentagon, Harvard University, the Cloud and much more, who could act at a pace that literally defied the speed of light. Putral could do a trillion things without a sweat. A reader once said to me that the only mistake I made was misnaming Putral—he said I should have called him Google.

Actually, *The Tenth Planet* was not the first time I let my imagination loose in written form. In 8th grade at Lowell grammar school, the teacher, Ms Fee, asked our class to write a story for the upcoming Thanksgiving holiday. I won the prize with a story where turkeys went on strike and would not let themselves be slaughtered for Thanksgiving dinners. This was in 1945, long before Doreen Cronin in 2000 published her award-winning children's story *Click, Clack, Moo*,

86 As described in *For Crying Out Loud*, John Wiley & Sons, 2009.
87 Ibid.
88 *The Tenth Planet*, Bonus Books, 1987.

where the cows refuse to give milk and the hens stop laying eggs unless Farmer Brown meets their demands.

In truth, the idea for my story came to me from a tale by the great Yiddish humorist, Sholem Aleichem, when chickens went on strike before Yom Kippur. On this holiday, it was tradition for orthodox Jews to perform the *Kapparot* ritual, by wringing the neck of a chicken before donating it to the poor for their pre-Yom Kippur dinner.

My ability to fantasize and create such an entity as Putral wasn't based solely on a runaway imagination. In fact, I was largely extrapolating from technological advances that had occurred in our own civilization during the past decade and contemplating where it might be taking us. It brought me to this question: if I could imagine a computer of such incredible capabilities as Putral in an alien world, was it not possible that our civilization's current technological capabilities could produce a much, much simpler computer—one that could run the execution process of a futures exchange? And if not now, how long would it be?

In this way, my fictional creation, Putral, became a catalyst in my personal conclusion that the open outcry transaction process could someday soon become a relic. No surprise, science often followed art—Jules Verne took us to the moon in 1865 and a century later, in 1969, Apollo 11 took Neil Armstrong there.

THINGS CHANGE

Standing at my desk in 1986 and watching the scene as packed human bodies moved about the CME amid the shouting and pushing, I had an epiphany, the sudden realization that open outcry was a transaction system waiting to become an outdated memory. How much longer could it survive the world's technological advances that seemingly were progressing at the speed of light? It suddenly became for me a certainty that an electronic transaction system was around the proverbial corner.

The words of Maynard Keynes came flashing at me as if on a neon sign, "When the facts change, I change my mind. What do you do sir?" It suddenly became a holy command. Standing there, I suddenly knew my destiny. As chairman, I could not allow the Merc to become a prisoner of the past. I had to openly admit that my earlier opinion was dead wrong. And do something about it.

Today, with the benefit of hindsight, it is clear that my willingness to admit an error in my past opinion and follow Mr Keynes' advice saved the life of the CME. I had no doubt that an automated system would make the transaction process much faster, more efficient, much fairer, more accurate, and at a lower cost. Such a system would quickly overtake the open outcry architecture.

After huddling secretly with CME Vice President T. Eric Kilcollin and his sidekick, Kenneth R. Cone, an outstanding University of Chicago economist, and directing them to make a cursory investigation as to how close or far the necessary technology stood, the answer was very encouraging. Enough to make me believe that it was within immediate reach. I verified their opinion by daring to meet with officials from Reuters covertly. My vision of the coming world was clear, as was my mission. It was my duty to lead the CME in the indicated direction—a direction which became my sacred and most difficult goal for the better part of the next two decades.

I had no illusions about how difficult a mission that would be. In fact, I expected that such an effort would make my introduction of currency futures seem like child's play. As historian Barbara Tuchman said, "Men will not believe what does not fit in their plans or suit their prearrangements." My decision was final. Though electronic trade represented a heretical thought, it was inevitable. So convinced did I become that I could not get it out of my head. There was no way around it. If not me, then who? If not now, then when? It had to be done, and, as I told Professor Peake, "when it is done, it will be a major exchange that will do it."

Open outcry was very much like a religion, Paganism if you will, a belief validated by the fact that all exchanges world-wide operated in open outcry architecture and always did. To have even a ghost of a chance, I would need a carefully structured long-range blueprint, one that would work inside of the Merc as well as it would outside. It took me several weeks to cogitate and then touch base with some of my market insiders. Very few were willing to think about it, most told me I had gone off the rails and to *fuhgeddaboutit*.

To succeed, I would of course need approval of a membership whose income was forever based on open outcry. These were people that mostly viewed electronic trade as the work of the devil and Leo Melamed as someone who was out to destroy their jobs. In other words, I became Darth Vader.

CHAPTER 33

1984: The Camel's Nose

M Y mind was made up. The only question was how to go about it. I thought about it long and hard. I needed a plan that gave me the best chance to succeed, to use a metaphor, in a world that still believed that the sun goes around the earth.

I created an exploratory committee whose stated purpose was non-threatening: "To determine the demands of the coming era of globalization." As committee chairman, I appointed a carefully selected group of members. I wanted people who were respected by the board and our membership, yet not bound by the status quo and open to my belief in the technology that was coming. I wanted people who would stand to fight what may become an all-out war, but still be unafraid to oppose my views and offer their own.

For historical purposes, allow me to record their names: Barry Lind, my closest and most trusted advisor, who could extrapolate the present with a realistic view of the future; Jim Oliff, a Brandeis Liberal Arts graduate who received a law degree from Northwestern University, an honest and outspoken analyst who would openly argue with me if he thought I was wrong; Brian Monieson, an innovative thinker, knowledgeable, brilliant and outspoken. I planned for him to become the next CME chairman. Monieson was much more than a good friend, he was my bridge partner with whom we won the 1986 Nationals Team game. John Geldermann, a solid conservative, who was highly regarded by the floor community; Bill Shepard, a strong and logical thinker, although often difficult to alter his views even when wrong; and, of course, I included as ex-officio chairman Jack Sandner, as well as two trusted staff members, Rick Kilcollin and Ken Cone, who had in total secrecy embraced the idea.

A DAUNTING TASK

The committee's deliberations lasted about six months—I purposefully kept a slow pace so that everyone's thoughts could be evaluated and discussed. I wanted all stones turned. I made certain that everyone became acquainted with the known facts: that some securities markets were already toying with an electronic destiny; that the people at Reuters, who were ahead of everyone with such technology, were tinkering with Instinet and dealing FX systems, both with a potential electronic transaction process; and that some people based in Bermuda were examining an exchange with an electronic transaction system called INTEX, which had received no traction.

At the same time, I wanted everyone to recognize that no futures market heavyweight had considered, or was brave enough to embrace, the idea of a technological transaction solution. Instead, such ideas were considered suicidal and that if this committee offered this direction it would most likely be rejected. But, as I hoped, everyone's thought process led to several truths: first, that to compete in the era of globalization—and capture the coveted prize of Asian business—it was imperative to somehow extend the availability of our products beyond American business hours; second, that the world will continue down a technological path which will ultimately confront open outcry; and finally, that the CME must somehow direct its evolutionary process to a technological transaction architecture.

What helped our ultimate decision was the rumor, and later fact, that our main competitor, the CBOT, was planning a night-trading session.[89] Open outcry into the night. The idea wasn't all that new, trading hours were flexible and had been changed from time to time to accommodate new or changes in business. The idea found its way into the media, which discussed the pros and cons of extended hours and even applauded the Chicago markets for being "ahead of the game."

My committee agreed with me that a so-called *night market* was not a solution. In other words, to extend open outcry with an additional trading night session at best might work for a month or two, but it wasn't a permanent solution. For me, such a solution was more a joke than an answer. The CBOT went in that direction since it really had no choice. Its membership would never, ever support anything that threatened open outcry. Period. We agreed in unanimous fashion that the only solution was to adopt a technological answer.

---

89   I recall that on the CBOT launch, the exchange celebrated its decision with a FIA banquet called Night and Day, during which the song with that name was featured.

FORGING A NEW PATH

We were fully aware that to adopt an electronic solution we would have to get approval by way of a referendum. A daunting task. Even before that, we needed board approval. Counting votes, the committee was optimistic that the CME board could be won over. On the other hand, to pass a membership referendum was a near impossible task; *hell no,* was the most likely response.

However, I knew what might work. For me, the only solution to the problem was to provide an iron-clad guarantee to the members that the electronic transaction system would not ever threaten regular trading hours (RTH)—in other words, their current income flow. The committee unanimously embraced that idea. We agreed that the electronic system proposed would not list products presently traded in open outcry *without prior express membership approval by referendum*—it was the only proposition that would have a chance.

Everyone agreed. It was even considered that the membership might tolerate their protected markets being listed electronically *after* RTH. In fact, such a system would give members an opportunity of trading after RTH, one they presently do not have.

It seemed to us that members would tolerate an electronic listing of *new* products without any restriction. In this case, new products would not compete with their present income but would instead expand their trading opportunity. To underscore this key point, we agreed to call the system 'PMT', for post-market trade.[90] Our system would be geared to attract users in time zones we presently do not cover, i.e., beyond the American RTH. We agreed the electronic system would operate, say, after 6pm until the next business day before 6am. In my view, such a revolutionary system should appeal to CME patriotism, a sort of private-sector jingoism to preserve the future of the Merc. After complete deliberation, the foregoing was precisely what the exploratory committee unanimously crafted.

Finally, to give the plan gravitas, we agreed to officially approach Reuters Holding PLC, the most prominent communications enterprise of the time, to accept the idea.

90   The PMT name was very early on permanently changed to Globex.

NEGOTIATION AND DEVELOPMENT

Would Reuters accept this challenge? Nobody officially knew. I did. I took it upon myself to meet with Andre Villeneuve, a top Reuters' official, who was very encouraging. It was a daring request, one they were inclined to accept. I was made aware that Reuters was building Instinet, an electronic system for securities, so this would fit their plans. One Reuters' board member directly asked whether I honestly believed "that those hard-bitten open-outcry pit traders would ever give up their ways?" I crossed my fingers and answered affirmatively.

Reuters eventually entered into a long-range agreement with the CME to create a global automated transaction system for the trading of futures and futures-options before and after regular US business hours. Andre Villeneuve and John S. Hull, two of their top executives, were appointed by Reuters to carry out this revolutionary mission. Rumor had it that Reuters spent over $100m building the system.

Our exploratory committee then added a profit incentive to the plan, a sort of sweetener to the members. It proposed to create a PMT organization for collecting fees from non-member users. The fees earned would be distributed as dividends to the membership on a 3–2–1 basis, based on divisional ownership in the CME, IMM and IOM—70% of its net income to the members, 20% to the clearing members, and 10% to the PMT organization.

Armed with the plan and the unanimous approval of the exploratory committee, I went to the CME board in August 1987 for approval. Jim Oliff and I had already secretly leaked the direction we were moving in to some of the board, so when it was officially proposed it was not really a surprise. What helped immensely was that the media was erroneously convinced that we would follow the CBOT with a night market. And after a long discussion, the CME board unanimously approved our groundbreaking proposal. September 2, 1987 was the date set to unveil the plan to the membership, with a referendum to follow on October 6, 1987.

So confident was I of the plan I intended to follow that a year earlier, in a publication for the members in 1986, *Making A Market, Making History*, laid the foundation for what might be coming:

> Fifteen years ago, we made a commitment to ourselves and the financial world that the IMM would be the premier financial-futures exchange. We told banks that the IMM would be their dependable partner for foreign exchange. We promised business that the currency contracts traded

on the IMM could be used to offset the financial risk resulting from fluctuating exchange rates. We assured the media that futures contracts would revolutionize the financial markets. Most importantly, we promised ourselves we would make the IMM the leader and the envy of the marketplace.

The technological genius of our age has given rise to the 24-hour financial market. Continents literally half the world away have been inseparably bound by the microcircuit. The marketplace has become perpetual, and world finance is now a giant that dares not sleep. This is our future, and it is imminent. The global market offers opportunities to those with vision and initiative. We of the IMM have never shirked from the future. On the contrary, the IMM has always set the course of the future. Let others follow our lead.

THE BIG REVEAL

The unveiling of this plan was as important as the plan itself. I had learned that if proposals are exposed (by leaks, hints or rumors) before they were fully formed, they get twisted, attract falsehoods and gain unappealing gossip which often becomes a huge impediment to their acceptance. Accordingly, I prepared the material and slides for this presentation in total secrecy with my executive assistant, Alysann Posner, with the warning: "Any leaks are punishable by the equivalent to death." To my memory, for the first time perhaps in history, there were no leaks. In fact, David Greising, a prominent reporter for the *Chicago Sun-Times*, wrote a column published the day before our unveiling predicting that the CME was going to follow its rival the CBOT to open a night market.

Finally, it is the foot soldiers, who receive little recognition, that prove crucial to our success. For example, the production of the booklet introducing PMT (Globex) to the members and press for the first time was task was carried out by Ron Burton, head of the CME's center for production and creative services. Ron made certain it was produced totally in secret. Over 1,000 members attended the unveiling meeting entitled 'The Future of futures.' We used the second trading floor for the meeting, since it was as yet still not being used. I led off the presentation, Jack Sandner followed, and the two Reuters' executives closed. Together we explained how we visualized the electronic system to work. The booklet of *The Future of Futures* was passed out to members as they left. Written by Posner and myself, it served to reinforce what was presented and offered answers to any question that we could think of. In sum total, the meeting covered everything the committee and I could think of to give PMT a strong wind to its back for the referendum a month later. Directly after the unveiling, I planned to announce the revolutionary plan to the world at large.

After that, it was up to my team and me to convince the membership to vote in its favor. I followed the script we created by strongly assuring members on September 2, 1987, that turning the lights off on existing trading floors by way of open outcry would be unforgivably stupid. However, I was quick to warn that "it was equally suicidal not to seriously prepare for the technological tomorrow."

The favorable reaction at the unveiling notwithstanding, we were far from assured approval. Man thinks, God laughs. One thousand years of history does not vanish overnight. The opposition was going to have its day. And the opposition I feared would come from every quarter, whether securities or futures, the US or abroad—there would be naysayers with deadly ammunition claiming that what Melamed was doing represented "the proverbial camel's nose under the tent." Deep in my soul, I have to admit that I realized this might very well be so. But if this brought an end to open outcry, I mused, it would at least be the advance of technology and enlightenment of the members who would make it happen.

And I was yet to hear from the broker community. This community was certainly aware that execution automation meant their demise—their livelihood. As I prepared our team for the referendum, I warned that it could make the second world war look like a backyard squabble. And even if we won, it would only be the beginning of a major conflict that would last for many years.[91]

---

91   Please see the 1988 Annual Report, 'The Third Milestone'.

CHAPTER 34

Hiroki

I N 1985, my mentor and friend Milton Friedman invited me to join him as a speaker at a financial seminar in Tokyo organized by Mitchell Fulscher, the executive in charge of Japan for Arthur Andersen. To be featured alongside the greatest economist of the twentieth century was among the highest honors possible. It also cemented a life-long friendship with Mr Fulscher, an extremely capable market expert who became my eyes and ears for matters in Japan.

At the end of the Tokyo presentation, I was approached by a Japanese gentleman who seemed a bit hesitant as he offered me his hand. "Good evening Mr Melamed," he said in English, "my name is Hiroki Sugihara." An emotional chill went through my body. Standing in front of me was Chiune Sugihara's eldest son. Hiroki would have been five years old to my eight years when we were both in Kaunas, Lithuania. We had never met though, because I never entered the Japanese consulate.

Hiroki explained to me that he had decided to devote his life to the memory of his father's humanitarian deed. From that moment in Tokyo, a bond between us was formed and, at his suggestion, I volunteered to help promote his cause in every way I could. A promise I have kept.

A LIFE HONORED

Over the years, Hiroki arranged memorials, several in the US and others in Japan, where we would both tell our stories and honor his father. Hiroki would often tell of the moment, back in Lithuania, when his father called their family together to explain why he was issuing transit visas. His father said, "All my instincts tell me the right thing to do is give them a chance to survive." These words were etched into Hiroki's memory.

More than half of the 6,000 Sugihara-escapees were granted entry to other countries, most commonly to Australia, Canada and South America. The remaining refugees were transferred to the Hongkew district, a Japanese sector of Shanghai, where they survived the war with the US. This was equally true for the entire *Mir Yeshiva*[92] and scholars of the *Telshe Yeshiva*—Mir was the only eastern European Yeshiva to survive the Holocaust intact.[93]

Once Chiune Sugihara's act of heroism came to light, he became known as the Japanese Oskar Schindler. In 1984, Chiune Sugihara visited Israel to be included by the *Yad Vashem* as one of the 'Righteous Among the Nations'. I made certain he received similar recognition from the United States Holocaust Memorial Museum in Washington, DC. In 1993, Chiune Sugihara was awarded the Life Saving Cross of Lithuania. A Sugihara Street was also assigned in Kaunas and Wilno, Lithuania, as well as in Tel Aviv, Israel. He was also posthumously awarded the Commander's Cross Order of Merit of the Republic of Poland by their president in 1996 and many other such honors worldwide.

My experience of Chiune Sugihara and Japan is the reason for my long-standing friendship with, and respect for, its people. It should be recorded that they were extraordinarily accommodating in assisting the Jewish refugees, for the most part penniless and with only a slim hope of actually escaping the Nazi onslaught, who descended upon them.

REMEMBRANCE

Over the years, I continued in every way possible to recognize and preserve the memory of Consul General Sugihara. My office in Chicago became a regular stop for Sugihara's relatives, children and grandchildren, as well as Japanese government officials, writers and movie makers. I often collaborated with Masha Leon (née Bernstein) to help arrange such visitations. I continue to assist countless Japanese reporters, writers, and movie makers in their quest to memorialize the Sugihara story. In 1992, I helped arrange for the Sugihara family to visit and be recognized by the United States Holocaust Museum in Washington, DC.

---

92 A Yeshiva is an Orthodox Jewish college or seminary.
93 It is presently the largest Yeshiva in the world.

The officials of the Tsuruga seaport, where refugees like me all landed, undertook a special effort to give the port extraordinary recognition by establishing itself as the *Port of Humanity*—an attempt to gain world interest for cruise ships and the like. At the request of former mayor Akira Akita, Betty and I, together with Sara Bloomfield (director of the USHMM), paid a visit to Tsuruga for a commemoration ceremony where we planted a tree in Sugihara's honor. Appearing among the Tsuruga delegation was the Honorable Tsuyoshi Takagi, Japan's senior vice minister.

In 2015, I was invited to meet with Japanese Prime Minister Shinzo Abe. I was also honored by the prestigious Waseda University in Tokyo, from which Consul Sugihara graduated. The occasion included receipt of a Waseda honorary degree and my laying of a wreath in his honor. The following year I helped arrange a visit by Prime Minister Abe to the Holocaust Museum in the US, where he lit a candle in Sugihara's memory. Sugihara's granddaughter, Oriha Sugihara, has created a Tokyo Sugihara museum honoring her grandfather.

On November 3, 2017, I was honored to have the Order of the Rising Sun, Gold and Silver Star bestowed on me by the emperor of Japan. This represents the highest award the government of Japan can confer on an individual who is not royalty or a head of state.[94] Its standing is comparable in the US to the Presidential Medal of Freedom. I received this award for initiating financial-futures markets worldwide, for my outstanding contributions to Japan-US relations, and for promoting recognition of Consul General Chiune Sugihara's life-saving deeds during the second world war.

Many years later, my experiences as a child in South East Asia led me to a similar affection for the people of China. In 1983, as CME chairman, I paid my first visit to China.

---

94   After the Japan-Russian war in 1904, Jacob Schiff was the first foreigner to receive the Order of the Rising Sun from the emperor for his assistance in helping Japan to win the war.

CHAPTER 35

1985: The Chinese Connection

A S previously noted, on July 25, 1985, communism officially met capitalism when President Li Xiannian became the first Chinese head of state to set foot on US soil... and visit the CME. It was an unparalleled occurrence. In fact, the US Treasury called me to ask if it was true that the president of China was due to visit our exchange. It was.

We planned a tour of the floor for President Li and his entourage, as was customary for any dignitary visit. However, a few days before his arrival we were visited by a security detail from the US Treasury, whose responsibility it is to guard foreign heads of state. My assistant, Carol Sexton, who happened to be the sister of Chicago mayor Jane Byrne advised me that the Treasury men would be bringing their guard-dogs the night before the visit to sweep our floor.[95] Surprised, I asked her to determine what the dogs would be looking for. The response she got was "anything that might be a problem." I thought for a second or two and asked, "Like, for instance, a controlled substance?" Carol nodded in the affirmative.

It must be remembered that the floor was populated by traders and their employees, many of whom were in their 20s and 30s. I had no knowledge of what was kept in each desk—there were hundreds of them. It took me about ten seconds to imagine the potential headlines the next day, "President of China discovers Marijuana at the Merc floor," or maybe "Drug trading at the Merc?"

---

95   After Jane Byrne became the first female mayor of the city of Chicago in 1979, she was afraid of being accused of nepotism and asked if I could find a job for her sister, Carol Sexton, rather than have her work for the city. I agreed and as it turned out it was of great benefit to the CME, since Ms Sexton, extremely competent, quickly became the chief of our public relations.

I instantly told Sexton, "Tell the T-men that there will be no tour of the floor and that we don't need the dogs." President Li was received and remained in the balcony overlooking the trading floor.

STRENGTHENING RELATIONS

Li Xiannian's visit was the result of my visiting Beijing a year earlier. At a banquet there I was seated with the chairman of the Bank of China and, as is the custom, ready to down a dangerous small glass of Mai Tai. That done, I brazenly asked how to go about inviting the Chinese president to our exchange. Through the interpreter, I received the answer: I just did.

Rumor in China had it that Mr Li came to Chicago to visit Leo Melamed before he went to Washington, DC, to visit President Ronald Reagan. Not true. However, Li Xiannian did not go to New York, as was the case with most foreign dignitaries, but instead came directly from D.C. to the Windy City, where he spent a couple of hours on the CME balcony overlooking the floor with the CME chairman, Brian Monieson, and myself, asking a ton of questions.

He obviously enjoyed and marveled at the openness of the execution process. He also gave us a bit of information indicating that Chinese economics were turning a corner. It was part of the reason he came to visit 'the bastion of capitalism in Chicago.' As history is witness, Deng Xiaoping followed Li Xiannian to become the paramount leader of the Communist Party, who turned away from its past economic policies and set China on a course of market-driven economic reforms. In a matter of some 30 years, it brought their nation to its present-day standing in the world.

CHINA IN TURMOIL

Of course, four years after Li's visit, the world was witness to the ruthless suppression of hundreds of civilian protesters in Tiananmen Square. Also known as the Gate of Heavenly Peace, Tiananmen Square is among the top ten largest plazas in the world. The square includes the Monument to the People's Heroes, the Great Hall of the People, the National Museum of China and the famous Mausoleum of Mao Zedong.

In spite of his leading the devastating Cultural Revolution, Chairman Mao is considered the founding father of the People's Republic of China; he was chairman of both the Politburo and Communist Party from 1945 until his death in 1976. In this time, he led the civil war against the National regime, ousting Chiang Kai-shek and driving him and his followers off the mainland to Taiwan. His body lies embalmed in the mausoleum and is visited by millions annually. When I first visited the mausoleum, along with hundreds in line to pay their respect, I could not help but remember the almost identical scene in Moscow when, as a child during our escape, my father brought me to see the tomb of Vladimir Lenin.

On the night of June 3, 1989, tanks and heavily armed troops advanced toward Tiananmen Square, opening fire on all who stood in their way. Two days later, shamefully, the military secured complete control. The historic university-student led demonstration was triggered by the death of Hu Yaobang, then general secretary of the Central Communist Party (CCP) and proponent of democratic reform. On the day of his funeral, tens of thousands of students gathered in Tiananmen Square demanding democratic reform. The student-led demonstrations eventually grew to some one-million people and was widely broadcast to the world. The protesters were overpowered by troops led by Chinese Premier Li Peng and unfortunately supported by top statesman, Deng Xiaoping, who feared anarchy and called the protest *bourgeois liberalism.*

China had a long way to climb on the economic ladder and had many setbacks along the way—Tiananmen Square being the worst. Often there would be a visitation by one or more Chinese dignitaries whom I was pleased to host at the Merc. Over time, I began to be viewed in China as an adviser to help their development of capital markets as well as futures.

Clearly, the visit by Li Xiannian in 1985 was not only a great public relations coup for the CME, but it laid the foundation for my strong friendship with the People's Republic of China. But it was no accident, nor good luck. Just as every long journey begins with a single step, so too are relationships built over long periods of time—especially within the Asian world. In bringing leaders to the floor, I was actually following the conceptual truth first promulgated by the Chinese philosopher, Confucius, that one picture is worth a thousand words. For me, it read, one visit to the chaotic atmosphere of a trading floor is worth a thousand written explanations. I knew that by bringing prominent dignitaries to visit, we were educating them in the *how* and *why* our exchange operated and, at the same time, advancing the magnificence of the free-market system.

Futures trading in China had a long history. But most of that involved many exchanges that were not recognized as such by the world at large, they were more in the nature of bucket shops or gambling dens. Once the China Securities Regulatory Commission (CSRC) came into existence in 1999, its first order of business was to do away with most of them and authorize only three futures exchanges: the Zhengzhou Commodity Exchange (ZCE), established in 1993; the Dalian Commodity Exchange (DCE), also established in 1993; and the Shanghai Futures Exchange (SHFE), established in 1999. In 2006, the CSRC authorized the creation of the China Financial Futures Exchange (CFFEX), which I had a hand in creating.

A NEW FRIEND

Among the Chinese visitors to the Merc was Cheng Siwei, a highly regarded Chinese economist who spoke in perfect English and whose credentials included being vice-chair of China's Standing Committee, the ruling body of their National People's Congress (NPC). Mr Cheng held an MBA from the University of California and was known as the Godfather of venture capital—he was the driving force behind the creation of the Nasdaq-style ChiNext, an exchange to channel venture capital into high tech companies. His past endeavors mirrored some of mine, making it easy to become good friends. Once, at Cheng's request, I held a luncheon in Washington DC in his honor, which was attended by congressmen Paul Sarbanes and Michael G. Oxley of the Sarbanes/Oxley regulation fame.[96]

Most importantly, Mr Cheng took me by the hand to introduce me to his close friend, the erudite Mr Wang Qishan, a premier and rising star in the Chinese political arena. Mr Wang Qishan received world praise in 2003 when, as mayor of Beijing, he took the unusual step of releasing all information about SARS to the public. It reputedly held SARS from further spreading. Wang Qishan subsequently became best known for his appointment as China's anti-corruption czar, on behalf of President Xi Jinping's crackdown on corruption, and for later becoming vice president of China.

My introduction to the premier, courtesy of Cheng, was pivotal. Wang Qishan had a deep sense of history which he viewed with strong philosophical overtones and in the light of past similarities. We found a strong commonality in our respect for the rule of law and order, and our philosophy about markets. He had read my books and would often quote from them. He also had great respect for the genius of the US Constitution. He told me that he held four Americans in high regard: Henry Paulson, former US secretary of the Treasury; Maurice Raymond 'Hank' Greenberg, former chairman and chief executive officer of the American International Group (AIG); Larry Summers, a noted

---

96   Unfortunately, Cheng Siwei passed away in 2015 due to cancer.

American economist and senior US Treasury department official; and myself. I figured that it was reasonably good company. Our friendship blossomed to a point where he admonished that I must visit him whenever I am in China. On another occasion, he asked me to write his remarks for a forthcoming visit to the American business community.

Most importantly, Vice President Wang embraced my idea of developing futures markets in China, and eventually asked me to help create a financial exchange, the CFFEX, for the listing of their stock index and other financial instruments. I began by organizing a symposium featuring Nobel laureate Myron Scholes and Cheng Siwei on the value of futures markets. In time, I became well-known in China's financial circles and lectured often about the CME and futures markets. I received honorary degrees from both Peking and Tsinghua universities. Three of my financial-futures books were translated into Chinese and are used in the schools. In addition, the CME initiated a systematic visitation program to and from China, where Merc officials could teach and expound on the value of futures in the development of capital markets.

STRENGTHENING US-CHINA RELATIONS

Wang Qishan put my name forward to become a member of the prestigious Chinese Advisory Council of China's Securities Regulatory Commission (CSRC). He also commissioned me as "chairman for life in the creation of a futures crude oil contract for China." Indeed, CME executives played an important advisory role. It took over ten years, but the International Energy Exchange (INE) went live in March 2018, the first market in China with cross-border application—something I insisted on from the start. In a similar fashion, I put forth the idea of a cross-trading between the CME gold futures market at the Comex and the Shanghai physical gold market. A cross-border application that would serve both our nations.

To the surprise of few, in 2018 Wang Qishan was appointed the vice president of China. That appointment led to my involvement in international relations. Directly after the recent trade war between our two nations ensued, the new vice president asked that I organize a US Advisory Business Council (ABC) to provide him with what were the Chinese faults and errors, as believed by a cross-section of top US business executives. To help achieve this effort, Mr Wang put his request in writing. I believe Mr Wang intended to use this information to initiate a top-level negotiation undertaking to correct the differences between our nations.

To do so, I asked for help from Ivo Daalder, then US permanent representative on the council of the North Atlantic Treaty Organization and presently president of the Chicago Council on Global Affairs. We put together an advisory council composed of ten American business leaders. Several months later, with help from Chicago Council economist Phil Levy and some members of the ABC, Mr Daalder and I provided Vice President Wang with our impressions of what China must correct.

First on the list was to stop the theft of intellectual property. Other entries included addressing the alleged altercations in cyber security, inconsistency against foreign investors in enforcement of regulatory practices, the demand for equal access to domestic markets, the demand to stop using Chinese regulations to pressure foreign companies to transfer their technology, and the demand to open their borders in matters of trade. This effort was abruptly disrupted by the public demands and responses from the top of both nations. While I do not know whether Mr Wang's effort would have achieved its mission, it may have led to a newly created China-US Financial Round Table (CUFR), to which I was appointed. CUFR was fashioned by the Chinese government to discuss current issues and establish a permanent dialogue between China and the US private business sector.

MUTUAL BENEFITS

I am certain China recognizes that over the decades it has been significantly aided by favorable American policies which helped vault China into becoming the world's second-largest economy in an unequalled period of time. This has been of great benefit to both nations. For nearly every dollar spent on what we buy from China, the Chinese buy US Treasury-debt securities or equities. This long-standing trade relationship has allowed US consumers to buy goods at truly inexpensive prices and thereby run budget deficits that we could not otherwise finance or would have had to finance at a much higher rate of interest.

Regrettably, the China-US relationship has in recent times deteriorated. It is said that China's goal is to overtake the US as the world leader, especially in technology. That has created a very competitive environment. But competition is healthy and does not need to become hostile. The US has been in competition with many nations in many fields for many years without it affecting the politics between us. For one thing, China was strengthened by virtue of our open borders. China has not reciprocated in kind. It is alleged that China has used its knowledge to violate world standards in cybersecurity. In addition, China's actions with respect to human rights has been objectionable. In particular, recent actions by China against the citizens of Hong Kong have been unacceptable.

The above has engendered a hostile environment. That is not to the benefit of either of us nor the world at large. It threatens commercial relations between our two nations. As the two largest world economies, it is imperative that we find a path to overcoming our differences and advancing our common interests. I firmly believe that the people in China have only the highest regard for Americans and that this feeling is reciprocated. We both have a long history of accomplishments and love for our respective cultures. I for one stand hopeful that our good sense and shared intellect will persevere. But I have got ahead of the story.

CHAPTER 36

1986: The Globex Revolution

THE war actually began with an incredible victory. On October 6, 1987, history was made: 88% of the members voted in favor of initiating Globex (née PMT), 3,939 to 526.[97] This huge victory reinforced for me several principles: one, always go with an idea that you deeply believe in; two, carefully prepare its dissemination, explanation, and broadcast; three, give it every ounce of your intellect, time, and energy; four, be respectful of the opposition; and five, if you really believe in it, don't be quick to give up.

The victory was beyond monumental. Las Vegas odds may have been 10,000 to one. We changed the course of markets—nay, of the world. We introduced life into what was destined to become a relic of the past. If Bobby Thomson's 1951 home run was the 'shot heard round the world,' the electrification of futures may have been the shot 'heard round the solar system.'

Above all, I learned that it is not enough to simply have a good idea—success requires *execution*. What I mean is that I lobbied for this vote in every way I could think of: I personally met one-on-one with almost the entire membership; I held explanatory meetings with small and large groups; I took traders and traders' wives out to dinner; and I talked to their parents and former teachers. I talked to strangers on the street and even talked to a preacher and a rabbi! I lived, breathed, and dreamed technology. I never became angry responding to critics, cynics, and doubters in an honest and even-handed manner; and I listened to additional ideas.

---

97   Originally called PMT to explain that the electronic system would operate exclusively Post Market Trade.

The vote gave us the green light to proceed with technology. For a population whose livelihood was, to the largest degree, dependent on open outcry, to cast personal interests aside and overwhelmingly vote in favor of what had to be in the best interests of the exchange was testimony that common sense can prevail. It just required leadership that could be trusted. It was a spectacular victory, one that—if I was right—would lead to a change in the transaction architecture of all world markets.

It is nearly impossible today to comprehend just how revolutionary our victory in 1987 was. It was the beginning of a new reality, where Dick Tracy technology was not a figment of Chester Gould's imagination, but rather every teenagers' reality; where electronic screens are a ubiquitous fixture on the desks of all traders in every corner of the globe; where every nuance of market information is transmitted in continuous fashion at cyberspace speed; where major market values are transformed by a statement of some high-level government official before the utterance is hardly out of their mouth; where information is communicated by a network such as, say, the Bloomberg system; where contract settlements occur not by delivery of the product, but in cash; and where financial futures are traded on every continent from Argentina to Australia, from Italy to India, from Taiwan to Turkey.

To simply say this was revolutionary is like describing the Declaration of Independence as an inter-office memorandum. The departure from open outcry was not just a watershed moment for futures markets—it was an event comparable to announcing the concept of email to a world that only knew of the postal service.

THE ANNOUNCEMENT

On September 28, 1987, a week before the vote, I explained my rationale to the public at large in *Barron's* special edition on global markets:

> Marriage of the computer chip to the telephone altered the world from a confederation of autonomous financial markets into one continuous marketplace. No longer is there a distinct division of three major time zones (Europe, North America and the Far East). No longer are there three separate markets operating independently of external pressures by maintaining their own unique market centers, products, trading hours, and clientele.
>
> Today, news is distributed instantaneously across all time zones. When such informational flows demand market action, financial managers no

longer wait for local markets to open before responding. They have the immediate capacity to initiate or alter market positions—a capacity that has come to be known as 'globalization.' With globalization, each financial center has become a direct competitor of all others, offering everyone new opportunities, challenges and perils.[98]

Our announcement sent shock waves through every financial center across the globe. I was contacted by the news media from *everywhere*. I explained that our proposal was based on how we saw the future and what it would take to remain competitive in the coming era of computer technology and globalization. The critical question was how to convince our traders to vote in its favor. We solved this by taking a solemn vow that the trader's present source of income would never be touched without their approval. It was a holy promise never to touch the pits unless they allowed it. It worked.

Approval by the members of one of the largest exchanges in the world for electronic trade was much more than revolutionary, it was a signal to the worlds' exchanges that they too must follow the Merc's lead—be open to enormous advances in technology or become an antiquated fossil without much of a future. Sure enough, during the year that followed, there were announcements by nearly every exchange, including the CBOT, of plans to explore or build technological capabilities to advance their market's reach.[99]

I was totally aware that our announcement completely contradicted what I had written in the *Hofstra University Law Review* in 1977. Then, I categorically stated that an "automated transaction process cannot supplant the trading floor of open outcry." Ten years later, advances in technology turned much of the world upside-down. I was following John Maynard Keynes' admonition, "When the facts change, I change." This is what I said to the CME membership:

> The CME believes that to blindly assume that open outcry is the perfect system for all time is to be lulled into a false sense of security and forgo any opportunities to strengthen or advance our way of doing business. Such a policy would be both foolish and dangerous and could lead to disaster. While we must always respect our heritage, we must never let ourselves be held back by its limitations. We must recognize the greater truth that those who ignore or fear to embrace reality will quickly become history.[100]

98 Barron's Special Edition on Global Markets. Statement by Leo Melamed, September 28, 1987.
99 Most exchanges were considering LANs—advancement in Local Area Networks—unlike the concept of Globex, which represented worldwide connections.
100 1988 Annual Report to CME membership by Leo Melamed.

OUT WITH THE OLD!

Karsten Mahlman, chairman of the CBOT, the world's largest futures market at the time, likened the CME's announcement to the development of the H-bomb, stating that it would mean the end of futures markets. Really! Statistics dramatize the story.

In 1991, on the eve of the Globex launch, the total transaction volume of futures and options on US futures exchanges (including the CME, CBOT and NYMEX) was 325m contracts. In 2018, the total transaction volume of futures and options at the CME Group, which includes all the above exchanges, on Globex was 4.4bn contracts with an ADV of 17.4m.[101] Approximately 75% of which was from financial products. As these words are written, the E-mini S&P contract alone trades something on the order of $200bn in notional value each day on Globex. And it will continue to grow.

Ultimately Globex did mean the end of open outcry—our original referendum did represent the nose of the camel, as I was accused. However, I made certain that every step along the way, as electronic trade continued to encroach on open outcry territory via Globex, the members were given the final say in a referendum as promised at the outset. Let me be clear, in *every* instance where Globex was allowed to list competing products to those traded in open outcry on the floor, it was *first approved* by the members.

My faith never wavered in the ultimate good sense of our members allowing us to lead the CME in the correct direction. It was only a question of time, and how to convince the vast majority within our exchange and industry (and other markets) that it was a do-or-die proposition. It was not easy. They had to be led, lobbied, coaxed and taught. But I never doubted that at the end of the day, the efficiency, speed, fairness, comparative cost and unlimited volume potential of electronic trade would overwhelm Friedman's tyranny of the status quo. It took longer than I envisioned, but at the end of the day I was proven right.

Globex represented a dimension of growth and success for futures impossible to quantify—far, far beyond what open outcry could offer.[102] After all, how big a pit for traders can one build? On top of everything else, our eventual IPO could not have been as successful were it not for the potential Globex represented.

---

101   Those statistics are substantially greater today.
102   That is not to say that an open outcry system can never find some small niche for a given product that can remain viable.

PROGRESSION VS STAGNATION

Throughout history there are countless examples of dominant and hugely successful enterprises ignoring or neglecting to embrace technological change—and failing as a result. In no particular order: Kodak, Motorola, Blackberry, Polaroid, Barnes & Noble, Nokia, RadioShack and Palm are all good examples of highly successful enterprises that failed, or whose potential was decidedly diminished as a consequence of changes in technology which they failed to recognize or adopt. The list is endless.

Allow me just two standout examples of the exact opposite, people and companies that foresaw and embraced the opportunities provided by the emerging digital economy. First and foremost, Jeff Bezos, who understood the potential of online services and built Amazon into the unequaled powerhouse it represents. Second, Reed Hastings and Marc Randolph, who took a DVD rental home delivery service and built it into the giant media-service provider Netflix has become.

I was so certain of my opinion that I dared to say publicly to the CBOT:

> Anyone who has not seen the handwriting on the wall is blind to the reality of our times. One can no more deny the fact that technology has and will continue to engulf every aspect of financial markets than one can restrict the use of derivatives in the management of risk. The markets of the future will be automated. The traders of the future will trade by way of the screen. Those who dare to ignore this reality face extinction.

In time, the CBOT made what amounted to a minor gesture in the direction of automation called *Project A*.[103] However, rather than abandon open outcry, their actual response to the threat of globalization was to create an open outcry *night session* to operate from 6pm to 11pm.[104] On their opening night, they garnered full support from their membership and recorded a huge volume. Dr. Richard Sandor, their chief economist, hailed it as a "grand slam."[105] I thought it was a sad joke. It went downhill from there quickly.

103 Primarily by the hard work of CBOT member Bert Gutterman.
104 For me, the difference in response to globalization between our two exchanges was fundamental. The CBOT leadership was bending to the political will of its traders and ignoring the wave of technology that was overtaking the world.
105 Dr. Sandor was instrumental in launching the CBOT's most successful financial instrument, the US 30-year bond contract.

Few moments in history define the difference between our exchanges so well as the CME's bold announcement and the CBOT's contrasting embrace of the status quo. I was quoted as saying to our members, "A night session for a few hours each evening to ward off Asian competition, was like trying to hide from a tornado in a cardboard box." The *Chicago Tribune* saw it correctly:

> The Chicago Mercantile Exchange announced a revolutionary plan to capture global business through computer trading rather than resorting to night hours. If the proposal is approved as expected, the century-old futures industry will make a giant leap into high-tech electronics with its first major attempt at automated trading.[106]

THE UNSTOPPABLE MARCH OF TECHNOLOGY

In 2006, at the celebration when I was awarded the Melamed-Arditti Award, Tom Russo, my dear friend and former general counsel of AIG, said to the audience that my Globex announcement "could easily have come from Thomas Friedman's 2005 book, *The World is Flat,* except it came from Leo, a decade earlier."

As I stated, "Financial markets [had] become virtually unencumbered, continuous and worldwide. A company located anywhere in the world, can use resources located anywhere in the world, to produce a product anywhere in the world, to be sold anywhere in the world. Suddenly, every country on the planet is a competitor in the global marketplace."

I visualized that Globex would become the electronic transaction system for every futures exchange in the world. Indeed, in 1991, I went as far as getting John Phelan, NYSE chairman, to sit through an hour-long demonstration of a Globex prototype. As I recall, Mr Phelan's final words were, "Not in my lifetime."

John Phelan, like many other luminaries of that day, missed the point. Technological advances will not allow the status quo to triumph. Technological advances represent a myriad of effects on civilization, sometimes occurring in inches, sometimes in miles, sometimes in minutes and sometimes in years. They are infinite in number and impossible to enumerate; one invention giving rise to the creation of another and on and on. The status quo capitulates as in a tumbling row of dominoes.

---

106 Carol Jouzaitis of the *Chicago Tribune*, Oct 5, 1987.

Everything is relative, of course, but in all of civilization, I dare suggest we have never experienced the scale of technological advancement of, say, the last three decades, maybe even the last decade alone. Some years after Globex was introduced, Joel Mokyr, American-Israeli economic historian and professor of economics at Northwestern University, described it well:

> The responsibility of economic historians is to remind the world what things were like before 1800. Growth was imperceptibly slow, and the vast bulk of the population was so poor that a harvest failure would kill millions. Almost half the babies born died before reaching age five, and those who made it to adulthood were often stunted, ill and illiterate. What changed this world was technological progress. Starting in the late eighteenth century, innovations and advances in what was then called 'the useful arts' began improving life, first in Britain, then in the rest of Europe, and then in much of the rest of the world.
>
> The consequences are everywhere, from molecular genetics to nanoscience to research in Medieval poetry. Quantum computers, though still experimental, promise to increase this power by orders of magnitude. As science moves into new areas and solves problems that were not even imagined, inventors, engineers and entrepreneurs are waiting in the wings to design new gizmos and processes based on the new discoveries that will continue to improve our lives.[107]

CONTINUED ACCELERATION

I like to group technological effects into two categories: *size* and *speed*. I have often suggested that in the twentieth century, technology has led civilization from the big to the little. For instance, the last century began with Albert Einstein teaching us about the universe—the big. In time, computer technology led us to the atom, subatomic particles, and quantum mechanics—the little. In biological science we also began the century with the big—molecules. And as computer technology progressed, it took us to DNA and gene engineering—the little.

In a similar progression, this applied to investment management. In the early 1980s, quantitative analysts (quants) using computer technology were able to disaggregate, repackage and redistribute risks and their corresponding rewards,

107 *WSJ*, August 8, 2014.

exchanging one set of risk and reward for another. Derivatives were born. A derivative is a contract that derived its value from the performance of an underlying entity. This underlying entity can be an asset, index, interest rate, a group of assets, etc. The motivation was to enhance potential profit and make risk more palatable or more suited to a given investor.

Derivatives, if you will, became the financial counterparts to particle physics and molecular biology. The former chairman of Bankers Trust, Charles Sanford, dubbed it *particle finance*. They grew exponentially, becoming the hottest new instrument of finance. It is estimated that over 90% of the world's 500 largest companies now use derivatives on exchanges and over the counter to help manage their business exposure.

But not without serious risks to the marketplace, as we painfully learned in the financial crash of 2008. Banks and other financial institutions, in their quest for better returns, ignored internal safe-guards and common sense. Acting in a reprehensible fashion, they helped create a financial time bomb—especially in housing. Professor Bob Shiller of Yale, a Nobel prize winner, summed it up this way: "The housing bubble is the core reason for the collapsing house of cards we are seeing in financial markets in the US and around the world."

Former SEC chairman Arthur Levitt Jr correctly stated that "transparency in the sale of OTC derivatives is an unqualified requirement so that risks associated with all forms of structured investment vehicles will be fully disclosed."[108] Nobel laureate Gary Becker added that there was a need for increased capital requirements relative to assets of banks in order to prevent the highly leveraged ratio of assets to capital in financial institutions.[109]

SIZE AND SPEED

None of the above, however, nor the passage of the Dodd-Frank Act, hindered the continued advancement of mathematics and quantitative analysis in application of trade. Over time, it led to a brand-new trading methodology: *algorithmic trading*. This was a super-secret method using automated computer programs and artificial intelligence that follow a prescribed set of instructions—based on time, price, patterns, quantity, volume—to execute trades at very high frequency. It is the world that the likes of Jim Simons, Ray Dalio, Ken Griffin and others

108 Arthur Levitt, Jr., *The Wall Street Journal*, March 21, 2008.
109 Gary S. Becker, *The Wall Street Journal*, October 7, 2008.

fashioned and conquered.[110] Jim Simons, founder of the hedge-fund Renaissance Technologies in 1982, is believed to be the first of these giants. Known as quants, they became the largest market players, reputedly representing 30 to 40% of the market's annual volume.

The second grouping, speed, needs little explanation. Technology has made our ability to do *everything* incredibly faster. More than that, it has made everything faster and, in most instances, more efficient. This has been going on since the beginning of mankind, from the onset of intelligence. And it isn't about to slow down, Moore's law has already passed.[111]

The pace of technological change will continue to accelerate—an understatement if there ever was one. As Professor Mokyr indicated, we have achieved an incomprehensible (quantum) pace, a robotic age with artificial intelligence that existed only in science fiction. We will harness and exploit the amazing laws of quantum mechanics to process information—something "that can compute many orders of magnitude faster than the most advanced supercomputers."[112] The effects will be incredulous, sometimes open and notorious, other times slow and insidious.

When electricity came upon us, did it not change everything? Of course it did. Were we quick to recognize all that it entailed? Of course not. With gas light, we were forced to go to sleep at nightfall. With electricity, our daytime life expanded exponentially. How could we compare our daily chores, medical advances, efficiencies fashioned, jobs created, or the financial consequences between the two different lifetimes? We could not. There was a new normal.

Is the same true today? For example, take our Federal Reserve's current seemingly unattainable quest for 2% inflation. No one understands why it has not been reached. Has technology changed everything? Perhaps we have insufficiently factored in the effects of technology? Are we prepared to measure inflation with new tools?

Be warned, however, the luddites of the past were babes-in-the-woods compared to current and future anti-technology urchins. Destroying textile machinery as a form of protest against automation will be child's play in today's cyberspace world. Some are already proposing a technological tax to slow things down. It won't work. Advancing technology cannot be stopped.

I know this battle first-hand. The introduction of Globex, which replaced the trading floors and the brokers, was a battle I ultimately won, but it took over ten

---

110 Ken Griffin was the 2019 recipient of the Melamed-Arditti award.
111 Moore's law asserted that the number of transistors on a microchip doubles about every two years.
112 *WSJ*, The Quantum Computer Threat, November 11, 2019.

years and my receiving death threats. Over time, the war became so vicious I had to hire an off-duty policeman to guard my office door. What kept me going was the knowledge that to remain viable, there was no other course. I could point to competitive threats, both domestic and international, that were ready to eat our lunch if we stood still. I dare say, in all humility, that the CME Group is what it is today because of my stubborn persistence.

ADAPTATION

In our industry we were lucky, new jobs quickly replaced the ones lost. In a matter of a few years, proprietary trading shops, using new technologies such as algorithms, evolved to employ hundreds of past floor traders, technicians, theorists, teachers and many right out of school. Today these jobs have grown exponentially, with many thousands of traders and support personnel. Not to mention the multitude of employees retained by banks and other financial institutions as they built similar trading operations and the like. Consider also the growth of tangential jobs that evolved, like real estate brokers, architects, accountants, financial advisors, as well as many yet to come. Taken in its entirety, I dare say, the total of jobs created far and away surpasses the ones displaced on the trading floors. In truth, a whole new industry was born.

Sadly, I do not expect the job-replacement time gap in other industries to be as fortunate. Many will be of a much longer duration. The consequential tug of war, therefore, will be much more pronounced. It will take strong resolve, innovation and a huge educational overhaul to solve this dilemma. The American ability to innovate represents perhaps our greatest birthright, but we have no patent on it.

During the past several decades, many US enterprises, especially in tech, have outsourced their manufacturing to China and other places where labor was much, much cheaper. This has greatly benefitted the American public—providing us with new products at affordable prices. But it comes with a downside.

OF GRAVE CONCERN

Throughout these writings I have made it obvious that I am a strong proponent of technology and why. But my opinion does not mean that I fail to recognize that there are downsides to technology which must not be ignored. In most instances the constructive results far outweigh the negative, or they can be corrected or will, in time, be self-correcting. In the long run, technology creates more jobs than it destroys. However, I wish to underscore an inherent cumulative effect of technological advancement that gives me grave concern: technology has been a major factor contributing to the continually widening gap between rich and poor.

It starts in the classroom. According to a Pew report:

> Even as technology becomes more affordable and internet access seems increasingly ubiquitous, a "digital divide" between rich and poor remains. The rich and educated are still more likely than others to have good access to digital resources. The digital divide has especially far-reaching consequences when it comes to education. For children in low-income school districts, inadequate access to technology can hinder them from learning the tech skills that are crucial to success in today's economy. Fifty-six percent of teachers in low income schools say that their students' inadequate access to technology is a "major challenge" for using technology as a teaching aid.[113]

Of course, it does not end there. According to the Congressional Research Service, a nonpartisan think tank, "On the bottom end of the income scale, technology now performs some of the functions that once went to low-skill workers ... Furthermore, improved computer and telecommunications systems have enabled more US companies to send jobs to countries with lower labor costs. With more workers competing for fewer jobs, wages for low-skill occupations dropped."[114]

To state the obvious, with the move to more efficient technology, outsourcing, and digitization, the poor have been left behind. And this disparity doesn't merely remain with the low-skilled workers, over time it will travel upward and impact large segments of the skilled as well. According to the most recent Census Bureau figures, income inequality in the US has hit its highest level since reports began more than five decades ago.

As President George H.W. Bush once stated in a different context, "That will not stand." If nothing is done to alleviate or improve the US income inequality, our economic system may become the victim.

---

113 The Pew Research Centers' Internet & American Life Project.
114 CRS Report, March 2012.

CHAPTER 37

1987: Crash(es),
Part One

N IKOLAI KONDRATIEFF, a Russian economist during the communist era, was the first to suggest that industrial economies followed a cycle of change—expansion brought about major industrial change and then contraction. The Kondratieff cycle averaged 54 years between alternating periods of extreme booms and extreme busts. However, cyclic periods can expand and contract and are therefore inherently unreliable for precise timing.

I was not around when the so-called Tulip Craze of 1673 occurred, nor when the 1711 South Sea Bubble burst, nor during the Wall Street Crash of 1929. However, I was front and center on Black Monday, October 19, 1987, when the Dow lost 22.6%, the worst single-day percentage drop in US history.[115]

THE SCARIEST DAY OF MY LIFE

It is impossible today, three decades later, to recreate the absolute deathly fear that engulfed my body and soul on Black Monday. My first thought was that futures would be blamed; my second that it would be the end of the CME. We recorded a single-day drop in the DJIA of 508 points, which represented a loss in value of

---

115   I was also an advisor after the burst of 2001 Dotcom bubble and the financial disaster of 2008.

approximately $1trn—the largest single-day dollar drop in history. There were moments during the day when it felt like maybe the end of the world.

Afterwards, Treasury Secretary Jim Baker blamed it on the Germans for raising interest rates. Others, more realistic observers, blamed it on Baker for the Louvre Agreement, which he sponsored and signed on February 22, 1987. This agreement aimed to artificially halt the continued rise of the US dollar caused by the 1985 Plaza Accord, which Baker instigated in the first place.[116] The deal lowered the US dollar's value and sharply boosted currencies like the Swiss franc, Japanese yen and German Deutschmark. Alan Meltzer, chairman of the Shadow Open Market Committee and professor at Carnegie Mellon University, admonished the US Treasury, telling them to "cease efforts at targeting the dollar's exchange rate". But the loudest voice came from the New York financial community, led by the NYSE, who blamed it on something called Program Trading at the CME. This became a cause that many got behind—despite the fact that hardly anyone understood what it meant.

In truth, the US stock market had been spiraling upward for years, with less and less fundamental reason to back up the higher values. As the former chief of the CEA, Herbert Stein, quipped, "If something cannot go on forever, it will stop." Beryl Sprinkel, then chairman of the CEA, said that US monetary policy was definitely too tight: "US financial markets could buckle if things don't change". At his request, there was a top-level meeting with President Reagan on the Friday before the crash in which Beryl expressed his concern about the negative effects of the Louvre Agreement. He said, "It spelled danger for financial markets." How prescient he was. Alan Greenspan, the chairman of the Fed, had it exactly right when he later testified before congress:

> Stock prices finally reached levels which stretched to incredulity expectations of rising real earnings and falling discount factors. Something had to snap. If it didn't happen in October, it would have happened soon thereafter. The immediate cause of the break was incidental. The market plunge was an accident waiting to happen.

---

116   The Plaza Agreement was an agreement signed on September 22, 1985 at the Plaza Hotel in NY by France, West Germany, Japan and the US to depreciate the US dollar in relation to the Japanese yen and German Deutschmark by intervening in currency markets. The US dollar depreciated significantly until it was replaced by the Louvre Accord in 1987 signed at Louvre in Paris.

BAD NEWS

I had a 6am call from the NYSE chairman, John Phelan, advising me that in London, their market was down the equivalent of 200 Dow points, an unbelievable number. I knew what he was telling me. I had been up half the night following the market in overseas locations. In Tokyo the Nikkei 225 was down 2.5%, Hong Kong seemed to be in a panic and the FTSE index in the UK was down 10% by midday. It was going to be a very bad day.

Once I got to my office, I immediately called John Davidson, our clearing house chief; Don Serpico, our MIS chief; and Barry Lind, chairman of the clearing house committee, to alert them of what was coming. I then called for an emergency meeting of the CME Executive Committee, of which I was chairman.[117] The committee remained in session until 6.30pm the following day.

As soon as I could, I went down to the trading floor to get a feel from the brokers and traders who were gathering for the 8.30am (CST) market opening. The pit was composed of about 100 to 150 members who rushed at me as soon I appeared. The S&P pit included some of the most experienced brokers and traders at the exchange. Their market was the most volatile and called for well-heeled risk takers and competent brokers. I had never before witnessed the fear I saw in their eyes that day. They bombarded me with questions for which I had no answers. Several brokers privately told me their decks were filled with sell orders and no buys. "Do the best you can," was the only advice I could muster.

The S&P market opened over 2000 points down. Throughout the day, as the horror unfolded, nothing was certain. It was like living in a nightmare, events seemed to be happening in no rational sequential fashion, except for an eerie connection between each scene. I had never before seen a market collapse as I was witnessing. There seemed to be no bottom. There were few buyers. What did it mean? The knot in my stomach grew bigger with every passing minute. There were two main concerns: an immediate fear about the gigantic settlement call that would result and the amount of money necessary to square the pays and collect between longs and shorts—and if we could not, what would I do?—and second, the longer-term fear about the recriminations and blame that would surely be levelled at the futures markets, which I knew to be totally without foundation.

Because ours had been the first market on the American shore to actually open, we had the unenviable duty of flashing the horrid news to US investors. If

117   The Executive Committee included Jack Sandner, who was CME chairman at the time.

past is prologue, I knew the messenger had a real good chance of being beheaded. There was no one I could turn to; I was in charge and literally alone.

A NEW PROPOSAL

In February 1987, months before the crash, I met with Susan Phillips, chair of the CFTC, to propose that the agency allow the CME to establish a daily price limit on the S&P futures contract—as is the case in all our agricultural contracts. A price limit would establish a fixed amount the market could rise or fall in a given day. I knew it to be a weird, if not impossible, request.

Susan Phillips was an economist and a former professor of business administration at the University of Iowa. Years earlier, I went to visit her when she had proposed that Iowa University create an electronic election market where traders could put money on who would win in a prominent political election. I thought it was a grand idea, and came to congratulate her and support the idea.[118] Later, in 1983, I strongly supported Susan Phillips as CFTC chairperson, the first female in that role at a federal agency. She served with distinction and went on to become a governor of the Federal Reserve. Point is, Chairman Phillips and I had a grand relationship.

Still, to support a move that limits the market movement was a very tall order for someone who, like me, was a strong free-market proponent. When she inquired why I made this request, I did not fully explain. The real reason was that I was very much in fear that the stock market could crash and *futures* would be leading the event. A price limit would prevent futures from being blamed in an extreme situation—exactly as happened in October later that year. But for the chairman of the Merc to openly say that he feared a crash to a high-level government official (and respond to the certain media questions that would follow) was not something I was inclined to do. In doing so, I could even start a run in the market.

Susan Phillips was a very thoughtful person and responded that although her free-market persona would oppose such a rule, if the equities community agreed with the idea, she would not stand in the way. I arranged to address members of the major equity firms at the annual Futures Industry Association (FIA) conference in Boca Raton in March 1987. I quickly learned that my suggestion was DOA. There was no chance that the financial community would support my idea. "This is finance, Mr Melamed, not pork bellies." I refrained from explaining my personal motivation.

---

118 The market is still in operation.

TIPPING POINT

It is important to remember the backdrop to the 1987 market. The bear market of 1973–4 was a low point for the stock market, with hardly anyone daring to be bullish. It was not until 1982 that the stock market showed some life. While slow in the beginning, the bullish mentality spread quickly. By happenstance or luck, our launch of stock-index futures in 1982 was perfect timing. New markets develop much quicker in a bullish environment than otherwise. Let's face it, as Bernard Baruch explained, only the professionals are true bears. From August 1982 to August 1987, the DJIA had risen from 776 to 2722, an increase of 257%. By October 1987, the stock market was at a fever pitch.

So when it happened, I was not really surprised—stunned would be a better description. The surprise was the magnitude of the crash. I had been bearish for many months. Economic growth had slowed while inflation was ticking upward. Valuations climbed to excessive levels. Future earnings estimates were ticking downward. The market had been very weak the previous several weeks, showing signs of a market that was topping. The financial news and headlines over the weekend of October 17–18 was exceptionally negative. I was kicking myself for having covered my personal short position on Friday's close. Money-wise, this was a great mistake. But that mistake turned out to be providential.

During the course of that day, I ran between telephone calls, the executive meeting and the pit. They were dealing at a frantic pace. But I realized there was a major disconnect between our prices and the NYSE. I never had a doubt that the prices emanating from transactions in the pit represented where the actual market stood—the prices I heard from New York seemed like they were from another universe. When the inevitable congressional investigation followed, I was given center stage: not only was I the Godfather of futures, but I had led the creation of stock-index futures, as if I invented the idea. They were only five years old and still a controversial innovation. In many minds, they instantly became a potential cause of the crash. Had I, the super leader of the Merc, made a profit by being short in S&P futures, it would quickly have provided a causal, albeit false, connection. As I stated, it was providential that I had no futures position whatsoever coming into the day of the crash. The good Lord was in my corner.

KEEPING THE MARKETS OPEN

During the two horrifying trading days of October 19 and 20, 1987, I had enumerable conversations with the who's who of the American financial establishment: Alan Greenspan, chairman of the Federal Reserve; Beryl Sprinkel, chairman of the Council of Economic Advisors to President Reagan (CEA); Kalo Hineman, acting-chairman of the CFTC; John Phelan, chairman of the NYSE; as well as a large number of US Senators and US House of Representatives who knew me personally from either a visit to our floor or my visit to Washington. Although I did not keep a list of the Congressmen, I remember speaking with Dan Rostenkowski, Nancy Pelosi, Chuck Schumer and Jim Wright. And by the end of the day, I had a full list of Senators to whom I owed a return call if I had not already spoken to them.[119] When talking to them over the following days, I impressed that we should do everything we could to keep the markets open. If we closed, it would remove the most important gage in determining what the market was telling us.

When the closing bell finally rang, everyone silently thanked the Lord since the market could not fall further that day. The brokers were all spread out on the floor with their clerks and runners beginning the task of checking out the fills made and desperately hoping that the out-trades would be minimal. There are many differences between futures and cash markets. On the NYSE, trading is conducted on a multitude of individual stocks. The actual index, be it the DJIA, the S&P 500, or another, is calculated by using the last sale price of each of the stocks that comprise their index and publish the resulting price as its index price. In the case of the DJIA, there are 30 different stocks involved; in the case of the S&P, there are 500 different stocks involved.

In futures, trade is conducted on only one product, whether that is currency, cattle or the S&P 500 index. Thus, the last transaction immediately establishes the latest futures price of the product and is immediately published to the world. No further calculation is required. In futures, Black Monday was no different than any other day, except that the opening price of the S&P index was unbelievably lower. That was not the case on Black Monday at the NYSE.

Even in normal times, spot markets always take longer to digest news. On Black Monday at the NYSE, there were many bellwether stocks that remained

---

119 US Senators whose office called: Donald Riegle, Phil Gramm, Alan Dixon, Al Damato, Richard Lugar, John Melcher, William Proxmire, Richard Shelby, Paul Simon, Pat Moynihan, Alan Simson, Chris Dodd, John McCain, Alan Cranston, William Cohen, Rudy Boschwitz, and Chuck Grassley.

unopened during the entire trading session.[120] Many that did open were hours late. The prices used in calculating the DJIA and S&P 500 index were always the last transaction of the given stock.

On Black Monday, when many stocks had not yet traded, the calculation was based on the stock's closing price of the previous Friday. This created an immensely false result. For the better part of the morning, the DJIA and S&P indexes were indicating prices that were well above the futures price of the S&P index and totally inaccurate. In contrast, the price of the S&P index at the CME showed the actual price of the last sale of the index. The difference was humongous. In reality, the NYSE never fully opened on Black Monday.

To add to this dysfunction, eventually the huge order flow caused the NYSE Designate Order Turnaround (DOT)—an electronic system that increases order efficiency by routing orders directly to a specialist—to break down. This created a huge backup, serving to further exacerbate the turmoil.

FUTURES VS THE SPECIALIST SYSTEM

The 1987 stock crash revealed that the system used by the NYSE was old technology operating within a hugely under-capitalized system. The NYSE operates by virtue of a *specialist system*. The specialist is a firm or individual who acts as the designated market-maker for a given stock or stocks. The specialist thus has a franchise on certain stocks and in return pledges to maintain a fair and orderly market. In practical terms, a specialist buys and sells assigned stocks from his own inventory, when necessary, against orders from the public or other broker dealers, in order to maintain a fair and orderly market. It is the specialist's duty to provide actual bids and offers all the time.

Futures, in contrast, do not use a specialist system. Instead, individual brokers and traders make the market. They have no franchise on any given product or any obligation to make a market. Brokers execute orders transmitted to them by brokerage firms, individuals, or other dealers whom they represent. Traders, similarly, have no obligation to make a market. They trade for their own account in products of their choosing. In practice, traders normally choose to work in products that are most liquid and where they feel most suited.

To put it bluntly, futures worked while the specialist system at the NYSE failed to meet its obligations. It became increasingly apparent that the system was inadequately capitalized to cope with the deluge of sell orders that were coming

---

120   As later explained, many NYSE specialists failed to make a market.

at them. The sell orders were of such a magnitude that the specialists either couldn't or wouldn't provide bids as they were supposed to do.

As Donald Stone, vice chairman of the NYSE and a principal of one of the leading specialist firms, admitted to me afterwards, "Leo, when you saw a cannonball coming at your head, you too would duck." Or, as another specialist explained honestly, "It would have been suicidal to make a market." It is important to note that the 1987 stock crash served as the reason to revamp the NYSE specialist system from top to bottom—but that was much later.

LATE-NIGHT PHONE CALLS

As fate would have it, Jack Sandner and I had a long-standing dinner engagement that fateful evening with two Reuters officials to discuss the potential contract between us for the creation of Globex (then called PMT). How prophetic was it that on the worst historic day in open outcry, we had a meeting scheduled with representatives of Reuters, the people who would eventually build the Globex electronic system that would ultimately take over the transaction process. The meeting was held at the Metropolitan Club in the Sears Tower, with our guests waiting until nearly 10pm because of the crash. The meeting served to reach an eventual agreement.

When I returned to my office that day, it was past midnight. My assistant, Patricia Reiffel, was still there because I asked her to stay until I returned. By happenstance, it was her first day on the job. She inquired whether every day was like this and handed me a stack of telephone messages to answer. Aside from the Senators, on top were three calls from Alan Greenspan, chairman of the Fed, with whom I had spoken several times during the day.

"Will you open tomorrow morning?" he immediately asked. It was a loaded question. The Fed chairman was new to his post, having been appointed only several months before the crash. However, he knew how futures worked, having been a commodities trader. I was one of his fans; we were both of the free-market mold.

He knew that for the CME to open the following morning all trades had to have cleared, meaning all market positions had to be fully paid for, based on the change from the previous day's settlement price. The swing of value on Black Monday between the longs and shorts was $2.53bn. That may not sound so big in today's marketplace, but in 1987, not only was this amount a CME record, it was then an ungodly sum. Our normal average daily swing was about $120m.

The Fed chairman knew that if payment by some firm was missing, there would be a default and we could not open the next morning. In such case, word would get out that someone failed and, in Greenspan's words, "gridlock" would ensue—a situation where firms would be loath to make their payments in fear of not being paid on their collectibles. It is what happened in 1929.

"I won't know that answer until tomorrow," I responded truthfully. "We will have to wait and see." There was a heavy pause and the conversation ended with the Fed chairman asking me to call him as soon as I knew more. Then, in an afterthought, Greenspan asked whether there was anything else I could think of for him to do. It was a frightening question which made me even more concerned, if that was possible—the chairman of the Federal Reserve was asking me for advice! *Scary* does not do the situation justice. The only thing I could think of was for the Fed to keep their money-wire in operation all night. He thanked me for reminding him.

A LONG NIGHT

I remained in the clearing house quarters that night, no thought of going to sleep. To his credit, Chairman Jack Sandner stayed as well. Every hour I would ask John Davidson, our clearing house chief, to determine how much money had come in. He had been in constant touch with the people of the Continental Bank, the largest bank in Chicago and the Merc's settlement bank. The news was not encouraging, with only a sliver of the debt covered. Davidson, a totally reliable officer and one of the rising stars at the exchange, gave me comforting words but was unable to hide the fear that we both were experiencing. The biggest debtor was Morgan Stanley, whose customers owed the Merc a little over $1bn.

It was 2am on the east coast when I decided that we had to alert the Morgan executives of the situation. John Davidson had the private telephone number for the CEO at the firm. I asked Jack Sandner to stand with me as we dialed the number. It had to be one of the weirdest conversations ever recorded. We were waking the chief executive of one of the largest financial firms in the world at two in the morning to tell him that his firm owed the CME $1bn.

The stunned silence that followed our explanation was understandable. "Who is this?" the voice at the other end asked for the third time. We responded by explaining who we were and that we were looking for Morgan Stanley to pay the CME what their customers had lost that day—and that we needed the money before the morning's opening. If not, I explained, we will have to call Alan Greenspan to tell him why we cannot open the markets. There was silence for a moment or two, followed by some garbled words that I understood to mean, "I will look into it."

The first of our markets scheduled to open were the currencies at 7.20am. Thirty minutes before the opening I called Wilma Smelcer, the Continental Bank's officer in charge of the CME account. "How are we doing Wilma?" I asked with my heart beating loudly. She meekly responded that we were still short $400m. I was actually elated. It meant that $2.1bn came in from the longs.

Wilma, however, wasn't so elated. It meant the Continental could still not settle the Merc's account. Her own loan limit, she explained, was $10m, which was obviously far insufficient to cover the missing remainder. The moment was intense and we had words. I told her that she should know the Merc is good for the amount missing. I explained that if the Continental Bank doesn't make good on the shortfall, we could not open the markets and I would have to make that fact known to Alan Greenspan. "And," I added rather loudly, "the next depression will begin." I think I scared her half to death.

Suddenly, she shouted that Tom Theobald, the bank's CEO, just walked in. There was a brief pause before Wilma returned. "You are alright, Leo," she shouted at the top of her voice, "Theobald said the bank would cover the shortfall." I looked at the clock—it was 7.17am—and said to John Davidson to ring the opening bell on schedule. I then made the indicated call to the Fed chairman.

We dodged a fatal bullet. But I knew the war had just begun.[121]

THE USUAL SUSPECT

Late in the evening of Black Monday, John Phelan, chairman and CEO of the NYSE, gathered all the directors of the exchange, marched them to the rooftop of their iconic Wall Street building, asked them to face West, lift their right hand, and point to the cause of crash—the Chicago Mercantile Exchange!

Of course, that did not really happen. But in my mind, the above allegory aptly describes the aftermath of the 1987 crash and how our Chicago futures instantly became the culprit. Without any exaggeration, the CME's life was on the line. I felt like the captain of the Titanic. Condemnation of the CME by the NYSE was the iceberg. The Merc is only still alive today because I navigated our ship without hitting the damn thing.

---

121 For a full description of Black Monday and its aftermath, I humbly suggest reading chapters 30, 31 and 32 in *Escape to the Futures*, by Leo Melamed. John Wiley & Sons, 1996.

In a near-universal knee-jerk reaction, *guilty as charged* was the immediate verdict by most in the media. Their business writers, pundits, and the self-appointed financial *cognoscenti* all came down on the Merc. One must remember, 30 years ago, the NYSE was the most respected and authoritative voice in finance in the world. To paraphrase the old E. F. Hutton advertisement: when the NYSE talks, everyone listens. When it came to financial matters, the NYSE was succinctly defined by John Damgard, the first president of the Futures Industry Association (FIA): "The NYSE was an 800-pound gorilla, that was motherhood and apple pie in the eyes of Congress." It became a classic David vs Goliath affair.

In truth, because of its arrogant existence, the NYSE hardly ever needed to be represented in Washington, DC. The voice of their chairman in the *New York Times* or *The Wall Street Journal* would carry the day. But for once, their voice was maybe not enough. I silently thanked Bill Bagley, the first CFTC chairman, for giving me the idea of a voluntary political-action committee. My own instincts to withhold political support unless the Senator or Congressman came to our house to see how our market worked was a masterful idea. It gave me and other Merc members a chance to explain and bond with the federal officials to a point that they understood the beauty of the free-market process. Due to this, I would estimate that before the crash better than one third of the House and a quarter of the Senate had paid us a visit. Pretty much every one of them knew me personally. This must have come as a shock to the NYSE chairman.

After the crash, Arthur Levitt, then chairman of the American Stock Exchange, publicly recognized that "Chicago has been much more active and much more sophisticated politically than any exchange in the country." How true! The lesson here is that every large business enterprise should prepare for the worst and maintain a strong presence in Washington DC.

HISTORY REPEATING

Blaming the messenger for bad news can be traced back to ancient times, when beheading the messenger of bad tidings was an accepted consequence whenever something unwelcome occurred. And unfortunately, futures markets are often the messenger. It is their salient trait. Their instantly available price, transparent structure, broad availability, ease of accessibility and efficiency, made them the first-responder to new information—for good or bad.

Two hundred years ago, the crash of 1792 was widely believed to be caused by—guess what—leveraged speculation in bank stocks. A few years later, the New York legislature passed an Act declaring short sales of securities void. Not to be out done, Pennsylvania passed a law in 1841 making short selling for future delivery a criminal offense. And in 1879, California went all the way with a Constitutional amendment invalidating all futures contracts. While all of those enactments were ultimately declared without merit or unconstitutional, the allure of blaming speculators for national problems never went out of style.

Think about it. The first market to crash on Black Monday was in Hong Kong, where the market went into a free-fall. From there, it instantly travelled to Japan and Singapore. It then crossed the Pacific to reach London, which shed 10% by midday. Next it crossed the Atlantic, where word on the street in New York was that the Dow would open an (unheard of) 200 points lower. *Finally*, it reached Chicago, where the CME's S&P index told the world what was happening. By what twisted logic—given the time-differential between Hong Kong and Chicago—could anyone put the cause of the crash on the Merc, at least 12 hours after its inception on a separate continent?

The trigger for that "snap" that Alan Greenspan spoke about can be almost anything. When I was but a runner on the floor of the old Chicago Mercantile Exchange, long before futures became an indispensable business risk-management tool, Elmer Falker, my personal Old Turkey and an old-line CME member who had made and lost many a fortune in the market, took me by the hand and warned, "When you become chairman, don't let our futures markets get too successful."

"Why not?" I innocently asked. "Because," he replied, waving his cigar in the air, "futures markets tell the truth and if the truth is too severe, they'll close us down."

THE ARBITRAGE ISSUE

Another reason for NYSE hostility was, as previously noted, a market technique known as *index arbitrage*. Some savvy market players, primarily at Solomon Brothers and Morgan Stanley, hit upon a very profitable trading tactic. The strategy involved arbitrage transactions between a basket of stocks at the NYSE— carefully chosen because they replicated the full index to a very high degree—and the futures S&P index.

Arbitrage between markets is, of course, as old as markets themselves. It is a strategy designed to create profit through taking matched opposite positions in two investments that have identical payoffs but are trading at different prices. The stock-index arbitrage version exploited price discrepancies between the cash market (the basket of stocks replicating the S&P index) and the futures S&P

index. If the futures-index price was less than its fair value, the arbitrageur will buy the futures index and sell the basket of stock, and vice versa. Aside from the huge profits this strategy generated, it also served to create liquidity and act as a market policeman forcing cash and futures prices to stay in line.

However, the majority of NYSE brokers and traders, and those who did not understand futures, felt it was an unnecessary innovation—Chairman Phelan among them. Those who did not participate in this strategy felt that index arbitrage represented nothing but an unwanted headache. It caused unusual stock fluctuations which disrupted their normalcy and affected their orthodox strategies. It gave rise to the complaint that futures were the 'tail wagging the dog.'

Their *official* objection, however, was that index arbitrage created volatility— meaning on the sell side of the market. Let's face it, the NYSE was the guardian of status quo, which secured their pre-eminent place in world markets in securities. The 1987 crash, in my opinion, proved to be the beginning of the end of the NYSE's grandeur.

UNFOUNDED COMPLAINTS

The NYSE's claim that selling caused by index arbitrage from Chicago was dragging down prices on the NYSE is laughable. On Black Monday, arbitrageurs could hardly perform this operation; to do so required simultaneous buying of the S&P futures contracts while selling (or vice versa) a basket of stocks (replicating the index) on the NYSE. With few real stock bids in New York on Black Monday, index arbitrage was difficult to execute. Subsequent studies determined that less than 10% of the volume at the NYSE that day was based on index arbitrage.

Stated another way, the competitive nature of our Chicago index market was making its mark. The new market provided institutional investors with a tool for quick broad-market risk management—purchasing or selling one futures contract as opposed to buying or selling 500 individual securities in the proper weights at the same time. The cost reductions were very significant, approximately 90% when using equity-index futures versus using underlying stocks for a given market strategy. Although the NYSE developed a routing system for sending trades quickly to individual specialists for execution, the system was laborious and costly by comparison.

Most significantly, the futures market was designed with a critical feature which assured that the underlying cash-index price and the futures-index price converged on expiration. Thus, the futures-settlement price and the closing cash-index price (calculated by the S&P on the closing prices of the securities in the cash index, i.e., at the NYSE) were the same.

Phelan also feared that the creation of Jack Bogel's Vantage Fund, which launched index investing, would benefit from the launch of our S&P index futures. It did, by promoting the creation of new applications in the form of index funds, arbitrage funds and hedge funds with a universe of new participants. In turn, these new participants served to produce a host of new trading strategies and an explosion of new indexes and index funds globally.[122] When taken together, these reasons were compelling and seemingly represented a real competitive threat to the NYSE. Except it *really* did not. As statistics bore out, futures served to greatly liquefy the equity cash market, resulting in major volume growth at the NYSE.

The NYSE complaints also included something known as *program trading*— automatic strategies with a high-speed electronic communications capability programmed into computers by financial engineers. Computer technology was opening the gates to a variety of brand new and sophisticated trading applications. Advances in technology cannot be stopped.

That said, while I was a strong proponent of technological advances, it was only with the proviso that I have both a thorough understanding of how they work and contain remedial provisions for times when things go wrong. In other words, I accept rules that limit certain freedoms to further the best interest of the market.

THE GREAT ILLUSION

The foregoing was particularly true with respect to something called *portfolio insurance*. For background, by 1987 the market had rallied smartly for the past five years and, in light of the crashes in the 1930s and 1970s, portfolio managers and pension trustees began to worry about the large profits the bull market had provided. In particular, they looked for ways to protect their profits without actually getting out of the market. By October 1987, the stock market seemed to have run way ahead of the fundamentals. *Hedging* was the watch word, and our futures market looked like the way to protect profits. You will recall that I too was nervous about the market and tried to find a way to limit its daily price movement should a panic develop.

Enter professors Hayne Leland and Mark Rubinstein from the University of California. As experts in the equity markets, they joined up with John O'Brien,

---

122 Jack Bogle was the 2018 recipient of the CME Melamed-Arditti Innovation Award.

a financial industry salesman, to co-found Leland, O'Brien & Rubinstein Associates (LOR) in 1980 to provide portfolio protection without actually selling stock. Called portfolio insurance, it basically provided a stop-loss methodology by way of put options.

When the S&P futures market was launched in 1982, LOR quickly realized that their protection strategy could be executed in a much less costly and cumbersome methodology by way of S&P futures. And while it was never really insurance, and never tested, portfolio insurance was designed to limit an investor's loss in stocks in a falling market with the application of derivatives—options and stock-index futures. The theoretical concept was an immediate success. LOR's asset base grew quickly, reaching over $500bn (in today's approximate money values) by mid-1987. Leland and his partners, Rubinstein and O'Brien, were co-named Businessmen of the Year in 1987 by *Fortune Magazine*.

During the crash of October 19, 1987, equity investors with portfolio insurance were contractually obligated to sell into the falling market in accordance with their LOR agreements directed by way of a mathematical formula. On that fateful day, these computer programs automatically began to sell S&P futures as certain loss targets were hit, pushing prices lower. It led to a domino effect as falling markets triggered more and more stop-loss orders. Each sell obligation further exacerbated the situation.

It turned out to be an unmitigated disaster. Portfolio insurance was an illusion. For it to work as promised, the futures market alongside the options market, the specialists on the NYSE *and* the rest of the world had to stand still while LOR sold out billions of dollars' worth of stock.

Fischer Black, the great market economist, in an interview with Nigel Foster, former chief investor of BlackRock Funds, suggested that a good analogy for what happened in 1987 would be if an untested drug was launched on the market to elderly pensioners by a pharmaceutical company without tests or trials.[123]

After he recovered from a deep depression, Mark Rubenstein admitted, "The portfolios that were being insured in 1987 were so large that it was impossible to sell enough futures in such a short period of time to keep the portfolio insurance strategy on track." No kidding!

The Brady Report, produced by a presidential task force established by President Reagan to report on the crash, had it right: portfolio insurance was not the initial cause of the crash. Instead, the report blamed automatic trading programs for generating huge sell orders that culminated in a 508-point drop in the DJIA on October 19, as more than 600m shares changed hands. Market

---

123　*The Derivatives Game*, Nigel Foster, 2018.

mechanism failures, such as the failure of the NYSE DOT system, were also held responsible.[124]

On the other hand, since insurance selling represented roughly 15% of total stock and futures sold that day, many experts, such as Burton G. Malkiel, a highly regarded professor at the Yale School of Management, concluded that the "Problem does not lie in the newly developed trading instruments and techniques." Whatever the actual cause, futures markets were totally exonerated.

I have said this many times, but it is worth repeating. Overcoming the 1987 crash was the most critical victory in our history, a success on which today's CME Group stands. For me, it was nothing less than the Miracle of Dunkirk.

---

124 Nicholas Brady, a former secretary of the Treasury, was appointed by President Reagan to lead a task force on market mechanisms to determine the cause of the 1987 crash.

CHAPTER 38

1987: Crash(es),
Part Two

IF Black Monday in 1987 was the scariest day of my life, the Tuesday following was the most critical. To everyone's relief, the market started higher—but it soon reversed with a vengeance. And it turned *ugly*. The CBOE and AMEX had officially closed their markets. For all intents and purposes, the only two exchanges still in operation were the NYSE and the CME. And given the fact that many of the NYSE stocks were not trading, the Merc was quickly becoming the *only* functioning market.

A few minutes after 11am, I learned what I feared the most: the NYSE had informed the SEC that it was considering closing the exchange. It was a terrifying thought. In truth, they were hardly open anyway, but at least the perception was there. In my opinion, if the NYSE *officially* closed, uncontrollable panic could follow. In such a case, the Merc would be left alone out there and the world would dump on us.

It presented me with an imponderable dilemma. I knew that it was critical to keep our market open, but if we became the patsy for panic-driven selling, it would be an equally intolerable eventuality. Our market theoretically could go to zero—as, it was rumored, happened to the Nikkei in Singapore. I could not allow that to happen. I had given Beryl Sprinkle, chairman of the president's CEA, my assurance that we would remain open, and so he had advised President Reagan accordingly. However, he could not assure me about the NYSE.

I called NYSE chairman John Phelan for the third time. I made the call alongside Jack Sandner and CME president, Bill Brodsky, through a squawk box in Brodsky's office so that everyone could hear the conversation. If the NYSE was to close, I wanted witnesses to the decision. I told Phelan that I heard rumors the NYSE was considering closing, was that true? Phelan sounded like death warmed over, "It is getting very close to that," he responded, "there are no buyers. We are going into a meeting to decide. We may be very close to that decision."

He left little doubt that the NYSE was very likely to close. Our market was about to be left alone in the world. Panic could certainly ensue. Even a rumor that the NYSE might close was enough to trigger a disaster. I concluded the unthinkable, that it would be suicidal to stay open alone. He agreed to call as soon as they decided.

I made the following calculation: from the moment the NYSE advised us of their decision to close, even if they did not act to do so before advising us, there may be a five to ten minute lag. Either way, we would need a couple of minutes to make our announcement to do likewise, and then at least 20 or so minutes to give the floor warning and additional time to warn the world of our decision. During this potential time lag, with the NYSE announcement ahead of ours by ten or 20 minutes, there would be no telling where the Spooz price would be driven—I did not even want to speculate. That was a risk we could not take.

I decided to ask the executive committee for the authority to temporarily halt our market until the NYSE decided one way or another. "At the most for one hour," I suggested. It was an agonizing decision, one I never thought I would make. But, then again, closing the NYSE was the market equivalent of the end of the world. At 11.30am, I told pit traders of the temporary halt. It was received in horrific silence. Fifteen minutes later, John Phelan called to say the NYSE would not close and that instead a *corporate buy-back* program was about to begin under pressure from the White House. The executive committee agreed with my instantaneous decision to reopen. Thirty-five minutes had elapsed from our halt to our reopening. The crisis moment had passed.

Arthur Levitt, chairman of the AMEX at the time, confirmed later that the NYSE was close to closing the market. Then came the buy-back program. The hold-up was that it needed SEC approval. Levitt praised our decision to reopen instantly. The Dow ended the day up 102 points.

DEALING WITH THE MEDIA

During the crisis, I took very few media calls. My reason was that I had a reputation for speaking frankly without evading difficult issues. It was too soon for that. I could not speak truthfully and say with any degree of certainty that everything would turn out well. Although I knew that the CME was not at fault, I could not speak confidently on how things would be interpreted. And if I hedged, the media could run with an indecisive answer and make it sound like the world was ending. Better less said until all the facts are understood.

The market was in a chaotic state and we were being accused from every side. Deep down, I was not certain we would overcome. Still, we had overcome erroneous accusations before. All I had to do, I kept telling myself, was to not panic and make decisions based on a reasoned judgment. I put on a positive face to the traders in the S&P pit. They were desperate for my guidance—they had an inherent belief that I would find the way. Knowing this, I would go to the pit every half hour or so and give them encouraging updates.

I recall taking a call from my dear friend Terry Savage, a national news commentator, and how I carefully crafted my words to give her a fairly positive response. Savage was, and remains, an outstanding, level-headed reporter for the markets. She actually cut her market-lore teeth on the floor of the Merc. As one of the earliest women to become a member and knock heads with the all-male rough-and-tumble trading pits, Savage learnt fast how to survive.

For someone whose eventual career was to become a public journalist and author, learning the game first hand rather than in school or from the books represented the best and sometimes only path to actually understanding how information is interpreted and becomes transmuted by the great unwashed public. Those early lessons served Terry well as she went on to become a widely-respected national market commentator. Indeed, our friendship has remained strong throughout the ups and downs of futures, becoming my go-to market expert when choosing a moderator for the numerous public events I sponsored. Eventually, Savage became the obvious choice for appointment to the Merc's board.

John Phelan was much more positive to the media. I guessed he would prefer to keep the difficult truth to himself or, because the NYSE was king on the hill, he would later retract or cover up his previous statements. As equities plummeted, and while he was as greatly concerned as I was, Phelan found more encouraging words that "things were just fine."

Felix Rohatyn, managing director of Lazard Frères & Co., told the *New York*

Times in 1990 that this was Phelan's "shining hour." Similarly, Tim Metz, in his 1988 book on Black Monday, stated "This is a time for statesmanship, for class. And Phelan is at the top of his game." On the other hand, given that ours was the only market that continued to function, Alan Greenspan once quipped that by keeping our market open during the crash, Leo Melamed may have "saved the world."

A QUESTION OF BLAME

At the instant the crash officially ended, the probers and pundits began poking at the corpse with the belief that the October 1987 stock-market crash was caused by a specific villain. Nicholas Brady, a former US Senator and subsequent secretary of the Treasury, was appointed by the president to chair the newly created Presidential Task Force to investigate the cause. I was pleased with the president's choice, since the Senator was a highly respected Wall Street pro and known to be fair minded. Importantly, Brady appointed Robert Glauber as his Task Force executive director. Glauber was a Harvard professor with a deep understanding of the marketplace. Within days, Senator Brady appeared in our board room on a fact-finding mission. It again occurred to me that it was providential that I had come into October 19, 1987, without any positions. Had I been short, it surely would have given our detractors 'evidence' of suspicious shenanigans.

We made certain that Senator Brady was provided with all the information he requested. In fact, he was amazed that the CME could give him the information he needed the very next day, including the name, quantity and time of the sellers and buyers during the crash. He learned that our markets were using cutting edge technology while, in the case of the NYSE, it would take them months, if not years, to provide the same data. The accusatory process lasted over two years.

Remember, in many quarters the Merc represented an *untested* idea, whereas the NYSE was trusted as though their word was from God. Never mind, as I later testified, that the crash was global in scope. It was equally severe, even much worse, in countries that had no derivative market and in which the strategies blamed in the US played no part.

Moreover, the drop in all the Asian markets, as well as the UK, occurred *well before* the New York opening, setting the stage for the American market to follow suit. The Japanese market dropped 15%, while the UK market dropped 11%, with a further 12% drop the following day. In Sydney, the market shed nearly 25% and in Singapore, which traded the Japanese Nikkei index, had no bids at all for a brief moment. The worst, however, occurred in Hong Kong, with a record decline of the Hang Seng index by 11%. It caused a number of failures, which prompted the exchange to make the critically bad decision to close for the remainder of the week. When it reopened the following Monday, on October 26, the Hang Seng index dropped 33%. It took a $4bn government bailout to resurrect the HK financial market which remained moribund for the next several years.

But for those who wanted an end to futures, it was a case of 'don't confuse me with the facts.' A two-pronged plan was concocted. It was correctly reasoned that if futures fell under the regulatory authority of the SEC, instead of the CFTC, their growth would surely be impaired. The SEC is a very important agency, but, at the time, it had no understanding of what futures were, how they worked, or why they were valuable to the national economy.

Some anti-futures folks—read: New Yorkers—sought to put our margins so high as to effectively kill our market. Without going into a discussion about the colossal difference between *futures margins*, which are a security deposit to cover potential immediate losses, and *margins in securities,* which represent a down-payment on the purchase of stocks, allow me to state that futures margins are carefully calculated on a Standardized Portfolio Analysis of Risk (SPAN) formula.

SPAN, a calculation for determining the risk involved in taking a position in futures, was invented at the CME by analyst David Emanuel. Today, SPAN is the world's standard calculus for evaluating margin risk. However, the NYSE was hell-bent on raising the futures equities margin to 50%. A certain death-knell to S&P futures. As Nobel laureate Merton Miller stated, "The margin issue is a code-word for killing the futures markets."

REPORTED FINDINGS

So, the battle lines were drawn, it was to be a New York vs Chicago brawl—our very existence came into question. The designated umpire was to be US Congress. Hearings were called even before the ink was dry. Program trading quickly became a market villain, and futures the villain's habitat. Within days after the crash, Massachusetts Congressman (now US Senator) Edward J. Markey, whose House subcommittee had jurisdiction over the SEC, had his mind made up: "Program trading," he stated to the *Washington Post* before anyone knew for certain what that was, "was caught red-handed behind the meteoric velocity of the decline."

He was not alone. In newspapers and magazines, on television and in hearing rooms on Capitol Hill, there were calls for a return to those halcyon days before there were stock index futures, before program trading, and before computers. At that hearing, barely ten days after the crash, I did not mince words:

> Because our markets are different, shall we be forced to become the same? Because we have advanced into the information standard, shall we be forced to retreat to a less technological past? Because we dared to enter an arena that some viewed as the exclusive domain of New York, shall we be forced to relinquish our market achievements?

All in all, there were some 77 different reports and studies about the crash. The *official* one, the Brady Report (published January 1988), exonerated futures as the cause of the crash but did recommend a single regulatory agency and *consistent* margin requirements. Its main conclusion was that "what have been traditionally seen as separate markets—the markets for stocks, stock index futures, and stock options—are in fact one market." That was an important conclusion for Professor Glauber. And while that was not news to us in Chicago, to the general public it was an important concept which gave the Merc some standing.

I also gained some significant knowledge. While those 35-minutes may have taken some years off my life, I learned that a temporary market halt was a workable procedure. It was an important lesson learned under fire and it led to my subsequent advocacy of circuit breakers. During Senator Brady's visit in the aftermath of the 1987 crash, I told him about price limits like those in our agricultural products and the temporary trading halt we applied on October 20, 1987. I contended that such a stoppage did not injure market performance and in fact had a salutary effect.

I continued to advance this idea so long as the break was of short duration, instituted in a coordinated fashion across all equity markets, and established well in advance of any emergency. I contended that the measure allowed the market to digest whatever had happened, offered time for the entrance of new participants and invited the accumulation of new orders. Brady seemed to embrace the idea. However, I believe that Robert Glauber should be credited in convincing the Senator of its value.

Jumping forward, Phelan recommended that in our testimony before Congress we find common ground to prevent another crash. I mentioned I had become a proponent of temporary stoppages. Phelan was a free-market proponent and at first he scoffed at the idea of interfering with the free-market process. However, when Senator Brady brought it up as an idea he would favor, it at once became Brady's idea and Phelan immediately agreed. The two of us ultimately presented the idea to Congress. It was, of course, enacted by both our exchanges and is now part and parcel of the rules in trading equities, future or securities.

Milton Friedman, on the other hand, privately told me that he could not support an artificial halt to a market. I responded that I knew that, but suggested practical application in a living marketplace sometimes trumps the theoretical. In other words, I would compromise a principle to a degree for what is the greater good. I had in mind my daughter's wedding and my father's principle. In this instance, to save our market from onerous federal legislation, I was willing to bend the free-market doctrine just a touch. The disagreement remained between us, but he agreed to stay out of the issue.

This was one very rare instance when Friedman and I disagreed. There was only one other. It was on the issue of what is called *conscious capitalism*. Here Milton applied his pure free-market theses, that the board of directors of a private-sector corporation only had one obligation to the stakeholders. Friedman said that any other path is short-sighted and advances the idea that profits are wicked and immoral.

He did not change my mind. While I agreed without any reservation that free-market capitalism was the most powerful system civilization ever devised, I am of the view that a private-sector corporation is also a citizen of the country and community in which it exists. It was my view then, and now, that big businesses should have a social conscience and when the opportunity arises, should contribute with money or in other ways to advance the interests of the general public.

ACADEMIC CONCLUSIONS

The vast majority of studies found no fault in the futures market or with index arbitrage, nor supported a single regulator or higher margin. Dr. Alan H. Meltzer, the John M. Olin professor of political economy and public policy at Carnegie Mellon University, who participated in a study of the crash by the Mid America Institute for public policy research, found no evidence to support efforts for any new futures legislation.

For me, the most telling study was the 'Findings of the Committee of Inquiry,' an examination of the events surrounding October 19, 1987, authored by four premier market experts, Nobel laureate Merton Miller, John D. Hawke of Arnold & Porter, Burton Malkiel of Yale University, and Myron Scholes of

Stanford University. Their unqualified conclusion was that futures were not the cause of the crash. Indeed, their study indicated that, on balance, futures actually absorbed selling pressure.

Other market-informed studies decided that there were an infinite number of factors to produce a 23% drop in the market. It certainly couldn't happen again. In fact, it didn't happen. Jens Carsten Jackwerth, a postdoctoral visiting scholar, together with Mark Rubinstein, offered incontrovertible proof that October 19, 1987, did not happen. According to their probability formula, published in 1995, the likelihood for the crash to have occurred was 10–160. "Even if one were to have lived through the entire 20-billion-year life of the universe, the probability that such a decline could have happened even once in this period is a virtual impossibility."

However, anyone that thinks that such academic studies ended the argument between New York and Chicago is delusional.

A STAKE TO THE HEART

The odds were of course against us, but our strong presence in Washington made John Phelan go the extra mile and put his thumb on the scale. He organized what was officially called the NYSE special panel on market volatility and investor confidence—better known as the *blue-ribbon panel*. Its official charter was to examine, analyze and discuss the reasons for the 1987 crash, and to draft recommendations for Congress to enact. Unofficially, it was a lynching party with John Phelan as the sheriff.

The panel included 19 marquee names representing the who's who of American finance and industry. Its chairman was none other than Roger Smith, chairman of General Motors (GM). The overwhelming majority of other appointees were members of the NYSE.

Seven of them, including Chairman Smith, were chief executives of major US corporations who were also serving as members of the NYSE governing board of directors. What most of them knew about futures is what John Phelan told them. An eighth panel member was Donald Stone, the NYSE vice chairman and former specialist-partner of John Phelan. Six other members were chief executives of major securities firms covering investment banking. Most of them also served on the Securities Industry Association—an entity with an engrained bias against futures. The remaining panelists consisted of two large institutional investors and one to represent the organization of individual investors. It was a stacked deck. There was no doubt that many, if not most, of the appointees came with hardened anti-futures views that were near impossible to change. Basically, the panel represented a potential 'hanging posse' to the CME.

The creation of the panel was a classic case of overkill. At the time of the crash, the CME was already on the receiving end of incoming negativity. Its checkered history; the multitude of published pejorative narratives about them; the relative youth of index futures compared to the long-established existence of securities markets; the nearly complete misapprehension of the economic value of futures to the national economy; the lack of understanding about the strength provided to the underlying market, which ensued from the combined use of cash and futures; the reputational credibility of New York as the center of finance in the US, compared to that of Chicago's *second-city* status; and the accepted importance of capital formation by way of the NYSE was more than enough to achieve the result Phelan was seeking—but he could not be certain so he devised a plan to drive a stake through our heart.

Once nearly everything was in place, Phelan called me to explain what he was doing, "To once and for all end the public discussion about the crash and offer some expert opinions to Congress." He asked if I would serve to represent the futures market's point of view. It was laughable. What chance did I have against 19 appointees who were part of the NYSE family? Still, if I declined, Phelan could say that he tried but failed to get a futures market point of view.

I accepted on the condition that the panel also include one notable academic, Nobel laureate in economics, Merton Miller. Professor Miller sat on the CME Board. I figured that one Merton Miller was worth *at least* ten executives from the equity world.

SKULLDUGGERY AT WORK

Fate does some funny things. Although the unwritten mission of Roger Smith was to carry out Phelan's plan, his company, General Motors (GM), was the first major US enterprise to successfully apply index futures to the management of its pension fund. Such an incongruity resulted from the early-1980s appointment of two talented executives to head up their pension-fund investments: W. Gordon Binns Jr as vice president and chief investment officer, and William P. Miller as pension fund manager.

Bill Miller joined GM as an engineer at Oldsmobile Division in Lansing, Michigan. Later, courtesy of GM, he received an MBA from Wharton with a master's degree on a thesis related to foreign-exchange risk management. GM promoted him to its treasury department to manage its foreign exchange exposures globally. Spotted by Gordon Binns as a budding star in risk management, he recruited Miller in 1983 to join his investment staff.

There, Bill Miller developed a plan for asset allocation and became the overall manager of GM's huge US pension-fund investment strategy. Miller saw the potential of applying futures to asset allocation and became the first major US fund manager to use the CME's S&P futures index as a strategic component of pension fund investments. His first financial-futures trade occurred in mid-1985, two years before the crash. The strategy proved extremely successful. Bill Miller soon became the manager of the overall asset allocation of GM's pension funds.

In subsequent years, Miller's role for pension-fund investment was expanded to Canadian and other international-fund investments. Although generally unknown to the members of the panel, GM's Bill Miller had become a leading supporting voice for the use of futures in pension fund management. On July 23, 1987, a couple of months before the crash, in testimony delivered by Gordon Binns and written by Bill Miller at a hearing before the US House of Representatives, Mr Binns testified that, "Program trading is a very useful trading strategy and investment technique that permits pension funds both to control market risk and substantially reduce transaction costs in investing or disinvesting in the equity markets."

The blue-ribbon panel was officially formed in December 1989. For all the foregoing reasons, its newly installed chairman, Roger Smith, appointed both Binns and Miller as his assistants for processing the panel's procedures and responsibilities. This action inadvertently placed both executives in a most difficult position. Not to put too fine a point on it, but their responsibilities at GM required them to *protect and enhance* the value of GM's pension fund. It was similarly a requirement under ERISA (the Employee Retirement Income Security Act) and the Code of Ethics and Standards of Professional Conduct.

However, from their vantage point at the panel, they could see that their boss, the chairman of the panel, was being largely influenced by the NYSE chairman and moving in what they deemed to be the wrong direction. If the panel's decision served to diminish or terminate the effectiveness of index futures, it would adversely impact the GM's pension fund and clearly act against the best interests of their responsibilities under ERISA. They were caught in a classic catch-22 dilemma.

THE NUCLEAR OPTION

The blue-ribbon panel held three meetings, the first on March 20, 1990; the second on April 17, 1990; and the final, scheduled for May 17, 1990. A week before the final May meeting, I received a strange telephone call from Bill Miller. At the time, I was at my home in Arizona. He began by explaining that the call must be kept highly confidential since his job at GM would otherwise be in jeopardy. He told me that this was the most difficult call of his life, but he thought it imperative to make. He was acting "on behalf of the best interest of the beneficiaries of the GM pension funds," he explained, in giving me a heads-up since, in his words, there was "absolutely nothing I could do to change the outcome."

Bill Miller then went on to tell me that at the very next meeting of the panel, scheduled for the following week, the GM chairman would seek conclusion of its deliberations. He would propose the panel approve two recommendations for which he sought their vote. First, that Congress legislate an increase in futures index margin to 50% of the contract value. Second, that Congress legislate to merge the futures regulator, the CFTC, into the much more powerful securities regulator, the SEC. As my heart sunk, Bill Miller concluded our conversation by saying that Roger Smith was certain of the outcome. The vote would be 16–6 in favor of both motions.

It was my ultimate nightmare. Either one of the above recommendations, if adopted, would be the beginning of the end of futures markets in America. While it was something that Professor Merton Miller and I feared from the beginning, the reality hit me like a thunderbolt. We had both hoped for something much less contemptible. An official recommendation of this nature by the captains of corporate America, with the full weight of the NYSE behind it, represented a force that members of Congress could not ignore. Any objection Merton Miller and I raised would be voices in a hail-storm. I would soon hit the iceberg as captain of the Titanic.

Desperate, I took what may be regarded as the nuclear option: I called Dan Rostenkowski, US Representative from the Illinois 5th District.

Congressman Rostenkowski was chairman of the House Ways and Means committee; to say that he was one of the most powerful legislators in Congress would be an understatement. As the chief tax-writing and appropriations committee, Ways and Means had untold influence across almost every Bill in the House of Representatives. And Daniel Rostenkowski ruled that committee with an iron fist.

Rostenkowski was a personal friend of mine, but his friendship with Tom Donovan, president of the CBOT, was even stronger. The two had worked together when Donovan was a very high official in Mayor Richard J. Daley's administration. Donovan and I were also good friends, having successfully worked together on behalf of Chicago's markets.

However, in this instance, I did not call Donovan. First, I did not want my action to get around. Second, I was positive Donovan would fully support my call to Rostenkowski. Third, the CBOT had no equity futures. And finally, the less people who knew of my nuclear option, the better. It took about ten minutes to explain all the details. Rosty listened without saying a word. When I was finished, he simply said, "Thank you," and hung up. I did not know what would happen and told no one of my call.

PANEL RECOMMENDATIONS

To say the least, Rostenkowski was Chicago's strongest futures-markets champion and an unequalled guardian of all things Illinois. He recognized that our futures markets had become a driving economic engine for the city and the nation. We were effectively changing Chicago's international status from the old Al Capone gangster image into America's *innovator*. Rosty was also acutely aware that the Chicago Civic Club of the day estimated (in 1975) that between the CBOT, the CME and the CBOE, our industry was responsible for a minimum of 150,000 city jobs. As dean of the Illinois Congressional Delegation, I once heard Rostenkowski explain to the delegation: "Never forget that what wheat is to Kansas, and what oil is to Texas, futures is to Illinois."

The following Saturday, I was back home in Chicago when the telephone rang. It was the unmistakably screechy voice of Roger Smith. "Leo," he screamed, "you violated our deal." "What deal was that?" I innocently inquired. "You damn well know what deal." I asked him to remind me. "That we will not go outside of the panel members to discuss our issues." I responded that I did not know what he was talking about. "You went to Dan Rostenkowski," he screamed at the top of his voice. "Do you know General Motors has 14 Bills before the House Ways and Means Committee?" I reiterated that I did not know what he was talking about—it was a very short conversation.

The blue-ribbon panel held its last meeting, as scheduled, on May 12, 1990. There were no motions, or actions made or taken; instead, there was a NYSE news release dated June 12, 1990. Its headline read: "Panel recommends initiatives aimed at reducing volatility, enhancing investor confidence." The findings, announced jointly by panel Chairman Roger B. Smith and NYSE Chairman John J. Phelan Jr, explained that the recommendations involve easing restriction on stock buy-backs and hedging by market makers; educating the public about program trading; introducing new products to protect individual investors; improving surveillance for intermarket trading abuses; and consolidating market regulations.

Its main conclusion was that "Markets are essentially sound, but there is room for improvement." In a minority report, Merton Miller and Leo Melamed complimented the work of the panel but dissented from the recommendation for "consolidating market regulation." The report made the papers the following day and then quickly faded into history.

In the interest of full disclosure, it should be noted that Dan Rostenkowski's political career ended in 1994 when he pleaded guilty to having converted office funds to his own use for gifts such as Lenox china and armchairs. I was one of the proud recipients of those gifts—a replica of the original Congressional House chairs. Rosty was later pardoned by President Bill Clinton. Gordon Binns and, subsequent to his passing, Bill Miller, served as members of the CME group board of directors.

RECONCILIATION

On the twentieth anniversary of Black Monday, John Phelan told *Associated Press* he was pleased that regulators and Congress, 20 years back, "didn't overreact with legislative cures." The 1987 crash he said was "An inevitable correction. The market was just too high and it was looking for some excuse to react." Hindsight makes everything clearer. By then, of course, financial futures had proven their worth as a most efficient risk management tool, one that was literally copied by every center of finance around the globe.

In the end, New York and Chicago came together. John Phelan, chairman of the NYSE, and Leo Melamed, CME chief, even became *friends*. Credit for that goes to Richard Grasso, then EVP of the NYSE, who later became its chairman and CEO. Grasso had an internal balance of things. He instinctively recognized that what we were doing in Chicago was an extension of what the NYSE represented. He had no problem embracing the concept of stock-index futures and their value to capital formation. We both were able to rise above the narrow instincts of regional partisanship to develop a close relationship that has lasted to this very day.

In my annual Member's Report, I filed this summation:

After all the studies were in, after all the evidence was presented, after all the analysis was made, after all the misinformation was laid to rest, futures markets were not only exonerated from blame, they were vindicated by receiving the highest of praise from most academic studies and from most knowledgeable experts. The frightening process served to strengthen, rather than weaken, futures markets worldwide.

Indeed, one doesn't hear much these days about the imminent demise of financial futures. Quite the contrary, new financial futures markets have been instituted or are scheduled in every corner of the globe. It seems as if the pronouncement by Professor Miller of the University of Chicago, i.e. that financial futures were "the most significant financial innovation of the last twenty years," has become accepted gospel.[125] Futures markets have become establishment.

But wait! More news. Kondratieff-wave theorists have found four of his waves since the eighteenth century. The first, from the 1760s to 1830s, driven by the invention of the steam engine. The second, from the 1830s to 1880s, featuring the advance of railroads. The third, from the 1880s to the 1930s, triggered by the advance of electricity and the age of automobiles. The fourth, from 1930, which is perhaps still *ongoing*, giving birth to computers, the internet and the smartphone.

---

125 Merton H. Miller, 'Financial Innovation: The Last Twenty Years and the Next,' Graduate School of Business, The University of Chicago, Selected Paper Number 63, May 1986.

CHAPTER 39

1989: The Misdirected Hedgeclipper!

THERE was yet one more call on my leadership before the 1980s came to an end. This came in 1989, in the form of a surprise attack (code name: Hedge Clipper) by federal authorities—the CFTC, FBI and US attorney—on our brokers and traders, accusing them of trading violations. It made front page headlines throughout the US. It was the most disquieting, even frightening, period in the modern history of our industry.

The accusations levied at both Chicago exchanges came without warning in a totally surprising fashion. It alleged that our brokers and traders violated the rules to the detriment of the public. There were no specifics, but among the accusations, the one the media fixated on was that so-called 'broker groups' (a group of order-fillers who banded together) did business in a manner that violated CFTC and exchange rules. I was aware that from time to time some of the broker groups were accused of applying strong-arm tactics to monopolize acquisition of business, but that fell far short of the charges being made. The Merc's enforcement department had no records of violations relating to the public trust. I knew broker groups found ways to get around the Merc's rules to prevent unfair advantage stemming from their simultaneous right to be a broker and a trader. Such practices were a serious problem, but internal to the Merc and a long distance from violating federal or CFTC rules relating to customers.

Trouble was, although I did not believe the charges, our growth was of such magnitude that it was possible rules and enforcement of them could not keep up. There was nothing specific, and no one could be certain what proof the FBI had.

I will always believe that the Feds saw the findings from the New York "Insider Trading scandal," perpetrated by Ivan Boesky and others in the mid-1980s, and reasoned that a much bigger scandal was awaiting them in Chicago's futures markets. After all, Chicago was the home of Al Capone.

It was up to me to put together a defensive strategy in order to prevent the crippling legislation that might otherwise be introduced if indeed there was something to the charges. I got advice from my New York friends, Henry Jarecki and Tom Russo. They suggested that I organize a blue-ribbon panel of stalwart members and known dignitaries, who would review our rules and make recommendations.

It was very effective advice. I did just that, making certain the panel was beyond reproach. It included former-Senator Tom Eagleton, a public director on our board and the US vice-presidential candidate under Walter Mondale in 1972. The panel was free to investigate the accusations and propose new rules where necessary. The creation of this panel was mostly unpopular with the membership. But I held my ground, believing that to prove our case, a super-clean jury was necessary. Here is what the *Chicago Tribune* wrote in their editorial on April 26, 1989:

> Leo Melamed, architect of Chicago's financial futures markets is an outspoken champion of self-regulation, and it is easy to see why. With Melamed as its chief policy maker, the Chicago Mercantile Exchange has been a consistent industry leader in new products and services while remaining largely free of heavy government interference. But Melamed knows that self-regulation is a right that can disappear rapidly if an institution doesn't act responsibly. Faced with increasing global competition and a government investigation of industry trading practices, he's fighting hard to preserve that right.

The Blue-Ribbon Committee selection ran into an unexpected difficulty that served for many years to sour my relationship with Jack Sandner. Nobody with a conflict of interest could serve on the committee I formed. As it was subsequently determined, Jack secretly owned an equity interest in a broker group and kept that information from me. Since much of the FBI focus was on broker groups, putting Jack on the Committee could have undone the sanctity of this undertaking. It could have wrecked my efforts to prove our integrity to the FBI.

That was a very difficult moment in my leadership. Jack and I were a close team until then. Jack's conflict of interest was obvious, even if it did not violate any specific rule. I had words with Jack, but it went nowhere. I guess it put Jack on the horns of a dilemma. It also brought to light a tangential issue. The broker community opposed Globex. Jack publicly was in its favor. I had always believed that Jack Sandner would strongly deny any adverse role in the development of Globex. I am quite certain that, intellectually, Jack knew I was right about our electronic future. He could point to countless public statements strongly in support of the Globex concept. However, broker groups were in an opposite camp. And the facts speak for themselves.

UNINTENDED CONSEQUENCES

I was grateful for the Tribune editorial because it put me on the side of law and order. Although Senator Eagleton turned out to be off-base (believing the charges without any proof) and had heated words with Jerry Salzman, neither the FBI nor the panel found anything serious. The federal onslaught of undeserved and unfounded federal accusations turned out to be much ado about nothing. When the smoke cleared, Operation Hedge Clipper's findings were negligible and the attack ended in a whimper. After two years of intensive investigation of some 6,000 traders and brokers (between the CME and CBOT), no more than 46 people were accused of violating exchange rules—of them, less than ten were found guilty. Tom Eagleton resigned as a CME public director stating that "the CME is run by insiders for insiders."

While the sting operation turned out to be a farce, it did bring to the forefront the dual-trading problem. This practice, allowing a broker to act as an order-filler (an agent of a third party) at the same time as trading for his own account, was not something limited to futures. The practice was similarly true for the cash markets, in securities, real estate and other fields of business. But in the frenzy of pit trading, the duality took on a much more serious dimension. Brokers were able to unfairly enrich themselves to the detriment of the exchange, local traders, and the competitive open outcry process.

Four of our local traders—Bill Shepard, Ed Charlip, Cliff Kabumotto and Joel Stender—sought to ban dual trading entirely. The petition did not have a chance since it would single-out our industry rather than a questionable practice in many other endeavors. However, it did lead to a compromise rule Bill Shepard and I crafted and enacted which would prevent the worst of the dual-trading activities. Called the Top-Step rule, this regulation prohibited brokers from dual trading while standing on the top level of a pit from where they could readily take advantage for themselves. The rule was effective for a time and resulted in a strong friendship between myself and Shepard. But the dual trading issue never went away.

ENTERING INTO NEGOTIATIONS

For me, the Hedge Clipper investigation actually bolstered my efforts to concentrate on Globex. An electronic transaction system would do away with many of the open outcry ills and potential mischiefs.[126] My grand design was for Globex to become the accepted universal transaction system in futures markets. Sure, customers would pay us a small fee for its use, but in return their exchanges' products would reach every corner of the planet. The French MATIF exchange was already onboard; negotiations with NYMEX and COMEX were well underway; the British LIFFE was deliberating (ostensibly waiting to see what the CBOT would do); and discussions with the Brazilian Mercantile and Futures Exchange (BM&F) were scheduled.

However, I knew without a doubt that the surest way to achieve my goal was to get the CBOT onboard, the rest will follow. Tom Donovan, CBOT president, knew this as well and made a difficult demand: drop ongoing negotiations with all other exchanges until negotiations between the CME and the CBOT were successfully concluded. I agonized over this demand, since we were very near to an agreement with the New Yorkers. And this demand could easily be a ruse calculated to stop Globex momentum. Still, bringing the CBOT on board, by far the world's largest exchange, represented a huge prize, one bound to attract futures markets everywhere.

I bowed to his demand. I am forever grateful to Vincent Viola and Danny Rappaport, leaders of the NYMEX at the time, for understanding without rancor the reason I stopped and withdrew from further NYMEX negotiations. It was a measure of his intellect that Viola and I remained friends throughout the years. We agreed to resume negotiations upon the CBOT's entry.

Negotiations began, starting with the leadership of the CBOT, Tom Donovan and Billy O'Connor, its chairman. O'Connor was a most enlightened CBOT official. He and his brother, Edmund, strongly embraced technology and were the moving force behind the creation of the CBOE, the CBOT's options exchange. The brothers also strongly supported the creation of the IMM.

The negotiations committee also comprised of Jack Sandner and Charles Carey, both of whom were destined to become chairman of their respective exchanges. Charlie Carey, with whom I found it easy to develop a personal friendship, presided over the CBOT a few years down the road when the merger between our exchanges occurred. Representatives from Reuters were also on

---

126 No doubt electronic trade would create its own set of shenanigans.

the negotiations committee. I point out the foregoing to prove the serious nature of the negotiations that followed. We met weekly for over a year. In the end, we reached an agreement—a monumental achievement.

BRINGING MY VISION TO LIFE

On October 27, 1990, both the CME and CBOT memberships overwhelmingly approved the tripartite agreement. A Globex Corporation was formed to jointly operate what became known as the JV (joint venture) enterprise. The JV included a set of hammered-out specifications that Reuters undertook to devise. Today those specifications look simple and primitive, but in 1989, a four-second demand for response time (RPS) in trade execution was considered near impossible. The RPS today is in the order of less than two milliseconds.[127] Thus, the Hedgeclipper and the JV closed out the decade of the 1980s.

The Globex Corporation included a board composed of illustrious members of the entire futures industry. At its first meeting, I was elected as chairman.[128] As it turned out, I was the one and only chairman of the IMM, as well as the one and only chairman of the Globex Corporation. As arrogant and boastful as this may sound, I am stating that during the 1980s I initiated, led or executed all of the actions as described. It forever transformed the Merc along with the futures industry.

Such a reflection increased my urge to step down. I consulted with my wife, Betty, and my three children, Idelle, Jordan and David, who had lived through all of my critical moments and achievements and were always on my side.

THE END OF AN ERA

My decision to finally step down from the Merc at the end of 1990, perhaps for the third retirement in my career, became final. But was it really? My firm belief was that the next decade would be defined by the difficult transfer of our markets to the electronic screen. As chairman of the Globex Corporation, I expected to

---

127 A millisecond is one-thousandth of a second, faster than the blink of an eye.
128 The board included Jack Sandner, John Geldermann, Scott Gordon, Tom Dittmer, Barry Lind and William Shepard from the CME, William O'Connor, Dale Lorenzen, David Brennan, Charles Carey, John Conheeney, John Gilmore, Burton Gutterman and Neal Kottke from the CBOT. In addition, serving as ex-officio board members were, William Brodsky, CME president and CEO, Tom Donovan, CBOT president and CEO, and David Vogel, chairman of the Futures Industry Association (FIA).

lead this effort, knowing that it would be a Herculean undertaking and take many years. I was not wrong.

To say that my CME retirement celebration was an earth-shaking event is a big overreach. However, few would deny that anything of significance occurred in the realm of markets during the previous two decades without my leadership. One might even go so far as to say my name had become a sort-of household moniker in matters of markets.

The magnificent retirement bash the CME orchestrated is hard to describe. It was an undertaking carried out by Carol Sexton, the Merc's PR chief, and Alysann Posner, my executive assistant. It was the event of the year—quite literally, since the who's who of the financial community and beyond came to the black-tie event on January 25, 1991. Many a political and elected official, from Senators far and wide to international financial dignitaries, took time out to attend. I maintain bound volumes of congratulatory letters, as well as a voluminous picture album of the people that came.

CHAPTER 40

The Tyranny of Status Quo—Again

AFTER five years of excitement, after hundreds of speeches, thousands of articles, millions of words, statements, promises and missed deadlines, Globex finally became operational on June 25, 1992. I made certain to make the first trade by bidding for ten September-yen contracts a hundred or so points above the current price. It took me a year to get out of that losing position. Professor Merton Miller came to the floor to celebrate the event. Standing next to me, he said: "I missed standing by you in 1972 when you ushered in the modern era of finance. At least I didn't miss Globex."

As one might expect, the event was very anticlimactic. I had lived with the idea for the last six years, since 1986, and had worked through holy hell to get there. For me, Globex was a long time coming and had something less than a robust beginning. It took Reuters five long years to build the system—perhaps our specification demands were too much for the times. There were many who cynically believed that the difficult specs, emanating mostly from the CBOT, were a tactic to undermine the project. Perhaps so. By the time Globex was officially launched, many foreign exchanges had followed our lead and built electronic local area networks (LAN). While such systems were a step in the right direction, my vision of Globex went far beyond LAN.

Globex was functioning thanks to Jim Krause and Don Serpico, our tech wizards, but most everyone went back to business as usual. For many members in our industry, it was more or less a non-event. They took it in stride and shrugged it off. After all, the majority of brokers, to say the least, were never thrilled with the concept in the first place. Nor did they believe that it would ever take hold. I accepted and expected such sentiments. But I never wavered in the belief that the electronic transaction system *will* be victorious—what it embodies is inevitable. If it isn't our Globex, it will be the son or grandson of Globex. My only fear was that it would be owned by someone other than the CME, but succeed it would.

It must be remembered that open outcry put the bread on brokers' tables. Globex would take away their execution fee, which was not small potatoes. In 1990, it was estimated that between the three major Chicago exchanges, the total annual income to brokers was in the neighborhood of $1bn. So many brokers figured, if Globex was inevitable, they should delay it as much as possible to preserve their income. And to a very large degree they could control the outcome. As I explain fully in the following chapters, unless the customer directed a preference, it was the brokers who determined whether an order was executed on Globex or in the pit.

One should not forget this was 1992. Sure, computers were all around us, but it was still impossible to imagine or visualize the world we live in today, some 30 years later. The technology revolution that ensued changed the world in unbelievable ways, putting most everything on some sort of smart screen. None of that existed. Sure, there were some in the technological arena, who could imagine such a transformation—but there weren't many, nor were they in the futures business, and certainly not brokers at the CME/IMM.

You had to be the likes of Bill Gates, Steve Wozniak, Jeff Bezos, Jack Ma, or Mark Zuckerberg, who let their imagination loose and extended what they knew or what they were doing into the future. Remember, this was five years *before* the E-mini showed the whole world that they were dead wrong. In 1992, the vast majority continued to believe that liquidity was created in open outcry— period. I was in a tiny, tiny minority without real proof.

GLORIOUS GLOBEX

Flash forward with me for a brief moment. The statistics will continue to change, but as I write these reminiscences, Globex records some incredible daily volume numbers. For example, Globex records between 17–21m contracts traded per-day, representing about $300bn turnover in notional value. Globex provides access to 150 countries, with connections through 11 global hubs, and relationships with 12 partner exchanges. We have global-distribution capabilities through our trading hubs in key market centers, and our international network of strategic partners provides further opportunities to serve a broad range of clients worldwide.

Globex represented an earth-shattering departure from the norm—its initial volume could not be compared to simply a new contract of trade, a new product or a new asset class. To make a fair comparison, Globex should be equated to (say) the first powered and controlled airplane flight in 1903 at Kitty Hawk. In my opinion, it would take another decade before a clear assessment could be made.

Besides, it wasn't *volume* I was after. There were no volume targets or expectations. What we were after was to prove that an international interactive trading system—the first of its kind anywhere—could be *viable*. And we proved it. Except for some minor glitches, Globex performed extremely well and received high marks from the priests in the tech world.

A GENUINE BLACK SWAN

While I could wait for the system to show volume, I encountered what Nessim Nicholas Taleb would surely tell me was a Black Swan—an event I could not predict, nor envision.[129] Maybe I should have.

Almost immediately it all went awry. The CME board, led by Jack Sandner, its chairman again, enacted a dastardly new rule: any action by the Globex JV board must receive the approval of the CME. In other words, the CME board would hold a veto right over actions taken by the Globex board. The CME board could veto any action or intended action of the Globex Corp. It served a tactical death-blow to the viability of the Globex JV.

Given that the CME had passed such a rule, Tom Donovan advised me that he had to follow suit at the CBOT. By instituting the power of a veto over actions taken by the Globex Corporation, the two exchanges effectively neutered the viability of Globex to succeed. Every one of the newly appointed directors on the Globex board objected but could not overturn this action. Clearly, I was outmaneuvered. It was an action to preserve the tyranny of the status quo. It was where the brokers money was made. Could I have, or should I have, envisioned this could happen?

I was deeply wounded. I wrote letters of protest. I wrote an editorial to the *Chicago Tribune* but was talked out of sending it by Bill Brodsky, who said it would not change anything. Finally, in protest, I resigned from chairmanship of the JV. The effort to unify and globalize electronic trade in the futures industry was derailed. The broker community had an enormous victory. What mattered

---

129 See chapter 38.

to me is that the Merc would be the ultimate loser. Not for one second did I ever doubt that automation would win in the end.

At that moment, Globex was the innocent victim. I needed time to regroup and perhaps mount a counter-offensive. Only time would tell. As Milton Friedman might have said, the tyranny of status quo had won the battle... but surely not the war.

CHAPTER 41

Hillary's Roundup

A T the annual CME Global Leadership Conference in 2014, Hillary Clinton was the keynote speaker. And on the stage with her was a *great big elephant*. The by-invitation-only audience was composed of about 250 officials representing the highest levels of the American financial service sector whose business related to futures markets. Virtually everyone in the audience was aware of Hillary's 1978–9 exploits in cattle futures, where media reports across the nation reported that she turned $1,000 into $100,000.

To her credit, Hillary took on the big elephant directly at the conference. "As everyone here is aware," she began with a smile on her face, "some years ago I made some money in cattle futures." The audience laughed and applauded in recognition of that memory. She then went on to tell her version of the story and how the media made a big deal out of it "until Leo Melamed said it was a tempest in a teapot." She concluded by saying, "Leo Melamed was my savior."

SO WHAT'S THE REAL STORY?

It began during the run-up to President Clinton's re-election with a phone call in early April 1994, from Rahm Emanuel, who was then assistant to President Clinton. Emanuel and I knew each other fairly well. As an assistant to Chicago's Mayor Richard M. Daley, he often had reason to ask for help from the Chicago business community, which certainly included the CME. Our friendship preceded his fame as Obama's chief of staff and his eventual election as mayor of Chicago. In addition, we had common family friends, which resulted in my once watching Rahm in his youth dancing in the Joffrey Ballet, Chicago's premiere ballet company. He was good.

Our phone conversation was brief, "Would you please take a call from John Podesta?" Emanuel asked. Instantly I knew it must be about Hillary Clinton's escapades in cattle futures. It was an old story that refused to go away. On October 11, 1978, Hillary Clinton opened a futures account at Refco, a large Futures Commission Merchant (FCM) and clearing firm of the CME. She made trades during the following ten or so months, before closing the account on July 20, 1979. Her profits at that time totaled about $100,000.[130]

The profits came to the public's attention 15 years later in a March 18, 1994, report by the *New York Times* during a review of the Clintons' financial records coinciding with congressional hearings over the Whitewater controversy. The press was highly sceptical that Ms Clinton knew enough in the treacherous arena of cattle futures to make that kind of profit. The implications were that the first lady must have violated a host of regulations to turn $1,000 into big money, or that it was a *payoff* by someone who gave her winning trades. In response to the criticisms, the White House released Ms Clinton's trading records. However, that did not satisfy the critics and forced the White House to explain that during the period in question, she was advised by James Blair, a futures expert, and that Hillary learned about cattle trading by reading *The Wall Street Journal*.

That made things look worse. First, reading reports in the *WSJ* will not provide an education in futures trade. Second, in 1978 Bill Clinton was state attorney general in the process of running for governor of Arkansas, and Jim Blair was the outside counsel to Tyson Foods, a major Arkansas poultry producer. The media made the obvious connection. The possibility of a *payoff* or *conflict of interest* and *influence peddling* was bandied about, and the cattle issue became a louder and more worrisome problem.

A SIMPLE REQUEST

John Podesta knew me from the time he was chief counsel to the Senate Agriculture Committee, before which I appeared in hearings relating to the 1987 stock crash. His request to come to their assistance was made in a friendly and honest manner: "Leo, we know nothing about futures, please help us determine what she did or did not do. After we provide you with her records and you decide

---

130 A full description of this incident can be found in the chapter 'A call from the White House', in *Escape to the Futures*, Leo Melamed, John Wiley & Sons, 1996.

not to help us, we will accept your decision." He then said, over my objections, that the White House communications chief, David Gergen, would call me to further the explanation.

Mr Gergen eventually did call. It was difficult for me, an immigrant, not to accept such a reasonable and "patriotic request," as Gergen put it. However, I did make three provisos: first, my report, *good or bad*, would be made strictly from what I learned from her trading; second, I would make no assessment as to how Ms Clinton made her decisions on what trades to make; and third, I would not delve into the relationship between Ms Clinton, James Blair or Tyson Foods. I also reserved the right to say nothing. To tell the truth, like most other people, I found myself siding with those who believed that something nefarious had occurred.

As promised, Hillary's trading records were delivered the following morning—I did not need them, nor did I trust that they were complete. Instead I asked the CME exchange to provide me with a complete record of her trading at the Refco firm. I then asked my special assistant, Alysann Posner, and the COO of my trading firm, Valerie Turner, to help me analyze the trades. After several days of review, our conclusion was that Ms Clinton was a small trader who had winners and losers and paid normal commissions.

On balance, she did well, and it was clear to me that she must have received expert advice before making any trade, presumably from Robert 'Red' Bone, the Refco broker who also conducted Jim Blair's trading. I asked Mr Bone to fly into Chicago and meet with me before I made my report. He agreed and ultimately confirmed the fact that he had discretion from Mr Blair to make the trades on behalf of Hillary. Mr Bone actually laughed after the interview, stating, "I don't know what the whole thing is about. She made one hundred grand—during that same timeframe, I made five million."

AN INFORMED JUDGMENT

The other thing I discovered was that out of some 32 important transactions, all but two were overnight positions. The distinction between a *day* trade and an *overnight* trade is material. If someone intended to allocate winning trades to a client, it would be done in a day-trade manner. One cannot control the result of an overnight transaction, since there can be no guarantee where the market will open the next day. Her positions were overnighters and at risk. Were there violations in her trading account? *Absolutely.* Hillary was thinly margined and, on some occasions, had insufficient margin to trade. But there was a catch.

As I later explained to John Podesta, nothing in the trades I examined reflected any violations on the part of Hillary Clinton. Margin violations and the like are never attributable to the customer. The exchange cannot expect customers of brokerage firms to know or understand the rules. That is the responsibility of the clearing firm.

I was, of course, well aware that I had found the perfect political solution for what Hillary was facing. I fully understood that there could be much more behind Hillary's profit in cattle. Nevertheless, I could state with a straight face that she personally had violated no regulations. I was not a political analyst, nor a psychiatrist, or a federal detective. And in the case of Refco, the CME firm where her trades were cleared, I was cognizant of the fact that the firm had a sordid record.

In fact, as Merc chair, I was instrumental back in 1979 of finding the Refco firm guilty of committing a multitude of margin and other trading violations. Hillary Clinton's account was so small it was not even visible on the Refco radar among the thousands of accounts in which violations occurred. But, again, Refco's violations were not attributable to their customers. Back in 1979, I authorized a fine of $250,000 against the firm, at the time the largest monetary punishment in CME history, and a six-month suspension to Tom Dittmer, Refco's chairman (although he was a friend of mine), as well as a three-year trading suspension to Red Bone.

A PATRIOTIC DUTY

John Podesta then asked if I would be so kind as to make a verbal report to the White House staff. I arrived the next day with Ms Posner. The scene was right out of the *West Wing* TV series, as I faced some 20 or so staff members which included David Gergen, White House counselor; George Stephanopoulos, senior presidential advisor; Lisa Caputo, Hillary's press secretary; and David Kendall, her attorney.

My report lasted about 30 minutes. Then, after a brief Q&A, David Gergen asked if I would be willing to submit my report in writing. I resisted at first, stating that I did not want to become a political analyst. "Besides," I said, "I am not really a true-blue Democrat." It was a fact, I was more an Independent than anything else. Indeed, when I organized the Merc's highly successful political action committee in 1976, I made certain that we divided our support more or less equally between democrats and republicans. David Gergen, known to be right of center, laughed at my objection. He retorted, "Do you think I am a democrat? You are not being asked as a democrat or a republican. You are doing this for the White House."

Ouch! As a refugee who found safety in America, and who considers himself an ardent patriot, I had no choice but to accept this patriotic rationale. Besides, as the saying goes, 'in for a penny, in for a pound.' Alysann and I soon found ourselves in a nearby room with a keyboard. Before we wrote the report, I called Tom Dittmer to explain what was being done. His only question was whether this would expose him again personally—I assured him that the beauty of his CME suspension and fine would dissuade the CFTC from going any further.

On April 22, 1994, Hillary Clinton held a press conference in the state dining room at the White House. It was broadcast live by all the networks. She reported what my independent examination had concluded and said that she relied on the trading advice of James Blair, a friend who was an expert futures trader. Having an advisor or consultant for trading is no violation—it is how much of futures are conducted. The matter, for all intents and purposes, was laid to rest. *Time* magazine called the press conference "open and candid." The *WSJ* ran an editorial stating that they would not argue with the expertise of Leo Melamed. The *Journal of Economics and Finance* of the University of North Florida, on the other hand, concluded that the odds of such a financial return in so short a time were 1 in 31trn.

CHAPTER 42

Revolt

D URING the next several years I remained in my private world. I was building a futures company named Sakura Dellsher—the result of Japanese bank Mitsui Taiyo Kobe (called Sakura) buying 60% of my small trading firm, Dellsher Investment Company. The competition for futures business was tough, but since I had exclusive rights to the bank's futures business, our new firm was doing very well.

However, all was not well on the floor. When I resigned in protest from the brand new Globex Corporation, I expected some negative fallout in the drive toward electronic trade. But as I understood it, the problems that evolved went far beyond Globex. It was believed by many that my absence from the trading floor, as well as the lack of my voice in the boardroom, served to have a negative effect on the fortunes of the Merc.

This grew into a major rift within the membership. Some went as far as telling me that an internal war was brewing. It wasn't that my presence in the boardroom was magical, but I knew the membership better than almost anyone— my presence on the board gave members comfort and someone to talk to about problems. That avenue was now missing.

PREFERENTIAL TREATMENT

There were a multitude of causes for the rising tension on the floor, but the main source was the old fight between local traders and brokers (order fillers). Specifically, a bitter schism had evolved between the so-called broker groups and that of independent traders (the locals). This division in our membership ranks was not new—it reared its ugly head during the FBI sting operation in 1989. The problem never rose to a level of federal crime, but nevertheless was hugely disruptive and often a violation of existing exchange rules. During my absence, it rose to an untenable level.

Beneath it all, the issue was dual trading, which gave every member the right to be both broker and trader for his own account. As I previously pointed out, dual trading was not a right limited to futures—it was an allowable tradition in other fields of business. But in futures, which is often conducted in the hectic conditions of a trading pit, it offered many opportunities to make money by virtue of unethical practices. You will recall that in the aftermath of the FBI sting, Bill Shepard and I had developed the top-step rule, which limited a broker's use of dual-trading privileges. For a number of years, the rule worked. However, the growth of broker groups severely cut down the top-step rule's effectiveness. Brokers found ways around it.

By definition and in practice, brokers controlled the incoming order flow, since they determined with whom they made the trade: another broker or a local. If they intentionally ignored a local in favor of a member of his own broker group, the local lost a profit opportunity. The broker with whom the trade was made suddenly became a local and the trade, if favorable, went to his personal account. This exploit kept growing. If an arrangement existed between the two brokers, they could split any resulting profit from the trade— or the broker-turned-local would reciprocate the action on another order. Further, if the local trader made noise about it or filed an official complaint, which some did, the broker could put out word to avoid trading with that local. In other words, fear of reprisal became a serious deterrent toward whistle blowing.

A survey made by the audit and compliance department determined that, yes, a large portion of business was executed between members of a given broker group to the exclusion of locals. When we put limitations on this practice, broker groups simply went beyond their own circle to make corresponding arrangements with other broker groups. Not only did this underhanded practice cause a serious loss of income to the local trader community, it was deleterious to open competition and therefore had a negative effect on liquidity. Obviously in an electronic environment, every trade is made on a first come, first serve basis. The ability to choose with whom to trade—an associate of your broker group, your brother-in-law, or girlfriend—is entirely removed.[131]

---

131 *Crain's Chicago Business*, Michael Fritz, August 5, 1996.

The exchange was, of course, aware of the problem and over the years tried to pass various rules limiting this broker-group advantage. But, short of banning the dual-trading capability, no rules seemed to effectively cure the broker's inherent advantage. Over time, this problem grew to an intolerable level and affected business flow to the Merc. From 1992 to 1996, the Merc's transaction volume fell precipitously. Equally significant was the fact that falling volume reflected badly on the value of CME, IMM and IOM memberships. During this timeframe, membership values fell by as much as 50%.[132] Suffice it to say, this was a critical reason for furthering the rupture between the two factions.

Likewise, when Globex was launched, the system too fell victim to the reality of this procedure. This was because the broker, or his group, could make the decision to trade with someone in the pit rather than use a terminal on the floor to execute an order on Globex. I don't think I need explain why Globex had only a very small volume during its fledgling existence. In truth, this became the central problem for Globex. The broker community held Globex hostage.

WORSENING RELATIONS

The locals knew that Globex could cure their disadvantage. But since I left Globex was not moving forward. Our technology team, led by Don Serpico and Jim Krause, who were absolutely the best in the business, were held back by the board's rule that nothing relating to Globex could proceed without the board's approval. After all, it was the same board that brought down the Globex Corporation.

As the locals saw it, the Merc was losing ground to world exchanges. Their original stance against technology had ameliorated and they were moving forward with plans to build electronic-transaction platforms—although these were Local Area Networks (LANs), rather than global systems. Still, the CME's first-mover advantage was being severely damaged.

There was also another issue which remained mostly unspoken for fear of reprisal by the brokers. It was known that Jack Sadner's clearing firm, RB&H, earned much of its income from the fact that many broker groups cleared their business there. This was also true of the Merc's largest broker group, the International Futures and Options Associates, in which it was believed that the

---

132 To adequately describe this distressing period of CME history required a book, which resulted in my writing *For Crying Out Loud*. John Wiley & Sons, 2009.

chairman owned a 10% interest.[133] The broker group affiliation put Jack and me at loggerheads. It was the reason our long-standing friendship fell apart for a number of years. It put us on separate poles on the destiny of Globex.

TAKING SIDES

In the fall of 1996, a group of alienated locals formed the Equity Owners Association (EOA) for the purpose of going public with the issues and gaining a stronger voice about the future of Globex.[134] Broker opposition to the EOA was immediate: they formed the National Alliance of Futures and Options Brokers. This resulted in a highly charged environment ready to boil over. As a consequence, the Globex war openly returned and Jack and I again fell further apart. On August 5, 1996, Michael Fritz of *Crain's Chicago Business* summed it up well:

> Independent traders at the Chicago Mercantile Exchange have long complained that powerful floor brokerage groups have too much clout and control of the action of the futures mart. Merc leaders downplay the criticism, insisting the exchange does a good job of ensuring a level playing field between independent traders and broker groups. But the Merc's position may resemble the fox guarding the hen house.

It was at this point that I was visited by a delegation from the EOA. They knew I was fully aware of the battle going on and wanted to ask whether I "would return to leadership of the CME?" I was not surprised and responded truthfully that, as everyone was aware, the CME board was controlled by broker elements. Unless there were sufficient votes to have a balanced board, it would be futile for me to return.

I suggested that they should create an EOA slate of candidates for the coming board election in January 1997. I counselled that the slate be composed of members of the highest ethical reputation, ones for whom I would be happy to lobby. I proposed that they should organize an all-out campaign to get the votes. The EOA delegation accepted the challenge and made me promise that if they

133 It was true and Jack Sandner was required to disinvest his interest. Crain's Chicago Business, Reuters, Dow Jones Commodities Service, December 9, 1996.
134 Original members of the EOA included: Bill Shepard, Don Karel, Joel Stender, Richard Ford, Steve Goodman, Joe Gressel, Sheldon Langer, and Kirk Malcolm.

were successful in unseating some of the broker elements that I would return. I agreed.[135]

The EOA slated their best candidates for election and an intensive campaign followed. I gave them my full support but concentrated on the election of a few who were in a weak position on that slate. In particular that meant Bill Shepard, who was most vocal in favoring Globex and an antagonist of Chairman Sandner.

I gave it my all. My special efforts on behalf of Bill Shepard proved successful. He squeaked in by no more than a handful of votes. In landslide proportions, the EOA got the support of a majority of the membership. Fifty percent of the hard-bitten broker elements were ousted from the board—an unprecedented result.

BACK AT THE HELM

At the very first meeting of the new board, I was unanimously appointed as an additional board member in the *permanent* role of chairman emeritus—and for emphasis, I was made senior policy adviser too. The word permanent was insisted upon before the vote. On the following morning, the *Chicago Tribune* business-page headline announced: "Melamed returns to power at the Merc".[136] Three days later, they called it, "Leo's second coming."[137]

Jack Sandner still had one more year as chairman and, being no fool, he reached out to me. In turn, I had a decision to make. I could turn my back on Jack, let him finish his term but keep him ostracized. That would be satisfying for me as the winner, but it would continue the war and perhaps interfere with what I wanted to achieve. On the other hand, I could turn the other cheek, get some promises and lead the Merc to the promised land.

I knew that to lead it was necessary to have unity rather than strife, so I chose the former. In doing so I was fully aware that Jack would likely be central to the take down of the Globex Corporation. I could never forgive that action. But my return was not to take revenge, it was to put the Merc back on track and I was going to devote 100% of my effort towards rejuvenating Globex. Jack and I met at the Drake Hotel for a four-hour dinner meeting to iron things out and bury the hatchet. Once again, Sandner officially embraced my leadership and my vision for Globex. While our friendship never returned to the way it was, we

---

135 See *For Crying Out Loud* for full description.
136 George Gunset, *Chicago Tribune*, January 23, 1997.
137 George Gunset, *Chicago Tribune*, January 26, 1997.

worked together and were almost always on the same side of important issues. Sandner became pro-Globex again.

The first action I took upon returning to leadership in 1997 was to pass a board resolution called the *technology emancipation policy*. In other words, I wanted our board, our staff and our members to know that the past was no more. From this day forward, Globex takes highest priority. It was precisely what our tech guys needed. The second thing I did was negotiate Fred Arditti's return to the CME fold. To my overwhelming joy, he did later that year.

The third action I took was to create the Globex oversight committee, appointing an inner group who I trusted to guide the technical development of Globex. The committee included three of my strongest Globex supporters: Jimmy Oliff, Bill Shepard and Barry Lind. Also on the committee was Rick Kilcollin, an early advocate for electronic trade, who helped develop the PMT (later Globex) electronic system and provided critical assistance in proving that the 1987 stock crash was never the CME's fault.

It also included our technology experts: Jim Krause and Don Serpico. As I often stated, they were supreme technicians without whose talent and expertise it is highly unlikely that the development of Globex would have moved forward at the speed it did. They applauded the technological emancipation decree that I issued upon my return, which allowed them and our members to invent and innovate the technology of Globex without interference. They are to be credited with the actual creation of the Globex mechanism, applying their professional skills to achieve the revolution I was espousing.

No sooner had I explained my idea, they made it happen. It was a love affair. Their talents in technology made our electronic transaction system the most advanced in the world. Without their efforts, Globex might not have ever gotten off the ground. Consequently, Globex became one of a kind, with truly incredible functionality and unprecedented capabilities that the world followed and copied.

The CME's main volume came from the eurodollar contract, where the majority of the brokers were dyed-in-the-wool anti-Globex. Unfortunately, there was no method to control where trades were executed. That decision was still in the hands of the broker community. Business in eurodollars continued in open outcry fashion as before. In other words, the broker community was still in control and boycotted Globex.

It is impossible today with the entire world of markets totally electrified to imagine that there actually was a time, not so long ago, when but a precious few saw the vision of market electrification. The status quo is an unbelievably powerful force. I was not alone in the world battling for technological advancement though. I must say that Michael Bloomberg, in a parallel vein in the 1980s, visualized a similar transformation as it related to computer software in financial information. Michael R. Bloomberg was the 2008 recipient of the CME Melamed-Arditti Innovation Award.

A NATURAL WINNER

Fast forward with me, if you will. Proof of what I was predicting was on its way. By 1996, LIFFE had become the biggest futures exchange in Europe, followed by the MATIF in France—both exchanges were committed to open outcry.

Two years later, in 1998, the German DTB and the Swiss (SOFFEX) exchanges merged to form the European Exchange, Eurex. Because the DTB was launched as an electronic exchange, Eurex adopted the system. LIFFE's most successful contract was the Bund, a ten-year German-government bond instrument. In 1997, Eurex listed an identical Bund contract on their electronic system.

I spent some time with Sir Brian Williamson, LIFFE's chairman, cautioning him that Eurex will ultimately take away the LIFFE's Bund contract, simply because open outcry would naturally lose out to automation. And while I considered Williamson a very smart fellow, he was fixated, as was nearly everyone else, on the fact that the London Bund contract was extremely liquid. "Surely," he said, "London's liquidity would be the determining factor."

It was not. As we learned, liquidity can be created on the screen and is much cheaper to trade. By mid 1997, Eurex had less than 25% of the Bund contract; by October, it had more than 50%; a couple of months later, the fight was over.

To Williamson's credit, he wasted no time in recognizing the truth. It is said he spent $100m on converting LIFFE into an all-electronic exchange, called Euronext LIFFE. On November 24, 2000, open outcry ended in the UK. This saved LIFFE but not its Bund instrument, which became Eurex's prime trader. The LIFFE exchange never got back its Bund contract.

THE UNEXPECTED

In 1999, on the eve of the new millennium, I published the following manifesto for our membership and in particular, for our obstinate broker communit:

> "The evidence today is overwhelming that the twenty-first century will be dominated by the information standard. Today, millions of transistors are etched on wafers of silicon. On these microchips, all of the world's

information can be stored in digital form and transmitted to every corner of the globe via the internet. It is no leap in logic to assume, as many have, that information technology will be to the twenty-first century what electricity was to the twentieth century. The Digital Age will change, and is changing, the way we live, work, play—and the way the markets work. The markets of the future will be automated. The traders of the future will trade by way of the screen. Those who dare ignore this reality face extinction. Today's cyber-wizards have combined the magic of all electricity and physics to produce a sorcery that can carry a computer command, the human voice, or virtually any program including market information, quotations, analysis, and market orders from anywhere to anywhere at a speed of about three-quarters of the way to the moon with every second. And progress will be continuous and unyielding.

By unplugging us from existing infrastructures, networks of information and communication hook-ups, we will suddenly have many more choices about where we live, work, or how we trade. Telephones as we knew them will soon be history. Everyone will be connected, carrying small pocket devices that will not only be used to communicate, but as a computer, or a fax, or to download money, or to trade. The new technology will have merged the computer, communications, and the internet into a small wireless marvel. Wireless e-mail in the twenty-first century will be the dominant personal telecommunications instrument and the trading mechanism of choice. Tiny chips might even be implanted in our bodies that could act as a universal credit card, passport, driver's license, or even to transmit buy and sell orders.[138] Surely, national and economic borders which have already been blurred, may dissolve completely, as communication satellites enable consumers and traders to do transactions in cyberspace. And now that we have seen the birth of the Euro, representing a single currency for much of the European zone, and there is serious talk of a similar Dollar zone for the Americas, perhaps in the twenty-first century a one world currency will evolve—digital money.

To be sure, the cyberspace age will cause an enormous shift of power from the producer to the user. Technology is a force for democracy and individual empowerment. The consumer will become king because the internet changes the old rules. Consumers who don't like what they see will just click and move on to the next screen. Those corporations who are currently merging and betting that bigger is better may be looking in

138 *The Tenth Planet*, by Leo Melamed, published in 1987.

the rear-view mirror to find they are completely wrong. With the cost of entry lower and easy access to the global marketplace via the internet, competition may come from smaller entities with a flexibility to offer innovative services.

While all of this is exciting and promising, I must conclude by injecting a note of caution: 'the only certainty about the future is to expect the unexpected—which, by definition, is unpredictable.'"

With the benefit of hindsight, my predictions for the future were mostly right on. What I failed to include was the most serious danger: Global Warming. This represents a problem that will affect every aspect of the entire planet.

CHAPTER 43

The E-mini

T HE entry of futures into the US equities arena was a dramatic moment in our history. Many said this, but most memorably, those were the words of Myron Scholes on April 21, 1982. The S&P contract was like the bride we romanced until finally we stood under the *chuppah* at 444 West Jackson, in Chicago, Illinois.[139]

To say the least, the S&P futures contract was an instant and huge success. For comparison, the most traded futures contract in the world, eurodollars, took almost four years to gain credibility and volume. The S&P contract did it maybe in *four days*. It provided us with transactional volume we never had before and gave us clientele we could not even dream of. Exactly a decade after the IMM's birth, the CME had become big time.

THE RETURN OF A FAMILIAR PROBLEM

Right from the start, I had nagging reservations about the size of the contract. Was it too big? It reminded me of the size issue I encountered back in the launch of currencies. I was influenced by the commercial world to create large contracts that were the norm in the cash markets. Then it was bank traders who urged me to launch a big contract, something on the order of $400–500 value. This was the size traded in the FX spot market. Now it was the equity market advisers

---

139   *Chuppah* is a canopy under which a Jewish couple stands during their wedding ceremony.

who similarly wanted very large S&P contracts. I recall how the FX market had liquidity problems until the FX size was made much smaller.

I was not alone in questioning whether the S&P specifications created too large a contract. Others saw it too. With a multiplier of $500, it represented a notional value of $500,000 per contract. This size cut out the average investor, who could not trade or use a unit so large. Of course, unlike in FX, the S&P contract was an immediate winner and the credo 'if it's not broken, don't fix it' won out. Having no competition, we did nothing and for the next 15 years the S&P prospered.

All of a sudden, it became imperative to review the issue. The Dow company was under new management and very envious of the success the S&P company enjoyed. Their new board unanimously voted to go into futures. Who would win the Dow contract, the CME or the CBOT, became the hottest topic on the street. But one thing was certain, if the CBOT won, our very large S&P contract might end up with a sore thumb. We had to protect ourselves, and the idea of cutting our size in half became a popular defense. I too was in favor of the split, but the knot in my gut remained. I still believed that it would be far too large for the average equity player.

Nevertheless, after 15 years of debate, we moved to change the existing S&P contract by reducing the multiplier to $250, halving our S&P contract to the size it is today. In other words, a two-for-one split. This was easy to put into practice, since it meant that all positions were doubled. We waived all immediate commissions too, a move that was applauded by the equity players.

THE CBOT VS THE CME

Our proposal to the Dow included an explanation as to why they should go with the CME: we had the practical advantage. A Dow futures contract would develop much more quickly at the CME, as opposed to the CBOT, because it would provide instant spread trade between this new contract and the established S&P contract. This argument was very true; new markets did develop quicker when traders had the ability to spread their risk into another similar contract or asset class.

The CBOT countered that they represented the largest futures exchange in the world and that a Dow contract would never play second fiddle to the S&P like it would at the CME. They asserted that a Dow contract would become top dog at the CBOT and get the full attention of its marketing, as well as its trader's prowess.

That was a telling argument to the Dow people, but it was flawed. CBOT traders were mostly occupied with the hugely successful grain trade, and no one could be certain whether they would exchange their habitat for the new product. In contrast, the IMM was known to have a large trader contingent who were willing to put money where their mouth was in support of new products. We had earned our stripes as the innovative exchange. The CME also had the IOM, which was a new division I took a page out of my IMM book and created a new division specifically designed for new traders limited to options and indexes.

Nevertheless, Pat Arbor (CBOT chairman) was very persuasive and offered the Dow company a premium, reportedly of $100,000, to sign with them—an impressive amount of money in those days. We refused to follow suit and the CBOT won the bidding contest.

The media made a real big deal of this CBOT victory. The Dow index, after all, is the way the world measures movement of equities—watching what the Dow does on any given day is the way an average person follows the market. Many Merc traders agreed with this rationale and took the loss as a real bad hit. The media prognostications sent our membership morale, as well as our CME seat value, spinning downward. To members, the value of membership is the main thermometer of an exchange's future.

PREPARING FOR DISASTER

It was true, we lost an important battle—the first loss in our expansive history. It was also true that the Dow was the best-known name in the world of equities. Still, I believed institutional equity managers measured value with the S&P index, and that was not about to change.

But the problem was serious. The prospective CBOT-Dow product would be a much smaller size than our S&P contract, even if we split our S&P product in half again.[140] In other words, the Dow futures contract would very likely be more attractive to the general public. In creating liquidity, there is no denying that the retail universe in equities is much, much bigger than the institutional crowd. A fact that the CBOT wasted no time in promoting.

This was having an impact even before the contract was launched. I had to

---

140 The original S&P product was based on a 500 multiple, making each contract worth about $500,000. There was only a very limited universe that could afford to use this product. In other words, it was designed to attract the commercial user. Even after the split, each contract was valued at about $250,000. On the other hand, since the Dow only represented 30 stocks, its futures contract value would be about $50,000 and be attractive to a much larger universe of users.

accept that the loss of the Dow was real and maybe even critical for the CME. However, do not underestimate the Bialystok Syndrome that my mother had ingrained in me. It said: "Always be prepared for a disaster lurking around the next corner."

From the outset of this competitive battle, I had the feeling that the Dow Jones company would buy into the CBOT's top-dog argument. It was the kind of argument that a big company understood, even though I knew from experience that the spreading factor was huge and, in many instances, the determining influence. But I could not rely on this, nor prove it to be the case. And there was so much at stake.

To prepare for the worst, long before the Dow decision was made against us, I secretly devised a defense in case we lost. It was a two-tiered plan, daring and very radical, but with huge potential.

PLAN B

As stated, the defense had two parts. The first relatively easy, its second incredibly difficult. I only spoke about it to my three confidants, Fred Arditti, Barry Lind and Jerrold Salzman. Indeed, its second part could not be divulged until after the first was initiated. It was an instance where Salzman's support was critical—without it, I could not proceed. I expected some pushback but received none. In fact, Jerry immediately embraced the idea.

Fred Arditti called it brilliant and said that if executed, "the action will be historic." Barry Lind also loved the proposal. In fact, he wanted us to institute both parts at once. I explained why that was impossible. Once the CBOT news was out, I formed a tiny inner-elite advisory group, adding Bill Shepard and Rick Kilcollin, to explain the idea.

Part one was for the CME to create a brand-new S&P instrument—a mini S&P, one fifth the size of the halved S&P contract. It would be designed specifically for the retail trade and its notional value would be about $50,000 per unit. It would be designed to compete with the forthcoming Dow contract. No one to my knowledge had thought of the idea and that it could be the perfect defense.

Since there was no such index, I explained that I had privately met with S&P executives to explore the idea. I convinced them that such a contract would be the perfect competitive response to the CBOT-DOW product. I explained that it would protect the S&P's name and the CME's future. The miniature size should be attractive to the retail universe and a healthy arbitrage trade should hopefully develop between the big and the little. The S&P executives asked a number of questions which I answered, and although they would have to go to the S&P board, they saw no impediment to follow through. Their only concern was whether they could make the time table I suggested which was "in time to launch when the CBOT plans to launch theirs which I understand to be September." I was quite certain that my advisory group would like the idea although no one could be certain how effective it would be. I said nothing about the second part, keeing it to myself. The plan was unanimously embraced.

To proceed with the second part of the idea required favorable legal determination. I went to Jerry Salzman. Jerry felt quite certain we were on solid ground but wanted some research time. It was a thought I harbored from the very moment Globex was born. In the back of my mind was the knowledge that to succeed with electronic trade, we had to ultimately prove that liquidity could be produced electronically. That factor was always the most critical problem. The world was totally, and I mean totally, convinced that liquidity could only be achieved in a pit with eyeball-to-eyeball competitive confrontation. It was the same conclusion I had reached when I first broached the subject ten years back. In short order I learned otherwise. It became my unshakeable opinion that this was a fallacy. But how could I prove it? From the very beginning, I knew that in order to prove my case I would have to find a live condition. What was needed was a product that would trade electronically during regular trading hours (RTH).

THE FINER DETAILS

I realized that the CBOT winning the new Dow contract might actually be the opportunity I sought. However, it presented a legal conundrum. Ten years back, in 1987, when the referendum to launch an electronic transaction vehicle was approved, it contained one special clause. The provision guaranteed that no product currently being traded in open outcry would ever be listed electronically during RTH—unless first approved by the membership. In other words, our currency complex, as well as our financial and agricultural products, were safe from electronic competition during RTH. The prohibition guaranteed that traders were safe from electronic encroachment on their income from the products they presently trade, unless they approve otherwise.

To launch the mini S&P on Globex, I needed to contend and prove that it was a brand-new product and not one protected by the referendum. Either way I believed a referendum would be required. But, as Jerry and I saw it, would anyone suggest that soybean meal and soybean oil were the same product as soybeans? Or cornmeal, the meal ground from dried maize, derived from corn, the same product as corn? The CBOT lists them as different products for trade.

I could go on and on, and Jerry could do much better, but it became our solid opinion that the mini S&P we proposed was not the same as the S&P 500 contract we had been trading since 1982. We were in complete agreement that we would be required to apply to the CFTC for approval before it was traded. Yes, the mini proposed was related to the big S&P contract, but only in the way that the earth is related to the sun—they are different bodies in our solar system.

The large S&P contract was clearly directed at an institutional trade for hedging purposes, the mini was sized for the retail trade. The mini S&P had brand-new specifications—the S&P company would undoubtedly have to devise a new product and together we would have to agree a new contract. They even needed to give us a new license. Besides all that, we were not touching the big contract, which would continue to trade in open outcry fashion and be available for spreading.

When I asked Jerry whether he was prepared to go to court if necessary, his unequivocal answer was in the affirmative—and that we would win.

ANOTHER DO-OR-DIE REFERENDUM

To be clear, my idea went far beyond simply launching a S&P mini instrument. I believed this was our opportunity to launch a fully electronic contract. We called it the S&P E mini. It would be the first instrument traded electronically on Globex during the open outcry trading session and beyond. It would thus become the first instrument to trade on a 24-hour basis.

Barry Lind became my principal co-conspirator. Not only was he thoroughly steeped in the evolution of futures markets, he and I had the same unshakable belief in the future of electronic trade. One more point, his firm's customers were predominantly retail traders. Lind's strong opinion that his customers would actually prefer an electronic venue was the corner-stone of my championing a Globex listing for this mini contract.[141]

Another do-or-die referendum on the challenging journey to electronic trade. And if we lost, we would have to go to court. A fight with our membership was the last thing I wanted.

I went to my advisory group one by one: first to Fred Arditti, who always viewed things in an historical perspective, then the others. Fred said I was taking

---

141 Barry Lind was fatally struck by a car on January 24, 2013, in Southern California.

an historic step—one that needed to be taken and, in his words, "would change markets forever." He called it "heroic." The advisory members were fully on board.

With all my ducks in a row, I went to the Merc board to ask for approval. The meeting went on well into the night, with me explaining the concept and answering questions. Salzman and I were at our best. We received unanimous approval. I then made another request: that the board establish an E-mini board with me as its appointed chairman. That done, Rick Kilcollin, Jerry Salzman and I flew off to New York to gain a long-term license for the new E-mini. Within a week, we had a deal.

VICTORY

But would we win the referendum? Would the majority of our membership agree that the E-mini does not violate the 1987 referendum? As word spread about our plan, a revolt began to build. Wasn't this the ultimate threat to open outcry? The first live missile directed at pit-trading? I realized that this may very well be the case. It was, after all, the reason why I had put the membership approval clause into the original PMT referendum. I lived and breathed E-mini. I became an obsessed evangelist—the Billy Graham of finance—with but one holy mission:

> Wasn't this a step in the direction the world was moving? Wasn't this the exact reason I was returned to the CME board? Was it not my mission to convince the CME floor community that telecommunications had fashioned a global marketplace which demanded around-the-clock trading mechanisms? That by ignoring this truth they would simply be inviting the same fate that has historically befallen all who would deny the advances of technology? Those who were deaf to the thundering maelstrom of the technological avalanche around us? And that if we as leaders failed to take the indicated action to preserve our future, would we not be guilty of misfeasance or worse?[142]

In other words, I was all in and betting the ranch that liquidity would follow. Once again, my credibility was on the line.

I organized a floor marketing campaign together with members of the new E-mini board. We held meetings with members individually as well as in groups, on the floor, and offsite. We argued, cajoled, and implored. I called in all the chits

---

142 *For Crying Out Loud*, by Leo Melamed, John Wiley & Sons, 2009.

accumulated over the years. I went to speak directly to all relevant committees. I gave it my all.

When we held the mandatory open members meeting to discuss the subject prior to the referendum, the anti-E-mini crowd was very vocal. There were even some members who threatened a court battle. But fate smiled on me. At the end of the day, the majority of members approved.

This was not simply revolutionary. It was what Arditti called "heroic." The only way to prove to the world that electronic trade can create liquidity. If successful, it would, once and for all, settle the critical question of whether an electronic venue could generate sufficient liquidity to be a viable alternative to open outcry. It led the whole world, both futures and securities, to the promised electronic land. This was a defining moment in the battle against the status quo. And as Arditti said, it would change the history of markets forever.

THE FINAL HURDLE

There remained two other considerations. The CBOT had targeted a September launch for their new Dow instrument. If the CME was successfully going to compete, we had to be ready with our E-mini product in the same time frame. I huddled with Jim Krause, the head of our technology department, who was a straight shooter and a one-of-a-kind techie expert—he never disappointed me.

Krause stated that my emancipation policy for Globex advanced the Merc's technology far beyond what anyone could have expected and assured me that we could be ready for a September launch. We actually launched the E-mini several days before the CBOT.

There was still one more wrinkle to be ironed out. It was Bill Shepard who conceived of the great idea. It took only one conversation with Shepard for me to agree to his suggestion. Since the primary reason for the failure of new futures instruments was lack of liquidity, Bill had an idea to help assure liquidity right from day one of the E-mini launch. He convinced me that we should create a floor-based arbitrage unit for chosen traders who would provide immediate liquidity to the E-mini during RTH arbitrage between the small and big contracts.

It was a marvelous, innovative idea that I readily accepted. I authorized Bill to build a special section on the floor abutting the S&P pit which could hold the necessary screens and apparatus for arbitrage, a keyboard for input to Globex, and visibility for hand signals to the pit. Bill appointed a limited number of volunteers to act as official E-mini arbitrageurs. It worked like magic.

BIRTH OF THE E-MINI

The IMM's E-mini S&P 500 was launched on September 9, 1997. It was the first US and global futures instrument for electronic trade on a 24-hour basis. I got Richard A. Grasso, NYSE chairman, and Harold McGraw III, president of the McGraw-Hill companies (the new S&P owners), to do the historic ceremonial bell-ringing.

To say it was an instant success cannot begin to describe the triumph it represented. It recorded 8,000 transactions, the highest number of opening-day trades in the history of futures trading. It quickly became the dominant after-hours Globex instrument, as well as the equity market's directional indicator. Shepard's addition was no doubt an important factor in its immediate success. But most important, it proved that Globex can produce liquidity, with or without arbitrage. The following was my assessment to the members:

> The impact of the E-mini far, far outweighed its record volume. It constituted a watershed in the history of markets, single-handedly making Globex a household name in financial markets and forever changing the course of futures. Without fear of contradiction, the E-mini was the springboard for the CME's future success, putting our exchange indelibly on the world's modern financial map. It forever proved that an electronic platform could generate sufficient liquidity to support a futures instrument and act as alternative to open outcry. In a relatively short time-span, the E-mini-S&P 500 stock-index contract, whose volumes continued to soar, became the US equity market's directional leader— the price discovery 'pit' for equities. It also served as the compass for all markets, bringing the imperative of 'electronics' to the top of everyone's agenda—be it in futures, options, or securities. Not only were there a rash of new electronic mini products throughout the world. More than that, virtually no new contract at the CME (of any significance) was ever again launched other than on Globex. And of critical value: the success of Globex served as the foundation for the hugely successful IPO for the CME a couple of years later.[143]

143 Ibid.

CHAPTER 44

Diverse, Strong and Vital

THE education of officials—movers and shakers, elected or appointed, from both within the US or foreign domiciles—was key to establishing the dynamic role that futures markets play in the development of capital markets. I understood this from the moment I was elected chairman in 1969 to the day I retired in 2018.

It is said that reputation can take years to build and can be destroyed in an instant. This is true, but there is more to it. A positive image, while difficult to achieve, can become a nearly immovable force—unless you do something outrageously stupid, and then it becomes irretrievable.

Today, the CME's image is based on its diverse coverage in risk management, financial strength, safety in clearing, and unequalled speed and integrity in trade execution. In other words, the Merc became diverse, strong and vital to the US economy. This was achieved step by step in countless ways over the span of five decades. And the trading floors were a big part of it. Alas, they are gone now.

TRANSFORMATION

The collective noise of several thousand traders was replaced by the silence of a computer. Globex, which made trading faster, safer, unlimited in volume, and significantly cheaper, replaced the human factor. But there was a price to pay; we lost two important attributes that the floor inherently possessed: the creative atmosphere, the floor was often a crucible of new ideas, and the unique wow-factor that had defined futures for centuries.

That instant and lasting shock felt when you first saw an enormous crowd of human beings in colorful jackets, jammed together in pits and shouting at each other at the top of their lungs, was no more. Curiously, this sight maintains a long afterlife—to this day the media still flashes old floor shots when speaking about futures.

However, it did not take me long to realize that the computer silence could also become a characteristic of great value. The Merc's second trading floor, once housing the immense eurodollar pit complex, containing up to 1,000 traders and offering ten years of 90-day interest-rate coverage, had been transformed into the CME Global Command Center. Today, it is a vast expanse of technology, housing hundreds of silent computer screens which provide a continuous flow of technical information and monitor the millions of Globex transactions across the entire world.

There are people on that floor as well, but they say nary a word as they perform market operations and customer service for the CME's Globex electronic-trading platforms. This silent image provides a wow-factor too. I often bring dignitaries to the site and it never fails to impress. When showing the Command Center to US Senate majority leader Mitch McConnell, his immediate reaction was, "Wow! Is there anything like this anywhere else in the world?"

Needless to say, the CME can boast of an electronic transaction system that is second to none, with a supremely low record of outages. We have also provided a commitment to building what amounts to a cutting-edge system in global cyber security, which has become a primary concern in many industries but particularly in financial services. Real-time global-security monitoring, sophisticated protection mechanisms, and an instantaneous response, are now table stakes for a company like the CME; it is pivotal that the CME recognize their role in the global economy, as well as the importance of protecting their customers.

PROTECT YOUR INTERESTS

As mentioned before, the CME's image was immensely enhanced by the organization of a voluntary political action committee (PAC), which was formed under my direction in 1976.[144] The idea of a PAC came from a conversation I had with Bill Bagley, the first chairman of the newly formed CFTC. He was appointed in 1974 by President Gerald Ford. Aside from wowing Bill with our trading floor, his visit served another purpose.

144 First organized as the Commodity Futures Political Action Committee (CFPF) in 1976.

Bagley, a very nice guy and somewhat of a card, had not a clue about our markets. He freely admitted this. Such down-to-earth honesty was unusual for Washington and made it easy for me to become his friend. Bagley quickly realized that I was at the top of this pyramid and named me his spiritual guru.

This did have a downside though. Once, in Mirabelle, a London Michelin-starred haute-cuisine restaurant, Bagley spotted me across the room, waved, fell to his knees and, to the consternation of everyone watching, waddled across the floor until he got to my table. From there, he took my hand, kissed my imaginary ring and, in a stage whisper, said: "Thank you godfather."

But Bagley, a former California State Assembly member, knew quite a bit about politics. He quickly realized that future markets had little or no voice or presence in the Congressional legislative process. "Lee," he said to me after visiting our trading floor, "if your market is to become as big and important as you believe, you will need people in Washington DC who can tell your story and protect your interests. That will take some money."

What he was saying was that the Merc would need a voluntary PAC. I asked if he would speak to our membership and explain why this was necessary, and why they should support and voluntarily contribute to such a committee. He agreed. He addressed a room packed with some 500 members and did a terrific job. The rest is history. To this day, the PAC is one of our most important and successful undertakings, providing the CME Group with a voice and presence in the federal legislative process.

Right from the start, we introduced a proviso: "every elected official that we supported has to agree to pay us a visit to our trading floor." This provided us with a unique opportunity to bring to the floor elected officials and explain first-hand how the markets worked and how they contributed to the general economy. The program left the visiting guest with a priceless educational lesson, one that could never be duplicated through textbooks.

Of equal importance, these programs served to invigorate our members' political interest. A photo opportunity with a political official was a priceless memento and an incentive to continue their voluntary contributions.

EXPANSION

The Commodity Futures Political Fund (CFPF), now the CME Group PAC, became an invaluable tool for getting to know our Congressmen and gaining their respect. It raised the profile of our exchange. We took it one step further. We realized that although one visit to our Chicago home was important, our continuous presence would be much more effective. Accordingly, we moved to establish a Washington DC office.

This required us to hire someone who knew the ins and outs of Washington and could carry forward our message as well as be on guard for problems as they arose. As previously noted, we found and appointed Dayle Hennington, a 30-year Washington DC veteran and former chief of staff for William Poage, chairman of the House agriculture committee—which had become the watchdog over future markets. Hennington turned out to be the perfect choice.

He was affable, smart, respected, seemingly knew nearly everyone in D.C., and was flawless in bringing us to meet with the necessary officials as it related to legislative matters affecting our industry. Dayle even persuaded the US House agriculture chairman, Eligio 'Kika' de La Garza II, to allow the Merc to use the spacious House hearing room for an annual reception for members of the US Congress—a custom that continued unabated until very recently. In my opinion, this ritual should not have been abandoned.

FAMOUS FACES AT THE EXCHANGE

Our floor visitation program was so successful that at the suggestion of Congressman Dan Rostenkowski, leader of the Illinois Congressional delegation, the CBOT soon followed our lead. The program then quickly expanded to serve another purpose. Why not extend this rationale further and invite prominent dignitaries who were visiting Chicago? Such visitations would attract media coverage for our visitors as well as raise the visibility of Chicago exchanges. There can be no doubt that the CME, CBOT, and CBOE were vital to earning Chicago its international status. It is what I predicted and promised Mayor Daley.

Not counting the innumerable visits by US Senators, Congressmen and their staff, the CME hosted a multitude of national and international dignitaries and officials of every brand. The Merc's image as an innovative enterprise was greatly enhanced. The visibility and favorable PR we achieved is impossible to estimate. Beginning in 1975 with the visit by Hubert Humphrey, the Democratic candidate for vice president of the United States, there was a steady stream of US presidents and vice presidents, as well as foreign heads of state, visiting the Chicago exchanges.

Our guest list is impressive. Among the names are: Ernesto Zedillo, president of Mexico (1977); Li Xiannian, president of China (1980); Ronald Reagan, US president (1985); Robert J. L. Hawke, prime minister of Australia (1988); Mary Robinson, president of Ireland (1991); George H. W. Bush, US president (1991);

Mikhail Gorbachev, president of the Soviet Union (1992); William J. Clinton, US president (1998); Zhu Rongji, premier of the People's Republic of China and Keizo Obuchi, prime minister of Japan (1999); George W. Bush, US president (2001); and Richard B. Cheney, US vice president (2006).

Visits from US presidents to our floor were, of course, very special. Each visit generated enormous amounts of publicity before, during, and after, which was great for the Merc's image. Not many exchanges or institutions representing the free-market ideal had this kind of honor. It lifted the spirit of our traders and offered many of them a photo-op that would last a lifetime. More importantly, I believe that the spirit of each president also seemed to be lifted. After all, they were seeing first-hand an exceptional American institution—the scene of our traders shouting, applauding and trying to shake the official's hand leaves a strong impression, not quickly forgotten.

In the case of Ronald Reagan's visit, you could cut the excitement with a knife. Reagan visited the Merc twice. First, during his campaign for election and then later as president. We became personal friends. He was a staunch believer in free-market capitalism and recognized that the Merc and its traders epitomized that ideal. It also created a special relationship for me. In fact, I became a strong member of his team and was high among the members of his Illinois election effort.

Zhu Rongji's visit in 1999 was also of special consequence, because China's phenomenal development was finally getting widespread global attention. The world took note that once again China's head of state came to Chicago and the CME. And, for me, it presented an additional challenge, to help China understand the value of futures in advancing their embryonic capital markets.

LEAVING MY MARK

To explain and raise the value of futures had become my *raison d'etre*—my reason for being. I cannot place the moment it happened, but, quite literally, I became the futures market evangelist. I was Paul the Apostle, Billy Graham and David Livingstone all wrapped up in one, proselytizing on the value of futures and free markets. I took the word 'international' literally in the IMM title, by preaching futures markets everywhere in the world, and assisting or extending a nation's domestic financial prowess by helping it build a futures component.

I dare say that my fingerprints, my voice, my presence, my writings, my advice and my ideas, from the 1970s to my retirement, can be found across the globe.

It began with the UK in 1973, directly after the birth of the IMM, when John Berkshire, a British money broker, came to Chicago to ask about helping him create another exchange. I encouraged him to do so and agreed to help—this became the LIFFE. In 1980, I was invited by the Deutsche Bundesbank, the central bank of the Republic of Germany in Frankfurt, to speak to them on why they should consider overturning their rules against gambling and allow the launch of a futures market. That discussion led to the creation of the Deutsche Terminbörse, which later merged with the Swiss Options exchange to become Eurex, the largest futures market on mainland Europe.

I also went to Japan several times to establish the Merc's credentials. In particular, in 1988, when I journeyed to Japan with Sandner and CME president Clayton Yeutter to execute an historic agreement between the CME and the Nihon Keizai Shimbun enterprise. This was for the CME's exclusive license to trade futures contracts on the Nikkei stock average in Chicago. This idea of mine was virgin territory; imagine, the revolutionary listing of a foreign stock index on the shores of another country.

And in France, in March 1989, when I signed an agreement with Gérard Pfauwadel, chairman of *Marché à Terme International de France* (MATIF), on their exchange joining Globex. And in February 1994, when I went to Brazil at the invitation of officials from the *Bolsa de Mercadorias e Futuros* (BM&F) to promote their launch. And in Mexico City, in May 1995, to encourage its officials to embrace futures and the free markets and help them devise a futures market. And in Kuala Lumpur, November 1995, to advise the government of Malaysia about their need for futures.

And in 1996, when I was invited to be honored by In-Kie Hong, chairman of the South Korea stock exchange, for acting as their advisor in assisting the creation and listing of the KOSPI, the Korean stock index for trade. Within a year, I was in Taipei to celebrate the opening of the TAIFEX, the futures exchange in Taiwan. They had convinced me to help create their market and show the world that unlike their brethren in China, they embrace the free-market ideal. I was happy to oblige.

And in India, in 1998, where, together with the brilliant Professor Kshama Fernandes, I helped to develop their Nifty 50 Indian stock index for futures and promote its listing on the electronic venue of the National Stock Exchange of India (NSE).

And in Israel, in 2009, at the behest of Milton Friedman, I met with Benjamin Netanyahu, then finance minister, which resulted in the listing of their currency, the shekel, for futures trade on Globex. Finally, my ongoing efforts to develop and expand futures markets in China. In September 2006, I effectively created the China Financial Futures Exchange (CFFEX) in Shanghai and in March 2018, I established the International Energy Exchange (INE) for crude oil futures—

with the honor of being the only foreigner on the stage who dared to speak about opening China's borders to foreign competition.

A RETURN TO RUSSIA

My visit to Russia in 1989 was also of great importance. I was contacted by an emissary of Mikhail Gorbachev, the president of Russia, with a request: "Would I consider meeting with the president to discuss creating a futures market in Moscow?"

Imagine that? The bastion of communism that had enslaved half the world's population for nearly a century was crumbling and could no longer hide the truth about empty stores, rotting wheat and potatoes, collapsing roads and buildings, and its desperate people. Their leader asking for help from this refugee capitalist, who had miraculously escaped from their world to help build a better one, one based on the principles of free markets.

I agreed and the following year actually led a delegation to Moscow composed of officials from the Merc and the CBOT, the captains of capitalism.[145] Of course, it was all for show and nothing came of it. But, for me, personally, it was historic. On November 1, 1990, this refugee, who escaped the clutches of both Adolph Hitler and Joseph Stalin, delivered a full-blown free-market capitalist address to a very large audience within the shadow of the Kremlin walls.

As I said, nothing happened as a result of my visit, but we were treated well. What we witnessed was a poor country with a sad history, empty stores and long lines. One of the highlights was a meeting with Gorbachev's finance minister, Leonid Abalkin, when I managed to swipe a bottle-opener with the crest of the Kremlin on. It is on display in my office.[146]

When I wanted to, for historical purposes, make a trade on the Merc floor from the Kremlin, they apologized that it would take several hours to arrange such a telephone call—so much for their technology in 1990.[147] They suggested instead, in typical Russian make-believe fashion, that I hold a telephone to my ear for a fake picture. I declined. In another contrived set-up, there was a trading moment in a church which began with a blessing by the chief Greek Orthodox priest, and where I was given the honor of ringing the bell. The ostensible barter-trade occurred when a computer was traded for a million Marlboro cigarettes.

---

145 From the CME, Chairman John Gelderman and President Bill Brodsky. From the CBOT, Chairman Billy O'Connor and President Tom Donovan.
146 A souvenir proudly exhibited on my office wall.
147 I passed that information to Andrew Card, Chief of Staff under George H. W. Bush.

Upon my departure, I offered my guide, Sergey, who admitted to being KGB, two cartons of Marlboro cigarettes as a farewell present. He thanked me, but I could tell he was not happy with this gift. When I asked what would make him happy, he said, "I would like a copy of your science-fiction book." Surprised, I agreed to send him the book as soon as I got home. He shook his head, "You have a copy in this suitcase," he said, pointing to where it was packed. I opened the suitcase to where he was pointing and, sure enough, he was right—so much for privacy.

MISSED OPPORTUNITIES

My next visit to Moscow came 20 years later, in October 2010, at the invitation of none other than Vladimir Putin. The visit came as a result of a newspaper account describing the destruction of half of the Russian's wheat crop due to the summer heat and fires in August of that year. The article quoted Putin as saying, "I wish there was a way of insuring our wheat crop."

It rang a bell in my head—I could help insure the Russian wheat crop with some hedges on the CBOT or their own futures market, if they created one. I called my friend Hillary Clinton, then US secretary of state, and asked if she could put me in contact with Putin. This required me to contact the Russian ambassador, Sergey Kislyak, who was very helpful and made the necessary connection.[148] Putin agreed with one proviso, that I should also visit with his best friend, the chief Rabbi of Moscow, Berl Lazar. No kidding!

I arrived in Moscow Domodedovo airport on Sunday, October 3, 2010. The meeting with Putin was set for the following day. As fate would have it, Putin's office advised me early on the Monday, with apologies, that Putin had been called away to Berlin for an emergency meeting with German Chancellor Angela Merkel, because of an impending Greek government-debt crisis. (There went an anticipated and historic photo-op!) Instead, I would meet with Viktor Zubkov, the former prime minister of Russia. He complained that the CFTC ignored their Russian counterpart. I agreed to fix that.

It was a special treat to meet with Rabbi Lazar. Not least because we were able to converse in any one of eight languages. I chose Yiddish, since that was the language with which I associated my life in Europe. I asked the Rabbi whether it was true that he was Putin's best friend.

---

148 Ambassador Kislyak took the trouble of sending Mr Putin a signed copy of my memoirs, *Escape to the Futures*, which was by then available in the Russian language.

He explained that during the Refusenik era, when Russia opened its gates to Jewish people (like Natan Sharansky) to at last escape from their garden of paradise, thousands of Jews fled to the US and Israel. "It has caused a brain-drain," Putin complained. "These were Russia's most educated citizens. How can we stop this occurrence?"

Rabbi Lazar said he told Putin to stop Russian anti-Semitism. And, in fact, Putin adopted rules that made anti-Semitic statements and actions illegal for people in government. He also took it upon himself to help fund the elaborate Moscow Jewish Community Center, which was run by Rabbi Lazar.

KIEV

As a result of the notoriety my visit to Russia received, a delegation from the Ukraine—led by Leonid Kozachenko, a prominent Ukrainian agricultural dealer—arrived at the Merc to invite me to Kiev. They wanted my help to build a futures wheat market in the Ukraine. (Ukraine, Russia and Kazakhstan each produce about a third of European wheat.)

This invitation led me to arrange, with the help of CME's Ariel Hantin, a visit to Kiev in May 2011 with a CME group led by Timothy Andriesen, head of CME's agricultural products, and Charlie Carey, former chairman of the CBOT, a strong friend of mine and an expert on the grain market. I actually signed a memorandum of understanding with Ukraine's president, Viktor Yuschenko.[149] A Black Sea wheat-futures contract was eventually developed, primarily the work of Andriesen and his executive assistant, Ariel Hantin. Charlie Carey and I took the opportunity to take a train ride to St Petersburg, where we visited its world-famous Hermitage Museum—we were royally treated whilst there.

Like I said, I was a missionary on a sacred mission. I seldom declined a request to help and never accepted payment. And yes, I was creating competitors. But my belief in competition is not simple lip service. Competition fosters innovation—keeps you on your toes and enlarges the universe of futures participants, thereby helping your own market grow. At the same time, my international labors were central in establishing the big, strong and vital image the Merc represented.

---

149 It turned out that Yuschenko was a communist assisting in Russian's invasion of Ukraine.

CHAPTER 45

To Be or Not to Be

SCOTT GORDON was duly elected as chairman in 1998. I readily supported this selection, as Gordon was both a Globex advocate and a good friend. He previously served as a staff member at my firm, Sakura Dellsher, and later, with my introduction, as president of Tokyo-Mitsubishi Futures. As we neared the twenty-first century, I discussed with Gordon the need to deal with a major issue: we had to demutualize and move forward with an IPO. Trouble was, neither of us, nor anyone on the board, had the expertise necessary to go public.

Gordon agreed—he formed a strategic planning committee, whose principal responsibility was to demutualize the CME, and a search committee, to find the right CEO to lead us through an IPO.

Neither I, nor Jack Sandner were included as members of the search committee. The fiercely fought 1997 election had left many sores, especially between our opposing camps. Gordon felt that if he appointed me, he would also have to appoint Jack Sandner, the outgoing chairman. To show his impartiality, and shy away from the controversy, Gordon appointed *neither* of us.

His rationale was wrong. First, Jack and I had already agreed to work together rather than keep fighting. Second, to show my good faith, I made a motion to give Jack an official title (policy adviser) so that he could continue in an advisory role. In spite of our differences, there is no doubt that Jack Sandner is a very talented guy who contributed to the growth of the Merc. In the long view, I would place Jack high on my list of exchange officials who stood at my side throughout many years at the CME. Third, the Search Committee had little experience in understanding the role of the CEO. I am certain that neither Jack nor I would have recommended Jim McNulty for the post, but Gordon did just that and McNulty received board approval.

LEGAL INNOVATION

Demutualization was likely to be a very complicated process, given that the CME, a membership organization, would be the first exchange to do so and execute an IPO. Gordon asked Jim Oliff (his close friend) and me to lead the effort and negotiate with the membership to achieve their approval. I was fine with that, since I knew Oliff was a very smart and thoughtful person—he had been on my electronic referendum committee back in 1987. The team included Jack Sandner, Yra Harris, Bill Shepard and, of course, Jerry Salzman.

As it turned out, the legal part of the demutualization plan was relatively easy. I called upon Brad Ferguson, the brilliant attorney from Sidley Austin who helped us create the 60/40 tax rule during our 1981 tax-straddle issue. Ferguson again proved his innovative talent. Working together with Jerry Salzman and Craig Donohue, a legal structure was created for converting the exchange from an Illinois not-for-profit corporation into a Delaware for-profit stockholder entity—without incurring tax liability to the members. After which, we issued shares to the members, initiated an IPO, and got them listed on the NYSE. Ferguson's prototype became the model for every American exchange going public thereafter.

A LOOK AT WHAT WAS TO COME

Flash forward: the IPO made a bunch of money for our members when memberships were turned into shares. To make certain that the CME's highest-level executives did not abandon ship after the IPO, we offered them up to 100,000 stock options to remain with the company. The Merc's street value at the time was about $20 per share. The shares went much, much higher. In my mind, the overriding reason was Globex—it was like investors suddenly came to realize the great value of Globex, as opposed to open outcry, and its limitless transaction volume. This was how the exchange was able to attain its income. I was a hero again—even to the most ardent Globex opponent.

It has been said that I have created more millionaires than anyone ever. Who can say? When stock options were offered to me, I would not accept such an arrangement for myself or for any of the other key board members who led the

IPO. "I am not a CME employee," I would always say. I have often been told that this was one of my biggest mistakes—probably so.

Although I had gone through a sort of baptism from open outcry to electronic trade, I never forgot the truth. My knowledge of futures is based on what I learned on the floor. The trading pit was the womb from which the trader in me was delivered. I continue to hold market traders in the highest esteem. They know a lot about markets and trading: they understand which fundamentals affect price, they stand by their word, and they epitomize the risk-taking spirit that made our nation strong—they are a breed unto themselves. They were the cradle from which financial futures emanated and my ideas were born. Alas, the world moved on.

With heartfelt emotion, years later, on February 11, 2015, a sad but inevitable day came to pass. The camel had overtaken our existence. Here is my op-ed piece, 'The Day the Shouting Stopped', announcing the closure of the last futures-market pit in Chicago:

> The centuries old open outcry markets of futures and options—those boisterous forums where buyers and sellers gather on the floor of an exchange in arenas known as pits, to push and shove, wave their hands, and shout at the top of their lungs in order to make trades into the future— was not impervious to the transformations caused by today's computer technology and the internet. Indeed, futures markets that officially began in 1730, at the Dojima Rice Market in Osaka, Japan and transported a century later to Chicago in the United States, and still later to every corner of the world, are in the process of being transported once again, this time to an electronic venue.
>
> The consequences of the 'information revolution,' felt in every facet and niche of civilized life during the last two decades of the twentieth century, dramatically changed the nature and structure of financial markets. What were once dozens of scattered national economies are today inexorably linked into one inter-related, inter-dependent world economy. Sophisticated satellites, microchips and fiber optics have changed the world from a confederation of autonomous financial markets into one continuous marketplace. There is no longer a distinct division of the three major time zones. Today's financial markets ignore time of day as well as geographic and political boundaries. The second part of demutualization was much harder to achieve. It was the 'Political Deal' with the membership whereby they received sufficient legal certification that the board of directors would uphold certain member rights relating to the open outcry sanctity. The

members of course were giving up control of the exchange destiny as well as their membership in over 200 committees. The give and take took about four months to achieve.[150]

MCNULTY'S B2B APPROACH

Jim McNulty's credentials as the Merc's new CEO were very good. Prior to joining us, he served as managing director and co-head of the corporate analysis and structuring team in the corporate finance division at Warburg Dillon Read. He actually did an okay job in leading us through the IPO process. He was also a strong supporter of Globex, which should have given me good reason to support him. Gordon became obsessed with having Jim McNulty aboard; his rationale was that McNulty was reputedly very knowledgeable in matters of going public, which he was. He was also a good speaker and terrific salesman. But it turned out to be a colossal mistake, since McNulty and the team he brought with him knew next to nothing about futures.

McNulty took office at the height of the dot-com insanity. He strongly believed that the dot-com revolution was a great opportunity for the Merc to expand its customer base. On the other hand, I personally believed the dot-com phenomenon was a ridiculous mania. I hoped it would pass without doing too much damage to the nation's economy.

To achieve his mission, McNulty and his team became hell-bent on increasing our customer base by utilizing the so-called 'B2B' approach. That was the popular catchphrase of the time, getting huge amounts of recognition in the media. In my mind, it was just another passing fad that I tried to ignore. McNulty believed that we could greatly expand our customer base by getting the Merc to trade and clear all kinds of products—chemicals, for instance. However, many of the suggested products, to my knowledge, had no need for futures or weren't sufficiently standardized to safely clear at our clearing house. I guess you had to understand how futures clearing worked to see the problem.

150 'The Future of Open Outcry,' by Leo Melamed in *The Wall Street Journal*. September 15, 2000.

THE FIVE-YEAR PLAN

McNulty announced that the CME was in a great position to provide clearing services to B2B entities, we just had to quickly organize ourselves to capitalize on our position. In the name of moving forward, he introduced us to two new models: B2B Lite and B2B Heavy. For the B2B Lite, the CME would co-develop and market futures contracts with a B2B exchange. In B2B Heavy, the CME would structure a NewCo clearing house for a B2B exchange. It was clear that McNulty's team knew next to nothing about how difficult it was to launch a new product. Over twenty different product attempts, you are lucky if you find one that works.

To my understanding, the underlying thrust of McNulty's strategy for the Merc was a five-year plan based on, in McNulty's words, "the current shift in the ecosystem, one which would lead to a collaborative commerce among financial institutions." Ecosystem was the favorite word by his team members.[151] You think I am joking? You really cannot make this stuff up. And it got worse.

McNulty promised that over the next five years there would be a consolidation of derivatives, securities, B2B marketplaces and clearing houses—something that he referred to as the perfect storm. Consequently, he predicted that the future success of the CME would depend on whether it could position itself as a consolidator and "preferred partner in the new marketplace", as well as "its ability to be a world-class applied technology firm." We always were open to being a preferred partner, but as a *technology firm?*

After two years of nonsense, Scott Gordon continued to be awed by McNulty's vision. Knowing my opinion of McNulty, Gordon sent a letter to the audit and compensation committee suggesting that the Merc stop paying the stipend to "our two advisors, Leo and Jack." Never mind that the amount of payment was in itself a joke.

I was certain this was McNulty's doing. Removing us would undoubtedly make life easier for him, since he would be able to carry out his plans without critique. Bill Shepard, who was most vocal in opposing McNulty, once confronted Gordon to say that he was swallowing the BS McNulty was dishing out. He stated: "You are not nearly independent enough as chairman. You have become Jim McNulty."

---

151 My advice: beware people with five-year plans who use the word 'ecosystem' more than once.

A WELL-DESERVED LECTURE

For me, McNulty's plan was first-class gobbledygook. It revealed a total lack of knowledge about the Merc's history, rules, and referendums. And it kept getting worse. McNulty and his cohorts correctly understood that the Merc's income was based on transaction fees and they soon realized that this would be much, much larger if the middleman, the broker, was eliminated. In other words, broker's fees (or part of them) would become income for the Merc.

Did they think we did not realize this? What was Globex all about? "Why don't we just set a date and close the pits?" Believe it or not, this is what McNulty and his team suggested. This, after a *couple of years* of stewardship.

While McNulty was pleasant enough as a person and knowledgeable about matters of going public, he had very little understanding about futures markets or the Merc. After two years of McNulty's leadership, many of us believed that he was moving in the wrong direction. This led to a rather painful relationship between McNulty and myself. Indeed, the entire hierarchy of CME staff—Craig Donohue, Phupinder Gill, Kim Taylor, Jerry Salzman and many board members including, of course, Terry Duffy—reached a near unanimous conclusion that McNulty must be relieved of his CEO position. Mr Satish Nandapurkar, one of McNulty's guiding lights and then CME managing director, came to my office one day with a chart showing his calculations of how the Merc's income would rise like a rocket to the skies after the pits were closed. "Why don't we just set a date and do it?" he asked. I tried to stay calm. It occurred to me that McNulty's team really had no idea of how Globex came about. It was like they parachuted down from Mars. I went into lecture mode.

I began by explaining the referendum rule, passed in 1987, which protected brokers and traders from *exactly* that type of board action. Did McNulty not realize that without that provision there was not a chance in hell that the members would have approved any technology that threatened their livelihood, especially an after-hours electronic trading system. Without that provision, Globex would never have happened. Besides, there had to be a referendum—it was in the bylaws. We had to gain approval from a majority of over 5,000 committed open-outcry advocates. This rule holds true even today.

To consider closing the pits willy-nilly was not only against the rules, it was suicidal. We could be put in jail. Twelve years ago, the whole idea of electronic trade was beyond revolutionary. We had to deal with reality. Passage of the referendum would simply give us a toehold. The idea had to be nurtured. Even today you would never get approval to close the pits. And yes, even today you would need a referendum. To think that anyone could get a majority to agree to closing the pits was pure *mishigas* (craziness.) It wouldn't be much of a chore for a couple of brokers to find even a rookie lawyer to get an injunction—a legal action we could not possibly win. Some of us might get deported. Regardless, how would a legal battle look before an IPO? Would it not kill any chances of our success?

I then asked some rhetorical questions, ones that I was certain they had never even considered: "Satish, can you guarantee where the business would go after we close the pits? Could Mr McNulty ensure that the business would go to Globex? Did such an agreement with our customers or their brokers exist? Is it not likely that any one of our world competitors—say LIFFE, or Eurex, or a number of New York banks—would be licking their chops at our action?"

The banks were always poised to lure our business away, they had even created execution facilities to do so. They had already tried several insidious ways to steal our open interest. We had gone to court to stop them. Did McNulty's team simply believe that the banks would say, "Oh, it would be unfair to go after the Merc's people just because they closed their floors." Or would they not gleefully steal our brokers and their customers away? They might even introduce substantially lower rates to do so, or maybe no fees at all for a year or two.

Did the McNulty team understand that the brokers, more than anyone, control where the business *is* traded or cleared? It was the reason that Globex wasn't getting much of the business—brokers were executing their orders in the pit. Did they fully understand that the brokers community didn't want Globex to succeed?

Finally, I asked whether Mr McNulty's team had failed to understand that we had given all our knowledge, expertise and energy to the acceptance of Globex? And to achieve that, we had to guarantee our members that without their approval, the Merc would never close the floor. To gain that approval would take time and an honest rationale.

Satish Nandapurkar left without saying a word.

ABANDON SHIP

If that was not enough, on another occasion McNulty proudly told me that he was negotiating with Morgan Stanley to sell the Merc's clearing house. When I responded with: "Have you lost your sanity?" He told me that I simply did not understand. "It would be for $1bn," he proudly said—as if the amount would make a difference! I replied that it would have to be "over my dead body." The clearing house, I explained, was the Merc's holiest asset, a priceless jewel, and never, *ever* for sale. Without the clearing house, I said, "the CME would be worth next to nothing."

McNulty decided that he would have to bring me into their deliberations. He invited me to join a weekly Wednesday meeting that he held with his senior staff. I thanked him and said I would attend if they also invited Jerry Salzman. He reluctantly agreed. My reason was to have another pair of ears hear their ideas and plans—maybe I was too prejudiced and needed another opinion, particularly Salzman's.

I knew of course that I was not alone in feeling that McNulty was the wrong choice for CEO. Many of our board members had offered the same opinion. And some had privately urged me to do something about it before he destroyed our future. Fred Arditti, one of the smartest and most honest human beings I had ever met, resigned, saying to me, "I don't know where McNulty is going, Leo, but I don't want any part of it." To my total disappointment, Fred gave up his post and left.

Another trusted high-level staffer, David Goone, asked for my permission to leave and take a job offered at our competitor, the Intercontinental Exchange (ICE), because he could not continue working with McNulty as his boss. Goone went on to become a top executive at ICE. We remained close friends.

After several weeks of our attendance at McNulty's meetings, Jerry came forward to say "Leo, McNulty is taking the Merc down a destructive pathway. I hear nothing but nonsense." It was all I needed to hear. Jerry's opinion served as the final word I was waiting for. It gave me the courage to proceed with the plan I had in my head. After two years of nonsensical ideas about B2Bs, ecosystems, willy-nilly floor closings and selling the clearing house, one might ask what took me so long?

Well, there was a problem. McNulty had a contract stretching until 2004, another two years. And there was always the fear that our chairman would renew the contract. While preparing for an IPO, the last thing we needed was an open contractual dispute with the sitting CEO. Surely such a dispute would terminate the IPO process. Instead, I came up with a way to get around this problem. The idea was difficult but feasible. To avoid as much negative publicity as possible, we would leave McNulty alone. Instead, we would pursue an *internal* corporate takeover by electing a new chairman in the upcoming 2002 election.

A new chairman would stop McNulty from carrying out his ideas and ensure that his contract was not renewed. Switching chairmanship was a more normal process for our exchange. Still, I was very much aware that the odds were against us carrying this plan out. With Gordon's help, McNulty had taken control of the relevant exchange machinery during his two-year tenure. There were few left in upper management that I could rely on. Some had simply left, others were replaced.

AN ALTERNATIVE CANDIDATE

Of course, we also knew there would be media coverage. Changing chairman was common enough in futures but it did make headlines. The best we could do was keep our moves secret. If McNulty or his team actually believed we could achieve our goal, there was no saying what they would have done to stop it.

First and foremost, though, we needed a candidate—time was of the essence. I had ruled myself out, but felt it had to be a board member. I discussed the subject at length with Barry Lind, who was all for the plan. I confided in Gill too. He was very supportive of the idea, since he had been considering leaving like Fred. I very secretly spoke with Craig Donohue, who was wary but extremely in favor of doing something to remove McNulty. I knew I would have to exclude Salzman from the undertaking. He would have been happy with our success, but we realized that, as our legal counsel under contract, our plan would have placed him in a conflicting position. To test the water, I confided in a couple of trustworthy directors. They urged me on.

It was logical to select Terry Duffy as the candidate for chairman, his credentials were sound and he was then board vice-chairman so it was the natural choice. We were good friends. He had supported my leadership from the time he became a member in 1981. Duffy was introduced to me by a mutual friend, Vince Schreiber, who was one of my strongest allies from the start of the IMM. Schreiber's introduction of Duffy spoke volumes for me. Duffy started as a runner but a year later borrowed money from his parents to become a member—pretty much the same story as my own.

Duffy was first elected to the board in 1995. He became an expert on floor operations and was the first floor-broker to try the Merc's initial hand-held electronic technology, Galax-C. While he was untested (board vice-chairman was mostly a ceremonial post), he had a solid reputation and was popular with the floor crowd. What most convinced me was that Terry's instinctive response to the major Merc issues I touched upon during our preliminary discussions were identical to my own. And because he had openly embraced the Globex direction, I became convinced he was the right choice. Looking back, my instincts were very correct. Terry Duffy was smart, a quick learner and politically savvy. He was the perfect candidate.

Remember, what was *not* changing was the strength and capabilities of the Merc. We were a model for the world's markets with a solid and tested clearing house and unequalled diversification. Those truths were not being altered. More to the point, Duffy embraced the essence of a futures exchange—to provide product insurance for market exposure within a secure setting with world-wide access and acceptance. McNulty was on a path to violating the financial equivalent of the Hippocratic Oath, "Do no harm." The thought of selling our clearing house, the priceless jewel of an exchange, or changing its underlying purpose with something called B2B, was a serious violation of this credo. Terry Duffy understood this.

I had a long dinner conversation with Myron Scholes, a CME public director. Scholes was clearly the dean of the five Merc public directors whose votes I counted on. The fact that our board members and CME staff could boast of having a Nobel Prize economist in the fold was of immense prestige, not to speak of the value his ideas gave us. Scholes embraced the plan from the get-go, explaining that he was not impressed with McNulty and had often wondered how long I would tolerate his leadership. When I identified Terry Duffy as the candidate, he said he would rely on my judgment. With Scholes on board, convincing the other public directors became much easier. I privately met with every board member who Terry and I considered to be in favor of change. They all agreed that McNulty had to go. Not only did I assure them that Duffy was the right choice, but Duffy himself went to visit with them to ask for their support. It was a great move and made the right impression.

Right from the start I admired Duffy's decision-making ability. Sure, in the beginning I was at his side, but he made it easy. It was like he was always ready for the job. I learned to trust his intellect, knowledge and courage. He was particularly strong as it related to advancing Globex, my highest priority. We seldom had a serious difference of opinion. The long and short of it was, Terry was an outstanding choice. More than that, a year or two after the IPO, it became clear that Duffy could safely lead our institution. He has done a highly commendable job as chairman, avoiding pitfalls and advancing our growth with mergers and acquisitions. He was vital during negotiations with the CBOT and incredibly important when we executed the transition from open outcry to the screen. His talent for making friends with high-level US elected officials was exemplary and served us well in Washington DC. I am very proud of Terry's performance as CME chairman.

However, when I first approached Terry about running for chairman, he was hesitant. I would have been surprised if he hadn't been. The idea of governing an institution that big was an overwhelming undertaking. But once he saw Gordon's letter attempting to remove me from leadership,[152] Terry said to me, "That is the last straw. I am ready to go with your plan."

INTERNAL POLITICS

Another secret ally of critical importance was Craig Donohue. Coming to the Merc as an attorney in 1989, Donohue had since worked his way up the CME ladder, holding a broad range of positions with progressively increasing responsibilities in legal affairs, market regulation and strategic planning before becoming the CME's general counsel. It was impressive.

Over time I got to know him well and found him to be knowledgeable, quick thinking and trustworthy. He had the ability to think ahead and was hugely in favor of going public. Most importantly, along with the other top Merc officials, Gill, Salzman, Krause, and Taylor, Donohue was openly supportive of my return to leadership in 1997—and totally in the Globex camp. Our mutual beholdenship to the exchange and its future gave our relationship a strong common bond and made us close friends. Donohue had no hesitation in privately declaring his dislike of McNulty and the crew he had installed. In unison with the other Merc officials, he considered McNulty to be misinformed and misdirected. "They know very little about futures," he confided.

But, for all his faults, McNulty was smart and no pushover—he also sensed that something was up. The pre-election coverage generated a good deal of attention and became very antagonistic. As I mentioned before, McNulty was a good salesman and was able to win over the press. His spin was that the old guard, Leo Melamed and Jack Sandner, together with Terry Duffy, were trying to regain control and move against the advancement of electronic trade. And the media bought it. Imagine that—the guy who revolutionized futures with the initiation of Globex was suddenly the dude in favor of open outcry!

It shows how easy it was even before Twitter for the media to buy into and spin a totally false narrative. We were painted as trying to hold onto open outcry. In the final week before the election, a Dow Jones commodities service headline read, "CME's vote is about keeping old ties in the new world." The chief market reporter at the *Tribune*, David Greising, on April 17, 2002, had this to say:

> In their day, Melamed and his feisty protégé, Jack Sandner, helped make the Merc one of the world's most influential and innovative exchanges. Too bad

152 In a letter Gordan sent to the accounting department which suggested my stipend be stopped.

old times aren't what the Merc needs right now. The exchange is preparing to offer stock to public investors. It fights to adapt to electronic trading. It is a leader in Chicago's effort to control the new market for futures contracts on individual stocks. And in all these areas, the Merc is faring well. Under Chairman Scott Gordon and new Chief Executive Jim McNulty, the Merc has avoided the pratfalls that the Chicago Board of Trade has endured. It has a chance to convert electronic trading from a threat to ally for growth ... and yet, with all this on the line, what is the talk as the Chicago Mercantile Exchange heads into a vital annual meeting Wednesday? They are talking about Jack and Leo. They wonder if the two fading legends really will make their move, first to oust Gordon and later McNulty.

Think about that. One of those 'fading legends' was recently inducted into the Chicago Innovation Hall of Fame.

BEHIND THE SCENES

It was now up to us to secure the necessary votes.

I also had to decide whether to bring Jack Sandner onto our side or not. Duffy left this decision up to me. During McNulty's tenure, Jack had lost all influence. He was like a non-entity. But we still needed Jack's vote (and that of another director Jack could influence) and since my plan was best served with the least raucous as possible, I agreed to bring Jack in. His vote in this was more important than whether he did or did not fully support Globex. The three of us met in my office and once again I accepted Jack's oath that he was totally in our camp. He said the magical words, "I want to regain my dignity." In bringing Jack onto our side, it restored Jack's image as he hoped.

With many top-level Merc's administrative officials by then on McNulty's team, every move we made was executed in secret. It worked. It goes without explaining that because Leo Melamed was leading this effort, and with acceptance of Terry Duffy as his choice for chairman, coupled with the fact that many on the board had lost faith in McNulty, the election turned into a rout.

Before the election meeting, I went to Scott Gordon, who I still considered my friend, and told him that we had 15 votes and to avoid embarrassment he could withdraw from consideration. He did not believe me. The board voted as I knew it would. As history records, we won, as they say, in spades. Fifteen of the 20 board members voted in our favor. Terry Duffy became chairman of the CME.

I felt bad for Scott Gordon, I knew I had lost a good friend, but it was the only way to stop McNulty from leading the CME to God knows where. McNulty likes to point out that the day after the board appointed Craig Donohue as CEO, our stock fell over 6%. That may be true, but it was also on its way from an IPO price of $35 to $710 five years later, on December 21, 2007. Then went even higher after its 5–1 split. It was rumored McNulty sold out his shares at $100, making a ton of money.

THE FALL OUT

As promised, after the IPO I appointed Donohue the first CEO of our brand-new public company. Donohue was overwhelmed that I kept my promise made to him during the clandestine takeover. For Donohue, it was life changing. In my opinion, we could not have found a better official than Craig Donohue, who knew the ropes and complexities of a public company. His tenure as the first CEO proved to be outstanding.

I have to say that during the IPO, Craig Donohue, Jerrold Salzman and Brad Ferguson proved their salt. They were nothing short of outstanding in carrying us through the nightmarish legal rigmarole that is required. We could not have chosen a more knowledgeable team.

Duffy, Donohue, and I met at our house in Glencoe to iron out the hierarchy of the CME going forward. We sat in the kitchen and strategized for an entire day while Betty served countless cups of coffee. Both Terry and Craig thought that I should take the title of president, but again I made the classic mistake of declining. I still believed that the chairman emeritus title was more dignified. At my insistence, Craig Donohue became CEO and Phupinder Gill became president. I continued my role as chairman emeritus and principal advisor to the board until my retirement in 2018.

During our Glencoe kitchen-cabinet meeting, we decided to create a Board Steering Committee. Its purpose would be to vet and discuss major issues before they were presented to the board for a vote or otherwise. The need for such a committee singularly rested with the McNulty administration. Under his rule, it was common practice for McNulty's team to put important matters to a vote without giving board members the opportunity to examine issues beforehand.

Unfortunately, this lack of communication created problems. One instance of this was uncovered by Arman Falsafi, a stellar CME managing director, who alerted me to the fact that an independent study showed Globex with failing marks on performance. This was corroborated by one of the most trustworthy Merc officials, John Curran, someone who I often turned to for verification. I then went directly to Jim Krause, the chief of Globex technology, and learned that Falsafi was correct.

The steering committee was created and evolved to provide senior staff members with the ability to discuss what they are thinking and planning with members of the board, as well as hear from board members. It became a must-attend forum for the purpose of discussion before advancing ideas to the board for approval. I chaired the committee until my retirement.

CHAPTER 46

The Roadshow

T HE earliest form of an IPO is said to have occurred in the Roman Republic, with evidence of trading being found near the Temple of Castor and Pollux in Rome. A more modern iteration of an IPO is documented in 1602, when the Dutch East India Company offered its shares to the public. In the United States, the first IPO was the Bank of North America, which offered its shares in 1783.

The only roadshow I ever participated in was in November 2002. It was under the direction of our underwriter, Morgan Stanley, and just prior to the Merc's IPO on December 6, 2002.[153]

THE SET UP

For the uninitiated—those who do not fully know how capital formation works—a roadshow, an American phenomenon, is a most revealing exercise. In simple language, it is a method used to get buyers (institutional investors, analysts, fund managers) interested in investing in your company by committing to buy a certain number of shares in the forthcoming IPO.

The price and amount of your company's shares to be sold are decided in advance with your investment banker. Your banker then arranges a series of meetings between representatives of your company (the company's management team) and the investment community. If you can afford it, your roadshow representatives then lease a private plane to travel around the country, as well

---

153   To prepare for the IPO the CME demutualized in November 2000.

as off-shore, pitching to potential investors by explaining who you are and why your company is a good investment opportunity. A successful roadshow is critical to the success of the IPO.

In the case of the CME, we were the first exchange to ever go public, so there really wasn't any script to follow.[154] Morgan Stanley was the underwriter for the Merc and did a fine job. They quickly learned my standing at the exchange and the futures industry, and leaned on my leadership throughout the roadshow and IPO event. Although McNulty did the opening introduction, and Terry followed with a brief overview, I carried the exercise from then on. Terry's intellect quickly understood the ropes and he began to inject his thoughts more frequently as he became more comfortable with the process.

Believe it or not, McNulty tried to exclude both Jack Sandner and myself from the roadshow team. Morgan Stanley stepped in and offered their opinion that both advisors should be present and that I should carry the process. In their final review, Morgan Stanley noted that the roadshow was a huge success, but that without Jack and me the roadshow would have been a no-show.

In my opinion, our duo act was spectacular. The two of us became a one-of-a-kind sales team, presenting the beauty of the CME alongside the unquestionable potential of Globex and the transaction volume it was bound to generate—on which our income was dependent. We were also able to answer the myriad of questions tossed at us by individuals who, if convinced, would spend millions of dollars in a successful IPO.

THE PITCH

The following is a snap-shot of how we presented our truly fascinating history. I would begin, applying the passion I learned on the Yiddish stage. Jack would then follow in perfect harmony. We were often asked whether we were professional performers. The CME we described was one of a kind, and the first exchange to ever go public. Being a futures exchange, there was a dearth of knowledge of our history: who we were, why we were, and who we might become. Here is what we explained:

Until the Merc shook things up 30 years ago, futures markets were synonymous with agriculture—the grains, the meats, and other commodities. We would

---

154 There are some observers who believe our stock was mispriced. We went out at $35 a share. Our price nearly doubled in one year and reached $700 by its fifth year of existence. In defense of Morgan Stanley this was a first in the world and near impossible to know what we were worth.

recount that, in 1972, the CME launched the first financial futures contracts in foreign exchange. We changed the futures markets, as well as risk management, forever. If you didn't believe us, ask Alan Greenspan, ask Ben Bernanke or Myron Scholes.

And we didn't stop at money futures. Before anyone else even considered the concept, we created a brand-new division, the IMM, specifically designed for financial futures trade. In 1976, the IMM listed the world's first short-term interest-rate contracts—US T-bill futures. Milton Friedman rang the opening bell.

Before anyone else understood what we were up to, we achieved an agreement with our regulator, the CFTC, to approve the concept of cash settlement in place of the traditional requirement for physical delivery. It ushered in a new financial era in futures.

Cash settlement meant that futures products would be limited only by our own imagination. The world's first cash settled instrument—eurodollars—was launched by the IMM in 1981. It is today the most successful futures contract anywhere, trading on the order of $1trn in notional value every day. Eurodollars futures are today's benchmark for short-term interest rates the world over. And it trades at the Chicago Merc.

A year later, we launched today's most successful stock index product—the S&P 500 futures contract. Our S&P product, in one form or another, has been emulated throughout the world and on nearly every exchange. Today, before a specialist on the NYSE makes his first bid or offer, they are likely to check the overnight price of the Merc's S&P contract in Chicago.

And how does the specialist go about checking our prices? More likely than not, he checks it through Globex—the CME's international electronic transaction system. In 1987, before any futures market in the world dared take on the sacred cow of open outcry, the CME brazenly conceptualized electronic trade. It was launched in 1992. Globex today does about 40% of our trade—and it's growing.

In 1997, we revolutionized the futures industry once again by listing an all-electronic version of the S&P contract. The E-mini—one fifth of the size of its pit-traded parent—trading entirely on Globex, boasting a transaction volume near 1m contracts a day. And according to Goldman Sachs, is the trendsetter for American equity markets.

Leadership is our *tradition*, innovation is our middle name. That heritage will inexorably lead us to greater and greater heights. Little wonder we were the first American futures exchange to demutualize. Little wonder we will be the first to become a public company. Since 1970, our revenue has grown 100-fold. From 1970 to 2000, our annual compounded growth rate was at 14%. Since 2000, that rate jumped to 40%.

The CME is one of a kind. When you talk about your blue chips, when you mention innovation, when you discuss futures markets, it is the CME. We *invented* the game. We *transformed* the way the world manages its risk. I would then close with the following:

"Yes, we are biased. But that is our history. We invented the modern futures market. And—as you know—it's not boasting if it's the truth. More to the point, because past is prologue, our past innovations and our past growth *represent* the foundation for our future. As the guy said, "You ain't seen nothing yet!"

CHAPTER 47

Whatever it Takes

MAKE NO LITTLE PLANS

DANIEL BURNHAM, a renowned architect who designed Chicago's lakefront, was famously known to have said: "Make no little plans." Such a hallowed doctrine has been adopted by many around the world—myself included. Rudolf (Rudi) Ferscha, CEO of Eurex, was also a follower of that dictum. Rudi was a nice enough fellow, very smart and very ambitious.

Britain's LIFFE exchange was a committed open-outcry futures exchange. Its most successful product was the Bund, a ten-year German bond. In 1977, Eurex, a futures exchange based in Frankfurt, Germany, listed an identical Bund contract that used an electronic transaction system. I met with Sir Brian Williamson, LIFFE's chairman, to caution him that the electronic system would win. In what was surely a watershed moment for the markets, Eurex defeated LIFFE in less than a year, winning over the Bund contract and unequivocally proving what I had been preaching for over a decade.

It is near impossible today, given the incredible technological advancements that have occurred in our lives over the past two decades, to accept that there ever was a time when such an issue was in doubt. That proof was needed to confirm what is so obvious today. Liquidity can be created on an automated system.

Upon becoming CEO of Eurex in 2001, Mr Ferscha recognized that the foregoing history represented a great opportunity. Across the pond there were these two major futures exchanges ripe for the picking. Both were in Chicago and both were ensconced in open outcry. It was the opportunity of a lifetime and nearly a sure thing. He devised a scheme to capture both American exchanges and make Eurex the biggest exchange in the world. The plan was as clever as it was devious.

First, some history. The CBOT was in a very dangerous, yet comical, place; it had made blunder after blunder. The first occurred some 77 years ago when the CBOT created a separate entity, the BOTCC, to be its clearing house to avoid direct liability. Problem was, anyone who controlled the clearing house, owned its open interest. Remember when I told Mr McNulty that our clearing house was never for sale. Well, this was one of the reasons.

One part of Mr Ferscha's plan was to gain control of the BOTCC and thereby snare the CBOT's US bond futures. Not easy but possible. And Ferscha was not alone in this goal; a combination of NY banks were also on the hunt.

CAUGHT IN A TRAP

The second CBOT blunder was not owning an electronic transaction system. It made them the weakest of all the exchanges. Remember, the CBOT had recently completed a new $200m financial-trading floor. Then, after seeing their mistake, the CBOT sought an electronic savior to defend its markets against attack.

They rejected the Merc's Globex offer. I knew they would; it was far too big an embarrassment to their membership. After all, a couple of years back the CBOT had walked away from the Globex joint venture, in which they would have been a major partner. Instead, they romanced Eurex and, on May 18, 1999, CBOT membership approved their alliance (a step toward eventual merger). This included a technological 'cross-product' coalition, as well as use of the Alliance CBOT Exchange (A/C/E), a German-built electronic transaction system.

Rudi Ferscha, now in charge, shook up the futures industry by applying to the CFTC for a license to become an American futures exchange. It was a bold and very innovative action. It would enable Eurex to directly attack the contracts on both the CME and the CBOT.

The CBOT found itself caught in a trap of their own making. If Eurex was granted a license, nothing could stop the new entity (Eurex US) from launching a replica of the US bond contract and trading it on their electronic transaction system. We had seen that movie before, we all knew the outcome. Worse still, the majority (some 80%) of CBOT's bond-market trade was already operating on the A/C/E platform—a fact that made Ferscha a favorite to win the US bond contract. Ferscha was on a roll.

To show their cast-iron certainty, Rudi Ferscha leased 20,000 feet of office space in Sears Tower, directly across the street from the CBOT's headquarters. At night, Ferscha had Sears light up its top floors in Eurex's colors, green and blue, and beam a searchlight onto the CBOT's building as a taunt. He then staged press conferences and parties for CBOT traders. During the day, Hooters-like damsels passed out free coffee and Eurex T-shirts.[155] Honestly, you couldn't have made this stuff up.

In an act of desperation, the CBOT broke their contract with the Germans in favor of a similar contract with the Brits. In the nick of time, they were able to transfer their bond trading from the A/C/E to Euronext LIFFE's platform.

STRICTLY BUSINESS

Around that time, in March 2003, Charles Carey took over CBOT's chairmanship. Charlie was no old-line CBOT member, he was a down-to-earth guy, smart and professional, and a strong supporter of Les Rosenthal. We quickly become good friends. Charlie remained steady in his mission to save the CBOT from extinction, doing everything he could think of. He demanded that his board adopt a new and highly competitive fee structure, and energized floor traders to support the bond contract. But he also knew that these measures might not be enough.

On September 20, 2003, Rudi Ferscha was ready to do battle with the Merc. He came to the CME with a high-level delegation led by Hartmut Schwesinger, the mayor of Frankfurt. Other members of the delegation included: Dr. Burkhard Bastuck, a partner from Freshfields; Dr. Annette Messemer, head of the Public Sector Investment Banking, JP Morgan Chase; Dr. Karin Zeni, managing director of international business at the Frankfurt Chamber of Commerce; Mr Michael Gallagher, Deutsche Bank; and several others.

As per our arrangement, they appeared before our leadership, Terry Duffy, Craig Donohue, Jack Sandner and myself, as well as Colleen Lazar, the CME's director of Public Affairs. We went through the formalities of greetings and exchanging business cards. Given the size of their delegation, this took a while.

Mayor Schwesinger thanked us for the meeting and spoke pointedly to me. He explained in a most congenial manner that we should remain friends even though Eurex would surely win the futures business from us. "There is nothing personal involved," said Mr Ferscha, "It is strictly business." All eyes were glued

---

155   Bernie Dan, CBOT's president, pointedly refused to take the gift.

on me. I kid you not, this really happened—*chutzpah* (audacity) comes in many forms. Perhaps he had seen too many American mafia movies, where just before you kill your adversary, you assure him that "it is strictly business and not personal."

Coleen Lazar told me later that she wished she had a camera to record the look on our guests faces when I responded in a most courteous manner with: "You are correct, Mr Mayor, we will stay friends, because Hell will freeze over before Eurex wins our business."

The meeting had a very abrupt ending. Although I smiled while I said the words, it was not intended as an empty promise—I was ready to do whatever it took.

A SAFE REFUGE

For me, it was both sobering and disappointing to see just how easily the US media bought into the *braggadocio* being dished out by the foreigners. Kopin Tan, a highly regarded reporter for *Barron's Market Week*, wrote on September 22, 2003:

> The announcement [by Eurex] was long anticipated but still created a buzz. Even skeptics who talked down the Eurex plan heard the bigger message: that the next year could bring accelerated change for Chicago's futures markets, which despite recent electronic embellishments are still devoted to manual trading through open outcry.

I flew to New York to meet with Kopin. We had dinner, but I could not disabuse him of his conviction that we in Chicago were Neanderthals who would ultimately lose.

Not too many days later, Les Rosenthal told me that Charlie Carey was going to give me a call. Les knew that Charlie and I had become solid friends, but he wanted to be sure of my position. He said, "Leo, you can't let Eurex win." I remained silent, but my mind flashed back to my vow to Rudi Ferscha.

Les told me what I already knew. Charlie did not care about face, nor past rivalries, he just wanted to keep the CBOT alive and safe. When he called, Charlie and I talked for a very long time. It led to an idea. Charlie called Terry and me to make a deal for the bonds to be moved to the Merc clearing house where they would be safe. It was a shocker. I called it the CME-CBOT Common Clearing Link—the Merc would provide transaction processing, guarantees, and other business services.

"The achievement ranks up there with the seven wonders of the world," I said to Terry. But credit really goes to Kim Taylor, our clearing house president, and Phupinder Gill, our president, who made the transfer of positions happen. As Kim Taylor responded with a wry smile: "A problem? No problem, all that has to happen was that billions of dollars' worth of positions had to be moved on time without any interruption to trading."

Bringing the CBOT onto our clearing system brought real safety to their exchange, and I think that every futures cognoscenti understood what would happen next. It was just a question of time. As I said to the *Financial Times*; "This agreement is truly historic. The link represents the culmination of many years of efforts to bring the CME and CBOT closer together."[156] A near 50-year dream was going to be fulfilled. Les and I privately shared a glass of wine.

On February 4, 2004, after a long delay due to deliberations about whether competition stops at our shores, the CFTC made the right decision and granted Eurex a US license.

DECLARATION OF WAR

But wait, the story was not over. On May 16, 2004, we celebrated the IMM's 30th Anniversary. William J. McDonough, president of the NY Fed and an original member of the IMM board, presided over the event, reading out a special greeting from Milton Friedman in which the great man called me "the greatest crapshooter of them all."

We also received a congratulatory message from Alan Greenspan, US Fed chairman, who said: "What is clear is that participants in financial markets across the country and around the globe have good reason to join the IMM in celebrating their 30 years of accomplishment." What the Fed chairman may not have known was that there were forces in the world plotting against us, hoping we would not survive another 30 years.

What I warned would happen, happened. Ten days after our celebration, LIFFE announced that it intended to attack the CME. The lesson they learned in 1997 was about to be used against the Merc. Sporting a new name, Euronext LIFFE, and a brand-new electronic system, LiffeConnect, LIFFE decided to do to others what had been done to them—and our eurodollar contract was the target.[157] Hugh Freedberg, their CEO, made it official, "This is something

156 *Financial Times*, Jeremy Grant, April 16, 2003.
157 *The Chicago Tribune*, Mark Skertic, January 27, 2004.

we've always envisioned since we started the development and introduction of LiffeConnect."[158]

The *Chicago Tribune* carried the news to our traders with a front-page article: "A European-based exchange is planning to grab business away from the Chicago Mercantile Exchange by launching trade in ... eurodollar contracts beginning March 18." War on the Merc had officially been declared by both Eurex and LIFFE.

SHIFTING ALLEGIANCES

The lesson LIFFE endured in 1997 coincided with my return to the CME boardroom. It was exactly the scenario I feared and hoped to prevent with the initiation of Globex. But there was this insidious problem. Although Globex became operational in 1992, little trade came its way. As I explained, unless the customer instructed otherwise, brokers dictated where trades were made. And so the Merc's electronic system was generally ignored. We were in the same vulnerable position as LIFFE. I had to do something.

I sponsored a new referendum that would override the 1987 prohibition and allow for concurrent trading of all Merc products on both open outcry and Globex. I hoped that this would initiate a migration of open interest from the floor to the screen and create liquidity on Globex. But my proposal was hugely contentious, and the broker community actively opposed it.

Meetings were held—nearly two years were wasted in controversy. Finally, on January 14, 1999, the proposal was overwhelmingly approved. Futures trade in currencies and equities responded quickly with business to Globex. However, the eurodollar contract acted like it was in a different universe. Little had changed. The cold war was still on. The *WSJ* gave context to the meaning of LIFFE's threat:

> Eurodollar futures are the CME's most popular product. But while the exchange's equity-index futures and currency futures-products have seen explosive growth on its Globex electronic-trading platform, eurodollar futures haven't. Last year, a total of 309.6 million eurodollar contracts traded, with electronic trading accounting for only 4 percent of total volume.[159]

---

158   Dow Jones Capital Markets, Adam Bradbery, January 26, 2004.
159   *WSJ*, Kristina Zurla, January 26, 2004.

The reporter had the figures right. But it wasn't the full story. At the close of 2003, the IMM eurodollar *was* the CME. The eurodollar contract—futures and options—represented 50% of the total CME volume, 84% of its total open interest, and 75% of its net income. It was our worst nightmare. The London exchange was fully operative, with solid financials and an electronic platform near-equal to our own.

Clearly what was happening was no accident. The eurodollar brokers surely understood that the plight of our brothers across the street stemmed from the fact that they did not have an automated transaction system. And they had to know that an automated system would win the battle against open outcry. There had to be an unspoken shun. Their rationale was, "once we lose the income from open outcry, it will be forever." In other words, brokers must have been thinking, "let's keep our treasure for as long as we can."

THE BIG MOMENT

Terry and I agreed to take off the gloves. The rule against listing eurodollars on the screen was settled by the previous referendum and was no longer operative. We now had to force the issue with another referendum, one which would demand that, within the next 90 days, 25% of open interest be transferred to the screen or else we would close the pits. We believed that such a referendum would win.

I remember vividly the meeting with over 1,000 angry eurodollar brokers and traders. We were all there: Terry Duffy, Craig Donohue, Phupinder Gill, Jack Sandner and myself. It was *Gunfight at the O.K. Corral* all over again. Terry and I were prepared to go to the mat; we agreed not to leave until we had won. I made one of my most passionate speeches—I was Knute Rockne, asking those brokers and traders to "Win one for the Merc." You could have cut the tension with a knife. If you lit a match, it would have undoubtedly blown up the room.

Eurex listed our eurodollar contract onto their electronic system to no avail. In a referendum on March 16, 2004, CME membership approved the transfer of 25% of the eurodollar contract to Globex. The first 25% was like penicillin; within three weeks, the vast majority of eurodollar trade was made on Globex. It took a couple of months for Eurex to take down its tent and go back to Frankfurt.

Hell did not freeze over.

CHAPTER 48

Bingo

CME-CBOT MERGER ANNOUNCEMENT

STATEMENT by Leo Melamed, chairman emeritus of the Chicago Mercantile Exchange on October 17, 2006:

> It represents the culmination of a Don Quixote impossible dream. An idea that was born in the 1970s with the launch of financial futures at the CME and then at the CBOT. An ambition forged when our two exchanges ushered in the modern era of derivatives. A vision that ignited financial innovation within the American financial service sector and made it first in the world.
>
> It represents a goal that some of us harbored for the past three decades, logical and compelling. One that required time. Time for our ideas to be embraced the world over. Time for our institutions to mature and become public. Time for our cultural heritage to harmonize around the electronic architecture of today's information technology. And above all, it required a coalition of skilled leaders, beginning with the chairmen of both exchanges who had the good sense and fortitude to make it happen. We have today fulfilled a destiny that will preserve Chicago as the global capital of risk management.

REPUTATION

When I took over the Merc in 1969, Chicago was known for two things: its stockyards and as the center for organized crime, i.e., the mafia. Starting in 1865 and continuing for more than a century, Chicago's yards were the meatpacking capital of the US. The district was operated by a group of railroad companies that turned it into a centralized processing area. The great poet Carl Sandburg made Chicago's yards famous with his celebrated poem, 'City of Big Shoulders'.

> Hog Butcher for the World,
> Tool Maker, Stacker of Wheat,
> Player with Railroads and the Nation's Freight Handler
> Stormy, husky, brawling,
> City of the Big Shoulders

It was true. The stockyards of Chicago supplied meat for the tables of America. The city's location, smack in the middle of the US, was the perfect place to become the nation's railroad center and freight handler. As Sandburg wrote, "Tool Maker, Stacker of Wheat," transporting product east or west. It symbolized the windy city.

The other Chicago symbol was Al Capone, the underworld boss who made his headquarters there. He became the most infamous gangster in American history. In the 1920s, during the height of Prohibition, Capone's Chicago operation— bootlegging, prostitution, and gambling—dominated US organized crime. Capone's most infamous act occurred in 1929 when he ordered the assassination of seven rivals. It became known as the Saint Valentine's Day Massacre.

As I travelled around the world in my role as the main futures evangelist, Chicago's stigmas followed me. They made it that much more difficult for people to embrace my sermon. No sooner had I mentioned Chicago than someone in the audience put their hands together and rapidly shouted *ack-ack-ack*, mimicking the sound of an Al Capone machine gun.

It certainly didn't help my effort to advance the interests of the IMM. What it did was degrade the discussion to question the locale of the financial market I was proposing. "Why in Chicago? Why not New York? Or, better still, London?"

WHY CHICAGO?

The obvious answer was that nobody in New York or London had thought of the idea. Never mind that with current communications capabilities it did not matter where the actual market was located. I did not go with those answers though. I was there to convince the world of a new religion, that a futures market in finance was an outstanding idea whose time had come. Besides, I knew something that my audience didn't: between the CME and the CBOT, Chicago was *already* the world's hub of futures trading.

The CBOT stood front and center in Chicago's business district. Established on April 3, 1848, the CBOT very quickly became the largest and best-known futures and options exchange in the world. It was the first to list and trade standardized forward contracts, and became the world's benchmark for the grain trade. Since 1930, the CBOT operated in its 45-story building at 141 West Jackson Blvd. Designed by architects Holabird & Root, the building was the tallest in Chicago until the Sears Tower opened in 1973 to become the tallest building in the world—a title it held for 25 years.

The top of the CBOT building is capped by an Art Deco 31-foot (9.5m) statue of Ceres, the Roman goddess of agriculture and grain. The sculpture is faceless because the sculptor, John Storrs, believed that nothing would ever be built high enough to see her face. The building stands at the head of LaSalle Street, which for more than a century defined the Chicago business center—at least until the CME built its building on Wacker Drive the last piece of the puzzle. Today, the Merc's location has been transformed into one of the hottest Chicago business sites.

A STRONG BOND

Given my belief about the growth of the IMM, I would suggest that the question should be the other way around—why *not* Chicago? As I once promised Chicago's Mayor Daley, "the IMM will move the center of financial gravity westward toward Chicago!" All my instincts told me that the quickest way to achieve this was for the CME to someday merge with the CBOT. It would result in an unbeatable super-market power, making it clear that Chicago is the international capital for risk management.

My thought process was instinctive, it was just the right thing to do. Thus, from the very beginning, merging with the CBOT became my ultimate goal.

To get there, the CME would have to become as big—or even bigger—than the CBOT, both in volume and standing. Remember, my last piece of the puzzle in the chase for stardom was to own a building as big and as prominent as theirs.

I believed the Merc was there. We were big and prominent enough to do an IPO before any other exchange. As keynoter at the 2002 Chicago Federal Reserve Bank round table, with apologies to Carl Sandburg, I penned the following.

Our Middle Name

Risk Capital for the World,
Innovator, Conceiver of Markets,
Player with Concepts and the Nation's Futures,
Stormy, husky, brawling,
City of the Big Shoulders.

In the '60s we were called hustlers—
Bamboozling the last dime from widows and
orphans; Proprietors in a stacked game of corner the market;
And yet we grew!

In the '70s we were called arrogant impostors—
Pretending to be relations to the holy temples of finance;
Stealing the rightful markets of New York and London;
And yet we grew!

In the '80s we were called lucky—
Beneficiaries of the inflationary aberrations of the 1970s;
Catering to speculators, volatility and index arbitrage;
And yet we grew!

In the '90s we were called obsolete—
Archaic mechanisms of a bygone era;
Inefficient relics that could not compete with ECN technology;
And yet we grew!

You ain't seen nothing yet.

The CBOT was always the big brother I respected. My overall relationship with the CBOT, its officials and membership, remained strong throughout the years. Although we were sometimes competitors, the goodwill between us began even before I became a member of the CBOT in the late 1970s. It continued through the presidency of Tom Donovan and chairmanships of Les Rosenthal, Pat Arbor and Charlie Carey.

With Rosenthal, the friendship went even further. We had so much in common: our professions were identical, we held the same office, the challenges we faced were without difference, we were both foreign born—him in Romania and I in Poland—we both began our career as runners, and both borrowed money from our fathers to buy a membership. His father later became the Rosenthal Collins Group phone clerk on the CME floor.

CBOT president, Tom Donovan, and I got along famously well. He was not simply the titular head of their exchange, he had the backing of the vast majority of its members. While not a trader, he was very smart and his knowledge of our industry was complete. At nearly every critical turn, as it related to federal legislation and the like, we were in lockstep.

On a personal level, that was also true of my relationship with Pat Arbor. Sure, we were galaxies apart on the role of technology in the marketplace, I told him he was building the "last trading floor on planet Earth," but he was one of the most coveted people to hang around with. He knew everyone, and everyone knew him. And he was the life of the party, with or without his guitar.

Billy O'Connor and Charlie Carey, both former CBOT chairmen, represented the heart of Chicago. I love them both. At the launch of the IMM, Billy called to ask if he could buy 20 seats to support my idea. And he did. They were going for $10,000 a piece. That sounded like $200,000 of real support. Charlie was a down-to-earth kind of guy and a straight shooter. They both joined me in trips to Russia where we were going to build a futures exchange for the Ruskies, as Billy called them. It was a blast.

CLOSING THE GAP

My relationship with the CBOT was considerably advanced early on—upon the election of Ralph Peters as chairman in 1979, in fact. Peters, like myself, was first and foremost a trader, except that he was in a league of his own. If I had to single out the greatest futures trader I ever knew, I would have little hesitancy in choosing Ralph.

After his election, Peters offered me a directorship on the CBOT board. It was an unprecedented idea. In turning down the offer, I wrote to Peters that it "was one of the highest compliments anyone could have bestowed upon me." But it went much further. Peters was an all-business kind of guy and he offered me chairmanship in his firm, Peters & Company. This was so that we could merge our personal interests before working to merge the CME and CBOT. It was not an idle offer, he wined and dined both me and Betty. Although very appealing, I was very apologetic in my negative response.

The idea of a merger resurfaced in 1981, following Leslie Rosenthal's election as CBOT chairman. Once his chairmanship ended in 1983, I dared to put Rosenthal on the CME board for one term, as Peters had tried to do with me. It was a brazen act, given that he was known to be a devoted CBOT member as well as the chairman of the BOTCC.

I did it because it would advance my ambition of a merger. Rosenthal and I often collaborated our legislative efforts in defense of futures markets, which brought our two exchanges much closer together. And although the merger did not happen until some 30 years hence, we both were in total agreement that it was inevitable.

TO THE RESCUE

The merger between the CME and the CBOT officially occurred on July 12, 2007. It resulted in the creation of the world's largest and most diverse exchange, with all the major benchmark asset classes available on a single trading platform: Globex. This included futures and options based on interest rates, equity indexes, foreign exchange, and agricultural commodities, as well as energy and alternative investment markets such as weather and real estate. Sometimes dreams do come true.

One of the main reasons we were able to make it happen then was that both exchanges were demutualized, meaning our values were calculated in the public market—no guesswork necessary. Fortunately, both chairmen, Terry Duffy and Charles Carey, knew and respected each other. My long-standing friendship with Carey helped. We always maintained an open line to each other. And the CBOT membership knew me, as well as the Merc's history of success.

Sometimes the good guys win.

CHAPTER 49

What Have We Learned?

THE wonderful book by Nessim Nicholas Taleb, entitled *The Black Swan*, is a must read.[160] The bird's color was first used in literature in the second century by Roman poet, Juvenal. For hundreds of years it was presumed that black swans did not exist. The black bird thus became a metaphor describing a hugely unexpected and unpredictable event. As Taleb said: "We expect all swans to be white and are shocked when a black swan swims by."

Even though Taleb's book was published before 2008, many people retrospectively used its ideas to make sense of the crash. This was because there were a multitude of causes attributed to the crash that were thought to be unforeseen and unpredictable, i.e., black swans. There were a variety of people who disagree with this though—count me as one of them.

A SPECIAL RELATIONSHIP

Having lived through the 1987 stock crash, the one in 2000, the so-called 'dot-com bubble' and the big mother in 2008, it was impossible not to gain a good deal of information about how and why they happened. Was there something we could do to avoid a repeat of the ordeal? Or was it really caused by a bunch of black swans? This is what I learned. Alan Greenspan, a brilliant economist and disciple of libertarian icon, Ayn Rand, served as Fed chairman for nearly two

160   *The Black Swan*, Nessim Nicholas Taleb, Penguin UK, 2007.

decades—from 1987 to 2006. Before his appointment, I invited him to become a board member of the CME. He declined, citing his higher ambitions.

I believe that my admiration of Alan Greenspan was reciprocated. During the length of his tenure as Fed chair, he never failed to hear my requests about CME issues, nor to give me a private moment when necessary. He also made special notice of our friendship whenever he visited Chicago to meet with Michael Moskow, CEO of the Chicago Federal Reserve branch, who was also a good friend of mine. Upon his retirement, Greenspan made certain that the incoming Fed chair, Ben Bernanke, met with me for introductory purposes.

It is important to record that over many decades of leadership, I became friends with most of America's Federal Reserve chairmen—to the point that I spoke directly to them on economic issues. Starting with Arthur Burns, who was first to learn of the IMM's creation, and throughout the years with Paul Volcker, Alan Greenspan, and Ben Bernanke, the relationship remained strong.

FEDSPEAK

Greenspan deserves credit for keeping the 1987 crash from escalating into something global and unwieldy. As chairman, he became proficient in Fedspeak (also known as Greenspeak), statements that are vague and open to interpretation. According to Nobel prize winner Bob Shiller, Greenspan, in not wanting to publicly commit himself to anything, became "a modern version of the prophets who spoke in riddles."[161]

This created an industry of Fedspeak-Talmuden experts[162] who would try to translate what Greenspan and other Fed officials, like Paul Volcker, meant. According to Charles W. Calomiris, a finance professor at Columbia Business School, it is joked that Alan Greenspan once said to a US Congressman: "If you understood me, then I misspoke."

Throughout his reign Greenspan supported the US economy by actively using the federal funds rate as a lever to help companies recover from any given crisis. It worked. He even earned the name of a new financial instrument: the Greenspan put. It described a reliance on his helpful action in times of difficulty. Greenspan soon earned the image of a Fed sorcerer—a maestro. During most of his tenure the markets applauded and remained in a positive mode. And of course, Central Bankers favor bull markets.

---

161 Robert Shiller, *Irrational Exuberence*, Princeton University Press, 1997.
162 The Talmud is the central text of Rabbinic Law and sometimes subject to conflicting interpretation.

In one very rare instance, however, he became a black swan. On December 5, 1996, the maestro was brutally direct and spoke in plain English. At the American Enterprise Institute dinner in New York, the Fed chairman uttered an irreverence that has since become his most famous statement.[163] Speaking about the valuation of the stock market at that time, Greenspan said that the market was displaying "irrational exuberance."[164]

MARKET MANIPULATION

It was certainly a shocker. As expected, all the world markets fell precipitously the day after the statement. The Tokyo market, which was open at the time, fell immediately and closed 3% down. It was exactly what Greenspan hoped would happen. As he later explained, he wanted to spook the market because he believed it had entered into a dangerously overbought zone.

His statement proved to be only a temporary deflection in the market's unstoppable rise upward. Greenspan's warning was right though—three years later, the dot-com crash of 2000 became a horrid ending to the massive bubble created by cheap money and a near-maddening rush for shares in tech and tech-related companies.

In the US, a speculative frenzy had been brought on during the 1990s—based largely on the discovery of the internet and its incalculable potential for business. Between 1990 and 1997, the percentage of households in the US owning computers increased by 20%. This demand for new computers and computer-run devices was buoyed by the fear that Y2K (the new century) would make existing technologies obsolete simply because they had not been programmed to handle the new century date: a 20 in place of the previous 19. It was thought by many that computers would start to malfunction at midnight on New Year's Eve.[165]

Of course, this was nonsense, but a great time for anyone selling computers. More than that, brand new IPOs could raise a substantial amount of money even

163 Upon his retirement, the Daily Show with Jon Stewart held a full-length farewell program in his honor called, an "Irrationally Exuberant Tribute to Alan Greenspan."

164 There was some speculation for many years whether Greenspan borrowed the phrase from Nobel Laureate Robert Shiller without attribution. Shiller later wrote that he contributed "irrational" at a lunch with Greenspan before the speech, but not "exuberant". Greenspan said he coined the term in the bathtub while he was writing the speech. Robert Shiller later used "Irrational Exuberance" as a title to one of his books.

165 Further, reminders not to be in an elevator at midnight so as not to get stuck when the computer failed.

before their enterprise made anything. Sometimes even before they were listed for trade—as long as they were connected to technology.

In the five years before the millennium, the Nasdaq composite index rose 400%. It reached a price–earnings ratio of 200 before crashing in a death-dive beginning on March 10, 2000. And once the bubble popped, there was no stopping its demise until it lost more than 70% of its incredible gain. It caused some Silicon Valley Wags to carry placards saying: "I want to be irrationally exuberant again."

That could have been the end of the story. But no, these circumstances induced Greenspan to step in with even cheaper interest rates, rekindling the low-priced money process. The US Federal Reserve held its Fed Funds rate at 1% from June 2003 to June 2004. It is believed by many that this policy was a causal factor in the eventual 2008 collapse.

Since precious few predicted it happening, and it was of a dimension perhaps never before encountered in the history of markets, many commentators believed that the crash was caused by a Black Swan (or many) and was subsequently unpredictable. Others, myself included, would strongly disagree.[166] The way we saw it, there were more than a few reasons for the so-called Great Recession, reasons which were very visible and whose consequences were very predictable.

CAUSES OF THE GREAT RECESSION

For me, there were eight causes of the Great Recession. The reasons I outline here come with a strong proviso though: I am no economist. Far from it. My views and knowledge of economics are those of a layman, one who knows and understands a good deal about markets.

1. Easy money, the result of excessively low interest rates.

2. The creation and sale of OTC derivatives, such as collateralized debt obligations (CDO) and structured investment vehicles (SIV). These were sold with reckless abandon at enormous profit without fully understanding (or caring) about the potential dangers of the instruments. Ben Bernanke, in

---

166 'The Gray Swan' remarks by Leo Melamed. Peking University, Beijing China, April 12, 2009. *The Black Swan: The Impact of the Highly Improbable* is a 2007 book by author and former options trader Nassim Nicholas Taleb. The book focuses on the extreme impact of rare and unpredictable outlier events—and the human tendency to find simplistic explanations for these events, retrospectively.

response to a question about the housing panic, said this: "The subprime loans were packaged in these securitized assets, and investors, once they began to understand that the subprime loans would go bad, they began to fear anything that was wrapped up in these securitized assets. That created panic and fear, and that led to runs." Exactly, but the blame lies with the banks who created these useless securitized assets in the first place.

3. Rating agencies granting triple-A approval of the above.

4. Woefully low capital requirements for banks.

5. Creation of mortgages based on subprime lending requirements like the NINJA conditions: no income, no job or assets (no problem).[167]

6. Unconscionable financial leverage. As Nobel laureate Gary Becker later recommended, there was a need for increased capital requirements relative to assets of banks in order to prevent the highly leveraged assets-to-capital ratio in financial institutions.

7. *Greed.* Clearly banks and other financial institutions, in their rush for greater immediate returns irrespective of consequential long-term risks, were guilty of irresponsible behavior and worse. *Barron's* Randall Forsyth suggested OTC structured investment vehicles became the financial equivalent of steroids.[168]

8. The pressure of government officials and government agencies—especially at Fannie Mae and Freddie Mac—to support and encourage cheap mortgage funds for the general public. These government-sponsored enterprises were front and center in the affordable-housing mission, becoming the largest buyers of subprime mortgages between 2004 and 2007. The total exposure exceeded $1trn. Although unpopular at the time, I am proud to say that my opinion was in line with a number of distinguished economists, for instance, Raghuram Rajan, professor in finance at the University of Chicago's Booth School of Business and later governor of the Reserve Bank of India.

167 Word coined by Princeton's Professor Burton Malkiel.
168 Gary S. Becker, *The Wall Street Journal*, October 7, 2008.

PART OF THE PROBLEM

I placed my eighth condition last because it deserves additional comment. For me, this was the most provocative of all causes. Government, by virtue of elected officials or governmental agencies, were serious accomplices. Long after the crash, on October 12, 2012, I arranged a debate at the Merc on the US housing collapse and the financial crisis. It was to be between Congressman Barney Frank and Keith Hennessey, the former National Economic Council director under George W. Bush. It was a standing-room-only event with Terry Savage, the national media commentator, as moderator. As one would expect, neither side took blame.

However, after the event, I pointed out to Mr Frank that for a number of years he and a multitude of US elected officials were the parties encouraging the 'housing for everyone' ideal, as well as sponsoring legislation advancing the goal of cheap mortgages for everyone. He responded truthfully: "I had political blinders on." I give Mr Frank high marks for honesty. But it was the case. Elected politicians found it profitable in the ballot box if they were on the side of cheaper mortgages and less requirements, or less impediments, to buying a home. Never mind that when multiplied by millions it resulted in a fragile housing underbelly. Which is exactly what happened.

The enumerated causes for the 2008 financial collapse were undoubtedly known and visible—it was what one might call the perfect storm. Taken together, their eventual destructive consequence was predictable. Those consequences were no Black Swans. Perhaps any one or two factors on their own were not enough to blow the whistle, but the confluence of so many should have been more than enough to call in the fire brigade. I am far from alone with this opinion.

I know of many in the private sector who lived through the pains of the 1987 and 2000 crashes and recognized the similarities fermenting in the years before the collapse. I cannot recall many on the Fed or other government bodies who beat the drum, or beat it loud enough, to sound the alarm.

When the collapse came it seemed to some like a bunch of Black Swans appeared. But in my mind, those consequences were no Black Swans. According to a 2011 report by the Financial Crisis Inquiry Commission, the Great Recession was avoidable. The appointees, which included six Democrats and four Republicans, cited several key contributing factors, same as the ones I enumerated, that they claimed led to the downturn.

SOLUTIONS

Enter the Troubled Asset Relief Program (TARP) led by Treasury Secretary Henry Paulson to address the subprime mortgage crisis spiraling out of control. Signed into law by President George W. Bush on October 3, 2008, TARP gave the Treasury purchasing power over $700bn (later reduced to $475bn) to buy illiquid mortgage-backed securities and other assets from key institutions in an attempt to restore liquidity to the money markets. It is said that TARP saved us from an even worse disaster. Similar rescue programs followed in the UK as well as the rest of Europe.[169]

In theory, of course, the failure of any enterprise in a free-market system is an acceptable part of the bargain. Government should think long and hard before intervening to save a failing company—even when the failing company is called General Motors.[170] It is the way capitalism is supposed to work. Let the investor lose when he has invested poorly or negligently; force a failing enterprise to look for a partner, merge, raise some capital or file for bankruptcy.

In the 2008 collapse, however, we did not let the market do its natural thing. We stepped in with TARP and quantitative easing (QE), preventing the natural progression of failure and reconstruction from taking place. In doing so, we surely violated some fundamental market mechanisms. Perhaps our intervention produced consequences we do not desire, nor yet understand. Time will tell.

When I spoke about this afterwards to Senator Chris Dodd, he admitted that the action was unique to US history. It was just not the free-market way. But as he explained it, "Everyone was in the room, Paulson, Bernanke, the leadership from both the Republican and Democratic parties and an assortment of committee chairmen and financial advisors. We were told that either we agreed to Paulson's rescue plan, or our nation was about to go to hell in a handbasket. Nobody was prepared to argue."

---

169 TARP signed into law by President George W. Bush on October 3, 2008 with the passage of the Emergency Economic Stabilization Act allowed the US Department of Treasury to buy up to $700bn of troubled assets. It demanded that companies receiving funds lose certain tax benefits, placed limits on certain executive compensation and forbade them from awarding bonuses. It should be noted that TARP spent $426bn and recovered $441bn, earning $15bn in profit.

170 Well, yes, a while back Chrysler was similarly saved.

QUANTITATIVE EASING

Once the market crashed, Ben Bernanke recognized the calamitous nature of the problem and thought up a radical, unprecedented solution: quantitative easing. This was itself an unexpected black swan—a monetary policy whereby the Fed would purchase predetermined amounts of government bonds or other financial assets in order to inject money directly into the economy. It was considered about as groundbreaking a move as you can get.[171]

But it wasn't as surprising as one might think. Ben Bernanke was known in some quarters as 'Helicopter Ben' following his 2002 remark that you could cure deflation by throwing money out of a helicopter.[172] Indeed, Bernanke's QE was a steroid's leap into Keynesian economics, which similarly advocated in the 1930s that the cure for the Great Depression was increased government expenditures and lower taxes.

The financial community was in shock and seemingly paralyzed. It sort of accepted Bernanke's QE explanation to Congress: "This is a temporary measure which is intended to provide support for the economy in this extraordinary period of crisis and when the economy is back on the road to recovery, we will no longer need to have those measures."

I guess that after QE1, QE2 proved that the economy was not yet on the road to recovery, and QE3 perhaps meant that it was a permanent condition—one that created a Fed balance sheet of just under $4trn. Congress failed to ask when it would stop, nor question the process by which we would return to normalcy. We were on financial heroin. According to David Rosenberg, an expert market analyst, "for the entire 2009 to 2019, the economy was on life-support." In other words, we never returned to normalcy. Should another calamity occur, it may be much more difficult to put us together again.

THOUGHTS

Here is my fear: I am not alone. I think most knowledgeable observers will agree that the Greenspan Put was the right thing to do—an acceptable federal hand

---

171 Ben Bernanke received the Melamed-Arditti Innovation Award in 2014.

172 The phrase "helicopter money" was first coined by Milton Friedman in 1969, when he wrote a parable of dropping money from a helicopter to illustrate the effects of a monetary expansion. The concept was revived by economists as a monetary policy proposal in the early 2000s following Japan's Lost Decade.

to help the economy cross the street safely. I heard no one's fear that it violated any principles within our laissez-faire(ish) marketplace. Not so with Bernanke's QE. It made the Greenspan Put look like a kindergarten toy. There were many pointing fingers and voices complaining that QE was a serious violation of the US free-enterprise system. Some went so far as to say that it would open the gates for the end of capitalism itself. The Lord help us.

On the other hand, even if QE is a no-no, there are exceptions to most everything. Was this not such a moment? It certainly felt like it. And as I told Milton Friedman, "I would compromise a principle to a degree for what I believe is the greater good." President George W. Bush once put it more directly: "Sometimes you have to abandon free market principles to save the free market system." If so, Ben Bernanke may have saved the world. In the interest of full disclosure, the Fed chairman was the recipient of the CME Melamed-Arditti Innovation Award in 2014.

My concern, however, was that the Fed response to the 2008 crash, which one could say (my fingers crossed) worked, would be a red flag for the next financial debacle. With every disaster, the US seemed to move further and further away from free-market capitalism, which worked because we allowed the causes and 'bad guys' to be sufficiently punished, thus clearing the market of baggage so that the system could start fresh.

Since we did not permit that to happen in 2008, our version of capitalism will have been so weakened, that there may be hell to pay next time. And if push comes to shove, the Fed will likely print what is necessary to finance any rescues to contain risks to the financial system. I fervently hope there is no next time. But if there is, holy hell may break loose and capitalism may be at stake.

Nuff said. I will move on to a happier view. Francesco Boldizzoni is an Italian social scientist and historian. A professor of political science at the Norwegian University of Science and Technology, Boldizzoni had this to say:

> Capitalism entered the twenty-first century triumphant, its communist rival consigned to the past. But the Great Recession and worsening inequality have undermined faith in its stability and revived questions about its long-term prospects. Is capitalism on its way out? If so, what might replace it? And if it does endure, how will it cope with future social and environmental crises and the inevitable costs of creative destruction?

Professor Boldizzoni answered his own queries:

> Prophecies about the end of capitalism are as old as capitalism itself. None have come true. Yet, whether out of hope or fear, we keep looking for

harbingers of doom ... Capitalism has survived predictions of its demise not, as many think, because of its economic efficiency or any intrinsic virtues of markets, but because it is ingrained in the hierarchical and individualistic structure of modern Western societies.

That says a mouthful with which I agree. Similarly, Fredrich Hayek echoed that sentiment about the US free-market ideal: "It is a social philosophy encompassing ethics, moral values, jurisprudence, ideas and a way of life." And Sir Winston Churchill, the man of the twentieth century, reminded us in remarks to the House of Commons on November 11, 1947, that "democracy is the worst form of government, except for all those others that have been tried." I believe he would say the same about the free-market ideal.

Which brings me to my final question about moral hazard. I will repeat the answer the Fed chairman himself provided:

> The moral hazard is that if you bail out firms that they will imagine that they will always be bailed out and they won't have any incentive to be cautious or take risks. I think we've dealt with that in two ways. In real time, we weren't generous to the firms that were bailed out. They got very tough deals: shareholders lost most of their equity. Creditors took a hit in some cases. Some workers lost their jobs. It wasn't a pleasant experience. I don't think many firms would voluntarily choose the fate of Bear Stearns.

OUR CONTINUED EXISTENCE

This brings to mind the question of how the CME fared during the latest humongous crash? Here are two answers:

On March 14, 2008, the last day before Bear Stearns was acquired by JP Morgan Chase, Bear held $761bn in notional value in open futures contracts for both customer and house accounts at the CME. All positions were paid for and settled. Impressive? Yes.

Then how about this. On Friday, September 12, 2008—the last weekday before Lehman Brothers filed for bankruptcy—their total notional value of customer and house positions at the CME was $1.15trn. Paul Volcker called me the Friday before the bankruptcy filing to ask whether the CME would open for business the following Monday. My answer was "of course." More than that, the

CME conducted a Dutch auction for the positions of Lehman on that Monday—the whole portfolio was auctioned off successfully to a number of firms.

In other words, the CME continued as normal during a time when the world seemed to be coming apart. No defaults, no failures, no federal bailouts.

POSTSCRIPT

I SET out to tell my story—the story of how an immigrant child can succeed beyond normal expectations. As I stated at the outset, my personal goal was to leave a mark, to make a difference, to deserve a word or two in history.

According to Nobel Laureates, Milton Friedman and Merton Miller, with the help of countless others, I achieved that goal. Aside from any congenital talents I may possess, I mostly credit the beauty of America and its free-market ideal. It enabled me to experiment and innovate. By introducing finance into the futures marketplace, I created a brand-new biosphere enabling us and financial engineers to use their talents and imagination to design a myriad of financial instruments in furtherance of business and commerce. It resulted in the creation of the CFTC and the modern futures industry.

In time, I became one of the earliest pioneers to recognize the march of technology and to visualize its impact on the markets. I openly stated my radical opinion: "Anyone who has not seen the handwriting on the wall is blind to the reality of our times. Those who dare to ignore this reality face extinction." The Merc's transaction system, as everyone's, was based on open outcry. That made it highly vulnerable and an easy target. I initiated the creation of Globex, and took on the mission to transform our transaction process from open outcry to an electronic venue. It became the most difficult challenge I ever assumed and took about ten years to achieve.

Some 30 years after I was first elected as CME chairman, I believed it was time to leave. Except for its name, the institution I turned over to my successors, had no resemblance to the Chicago Mercantile Exchange I took over in 1967. The CME Group of today is a poster-child of efficiency and financial strength. We possess a time-tested clearing house, provide coverage for an unequalled diversified product line, and we own Globex, one of the world's very best electronic transaction systems.

Long may it prosper.

ACKNOWLEDGEMENTS

IT is dangerous to attempt to record and recognize the multitude of people who have stood beside me during this journey and deserve my gratitude. The obvious danger lies in neglecting to mention one or another individual who deserves to be included. The other danger lies in the opposite direction, in repeating a name both throughout the memoir and again in the acknowledgements. Surely both will be the case. Nevertheless, I am a risk-taker and, while I will attempt to give service to each individual across the course of this book, I shall also briefly mention them in this dedication.

Please also remember that I am describing events across more than a half century. Very few people were there from the beginning of this tale, some were there for a year or two, and others for a decade or more. Throughout these reminiscences, I have attempted to acknowledge those individuals who were essential to this extraordinary history.

Allow me to begin by praising my parents, who had the vision and courage to outwit both the Gestapo and the KGB to bring us to the safety of this remarkable country. My father was exceptionally talented, to say the least, and possessed an uncanny ability to predict world events and their impact on civilization. His life was influenced and modelled after the teachings of the great Jewish author and philosopher, Isaac Leib Peretz, who taught the Jewish people that morality can be an even higher virtue than religious teachings, and the Bundist leader, Shloyme Mendelson, who led the creation of a secular Jewish school system with Yiddish at its foundation. My father was first and foremost a Bundist and then an authoritative parent who held high demands for his son. He was a man who would not violate his principles no matter the consequence.

My mother was no less a Jewish intellectual—she was well read and educated. She graduated from the acclaimed Vilnar Teachers Seminary. Above all else, she was an exceptional teacher who loved her profession. She was also a leader in the budding Women Rights movement. At the same time, she was the soul

347

of discretion, with a gifted ability to understand human beings, their frailties, strengths, and internal compassions. Without my parents' combined intellect, insight and bravery, there would be no tale to tell. I trust that some of their talent in understanding the nature of human beings has rubbed off on me.

I cannot say enough about my wife, Betty, my high-school sweetheart. She became an incomparable advisor who assisted my career through all its twists and turns. Betty's great memory and knowledge over a wide swath of subjects has always been extremely useful—she substituted as an in-house Google, an invaluable tool for someone taking on the challenges I did. She reads constantly, devouring several books a month. Betty's unassuming nature is a façade, hiding her deep intellect and consistent good judgment, ideas and patience, especially when editing my written material—often in the middle of the night. Her good nature is also legendary, myself and our children frequently take unfair advantage.

Our daughter, Idelle, is extremely bright—a lawyer by profession and a public-school librarian by choice. She is nearly a carbon copy of her mother, except that she reads several books per week. Idelle owns a treasure trove of common sense which she applies liberally in her adopted profession. Rarely has a librarian offered their students such devotion and innovation.

In many ways I regard Idelle as my alter ego, often using her as the last word on complex political or delicate humane decisions. I am not alone. She is consistently sought out in both private and public affairs. After graduating from law school, John Marshall, and reaching high status in the old-line Sidley Austin law firm, she took a leave of absence to give birth to her first child, a boy. She later had two more boys and a girl—four of our grandchildren: Joshua, Aaron, Jared and Mara. All became stars in their own right. Finding that she had a great interest in computer science, Idelle left the field of law and went back to (night) school for a master's degree in Library and Information Science.

Like her grandmother, Idelle's talent as a teacher is boundless. Her ideas for advancing the learning of her young students have become a hallmark for librarians throughout the school system. Her level-headedness is in demand both in her professional and family life. Seldom can one find a mother so devoted to her offspring, who also has the ability to administer tough love.

Idelle's husband, Howard Dubnow, is a former futures broker, whose real talent blossomed after he left the world of trading to become an expert in information technology. Howard, whose knowledge in technological matters is extensive, is a hugely intelligent and well-organized individual. He assumed the role of husband and father as if he invented its rules and practices.

Both my sons, Jordan and David, were intimately involved with futures. It could not be otherwise, given that our entire household was wrapped in market lore, day and night. Although Jordan was a very successful trader, he eventually chose movie-making as a career. Having personally made a similar life-changing decision, I never objected to this choice, nor doubted his eventual success. He has made several well-regarded movies. One of Jordan's great achievements—aside from caring for his lovely daughter, Sofie Gavin Melamed, our fifth grandchild—was the documentary, *Futures Past*. In it, Jordan captures the raw beauty of the trading floor and its traders. His depiction of the transition from open outcry to the electronic screen, as well as my role in this evolution, will forever remain the last word on that remarkable history. Jordan also has a writing talent that is exceptional. He could easily become a highly regarded story teller if he decided to change direction. On the other hand, he has put it to use as a movie maker.

David, my youngest son, knows the markets—their history, complexity, and macro movements—better than most people in our industry. And he never hesitated to offer advice and criticism. David's ability to predict major market moves is nearly without equal. I have often embraced his ideas and followed his predictions.

My cousins, Arthur Tursh and Ariel Hantin, both grew up to become futures market aficionados and were always available for information and assistance. Tursh became an expert telecommunications engineer while Ariel, who is extremely intelligent, became invaluable to my efforts to advance futures in emerging nations. I treat and think about her as another daughter. I also have two cousins in New York, Carol and husband Rob, as well as their twins, Alexis and Elana, who provided the necessary element of familial comfort.

Throughout my life I have relied upon an inner circle to assist me in my odyssey and act as a sounding board when necessary. Most often, the circle was comprised of CME members or officials—some of whom I have recognized over the course of this recount.

Bear in mind that my inner circle changed over the years. In all humility, I was the only constant. I will now call out, in no particular order, those central to the history and record the chapter in which they first entered the story.

Barry Lind is the first name that comes to mind. As described in chapter 17, not only was Barry my bosom-buddy but, as I point out throughout the memoir, he was an important member of the inner circle right from the beginning of this history until his untimely death in a traffic accident in January 2013.

One of Barry's early traders/advisors was Dick Stoken, who helped create the Lind-Waldock firm. At the time, we were all learning how to trade. Dick Stoken was the first in my mind to actually create a system that worked. It brought clients to Barry Lind and made money for Stoken. We instantly became friends. It did not last long though, because Stoken made a lot of money in those days (reputedly $1m) and decided he had made enough to dial down his trading activities and try his hand at other ventures.

Nevertheless, Stoken followed our history and, after a number of years, returned to these environs and to trading. This proved what I already knew: once trading gets into your blood, it will never leave you. Dick was, and remains, an excellent trader. We resumed our friendship as though it had only been a day or two since we last saw each other. We found commonality and interest in a wide spectrum of life, culture, politics, and markets. Betty and I, together with Dick and his very bright and knowledgeable wife, Sandra, became a tight foursome.

Brian Monieson and Jack Sandner, described in chapter 26, both of whom I helped make CME chairman, are high on the ladder of our successes. I included their roles throughout this history although Sandner's role was at times problematic. Jerrold Salzman, in chapter 14, our general counsel, also belongs in the highest echelon of people who helped me achieve the revolutions I set in motion. I believe Salzman's values are well described throughout this memoir.

As I say in the book in chapter 24, my strongest friend and ally was the former CEO, Phupinder Gill. He had intellect and vision and was the brother I never had. He was also my partner in many of our efforts in China, believing as we did that it would provide the CME with business into the future. And of course, Fred Arditti, as noted in chapter 24, a brilliant and non-assuming economist who became a significant addition to the leadership team. Arditti brought the Merc solid economic ideas, among which was devising the eurodollar contract, the most successful futures instrument in the world. He also invented weather futures.

Clayton Yeutter, president of the CME from 1978 to 1985, is first mentioned in chapter 22. While never actually in the inner circle, he played a critical role in advancing the Merc's reputation. He was the only president the CME retained who was without futures market credentials. Jack Sandner and I recruited Yeutter, who had degrees in both agriculture and finance, and held a subcabinet appointment in the department of agriculture. Our understanding was that I would be Mr Inside while Yeutter played Mr Outside. He remained CME president for seven years and gave us an international presence.

Beverly Splane, an exceptionally brilliant economist and graduate from the University of Chicago, was the White House's chief of personnel recruitment in 1974, when the CFTC was created. She accepted the appointment by President Ford to the post of executive director of the newly created federal agency and was in charge of attracting a host of top-notch personnel. Splane and I developed a strong friendship as I became her chief advisor. In 1975, I recruited Ms Splane to become Executive VP for the Merc, becoming perhaps the first high-ranking female official at a major American exchange. I remember her saying, "you will never get your board to agree."

Of course, Terry Duffy. As I have described in chapter 45, I sought Duffy out to wrest control from Jim McNulty. My plan was to give Terry my full support if he would run for the position of chairman against Scott Gordon. The plan succeeded, our IPO was carried out, and we put the CME back on course. Terry Duffy went on to become an outstanding chairman.

Another official I held in high regard was our economist, Mark Powers, who was quick to design the original currency specifications. He enthusiastically supported the idea of currency futures from the very outset. He went on to become the first economist for the CFTC. Rick Kilcollin, the economist who succeeded Powers, was recruited from the Federal Reserve. Rick was an early supporter of my audacious idea to create Globex.

Of course, there are not sufficient words of praise to describe Jim Krause and Don Serpico in chapter 42. Their technical expertise was in a league of its own. They were first to applaud my return to the board in 1997, which served to untie their hands.

Craig Donohue, as I have described in chapter 45, was an exemplary thought leader. He was also of critical value in achieving our takeover. He played the role of 'deep throat', using his legal training and natural intelligence to assist me in carrying out our plan. He became our first CEO after we went public—the first exchange in American history to do so. We believed that our entrance into the equities space in 1982, with the launch of the S&P contract, required our employing someone with security-market expertise. Bill Brodsky fit the bill. Clearly, as noted in chapter 29, he was the perfect recruit from the American Stock Exchange on the eve of our equity-products launch.

Another important ally was my good friend, Nobel-prize-recipient Myron Scholes, who needs no introduction and is described in chapters 28 and 45. He helped convince the other public board members to embrace my takeover plan and elect Terry Duffy as chairman. It worked, of course. Strangely, in spite of his world recognition and his critical assistance in the McNulty takeover, Myron Scholes did not receive re-nomination from the CME nominating committee. In my opinion, it was a shameful act of ingratitude and a critical mistake. Myron and I remain strong friends.

There were some individual members who, at different times, played an important role within the inner circle or on assignment to special issues. Although it is not possible to name them all, I will try to call out a few who come to mind. Jim Oliff, a long-standing friend and devoted Merc board director, often played the important role of devil's advocate. He was also a talented source of new ideas. Oliff was a broker, but one who realized the importance of electrification and was extremely valuable in achieving this objective. His father, Hutch, was a legendary old-line member with a great sense of humor, which his son inherited.

An unforgettable and top loyal captain in my army was Harry 'The Hat' Lawrence, who I could trust with my life. He became my principal go-getter when it came to political action funds. He was also my most capable ally when it came to rounding up the troops for an undertaking that needed strong support. I also became a friend of his first wife, Michelle, who I helped get elected as a judge in the Illinois Circuit Court. As late comers to political action, I would credit William Hobert and his wife Julie. I would also give credit to Ron Pankau, a long-time member of the board, one I learned to greatly rely upon when speaking to visiting elected officials.

Another father-son duo, Yra Harris was physically dragged by his father Joey from liberal politics, where he was an assistant to Idaho Senator Frank Church, to join the real world. Now a national commentator, Yra was baptized into the free-market ideal by his father and became an ardent adherent to the teachings of Milton Friedman. He grew to become one of my closest friends. He had a gifted sense of market dynamics, with an accuracy hard to replicate, and whose opinion I learned to seek, often when he and his wife Janice joined Betty and I to discuss national and world-market issues.

Needless to say, at different times in our evolution, I deeply relied on the advice of people outside the CME. For instance, Les Rosenthal, who had a wealth of knowledge from being both CBOT chair, from 1981 to 1983, and chairman of the BOTCC. Rosenthal became one of my closest personal friends. He was the person with whom, as early as the 1970s, I first speculated about an eventual merger with the CBOT. And although it did not happen until some 30 years hence, we both worked for its fulfilment.

Speaking of the CBOT, after our merger in 2007, the Merc appointed Charlie Carey, its former chairman, to the combined new board. As I have indicated, Carey provided us with highly regarded grain expertise. In similar fashion was the addition of the CBOT's Bryan Durkin, who had been their workhorse under the leadership of Tom Donovan. I quickly learned that if I needed someone trustworthy with a high professional caliber to get something done, it was Bryan Durkin. Bryan deservedly rose swiftly through the CME ranks to reach the lofty position of president.

Speaking of people outside the exchange, Henry Jarecki, a psychiatrist by profession and silver arbitrageur in practice, played an important role. Until 1972, I had never heard of Dr. Jarecki; his psychiatry credentials were not exactly what I was seeking when forming the brand new IMM board. Still, once exposed to his intellect, experience and wit, I realized that in Jarecki I had found a kindred soul who understood the markets. We thought similarly on so many subjects that it was uncanny. By happenstance, our life experience was also alike. He was born in Germany and, as a young adult, moved with his parents to the US at the outset of Hitler's regime. And, of course, he had learned a thing or two as arbitrageur for Mocatta Metals. For one thing, he learned to make many millions of dollars. It wasn't too long before I became convinced that he should be included on the original IMM board.

Jarecki's breadth of market knowledge and general business acumen was often critical in providing me with advice on the ins and outs of our market arena right from the start of the IMM. Over the years he became one of my trusted associates and friends, who never failed to provide me with invaluable advice based on a world perspective. For instance, during the unwarranted attack by the US Attorney on the CME and CBOT traders for alleged trading violations in 1989, I relied heavily on his advice. I feel privileged to call Henry a very close, lifelong friend.

Another highly qualified executive that we were fortunate to gain from the CBOT was Julie Winkler, who was bright and filled an important role in the development of new markets. Speaking of Julies, the Merc's COO, Julie Holzrichter, a personal friend of mine who runs CME operations, has been, and remains, one of the most solid and devoted Merc officials. From the very start of her employment, I learned that she was totally trustworthy and hugely knowledgeable in the operations of an exchange.

As we prepared for our IPO, I made certain that Gill and other valuable exchange officials would not leave our domain by endowing upon them a large number of stock options. As has been the case throughout my career, I refused to be awarded similarly, claiming that I was "not an employee of the Merc." With the benefit of hindsight, this was not one of my smartest decisions.

Mitch Fulscher, an executive at Arthur Andersen, recognized from our earliest days that futures would become big business and so invested his time in becoming a special futures expert for his firm. He was among the first in the world to recognize the huge potential that futures represented for risk management. In time, he represented AA in Japan and the Asia region, where he organized a Futures Industry Association (FIA) chapter and served as its president for a multitude of years. Mitch became my eyes and ears in Japan, often relying on his advice and ideas as we both participated in the unprecedented growth of our industry. Needless to say, we became the closest of friends.

Sometimes I would test my ideas on professionals in tangential fields of endeavor to see how they would view what we were doing. Tom Russo, the former general counsel of AIG, was such a person—his ideas and advice were always welcome. My boyhood chums, Meyer Seltzer and Jerry Specthrie, were also in that category. In fact, Meyer, a talented commercial artist, designed the logo for my firm, the Dellsher Investment Company. His paintings of the old Merc floor hang proudly on my office walls. On top of that, we are fairly matched as chess players and have been engaging in never-ending games since high school. There was also Willie and Helen Boris, who were special because both of Helen's parents were survivors too—I knew them well. Helen's husband became a CBOT trader and would give me a deeper understanding of that exchange's point of view.

I often tested the water with friends in the legal profession too. For instance, Rikki Klieman, a notable and influential Boston attorney, and Kshama Fernandes, a professor in finance at the University of Goa in India. Fernandes and I collaborated to help India launch its Nifty 50 stock index. Another good example is Gila Bronner, a Chicago Business management consultant who served with me for 15 years on the executive committee of the USHMM. And, of course, my personal attorney, Matt Kluchenick, who became steeped in futures lore having served in the Merc's legal department.

Aside from having the right people on the inside, I was always aware that whatever we wanted done needed approval from the members at large. We were a membership entity; a membership that had a big say in everything I wanted to do; a membership with over 200 committees to use as levers of support or criticism. I often lamented that "everything down to the color of paint in the washroom" had to gain membership approval. I never forgot that it was the rank and file members who catapulted me to chairmanship. Thus, my modus operandi was to always explain what we planned and gain floor support on any action I considered of major consequence. To help achieve this result I relied on a group of members who were respected by the membership and were ardent supporters of my actions. There were dozens of such lieutenants, as I referred to them. I shall name but a few here:

It goes without saying that Robert J. O'Brien remained one of my exulted personal heroes. I will never forget that he and I successfully plotted the original takeover of the Chicago Mercantile Exchange, opening the door for me to become its chair and leading the institution to its incomparable standing today. His firm, R.J. O'Brien & Associates, remains the oldest and largest independent futures brokerage firm in the US. No one can match that history.

I have already mentioned guys like 'The Hat' who had leadership roles. But in the forefront there were others, like John Geldermann, who eventually became chairman; Morrie Levy, who was my first currency arbitrageur; Michael Sturch, a most devoted member on whom I relied for membership support; George Fawcett, my partner in Dellsher Investment Co. and the straightest arrow I ever met; Dick Boerke, who provided me with courage in launching currency futures; Terry McKay, a popular and successful trader; Billy O'Connor, an influential CBOT trader and eventual CBOT chairman; Bill Shepard, an able and ardent supporter and advisor.

I would also like to mention Glenn Bromengen, a highly regarded and successful cattle trader; Joe Fox, an enlightened old-guard representative; Bruce Johnson, a very capable and savvy cattle trader who was highly respected by the members; Louis Schwartz, who had great respect among eurodollar traders; and Lonnie Klein, a very smart member who embraced the new direction I had initiated. I could go on and on. This army of lieutenants is incomplete and I apologize to those I neglected to name. They all were highly regarded and were my voice to the members.

Last but certainly not least, there were four or five internal private assistants without whom I could never have carried out what I did. They came at different junctures in my history, but were all extremely capable and totally devoted to my efforts. First was Valerie Turner. Valerie came with me from my law practice Melamed & Kravitz to run my firm, Sakura Dellsher, as its COO, with an iron fist. She made certain that while I was carrying out my CME responsibilities, I did not have to worry about the well-being of my private clearing firm. She was one of the first African Americans to reach this high stratum in Chicago. I later needed an expert secretary and found Sue Chattler, who I stole from Henry Hall Wilson, president at the CBOT.

Around the same time, Alysann Posner came over from the CBOE to become my executive assistant. Alysann became my right hand for several decades in all matters concerning my responsibilities to the Merc, the futures industry, and my life in general. I have never before, nor since, found anyone who could anticipate my thoughts and next moves like she could. She became my alter ego. More than that though, Alysann often took one of my thoughts or ideas and added to it a personal dimension that undoubtedly enhanced it. For instance, in the early 80s as I began to write *The Tenth Planet*, a science fiction story, Posner insisted that I learn computer-based word processing.[173] I became one of the earliest business executives with that capability. Given the huge amount of writing that I did, this talent served me for the rest of time.

In the same vein, I was very lucky to have Pat Reiffel, who was my *upstairs* commander-in-chief. She knew at every moment what I was doing and

173 *The Tenth Planet*, Bonus Books, 1987.

where to find me, who I needed to talk to, with whom to make an immediate appointment and whom to stall, all the while always staying even-keeled without a hint of frustration. Appropriately enough, Pat started with me on October 19, 1987, the scariest day of my life—she waited till I returned to the office well past midnight, holding a stack of calls that needed to be answered, and calmly asking if today was a sample of my normal life? She began as a part-time fill-in and remained for the following 30 years.

Upon her retirement, there was an enormous void which I am filling with Nancy Appleyard, the former assistant of my buddy, Brian Monieson. To become an assistant to someone like me, with the myriad ideas and responsibilities that I entertain, is one of the most difficult assignments one can take on. I deeply admire Nancy's willingness and talent to take it on with a commitment to succeed. I also want to mention Jill Rogers, who has faithfully been in charge of my trading endeavors during the past three decades.

I cannot neglect to mention Carol Sexton, who became a main cog in the Merc's Public Relation department, following the work of its preceding chief, the able Barbara Richards. Carol Sexton got the job because her sister, Chicago Mayor Jane Byrne, the first woman to be elected mayor of a major city in the US, called me to see if I could find a job for her. It turned out to be a most fortunate request. Anything that came at us, good or bad, in any shape or form, was met by Carol Sexton, who would be waiting to respond. She would then use her versatile imagination and talent to make the bad turn good, and the good become great. She became the Merc's best voice and played a huge role in making our name the number one in the world of markets.

Throughout the years, I met with a host of people in the media, always attempting to maintain an open and responsive rapport. Such an attitude was a significant factor in advancing the 'educational' purpose and effect of my actions. There were, of course, many who did not understand or grasp how big a story futures were. For them it was but a momentary encounter. Fortunately, there were many who got it, and kept following our history and my career. I am of course speaking about Terry Savage, who I describe in chapter 38 and who earned her stripes on the floor of the Merc to become an outstanding national business news commentator, whom I have described separately in this book. Additionally, if I had to name one additional reporter who stayed the course and got it right, it would be John Lothian, a former CBOT bond trader who publishes the highly informative John Lothian News.

Today, public relations have taken on a very different role, given that we are a listed company with much greater visibility. These responsibilities have been carried out in style and with success in expert fashion under the professional direction of Anita Liskey. Early on in my Merc career I was approached by Daniel Edelman, the founder of the world's largest public relations firm, to seek our account. I was reluctant because we really did not have any money for this kind of effort. But Edelman was not in PR business without smarts. "I don't want your money," he responded to my hesitation, "I want your name." I greatly admired his honesty and immediately embraced his offer. We remained a client for the Edelman firm now run by his son Richard, who clearly inherited his father's talents and then some. They are clearly the best in the difficult promotion arena, finding ingenious ways to promote the CME as being vital to the American economy without delving into hugely complex explanations of how futures work.

In the areas where I continue to carry out responsibilities as chairman emeritus, I am fortunate to have the talents of people like Colleen Lazar, who may not always be found in the limelight of our undertakings, but who is a critical cog carrying out very difficult assignments which enhance the Merc's image and reputation. Colleen directs the Merc's Competitive Market Advisory Council, which I created with Myron Scholes. It is one of a kind in terms of high-level advisory institutions that include prominent officials and academics as well as Nobel prize winners. It takes a highly intelligent and capable person like Colleen to carry out this very difficult mission.

In addition, Colleen directs our efforts with the Mathematical Sciences Research Institute, of which a very long list of American colleges and universities belong. It is widely regarded as the world's leading mathematical center for collaborative research as well as the educational undertaking of futures fundamentals. Most important, Colleen Lazar is responsible for administrating the CME's highly regarded annual Melamed-Arditti Innovation Award.

Equally important, John Peschier, managing director for investor relations, made certain that our investors were kept informed of these developments. I am also very taken by Bluford 'Blu' Putnam, the current managing director and chief economist of the CME Group. Putnam is responsible for leading global economic analysis and monitoring developments in the price patterns, volatility and correlations of futures and options markets. He was acquired in 2011 and his performance has been simply outstanding. Of special consequence is that Putnam has also stepped into the role of administering the CMAC council—no small undertaking. My successful efforts in Japan could never have been achieved without the devoted assistance by the Directors who over the many years headed up our CME office, Yoshio Kuno, Hayami Shiraishei and Dr. Izumi Kazuhara.

I doubt if I could have achieved or continued my standing and responsibilities in China were it not for the special assistance of Lucy Wang, who became my eyes, ears, and voice in that nation. Not only is Lucy conversant in the idiosyncrasies of futures markets, gained from working with her mother Wendy Wang to operate a successful futures enterprise in China, but she is extremely talented, personable, resourceful, and known by many in the Chinese government and business circles. I clearly owe a good deal of my reputation in China to Lucy's handling of their affairs to this very day.

Point is, I had plenty of help!

INDEX

Comprised of notable people named
within the text.

CPSIA information can be obtained
at www.ICGtesting.com
Printed in the USA
LVHW032112150321
681639LV00001B/1/J